THE MORALITY AND GLOBAL JUSTICE READER

THE MORALITY AND GLOBAL JUSTICE READER

EDITED BY
MICHAEL BOYLAN
Marymount University

A Member of the Perseus Books Group

Westview Press was founded in 1975 in Boulder, Colorado, by notable publisher and intellectual Fred Praeger. Westview Press continues to publish scholarly titles and high-quality undergraduate- and graduate-level textbooks in core social science disciplines. With books developed, written, and edited with the needs of serious nonfiction readers, professors, and students in mind, Westview Press honors its long history of publishing books that matter.

Published by Westview Press
A Member of the Perseus Books Group

Find us on the World Wide Web at www.westviewpress.com.

Designed by Trish Wilkinson
Set in 10.5 point Adobe Garamond Pro

Library of Congress Cataloging-in-Publication Data

The morality and global justice reader / edited by Michael Boylan.
p. cm.
Includes bibliographical references and index.
ISBN: 978-0-8133-4433-1 (alk. paper)
1. International relations—Moral and ethical aspects. 2. Social justice 3. Human rights. I. Boylan, Michael, 1952–
JZ1306.M685 2011
172'.4—dc22
E-book ISBN: 978-0-8133-4514-7

2010047253

10 9 8 7 6 5 4 3 2 1

To those working on the front lines
assisting the victims of poverty, war, sickness,
and oppression wherever they are found.

CONTENTS

Preface *ix*

Part One: Normative Principles 1

Chapter 1 Global Human Rights 7
ROBERT PAUL CHURCHILL

Chapter 2 On Justifying Human Rights 27
JOHN-STEWART GORDON

Chapter 3 When Is Ignorance Morally Objectionable? 51
JULIE E. KIRSCH

Chapter 4 The Ethics of Otherness 65
WANDA TEAYS

Part Two: Normative Theories 83

Chapter 5 Consequentialism and Global Ethics 89
HALLVARD LILLEHAMMER

Chapter 6 How to Think About Global Duties 103
CHRISTIAN ILLIES

Part Three: Normative Applications 127

Poverty and the Global Economy

Chapter 7 Collective Responsibility and Global Poverty 135
SEUMAS MILLER

Chapter 8 Building Wealth with Conditional Cash Transfers 153
MICHAEL BOYLAN

Chapter 9 Ethics and Global Finance 169
KLAUS STEIGLEDER

Chapter 10 Global Business and Global Justice 185
NIEN-HÊ HSIEH

Global Health

Chapter 11 Global Health Justice 211
MICHAEL J. SELGELID

Chapter 12 Access to Life-Saving Medicines 229
DORIS SCHROEDER, THOMAS POGGE, AND PETER SINGER

Religion

Chapter 13 What Price Theocracy? 263
LAURA PURDY

Chapter 14 Global Ethics in the Academy 281
JAMES A. DONAHUE

War

Chapter 15 The Law of Peoples 299
DAVID CUMMISKEY

Chapter 16 Cosmopolitan Revisions of Just War 325
GABRIEL PALMER-FERNÁNDEZ

Gender, Identity, and Family

Chapter 17 Women on the Move 349
ROSEMARIE TONG

Chapter 18 Gender and Sex Development 365
SIMONA GIORDANO

Chapter 19 Duties to Children 385
MICHAEL BOYLAN

About the Contributors *405*

Index *411*

PREFACE

In *The Republic* Thrasymachus offers five arguments to Socrates why justice is the rule of the strongest. In each instance Socrates offers a refutation. The fault lines on justice have been thus set for some time: the competitive virtues of over-reaching for whatever one can garner versus the cooperative virtues of sharing. This reader stands in a long tradition of considering questions of justice from the dual vantage points of prudential advantage and ethics.

Traditionally, this discussion is carried on within the perspective of a single society. The ancient theorists such as Plato and Aristotle, along with the seventeenth and eighteenth century contract theorists (Locke, Hobbes, Rousseau, and Hume) all took a national perspective. In contemporary times, most theorists have maintained a national perspective (including my book *A Just Society*, 2004). However, perhaps because of better communication, global trade, and two world wars, perspectives that include the rest of the world have increasingly come to the fore. Peter Singer's shallow pond thought experiment in the 1970s initiated a wave of thinking in global terms about ethical duty and justice. No longer was it enough to get it right in one's own country. There is a whole world out there, and normative accounts have to take notice.

Like many authors, I have often situated claims about justice within the setting of a nation, which stands like a logical placeholder for any state. If I could prove that any person, *x*, has a right to *y*, then why does the specification of the venue matter? To some extent this is still true so long as one bases one's theory of justice upon abstract principles of morality.[1] But what this traditional philosophical approach misses is the importance of integrating timeless theory with contemporary needs: applied philosophy. From its beginnings in the Western tradition, theoretical philosophy was always attended by applied philosophy. For concrete-minded Greeks and Romans, there was a very limited value in speculation about that which had little to no application to action.

In our present era, applied philosophy made a resurgence in Continental Europe during and after the Second World War. The Anglo-American-Canadian-Australian tradition lagged behind. They were caught up in a fascination with logical empiricism, monist-materialist metaphysics/epistemology, and ethical antirealism. Application to the daily world was thought to be mundane. Theory and mental gymnastics were the sign of worth. It wasn't until the Vietnam War and the American Civil Rights Movement in the late 1960s that the relevance of philosophy to actual problems in the world seemed important to this segment. Enter Singer's essay. Enter bioethics. Enter business ethics. Enter environmental ethics. Enter philosophical feminism. The Anglo-American-Canadian-Australian world *moved.*

The ascendancy of global business, regional wars, and environmental disasters exacerbated everything. Philosophy split. A new wing of the discipline (the applied wing) tried to bring analytic tools to bear upon the suffering of humankind. The results are books like this one.

This is a book of original essays by a team of international writers. If you look in About the Contributors at the end of the book, you will find considerable diversity in international affiliations as well as gender and philosophical perspectives. These essays are divided into three groups: those dealing with core normative principles, those dealing with normative theories, and those dealing with normative applications. In each case the emphasis is upon an international perspective.

What is an international perspective? Here again there is some controversy. For some, the international perspective follows the precise meaning of the compound word: *inter* (between) and *national* (nations). This group follows the order of the world as it is to set policy goals in terms of the existing political structure.

A second perspective is theoretical. It looks at nations as only conventional. If nations have no *real* status, then underlying "oughts" of morality and justice may be justified independently of one's physical presence within a state. At root, this is the view of *cosmopolitanism.* The origin of rights is independent of one's fortuitous existence within a particular state.

Obviously, in carrying out policy suggestions, one must recognize that the world *is* divided into states, but it *does* make a difference in the way claims are justified. For the most part, the perspective of these essays is cosmopolitan, as so defined.

The following are distinctive features of this book:

- Original essays were written especially for this book by prominent scholars in the field.
- Essays are grouped according to pedagogical design moving from *normative principles* to *normative theories* to *normative applications.*
- Essays are presented in the format that readers would see in journals. This enhances the "primary text" experience with abstracts and key words (both of which give a centering on what the essay intends).

- Essays are all given lengthy editorial introductions within the context of each subsection (which make some references between essays).

This book is relevant to general readers interested in morality and global justice and their policy implications. Students should find this text engaging within the classrooms of philosophy, politics, and international relations. Our goal is to hook the reader to think about these issues with the hope that those so engaged will be moved to positive action for change.

I would like to thank the nineteen authors who have written essays for this book and those reviewers who have made constructive suggestions. I would also like to thank Karl Yambert, my editor on this project, for his expert assistance. Lastly, I would like to thank the production crew—in particular my production editor, Sandra Beris; the copy editor, Sarah Van Bonn; and the marketing manager, Erica Lawrence. These individuals and others at Westview are to be commended for their careful work in the creation of this volume.

Michael Boylan

Note

1. I use the terms *ethics* and *morality* interchangeably because the former comes from Greek and the latter is Cicero's translation of the former.

PART ONE

NORMATIVE PRINCIPLES

- Chapter 1 Global Human Rights
  ROBERT PAUL CHURCHILL
- Chapter 2 On Justifying Human Rights
  JOHN-STEWART GORDON
- Chapter 3 When Is Ignorance Morally Objectionable?
  JULIE E. KIRSCH
- Chapter 4 The Ethics of Otherness
  WANDA TEAYS

PART ONE
INTRODUCTION

Many normative principles can help readers frame the issues of morality and global justice. The ones I chose to highlight here play a pivotal role in being able to engage intellectually in the problems discussed in the third part of this book. These normative principles are human rights, epistemic obligations, and the status of those who hang on the fringes of the community of nations—the "other." There are, of course, additional important normative principles, and some of these are embedded within the applied essays that comprise two-thirds of the book. They will be discussed in the context of those essays.

Respecting human rights, we begin with essays by Robert Paul Churchill and John-Stewart Gordon. These essays differ in three key areas: the scope of human rights, the justification of human rights, and the motivation of peoples to act on their duties based upon rights claims. For Churchill, the scope of human rights is universal. A legitimate rights claim applies equally in China as it does in Iowa. Making reference to his 2006 book on global human rights, Churchill highlights the various competing ideas on the scope of human rights—such as "the rising tide of rights" approach. Ultimately, the scope of human rights depends upon how one justifies human rights. Here Churchill sets out what a good justification might look like (determinacy, coherency, claimability, separability, and feasibility) and then uses these to examine pluralistic, interest-based, and agency-based approaches. Churchill sides with the agency-based approach. Because the criteria for human agency are universal, so is the scope of the theory. Along the way he carefully sets out tenets of Carol Gould and James Griffin. The problem of motivation is addressed via the way we internalize human rights norms. The landscape here is broadly explored including my own *extended community worldview imperative.* Churchill suggests that engagement with this imperative would stimulate moral imagination that would solve the problem of moral motivation. This is because the personal worldview imperative works through a strategy of *integration.* By emphasizing a process of formal self-examination, the agent can create a coherent self that is both necessary and sufficient for self-recognition of these moral dimensions. But when the case is expanded to distant peoples, the problem is more complex. It is here that the extended community worldview imperative fits in. But though the extended community worldview imperative is a start, the motivational question remains very important vis-à-vis action and accountability; we are still at the beginning of such a process.

Gordon addresses the same questions. He begins by examining the various meanings of rights as being moral rights (with high priority over all else), legal rights, claim and liberty rights, and how rights and duties are related. Next, Gordon examines four categories of traditional justification. The first category is natural rights. In this category he draws upon his book on Aristotle's *Nicomachean Ethics* to set out an understanding of nature that filtered through to the Enlightenment. A second approach (that has some overlap with the first) makes an appeal to the will of God to ground human rights, for example, the Ten Commandments. The third way of justifying human rights is the interest-based approach. Fundamental interests are defined according to what is necessary for anyone's fundamental interests. The last sort of theory is the agency-based approach (advocated by Churchill and myself). Gordon examines Alan Gewirth and myself under this category (making use of his recent edited volume of essays on my *A Just Society*).

Each of these four traditional approaches has flaws according to Gordon. To remedy this he offers his own theory that he contends solves the shortcomings of the other approaches. He begins with Kant's *Groundwork for the Metaphysics of Morals* and the place of rationality in relation to morality. Rationality can dictate commands (duties). These commands are relative to a thought experiment that would be directed to a community about what they thought they needed for a minimally decent life with a Rawlsian veil of ignorance attached to it (they could not know idiosyncratic information about themselves—age, gender, talents, etc.). From this Gordon generates a list of rights that would generally apply—though later some of these are tailored to ideas formed from their particular societies (this might limit the scope, i.e., limiting universality—contra Churchill). After examining five possible objections, Gordon sets forth his program as a viable alternative to the four traditional approaches. The moral motivation piece of the puzzle turns again to the ancient world and the concept of a contented, flourishing soul, *eudemonia.* This amounts to an appeal of ethical egoism.

Gordon and Churchill situate their essays around these three touchstones: the scope of human rights, the justification of human rights, and the issue of moral motivation. There is some overlap, but also some critical differences in their claims.

Julie Kirsch's essay also addresses the issue of moral motivation via our epistemic duties. Following William Kingdom Clifford, Kirsch examines what a belief consists in and what follows from that. Kirsch argues that beliefs are connected to actions such that if one believes "that *P*," then this will result in an action concerning *P*. Some beliefs are unitary about some *P* (a particular event), while others are rather more general and affect a wider range; for example, racism would influence more than a particular event. This is a shorthand of Clifford's groundwork for an ethics of belief.

However, the nature of belief may not be totally voluntary. This can involve issues of self-deception. In order to sort this out, Kirsch distinguishes between direct and indirect control of beliefs. Such a distinction can lead to doctrines of *managing* beliefs through taking productive means to bring them about. Some of these strategies include seeking and evaluating evidence for and against beliefs, identifying and eliminating biases in belief formation, interpersonal and critical discussion, and creating nested hierarchies of beliefs.

When we apply these categories to ignorance of the moral world, then the status of moral beliefs becomes relevant. Kirsch then brings up my notion of the personal worldview and the associated critical apparatuses that fulfill doxastic responsibility: the personal worldview imperative, the shared community worldview imperative, and the extended community worldview imperative. Thus, belief formation and personal education are set out as important, separate meta-issues. Through a few examples, Kirsch links this position to Peter Singer's understanding of these issues from his classic essay "Famine, Affluence, and Morality."

Kirsch finishes her argument discussing exactly how this sort of education might occur and what burdens it could impose. Because much of the available information about the world comes to most people via the Internet, and because much of the material on the Internet may have unacknowledged biases, the imperative to educate oneself according to the criteria set out in the beginning of the essay may be steep. But perhaps the answer is to concentrate upon the priority of some beliefs over others.

A fourth normative principle concerns the status of those who are marginalized by societies and the world: these individuals are called "the other." Wanda Teays writes from her own original research concerning those whom the mainstream often does not see: the invisible humanity that suffers. Because they are "invisible," the rest of the world often does not plug them into their extended community worldview duty to self-education. Teays examines in particular three groups: refugees, detainees, and gays.

The United Nations says that a refugee is "a person outside of his or her country of nationality who is unable or unwilling to return because of persecution or a well-founded fear of persecution on account of race, religion, nationality, membership in a particular social group, or political opinion." However strong the duty is upon countries to assist refugees, their lot is often very difficult. For example, asylum seekers to the US are often detained in jails or buildings that are operated like jails. Elsewhere in the world many Somalis sought refugee status in Yemen, and thousands of Zimbabweans sought refuge in South Africa. While their requests were pending, they lived in squalid camps that are breeding grounds for disease.

Obviously, there is an expense to the host country to accept refugees and offer them sanctuary. Teays argues there are moral and religious reasons to do so. But these are often rhetorically challenged through the attack that refugees are only out for economic betterment and that economic betterment is not mentioned in the United Nations' definition. The self-interested cry of opponents is a careful linguistic twisting of the facts on the ground. Their tirades call for racial and religious profiling based upon straw men—such as linking sanctuary with terrorism. Teays argues that the countries of the world (including the United States) should accept their moral obligation to admit their fair share of the world's refugees.

Linguistic spinning also occurs with detainees. Teays argues that these individuals exist in a moral limbo. They are incarcerated though not charged with a crime. Terms such as "insurgents," "unlawful enemy combatants," and so forth are used to shape public opinion. Unlike prisoners of war (who have legal status under the Geneva Conventions), detainees have no protections. Even US citizens can be subject to rendition and questioning (sometimes via torture) for an indefinite time period. Mistakes can and have occurred resulting in the abrogation of human rights to the innocent. Because there is no system of dealing with these individuals under a canopy of law, terrible human rights abused have occurred.

Teays's last category concerns gays and lesbians. In most of the world, these individuals have had to fight for social, moral, and legal standing in the midst of oftentimes contradictory rules and regulations—such as being allowed to donate organs to save another's life but not allowed to serve in the military (USA) or being allowed to adopt children but not allowed to marry (most of the USA). The situation is similarly difficult for gays and lesbians around the world.

Societal and legal recognition involves the attribution of the inalienable rights of being a person in the world. Much of the opposition stems from ignorance and the assertion of inscrutable claims—such as gays being spiritually unclean (by the Boy Scouts of America). Teays argues that this is a smoke screen for unexamined, unfounded prejudices. Rationality alone may not be enough to dislodge these prejudices. What is needed, Teays contends, is a context of discovery around all the *others* who exist on the margins of society and the holistic ways they are marginalized and described. Through a wider lens that is sensitive to linguistic constructions, we may be able to recognize the human rights of these *others* and fulfill our moral duties toward them.

CHAPTER ONE

Global Human Rights

ROBERT PAUL CHURCHILL
George Washington University

Abstract

This chapter addresses justifications of the universality of human rights and the problem of motivating the affluent to care about the rights of distant others. I argue that lack of care for distant others does not signify failure to justify human rights as genuinely universal. On the contrary, we need to distinguish clearly between the problem of justification and the problem of motivation to avoid having unreasonable expectations for even the best justification of human rights. The problem of motivation must be addressed separately through processes of internalizing human rights norms and developing moral imagination.

Key Words

human rights justification, agency-based justification, interest-based justification, capabilities, universability, motivation

---

Human rights are here to stay; they have become the predominant moral resources for resolving problems between persons, their freedom and needs, and dominant power structures, whether public or private. It is nevertheless apparent that despite the advance of human rights, we confront resistance of many types and in many quarters, as well as the most appalling violations of the dignity all people are owed. The International Bill of Human Rights is accepted by the majority of countries as binding law, at least in principle, and through careful interpretation and argument, philosophers, theorists, and international lawyers have advanced support for plausible lists of human rights based on United Nations covenants and declarations. Yet, the diversity and complexity of issues human rights are expected to address and heightened controversy over the proper domain of human rights reopen questions, almost at every turn, about justifications of human rights, who holds them, and who must discharge correlative obligations.

Do we expect more from human rights than they can deliver? How far can we continue to advance respect for human rights through philosophical argumentation? At the heart of plausible answers to these questions, there has to be a credible justification for human rights. But we must ask, in turn, how much we can reasonably expect a justificatory argument to accomplish. A major feature of controversies over human rights, even among scholars, is confusion over what a justification should accomplish in contrast to a full-blown theory. Thus, following a brief overview of some of the reasons for the "globalization" of human rights, I offer some desiderata, or criteria, for a theory of human rights. My purpose is to demarcate the limits between theories and justificatory arguments so that we do not have unreasonable expectations about what the latter should accomplish. This discussion is followed by a review and evaluation of some leading justifications of human rights in an effort to identify the most comprehensive and satisfactory justification.

Surely the most perplexing problems associated with justifying human rights concern distant others. How can we be assured that human rights are truly universal? It is generally agreed that the "universality" of human rights, or the claim that human rights are possessed equally by all persons, poses the greatest problem for justification. Likewise, as noted above, given that human rights are based on what it means to be human, how do so many humans find it possible to ignore or violate them? Does this say anything about the weakness of our justification for human rights? Here I address both sets of questions head on but in different ways. I argue, first, that philosophers and theorists have weakened the persuasive power of justifications by mistaking what is involved in "universalizing" human rights so that they have conceived a need to close a gap between what one recognizes as "one's rights" and the rights of distant strangers. Second, drawing a distinction between the problem of justification and the problem of motivation, I argue that we must accept that, at best, justifications may have very limited efficacy in motivating action. Rational constructs, as necessary as they may be, cannot be expected to carry the burden alone: human rights norms must be internalized, inclinations to be partial or indifferent must be neutralized, and imagination, compassion, and the emotions of caring must be enlisted on behalf of distant brethren.

The Globalization of Human Rights

Among the many reasons for the burgeoning rise of human rights, we must acknowledge their continuing vitality in resisting unjust and abusive uses of power. The globalizing effects of media and information technologies have carried discourse about rights into areas not previously penetrated, such as the hinterlands of China (Gibney, 1999). Human rights norms are increasingly hailed as justifications for arguments against uneven development and gross economic inequalities generated by economic globalization (George, 1999; Pogge, 2002), and to demand that the affluent do more to alleviate the suffering of the poor (Chatterjee, 2004). States and international organizations such as the UN and NATO are less reluctant to engage in humanitarian intervention in response to genocide and other gross human rights violations, despite glaring lapses in will (Falk, 2006). Individuals responsible for crimes against humanity or crimes of war find it more difficult to evade the legal consequences of their conduct as indicated by wider acceptance of the doctrine of "universal jurisdiction" and the activities of tribunals at The Hague (Robertson, 1999).

On another front, human rights norms have a widening role in international law and the structure and justification of governments (Risse, Ropp, and Sikkink, 1999). For instance, given widespread knowledge of the benefits of democratic governments, such as in averting famine, and lively debates over deliberative democracy, there is increasing interest in a "right to democracy" (Crocker, 2008; Gould, 2004). One very important development is the stepped-up "justiciability" of human rights norms. The number of critical covenants and declarations passed since the Universal Declaration was adopted in 1948 are very extensive and provide both broad and ample material for legal interpretation. Thus, there has been considerable development of what can be characterized as "justiciable" or legally interpretable human rights norms, as they move successively from broad clauses in ratified documents such as the International Covenant on Economic, Social and Cultural Rights to applicable, or "actionable," principles and standards of positive law. The European Court of Human Rights has had an especially prominent role in this transformation because its decisions are accepted as binding by member states of the European Union and are increasingly accepted as precedents even by nonmembers (Weston, 2006). Rights principles and provisions are being included within the constitutions of newly independent states, are cited by appellate courts in deciding cases (in countries as diverse as Kenya and Russia), and are increasingly recognized as providing protection for certain traditional groups, such as indigenous peoples and ethnic and cultural groups (Simmons, 2006; Lyons and Myall, 2003; Steiner and Alston, 2000).

At the same time, it has to be admitted that some of the rising tide of rights rhetoric is a result of careless and inflated language, as well as confusion over the sort of activities human rights, as the justification for moral norms, should properly regulate. There is strong motivation for the inflation of human rights, for, as James Griffin reminds us, "One is transformed from beggar ('you ought to help me') to chooser ('it is mine by right'). If one can claim by right, one is not dependent upon the grace or kindness or charity of others" (2008, 92). A possible example of this kind is the so-called third generation right to development proclaimed by the UN General Assembly upon the initiative of developing countries but widely decried as merely an "aspirational" or "manifesto" right. However, while Arjun Sengupta (2006, 249–259) admits that the right to development is at present only an "in principle valid" human right and not yet a justiciable "legal" human right, he believes it can become legally binding "if an agreed procedure for its realization can be established" (250). Thus Sengupta believes the right to development can become legally binding even if it is not officially legislated by the UN General Assembly and then ratified by UN members. The cause is likely to be taken up by some of the numerous rights-advocacy NGOs, characterized by Howard Koh (2006, 312) as "transnational norm entrepreneurs" because of their vested interests in advancing the human rights agenda.

Of course, far more serious than possibly inflated rights claims are glaring failures to respect and protect human rights, including China's staunch resistance to civil and political rights (Foot, 2000) and the United States' checkered record on social and economic rights (Mittal and Rosset, 1999). While it is widely recognized that justification and theory can have limited effect when political will is absent or, worse, perversely self-interested, commentators have not fully appreciated the limited motivational effects of justifications. This is a subject I address below. At present we should also note that much of the global controversy over the universality of human rights versus cultural or moral relativism, highlighted by the "East Asian challenge," seems to be related to perceived inadequacies in justifications of human rights or the view that, in trying to make human rights theory do too much, human rights advocates have gone too far (An-Na'im, 1992; Bauer and Bell, 1999; Bell, Nathan, and Peleg, 2001; Churchill, 2006; Van Ness, 1999). The same can be said, I believe, about controversies over the human rights persons actually possess, priority rankings, supposed "trade-offs," and who ought to be obligated by rights claims (Donnelly, 2003).

Justifications Contrasted with Theories

If we do face something like a "justificatory deficit" (Buchanan, 2004) for human rights, we need to reconsider what it is reasonable to expect *justificatory arguments* to accomplish in contrast to *theories* of human rights. Allen Buchanan (2004, 127–128) and Simon Caney (2005, 65–66) have taken the helpful step of identifying criteria, or desiderata, but they continue to speak ambiguously about a satisfactory "account" fulfilling these criteria. We want a justification of human rights to be robust and compelling, but it will never be more than one element of a theory. In brief, we justify human rights by showing what it is about persons that has intrinsic worth, or that comprises their dignity, and by showing how this worth, or dignity, suffuses the life of human beings as evaluative, purposive, and self-directing agents. This is a justification best elaborated, as I show below, in terms of what Griffin calls "normative agency" (2008, 32–33). Before continuing with issues of justification, however, it is helpful to look at desiderata for theories of human rights to see what is *not* to be included in a proper justification.

In the first place, it seems highly desirable that a theory have *determinacy*. In addition to a justification, or argument, showing why human beings have human rights, a theory should enable us to determine what specific rights humans possess as a result of their normative agency, or how specific human rights can be derived from our status as normative agents. Determinacy pertains to the applicability of human rights norms as guides for life. However, providing complete "lists" of derivable rights to fit the contingent conditions of life goes well beyond what can be expected of a justification. At most, in specifying what is necessary for our status as normative agents, that is, the basic liberties, needs, and interests that must be met in order for life to qualify as a truly human life, a justification will yield only the basic or fundamental human rights. Moreover, the rights specified by a justification will remain abstract; it is the function of more specific theories and policies to show how human rights can be realized in the particular, concrete conditions of life.

Second, it is necessary that a theory have *coherency*: The human rights derived from our understanding of human dignity, and all human rights norms derived from a set of basic and general rights should be internally coherent. Moreover, a theory should provide a clear distinction between human rights and claims (e.g., for entitlements, liberties, privileges, immunities) that ought not to be regarded as human rights claims or entitlements. This tenet applies to theories, but to justifications as well. Proposed "pluralist approaches," as noted below, seem particularly prone to miss this mark.

Third, a theory of human rights ought to have *claimability* (Griffin, 2008, 107–110). This condition requires that it must be possible that the duty-bearers corresponding to rights-holders be specifiable. Of course a good theory will go farther and indicate how to understand the differences between types of duties and the various ways in which individuals and institutions bear correlative duties, as well as which rights require duties to refrain or abstain (negative duties) and which require duties to assist, aid, or provide (positive duties). However, some theorists seem to have proceeded in the reverse order, and have claimed that, because actual agents with correlative objects cannot be identified, human rights requiring positive duties, often dubbed "welfare rights," cannot be justified (O'Neill, 1991, 131–134; Wellman, 1982, 181). Among Henry Shue's accomplishments in *Basic Rights* (1996) is a persuasive demonstration that apparent limits to the claimability of human rights can often be overcome by drawing more careful distinctions between possible duties, and in particular, distinctions between duties to protect, to provide, and to promote.

A further desiderata for a theory of human rights is what, for lack of a better term, might be called *separability.* The point is that while human rights are justified as an indispensable part of our moral lives, they should not be regarded as coextensive with the realm of morality concern and behavior. As Griffin notes, "It is a great, but now common, mistake to think that, because we see rights as especially important in morality, we must make everything especially important in morality into a right" (2008, 43). A good theory ought to draw boundary lines and show how important elements of compensatory, distributive, and retributive justice fall outside the proper scope of human rights. Neither should a good theory confuse human rights with some conception of virtuous living, the good or flourishing life, or human perfection.

A fifth proposed criterion for a theory of human rights is what James Nickel refers to as *feasibility* (2007, 80–82) and what Griffin calls *practicalities* (2008, 37–39). Both terms pertain to the conditions, some relevant to human capacities—physical and psychological—and some social and material, but all prerequisites for enabling human rights to yield, in Griffin's words, "effective, socially manageable claim[s] on others" (38). It is a mistake, however, to suppose that feasibility is part of the justification of human rights. The grounds for human rights remain the same as long as human beings, or moral persons, exist. The inherent worth of humans does not cease to justify certain forms of respect due to them, and thus human rights do not cease, even when addressees are genuinely unable to fulfill correlative obligations and therefore have legitimate excuses. Practicalities are subject to changing conditions; what we cannot do on behalf of impoverished, injured, and diseased Haitians today, we may well find possible to do for Haitians or others with similar needs tomorrow.

Nickel also speaks of human rights as justifiable only if they pass a feasibility test that includes consequentialist considerations about costs, such as the costs of their implementation (2007, 82–86). But this notion and Nickel's talk of human rights sliding between the categories of "almost justified," "fully justified," and "unjustified" based on the consequences of protecting them (86) confuses issues that ought to be kept distinct. There are a number of moral considerations for deciding, at the end of the day, what it is morally best to do. A moral argument might show that a human right must be derogated—that is, that it is morally permissible in specific circumstances to restrict the exercise of a right—especially if this argument shows that exercising the right in question would result in the violation of the equally basic human rights of a greater number of people.

Of course, reaching such a decision does not involve justifying (or un-justifying) the right in question, as the status of the right does not change. It has not been frequently recognized but needs to be emphasized that while prudential, pragmatic, and utilitarian arguments are arguments *for* accepting human rights norms, they are *not* arguments justifying human rights. One can accept the view that countries that protect human rights are likely to be more stable, peaceful, and prosperous (Talbott, 2005) without needing to be persuaded that persons have inalienable human rights. Perhaps inability to appreciate this point results from failure to appreciate the "separability" condition for human rights, that is, that rights norms do not encompass all that is important in morality, including consequentialist considerations and facets of fairness or distributive justice.

Justifying Human Rights

The preceding outline of some recommended features for theories of human rights should make it clear what it is reasonable to expect theories to do but unreasonable to require of a justification. All the same, there are different approaches to the justification of human rights. It is natural therefore to consider which of the most plausible approaches is best. One way to proceed is to inquire first about the merits of "pluralistic" approaches to justification, that is, those approaches that attempt to combine different kinds of arguments. We should then ask, "Do human rights form a coherent set derivable from a single theory or a set of fundamental, consistent principles?" If the answer is no, then different human rights will have to be justified by appeal to very different features of persons or very different basic moral principles. For instance, the right not to be tortured might have to be justified by appeal to basic needs or interests or moral principles very different from the needs, interests, and principles to which we appeal when justifying another human right such as the right to minimal sustenance. If this is the case, then a pluralistic justification will be needed. So far as I can tell, however, the only approaches that suggest that the moral principles or considerations grounding human rights form an inconsistent set are pluralist approaches themselves. Thus, since a pluralistic justificatory framework is not necessary and might involve some inconsistency, we need to consider whether it offers significant offsetting advantages.

Both Allen Buchanan (2004) and James Nickel (2007) advocate pluralistic approaches. The diverse grounds for justification Nickel endorses include prudential reasoning, utilitarian and pragmatic justifications, arguments from plausible moral norms and values (for instance fairness, dignity, minimal well-being, security, and liberty), and what he calls "linkage arguments" that one right is necessary for the effective implementation of another (2007, 53). Buchanan embraces arguments based on the moral equality of persons (in which group he includes well-being or interest arguments, autonomy arguments, and composites of the two), arguments from central human capabilities as propounded by Amartya Sen and Martha Nussbaum, utilitarian arguments, and religious justifications (2004, 131–142).

Why promote a medley of arguments over a single robust and persuasive argument? Here is Nickel's response: "When one pushes good ways of justifying human rights off the stage and puts one's own single favored way in the limelight, one's justification may look thin and vulnerable. Alone under the spotlight, its weak spots are likely to be apparent. Readers may think that if this is the best justification for human rights, those rights are really shaky" (2007, 53–54).

Appeals to pluralistic approaches to justification are thus pragmatic or strategic; they seem to suggest to wary readers that somehow the cumulative effect of several arguments should compensate for any single argument that might look too "shaky" on its own. However, what a reader might want is a commitment from the author to provide the best possible argument. This objective is thwarted by the risk pluralistic approaches run of increasing incoherency in argumentation about rights. It seems unlikely, for example, that a utilitarian approach can be compatible with any justification of human rights according to which human rights are seen as "trumps" (Dworkin, 1977) over considerations of maximum utility. Moreover, increased confusion may result if fundamental but incompatible principles support the derivation of equally incompatible rights claims.

Despite recognizing that different arguments "rest on incompatible ethical or political theories," Buchanan claims they converge in support of a fairly standard list (2004, 128). One major difficulty with human rights discourse today, as noted above, has to do with concerns about "rights inflation" and "manifesto rights" in connection with contested rights claims and the resulting dispersion cast on rights as moral resources. Unless we are circumspect about the theoretical grounds that justify human rights, persons may be tempted to throw their own preferred arguments into the heady pluralistic "brew," further confusing the mix. Fortunately, the sensible list of "basic human rights" Buchanan himself identifies does not require anything like this heterogeneous plurality of justifications; this list can be derived from a single perspective, either respect for persons' fundamental interests (the so-called interest account) or, preferably, respect for normative agency.

Interest-Based and Agency-Based Justifications

While Kant emphasized that human beings have a certain status as persons, namely dignity, or inherent worth, that requires treating them with respect, Caney (2005, 75) notes that saying this does not indicate what aspects of persons merit respect. Yet it seems uncontroversial that human beings share both interests in avoiding debilitating harms or incapacities that make life less than minimally decent and interests in the freedoms and opportunities necessary for at least a chance for a fulfilling and rewarding life. Thus some theorists propose that treating persons with respect requires respecting their basic interests. Caney says that such an argument "moves in a fairly uncontroversial manner directly from a core interest to an important right and does not require any additional premises" (2005, 73). Indeed such core interests seem sufficient to justify protecting the goods or objects of these interests as basic human rights, whether this is freedom and bodily security (e.g., freedom from deadly force, assault, torture, imprisonment without trial) or interests in subsistence and avoiding starvation, malnutrition, and disease (Jones, 1999, 61–62).

Like Caney, Joseph Raz (1986) offers an interest-based theory of rights, claiming that a person has a right if and only if an aspect of the person's well-being—his or her interest—is a sufficient reason for imposing correlative duties on other persons (166). Ronald Dworkin (2000, 242–276) and Will Kymlicka (2002, 13–20, 214–217) likewise offer versions of interest-based justifications for human rights. Amartya Sen (1999) and Martha Nussbaum (2000) direct attention to the functions that are of "central importance to a human life" and interpret human interests and well-being as having the capabilities for these central functions. Nussbaum calls attention to "central capabilities" in ten areas of human life (2000, 78–80).

Efforts to ground human rights on core interests or central capabilities do move us in the right direction. Obviously any reasonable account of human rights must advocate protection of those goods or objects without which human life is impossible—air, food, water, shelter, rest, health, and companionship. Yet, it is not clear that emphasizing fundamental interests, or needs, or capabilities takes us as close to the basis of the inherent value in being human as we can get. The category of interests is very broad: though I have a fundamental interest in whatever is indispensable for my dignity, the reverse does not hold; not all my interests can be dignified. Yet, interest-based accounts of human rights also risk being too narrow, for persons may be unjustly denied some rights such as civil and political rights, for example, due process or freedom of association, although they may not have an interest in them for they do not see themselves in need of them. As Griffin notes, were he denied his freedom of religious observance, then "I am not thereby ailing or malfunctioning. What is functioning badly is my society" (2008, 89).

As this example suggests, what we regard as basic interests are not only empirical; they also seem worryingly contingent. The standard response to this worry is that when we speak of persons' *basic* interests we are referring to what all reasonable people recognize as necessary for a minimally decent human existence, provided they have knowledge of serious but standard threats to human well-being. As Caney (2005, 76–77) shows, we can block the challenge that, because any account of human interests will be partial, the interest approach is unsatisfactory. At the same time, however, because our emphasis is not just on "interests common to all people" but also those interests that are "constitutive of a decent life"

(Buchanan, 2004, 127), then ought we not to inquire why some interests are of such special worth that we recognize moral value in our responses to them? In other words, either it just happens to be a fact that humans agree on matters regarding fundamental interests, or these interests are "uncontroversial" for some deeper reason, namely, that it is morally wrong not to respect these interests.

Thus it is not our core interests *per se* that ground the morality of human rights but features of human beings that endow these interests with moral significance. In my view, justificatory arguments that provide this extra but necessary step focus on the inherent worth of persons as autonomous and purposive agents (Boylan, 2004; Churchill, 2006, 28–32; Gewirth, 1996, 14–19; Gould, 2004, 33–34; Griffin, 2008, 32–37, 44–48). The features of human existence that make humans worthy of special respect pertain to our capacities for choice among alternatives, the importance to us of having purpose and forming plans and of activity, of doing, and not just having certain things, or being in certain states; of taking charge of our lives and making our own decisions; and of evaluating, forming conceptions of a worthwhile life, and attaching meaning to experiences with others as we seek to meet our ends. As Griffin says, "We have a conception of our past and future. We reflect and assess. We form pictures of what a good life would be . . . and we try to realize these pictures" (2008, 32). Gould speaks of "transformative power" (2004, 71) in referring to the ability of humans to realize long-term projects and participate in their development. For similar reasons Griffin refers to humans as "self-deciders" and speaks, quite appropriately, of human beings as "normative agents" (2008, 33).

Justification and the Problem of Universality

Justifications of human rights as grounded in normative agency are superior to interest-based arguments as they can subsume the latter and they reveal not just that we have core interests, but why these interests matter. Here I shall not attempt to present a fully developed normative agency-based argument. Instead, I turn to a critically important feature of justificatory arguments that has hitherto seemed problematic. This problem concerns the universality of justificatory arguments, that is, demonstrations that all persons everywhere possess human rights equally. As Nickel notes, prudential reasons are those relating to a person's own prospects for a good life, and Nickel asserts that in taking others' interests and well-being into account we are "moving to the moral point of view" (Nickel, 2007, 54, 58). Even advocates of agency-based justifications seem to be at a loss over how best to close the apparent "gap" between prudential and moral reasoning. For instance, Griffin speaks of the "transference" of reasonableness from the first-person case to the universal: "a reasonable person who recognizes the prudential value of autonomy will also recognize the respect that it is due" in others generally (2008, 135). Yet, Griffin admits, "I find it very hard to understand the nature of the transition from prudence to morality" (2008, 134).

For the most part, theorists have proceeded as if they understood the problem as first convincing the reader about the justification of human rights and then showing why, if one agrees that one is a rights holder, denying the same status to others involves logical inconsistency. Given this strategy, let us call these *first-person* arguments. Now, such efforts seem rather strained and unsatisfactory, depending as they do on a rather stark principle of rationality famously associated with applying Kant's categorical imperative and generally called the principle of "universalizability." Some version of this logical principle is widely used in theories of human rights; for example, I rely on it in my book (Churchill, 2006, 10–12) and Caney offers a logically comparable "scope requirement" (2005, 65) to show that any justification successful in demonstrating that some persons have civil, political, or subsistence human rights also succeeds in showing that relevantly similar others must have these rights as well.

The principle does its required job in establishing a conceptual point, that is, in showing that human rights norms must be *conceived* as applying universally: in exactly the same way to all relevantly similar persons. But let us ask, "What more can we expect this merely formal principle to accomplish?" Universalizability as a formal principle is too weak to justify respecting the rights of others and first-person arguments are misconceived. They proceed by making a case for the importance of my interests or my agency as if I were a solitary individual, and then assume that a further appeal to logical principles can persuade me that I ought to have an interest in the welfare of complete strangers. The gap between the individual and others is increased, not diminished, by dwelling on the interests and agency of the solitary individual; given the emphasis on self-interest in a world in which scarcity is a fact, and life often fragile, appeals to logical consistency will hardly be effective.

Anyone not already sympathetically motivated to respond to the plight of others is likely to remain unmoved. I want certain protections from harm and certain necessities for life, and if the grounds for my wanting these things is sufficient warrant for my claiming them as my rights, then the fact that others claim their needs and interests warrant the same claim suggests that they may be in competition with me. My interests stop with the limits of my consciousness, body, family, nation, and so forth, and if it appears that respecting the interests of others in Africa or Asia will result in net losses for me, then I will not think I have sufficient reason for making the interests of strangers my own. Showing me that I am being logically inconsistent by violating some universalizability or scope requirement will hardly affect me if I believe the sacrifice of my own core interests or duties to my family or compatriots are at stake.

We can distinguish two difficulties related to first-person arguments. By starting first with the prudential case and then "moving" to ethical concern for others, first-person arguments reinforce widely held intuitions about the differences of duties to peoples. These arguments reinforce the impression that it is more difficult to make the case for the human rights of distant others or that others' rights impose either no obligations or much weaker obligations on us. Second, first-person arguments suffer from a defect analogous to the central difficulty in convincing self-interested state actors to respect human rights. Prudential appeals to agents, whether individuals or states, to "go moral" by taking the interests of others into account, face the difficulty of attempting to convince agents that respecting the interests of others is in their own self-interests (Schulz, 2001). This way of proceeding subjects our thinking about human rights and our obligations to the vagaries of fortune, to the notorious difficulties of determining what will promote our best interests, and to temptations to engage in means-end calculations.

Solving the "Problem of Universality"

There is an alternative way to solve, or dissolve, the "problem of universality" and this involves demonstrating that there is no gap in the first place. That is, I do not first accept prudential reasons for claiming my rights and then seek moral reasons for respecting the rights of others. On the contrary, I argue that coming to understand myself as a rights holder necessarily requires an understanding of humans in general as rights holders. Thus, I maintain that the normative perspective logically precedes the prudential and the universal condition logically precedes the concrete or individual case. In making this argument, I develop certain insights and ideas in the works of Gould (2004) and Griffin (2008), although I accept full responsibility for any errors of interpretation. It must be remarked as well that, although I believe dissolving the problem of universality endows the normative agency justification with greater effect in motivating respect for human rights, there are, as I explain in the last section, significant limits on the ability of any justification to motivate behavior.

Carol Gould grounds human rights on agency, which she characterizes as "a normative imperative." She says, "There is an equal and valid claim—that is to say, a right—to the conditions of self-development on the part of each human being. On this view, to recognize others as human beings is to acknowledge their agency" (2004, 33–34). Gould adds that seeing other persons as rights bearers is "ingredient in our recognition of the other as a human being" (34). I interpret Gould as saying that our *recognizing* others as rights holders emerges, and thus, is partly constitutive of our understanding of them as human beings. Beholding the face and presence of another as human necessarily puts me in a normative relationship with this other. Moreover, my understanding of my needs or my interests as vital for me necessarily entails my understanding the vitality of these needs and interests for other persons and vice versa. As Griffin says, "For me to see anything as enhancing my life, I must see it as enhancing life in general in a generally intelligible way, in a way that pertains to human life and not just to my particular life" (2008, 114).

Griffin points to continuity between the necessary conditions for the intelligibility of our language and the intelligibility involved in understanding our activities and in appreciating value (2008, 111–128, and especially 113–119). Drawing on the thought of Wittgenstein and Donaldson, Griffin reminds us that we cannot even interpret the language others use without assuming that we share beliefs, attitudes, and emotions in common with others (113). What we might refer to as the "bounds of intelligibility" is publicly shared among persons. For instance, as Griffin notes, if I want to accomplish something significant with my life, I do not decide about the value of my objective by appeal to my own subjective states, at least not wholly. Rather, "what plays a key role is my understanding of what accomplishment is." Moreover, this sort of understanding comes with its own standards of success that are, in this sense, independent of me and experienced as making demands on me. For this reason, Griffin refers to my apprehension of these standards and the values they represent as a kind of "perception" (114).

In recognizing values, we exhibit our peculiar sensitivity as a species to the sometimes dangerous, sometimes fulfilling goings-on in the only world humans can inhabit. We perceive some activities as purposive and some events as fulfilling or beneficial because we share a reservoir of human experience and knowledge. Likewise, it is not just my desiring physical security or sustenance that makes them valuable to me, nor are they valuable because I first have an interest in them. Griffin makes this point clearly (in a way that echoes the question Socrates posed to Euthyphro): "For anyone to see anything as valuable, from any point of view, requires being able to see it as worth wanting. This is a perfectly general requirement on values" (115). The distinction between merely wanting or desiring and the sort of wanting connected with value (wanting what is *worth* wanting) corresponds to the distinction between intentions arising from our subjective states and cases in which our subjective experiences, beliefs, attitudes, and subsequent actions are intelligible only in terms of shared perception and experience. To perceive something as valuable, as worth wanting, "is to see it under the heading of some general human interest" (Griffin, 2008, 115). Griffin adds, quite aptly, "To see anything as making life better, we must see it as an instance of something generally intelligible as valuable and, furthermore, as valuable for any normal human being" (115).

If this interpretation is correct, then the upshot is that the general, or universal, case is logically and normatively prior to the individual and prudential case.

Thus, the first-person account gets things backward. Every particular case in which a human right is justifiably claimed can be regarded as a particular instantiation of a universal condition and derives its normative force from the universal. The intelligibility of my claiming certain liberties or certain goods (the objects of subsistence rights) as *human rights* presupposes understanding oneself as a person who, as a normative agent, possesses inherent worth or dignity. And this understanding presupposes, in turn, that I see myself as a being of a certain *kind* and as representing or standing up for—when I must claim my rights—what is truly valuable about human beings generally.

Let us note what takes place if I am accused of a crime, for instance, or I am in need of food, water, shelter, or I desperately seek to avoid torture, and I claim as a right to be presumed innocent unless proven guilty, or I claim food, water, shelter, or not to be tortured as my rights. If I claim these liberties or necessities *as human rights*, then I claim them not for who I am in my concrete particularity as an American, a citizen, a resident, a university professor and so forth, but *as a person*, that is, my claim is that this is not the way a human being is treated, and thus, my claim is made in the name of all of humanity. Interests in preserving normative agency that arise as *mine* in a particular case, if I am arrested or find myself without subsistence, for example, are intelligible only because normative agency is inherently valuable, always and everywhere.

Because we are goal creating, purposive, and evaluative agents, we are able to contemplate and anticipate various ways in which life can go wrong and our normative agency might be defeated or obstructed by others. Because we cannot know in advance when serious threats to agency might arise, what we can recognize as "standard threats" (Shue, 1996; Donnelly, 2003) must be condemned as wrongs by normative agents. The moral force of the ought attaching to respect for agency thus arises in conditions of generality, or universality: it arises from recognition of the incompatibility between the "existence conditions" (Griffin, 2008, 44) for persons as normative agents and conditions or states of the world that drive humans below the threshold of effective agency.

The Problem of Motivation

Why did first-person arguments starting with prudential reasons appear plausible in the first place? Surely this had to do with the fact that ordinarily individuals have no occasion to claim their rights except when they are being violated or when a serious threat lurks. So practicalities determine when rights come into play: when entitlements are claimed, and others either respond or fail to do so. For instance, most people will not recognize the universality of the right to subsistence when they and those they know and care for have food and water sufficient to ward off hunger or chronic malnutrition. Of course, whether or not persons claim their rights depends on a multitude of contingencies, including one's understanding of rights and the nature of the threat, the availability and saliency of the discourse of rights in one's society, whether invoking the right is necessary to avert a threat or assuage a loss, and rather grimly, whether or not there is any basis for hoping that in claiming one's rights one will be met with a positive response. Yet when a person feels up against some wall, her needs are desperate, and others fail to respond adequately, a demand that was first expressed as a right may, over time and with the continued indifference of strangers, come to be felt by her in very much the same way it is seen by those who do not respond—as no more than a matter of her own personal interests. Tragically, she may come to see herself as others treat her—as isolated, worthless, and disposable.

As noted at the outset, despite the preeminence of human rights in our globalizing world, it is distressing that human rights are violated so frequently, so gravely and vastly. Though less ghastly, the capacity of so many of the affluent in our world to be so callous and indifferent about the grinding poverty and chronic hunger of a majority of humanity is almost as depressing. Given all of this evidence, it is tempting to conclude that justifications for human rights have failed. If only we had a better, more persuasive justification of human rights, one might think, people would be more strongly motivated to respect and to protect the rights of persons other than themselves or their own group. However, I believe this worry confuses the problem of justifying human rights with a further problem lying outside the scope of justificatory arguments. I call this additional problem the *problem of motivation.*

Now, unless we are prepared to be convinced rationalists and to reject Hume's warnings about the influence of the emotions, as well as a host of empirical studies, we ought to be skeptical about the ability of humans to be motivated by reason alone. We have to accept the reasonable limits of justifications in appealing to the intellect. Thus I propose we adapt Kant's strategy by undertaking a "Copernican Revolution" and changing our vantage point. We have been asking, "What is wrong with justifications of human rights such that they fail sufficiently to motivate people"? Instead we should ask, "What is wrong with people that they are not sufficiently motivated by arguments for human rights?" What is wrong with us does not have to do with reason or perception, at least not for most of us most of the time. Yet why do humans defect with such distressing frequency from normal, expected behavior? We do not need to be persuaded that, although healthily endowed with sympathy and benevolence, as Hume noted, we often allow self-interest to prevail in ways that are detrimental to others. As Aristotle astutely observed, "It may well be that regard for oneself is a feeling implanted by nature, and not a mere random impulse. Self-love is rightly censured, but that is not so much loving oneself as loving oneself in excess" (Aristotle, 2005 [c. 325 BCE], 186).

More surprising, if not alarming, are the destructive effects of a whole array of phenomena first introduced to philosophers as the "banality of evil" by Hannah Arendt (1963). Subsequently, dozens of studies and experiments in the social and behavioral sciences document the capacity of ordinarily cooperative, caring, and respectful persons to be indifferent to others and even to commit abhorrently destructive acts. This is not counter evidence against my claims about the universality of human rights, for these research results converge in showing that these alarming effects are due to *situational factors* commonly characterized as the "power of the situation" such as conformity or peer pressure, obedience to authority, depersonalization, the diffusion of responsibility, anonymity, the bystander effect, and social contagion (Glover, 1999; Zimbardo, 2007). Nevertheless, it is an ugly fact about us that, in addition to our partiality for ourselves and those we know and care about, it is difficult to imagine the plight of those we cannot know as individuals, and as our sensitivities and imaginations falter, so does our sympathy.

Sociologists Christie Davies and Mark Neal (2001) have demonstrated experimentally what we each must suspect based on anecdotal evidence, that is, without intentional bias, all persons are not assigned the same degree of consideration even within the same community. Davies and Neal distinguish between full particular persons, statistical persons, and potential persons. The salient characteristic of "full particular persons" is that they possess a recognizable "coherent self" whose existence others can discern, understand, and appreciate. Of course, those defined as "statistical persons" also possess these properties but, "since no one knows who they are" as individuals, "their personhood is less visible, vivid, and capable of comprehension" (69–70). Mere "potential persons" (fetuses, babies, very young children, and those severely incapacitated) lack a recognizable, coherent "self."

Davies and Neal note that almost unlimited resources might be expended to save the life of a miner trapped underground when his plight is clearly visible to the nation via the media. Yet nearly a miner a week dies in Britain from routine causes. During World War II, major population centers full of statistical people were bombed with horrific loss of life without much public protest. At the same time, however, it was viewed as wrong to send a full particular person to absolutely certain death, however desperate the situation. For instance in 1941 when British pilots had to face almost certain death by charging Zeppelins to prevent the bombing of London, it was arranged that pilots draw lots for the task. "The British pilots had to be converted into statistical persons" and this was done "by reintroducing the element of chance into the situation, using the impersonal anonymous statistical procedure of drawing lots" (72).

It remains unclear whether the tendency to convert distant and unknown others into statistical persons is primarily a result of self-absorption and the absence of knowledge, effort, and imagination, necessary for effective compassion, or whether—more chillingly—the tendency to convert others into cold and abstract statistics reflects a limitation on our capacity to care. If we are social animals, are we capable of being fully human only in very small face-to-face societies? This is a dreadful suggestion, and Michael Boylan (2011), for one, has propounded an "extended-community worldview imperative" that, if implemented successfully, could demonstrate that this dark thought is false, as well as contribute significantly to overcoming the problem of motivation. Boylan's imperative requires that "Each agent must educate himself as much as he is able about the peoples of the world—their access to the basic goods of agency, their essential commonly held cultural values, and their governmental and institutional structures—in order that he might individually and collectively accept the duties that ensue from those peoples' legitimate rights claims, and act accordingly within what is aspirationally possible." This is a very good first step, but it needs to be accompanied by collaboration between philosophers and social and behavioral scientists across a range of issues—not least being questions of socialization and the internalization of human rights norms—if we are to realize the genuinely global reach of human rights.

References

An-Na'im, Abdullahi Ahmed, ed. (1992). *Human Rights in Cross-Cultural Perspectives: A Quest for Consensus.* Philadelphia: University of Pennsylvania Press.

Arendt, Hannah. (1963). *Eichmann in Jerusalem: A Report on the Banality of Evil.* New York: Viking Press.

Aristotle. (2005 [c. 325 BCE]). *Politics,* trans. Ernest Barker, rev. R. F. Stalley, in *Political Philosophy: The Essential Texts,* ed. Steven M. Cahn: 129–169. Oxford: Oxford University Press.

Bauer, Joanne R., and Daniel A. Bell, ed. (1999). *The East Asian Challenge for Human Rights.* Cambridge: Cambridge University Press.

Bell, Lynda S., Andrew J. Nathan, and Ilan Peleg, ed. (2001). *Negotiating Culture and Human Rights.* New York: Columbia University Press.

Boylan, Michael. (2004). *A Just Society.* Lanham, MD: Rowman and Littlefield.

Boylan, Michael. (2011). *Morality and Global Justice.* Boulder, CO: Westview.

Buchanan, Allen. (2004). *Justice, Legitimacy, and Self-Determination: Moral Foundations for International Law.* Oxford: Oxford University Press.

Caney, Simon. (2005). *Justice Beyond Borders: A Global Political Theory.* Oxford: Oxford University Press.

Chatterjee, Deen K. (2004). *The Ethics of Assistance: Morality and the Distant Needy.* Cambridge: Cambridge University Press.

Churchill, Robert Paul. (2006). *Human Rights and Global Diversity.* Upper Saddle River, NJ: Pearson Prentice Hall.

Claude, Richard Pierre, and Burns H. Weston, ed. (2006). *Human Rights in the World Community: Issues and Action, Third Edition.* Philadelphia: Pennsylvania University Press.

Crocker, David A. (2008). *Ethics of Global Development: Agency, Capability, and Deliberative Democracy.* Cambridge: Cambridge University Press.

Davies, Christie, and Mark Neal. (2001). "Ethics and the Person: Risk, Moral Recognition and Modernity" in *Virtue Ethics and Sociology: Issues of Modernity and Religion,* ed. Kieran Flanagan and Peter C. Jupp: 68–91. Basingstoke, Eng.: Palgrave.

Donnelly, Jack. (2003). *Universal Human Rights in Theory and Practice, Second Edition.* Ithaca, NY: Cornell University Press.

Dworkin, Ronald. (2000). *Sovereign Virtue: The Theory and Practice of Equality.* Cambridge, MA: Harvard University Press.

Dworkin, Ronald. (1977). *Taking Rights Seriously.* Cambridge, MA: Harvard University Press.

Falk, Richard. (2006). "Humanitarian Intervention: Imperatives and Problematics" in *Human Rights in the World Community,* ed. Richard Claude Pierre and Burns H. Weston: 401–410. Philadelphia: University of Pennsylvania Press.

Foot, Rosemary. (2000). *Rights Beyond Borders: The Global Community and the Struggle over Rights in China.* Cambridge: Cambridge University Press.

George, Susan. (1999). "Globalizing Rights?" in *Globalizing Rights,* ed. Matthew J. Gibney: 15–33. Oxford: Oxford University Press.

Gewirth, Alan. (1996). *The Community of Rights.* Chicago: University of Chicago Press.

Gibney, Matthew J., ed. (1999). *Globalizing Rights: The Oxford Amnesty Lectures 1999.* Oxford: Oxford University Press.

Glover, Jonathan. (1999). *Humanity: A Moral History of the Twentieth Century.* London: Jonathan Cape.

Gould, Carol C. (2004). *Globalizing Democracy and Human Rights.* Cambridge: Cambridge University Press.

Griffin, James. (2008). *On Human Rights.* Oxford: Oxford University Press.

Jones, Charles. (1999). *Global Justice: Defending Cosmopolitanism.* Oxford: Oxford University Press.

Kymlicka, Will. (2002). *Contemporary Political Philosophy: An Introduction, Second Edition.* Oxford: Clarendon Press.

Koh, Harold Hongju. (2006). "How Is International Human Rights Law Enforced?" in *Human Rights in the World Community,* ed. Richard Pierre Claude and Burns H. Weston: 305–314. Philadelphia: University of Pennsylvania Press.

Lyons, Gene M., and James Myall, ed. (2003). *International Human Rights in the 21st Century: Protecting the Rights of Groups.* Lanham, MD, and Oxford: Rowman and Littlefield.

Mittal, Anuradha, and Peter Rosset, ed. (1999). *America Needs Human Rights.* Oakland, CA: Food First Books.

Nickel, James W. (2007). *Making Sense of Human Rights, Second Edition.* Malden, MA: Blackwell Publishing.

Nussbaum, Martha C. (2000). *Women and Human Development: The Capabilities Approach.* Cambridge: Cambridge University Press.

Pogge, Thomas W. (2002). *World Poverty and Human Rights: Cosmopolitan Responsibilities and Reforms.* Cambridge: Polity Press.

O'Neill, Onora. (1991). *Towards Justice and Virtue.* Cambridge: Cambridge University Press.

Raz, Joseph. (1986). *The Morality of Freedom.* Oxford: Clarendon Press.

Risse, Thomas, Stephen C. Ropp, and Kathryn Sikkink, ed. (1999). *The Power of Human Rights: International Norms and Domestic Change.* Cambridge: Cambridge University Press.

Robertson, Geoffrey. (1999). *Crimes Against Humanity: The Struggle for Global Justice.* New York: The New Press.

Schulz, William. (2001). *In Our Own Best Interest: How Defending Human Rights Benefits All of Us.* Boston: Beacon Press.

Sen, Amartya. (1999). *Development as Freedom.* New York: Random House.

Sengupta, Arjun. (2006). "The Right to Development" in *Human Rights in the World Community,* ed. Richard Pierre Claude and Burns H. Weston: 249–259. Philadelphia: University of Pennsylvania Press.

Shue, Henry. (1996). *Basic Rights: Subsistence, Affluence, and United States Foreign Policy, Second Edition.* Princeton, NJ: Princeton University Press.

Simmons, Beth A. (2006). *Mobilizing for Human Rights: International Law and Domestic Politics.* New York: Cambridge University Press.

Steiner, Henry J., and Philip Alston, ed. (2000). *International Human Rights in Context: Law, Politics, Morals, Second Edition.* Oxford: Oxford University Press.

Talbott, William. (2005). *Which Rights Should Be Universal?* Oxford: Oxford University Press.

Van Ness, Peter, ed. (1999). *Debating Human Rights: Critical Essays from the United States and China.* London: Routledge.

Wellman, Carl. (1982). *Welfare Rights.* Totawa, NJ: Rowman and Allanheld.

Weston, Burns H. (2006). "Human Rights: Prescription and Enforcement" in *Human Rights in the World Community,* ed. Richard Pierre Claude and Burns H. Weston: 294–304. Philadelphia: University of Pennsylvania Press.

Zimbardo, Philip G. (2007). *The Lucifer Effect: Understanding How Good People Turn Evil.* New York: Random House.

CHAPTER TWO

On Justifying Human Rights

JOHN-STEWART GORDON
University of Cologne, Germany

Abstract

This chapter is a contribution to the philosophy of human rights and in particular to the vital issue of how to justify them. In the first and second part, I give a brief depiction of the nature of human rights and examine four different approaches to justifying human rights: the natural rights approach, the divine rights approach, the fundamental interests approach, and the personal autonomy approach. The third part broadly outlines and examines a novel approach, which can be called the rational rights approach to human rights, and is based on a modified version of Kant's notion of rationality and Rawls's idea of the veil of ignorance. The final part defends the rational rights approach against some main objections.

Key Words

human rights, justification, basic human needs, natural rights, fundamental interests, personal autonomy, rational rights

---

Introduction

In his principal ethical work, *On the Basis of Morality*, Schopenhauer rightly claims that to preach morality is easy but to justify it is complex. Likewise, to preach human rights is a rather easy task but to provide a sound philosophical

Author note: I am very grateful to Michael Boylan and Will Kymlicka for their helpful comments on earlier drafts of this chapter. This work is funded by the Heinrich Hertz Foundation (HHS, B41 No. 44/08).

justification for human rights is certainly one of the most challenging matters in philosophy. This is so because the burden of proof with regard to the concept of human rights is extraordinarily high. Broadly speaking, human rights are primary universal moral norms that bind all people in all places at all times; they are meant to be independent of legal recognition, and human beings have them simply because they are human beings. The long history of the justification of human rights is rife with different approaches, provided by philosophers such as Hart (1955, 1961), Rawls (1993), Shue (1980), Gewirth (1982, 1996), Nickel (1987), Rorty (1993), Walzer (1999), Orend (2002), Beitz (2009), and Griffin (2009). Many approaches, including the more promising ones, however, seem to fall short of providing a convincing justification for the ontological and epistemological problems concerning human rights. In this chapter, I provide a brief overview of a novel approach to justifying human rights based on Kant and Rawls. The first part contains a brief and general description of the nature of human rights. The second part deals with two classical and two modern types of justifications in the philosophy of human rights. In the third part, I present some general features of a novel justification of human rights as rational rights, and, in the fourth part, I discuss some objections concerning the approach. The chapter ends with some concluding remarks.

What Is a Human Right?

This part deals with the general idea of human rights in more detail by setting out the main defining features. The goal here is to answer briefly the question of what human rights are by providing a general description of the concept rather than a list[1] of specific rights.

Universality and High Priority[2]

Human rights are universal rights of high priority. The general idea is that they apply to all people in all places at all times. Although they are usually seen as having a Western origin, they apply to all human beings, whether they live in Africa, Asia, or elsewhere. Human rights have a high priority because of their general aim to secure the basic interests and needs of human beings and thereby set a minimal standard. According to Brian Orend (2002), human rights should secure *minimal levels of decent and respectful treatment* in order to establish the conditions for human beings to lead a minimally good life, and they do not represent a utopian ideal to create a morally perfect society. Any local tradition that does not comply with the idea of human rights, such as forced female genital mutilation or circumcision, has to be abandoned. In *Taking Rights Seriously* (1977), Ronald Dworkin coined the term "rights as trumps," which, he explained, in the context of human rights means that rights express the fundamental ideal of equality upon which the contemporary doctrine of human rights rests. Treating rights as trumps is a means of ensuring that all individuals are treated in an *equal* and *like* fashion in respect of the provision of fundamental human rights.

Moral Rights and Legal Rights

In the first place, human rights are universal moral rights, irrespective of whether they are enforced by local laws or not. They are typically seen as referring to moral facts that exist independently of, but with reference to, human beings, which is the view of moral realism. States (and people) that violate human rights or do not acknowledge their existence nevertheless act immorally by acting against this universal moral standard of basic rights (e.g., the former South African apartheid system, the caste system in India). In the second place, human rights are international legal rights, which should be integrated into local law in order to be most effective for human beings. Enforcement is necessary in order to avoid human rights becoming ineffective. Therefore, it is of utmost importance to put teeth into the law. Human rights need to receive universal legal recognition and the protection of the law (the US Bill of Rights in 1789, the French Declaration of the Rights of Man and the Citizen in 1789, the Universal Declaration of Human Rights in 1948, the International Covenant on Civil and Political Rights in 1966, and the International Covenant on Economic, Social, and Cultural Rights in 1966).

Claim Rights and Liberty Rights

Most scholars distinguish between two functional properties of human rights: claim rights and liberty rights. A claim right is a right one holds against another person or a group of persons (or the state) who owe a corresponding duty to the rights holder. Such a right can be positive or negative. A claim right is termed positive when a person has a right to some specific good or service, which another person or the state has a duty to provide. A negative right, in contrast, is a right one holds against other people or the state interfering in or trespassing upon one's life or property in some way. Both kinds of rights can be either held *in personam* or *in rem*. What does this mean? A claim right held *in personam* means that it is a right against a specifically identified duty holder; a claim right held *in rem* means, in contrast, that it is a right against no one in particular but applies to everyone. Liberty rights are primarily negative rights and exist in the absence of any duty not to perform some desired activity, and thus consist of those actions one is not prohibited from performing. Hence, a liberty right can be seen as a right to do as one pleases precisely because one is not under an obligation that is grounded in another person's claim right to refrain from so acting. Liberty rights provide for the capacity to be free without actually providing the specific means by which one may pursue the certain particular objects of one's will.

Whose Rights, Whose Duties?

One important feature that should be mentioned with regard to rights and duties concerns their relation. At first sight, it seems that rights and duties stand in a reciprocal and symmetrical relation to each other, but this assumption would be premature. Small children, for example, have rights but no corresponding duties. Reciprocity with regard to rights and duties holds only for the core area of morality depending on rational human beings. There is no reciprocity at the marginal areas of morality—only rights without corresponding duties. However, even in the core area of morality, some cases are an exception to the supposed symmetrical relation, such as the case of benevolence. Some people claim, not unconvincingly, that people do have a duty to be benevolent, but the duty of benevolence does not correspond to any claim right of a particular person. No person has a right to benevolence (see also supererogatory acts). The important point concerning human rights is that they correspond to basic duties. *All* human beings are protected by human rights and, at the same time, they also hold the corresponding basic duties ("doubly universal"). In practice, national governments and international institutions (the UN, the World Bank, the International Court of Justice, or NGOs such as Amnesty International or Human Rights Watch) secure human rights because they are most able to perform this task effectively.

On Justifying Human Rights

Human Rights as Natural Rights

The idea that there is a universal standard of evaluation of human behaviour and laws can be traced back to the classical Greek period, at least. Most notably it was brought to the fore by Aristotle, who distinguishes between "natural justice" and "legal justice" in the *Nicomachean Ethics.* He forcefully claims that "the natural is that which has the same validity everywhere and does not depend upon acceptance" (EN V. 10). Natural rights, according to Aristotle, exist before any specific social and political configurations, and can be determined by the exercise of reason free from the distorting effects of mere prejudice or desire. Any misconduct by governments against their citizens can be detected by the appeal of natural rights. In this context, Aristotle additionally refers to the case of Antigone[3] in order to illustrate his claims. Sophocles, a well-known classical Greek poet, in his tragedy *Antigone* (442 BCE), shows the conflict between the law and the reason of the state exemplified by Kreon and Antigone's "illegal" action of burying her brother Polyneikes against Kreon's decree. Antigone breaks with Kreon's decree because she believes it to be immoral. In her view, it violates the eternal law of nature and her conscience. How should one act in such a case? Is the immoral decree legally binding?

The doctrine of natural law in conjunction with the idea of human rights most clearly emerges during the seventeenth and eighteenth centuries in Europe. Analyses of the historical predecessors of the contemporary theory of human rights typically attribute a high degree of importance to John Locke, who provided the precedent of establishing legitimate political authority upon a rights foundation, which is an undeniably essential component of human rights. Locke's vital argument in his *Two Treatises of Government* (1688 [2005]) is as follows: Human beings possess natural rights, independently of the political recognition granted them by the state. These natural rights are possessed independently of and prior to the formation of any political community. Locke argues that natural rights stem from natural law. Natural law, in turn, originates from God. Accurately discerning the will of God provides one with an ultimately authoritative moral code. Each person owes a duty of self-preservation to God. In order to fulfil this duty of self-preservation successfully, each person has to be free from threats to life and liberty. In addition, this also requires what Locke presents as the basic positive means for self-preservation—personal property. The duty of self-preservation owed by individuals to God entails the necessary existence of basic natural rights to life, liberty, and property. Locke proceeds to argue that the main purpose of political authority in a sovereign state is the provision and protection of the people's basic natural rights. According to Locke, the protection and promotion of individuals' natural rights is the sole justification for the creation of the government. The natural rights to life, liberty, and property provide clear limits to the authority and jurisdiction of the state. States exist, in Locke's view, to serve the interests (the natural rights) of the people, not to satisfy the needs of a particular monarch or a ruling class. Remarkably, Locke argues that people are morally justified in taking up arms against their government in the event that the government systematically and deliberately fails in its duty to secure the people's natural rights.

According to the theory of natural law, natural rights are absolute universal moral norms that can be determined precisely by the *correct* use of reason. To cut a long story short, the natural rights approach faces two serious challenges. First, it is unclear whether there are any *absolute* universal moral norms (the ontological question) and, secondly, it is unclear what the exact criteria are to reason *correctly* in order to determine (true) natural rights (the epistemological question). Simply to state that there are natural rights is a *petitio principii* and therefore useless for a sound justification of human rights as natural rights. Likewise, simply to allege that there is a correct use to reason without providing a guideline or criteria for its correct use is pointless, unless one claims that common sense has enough power to do the work. However, the idea of common sense seems inappropriate to justify the high ontological demands of moral realism.[4]

Human Rights as Divine Rights

Aristotle's basic idea of natural rights was similarly expressed by the Roman stoics (e.g., Cicero and Seneca), who argue that morality originates in the rational will of God and the existence of a cosmic city from which one could discern a natural moral law whose authority transcends all local legal codes. The stoics argue that this universal moral code imposes upon all of us a duty to obey the will of God. Thereby, they posit the existence of a universal moral community, which is effected through our shared relationship with God. According to the stoics, there is a divine law that exists before all human contingent laws and functions as the ultimate standard of evaluation, which is a core feature of the idea of human rights, irrespective of whether these natural rights achieve the recognition of any given political ruler or assembly.

Subsequent to the classical stoic belief in the existence of a universal moral community, Judaism and Christianity certainly promoted the idea of human rights, but their influence has to be acknowledged with some caution for two main reasons. First, the Old Testament declares that every human being is created as an *imago dei* (God's image), but at the same time the Old Testament limits the potential of this thought by claiming that there is only one *chosen people*—the Jews. Secondly, Christianity extends the idea of the *chosen people* by extending it to *all* people, but finally it allowed the institution of slavery and the legal inequality of women. Despite this, according to the proponents of divine reasoning, human rights can be seen as being a part of divine law propagated in the Holy Scriptures.

The theological approach to human rights seems to answer the ontological and epistemological question. Human rights finally stem from God and people simply have to consult the Holy Scriptures (e.g., the Ten Commandments).[5] At first sight, this seems to be a sound line of reasoning. However, at second glance, it fails to be a proper justification for human rights for at least two main reasons. First, the very existence of God, who is the ultimate source of justification for human rights, is rather questionable given the flawed arguments about the existence of God. Thereby, the religious justification finally fails to show the existence of human rights. In order to prove the religious line of argumentation one has to address four vital issues: the proof, one, of God's existence; two, that God has a will; three, that God wants something from human beings; and four, that God wants the human beings to act in accordance with His commandments. Secondly, even if God's existence is true for those who believe in God, nonetheless it does not have the same standing for nonbelievers. The truth simply is that believers and nonbelievers do not share the same basis for exchanging arguments on the existence of God. Therefore, since both camps *speak* totally different languages—to use one of Wittgenstein's famous phrases—they will never come to a satisfactorily conclusion unless the existence of God has been proven by rational argument alone.

Human Rights Based on Fundamental Interests

The general line of argumentation with regard to the interests-based approach is as follows. The major aim of human rights is to protect and promote certain particular essential or fundamental human interests, such as: one, personal security (protection from unwarranted bodily harm, like murder or torture); two, the satisfaction of basic nutritional needs; and three, the provision of housing and clothing. These basic human interests are the social and biological prerequisites for human beings to live a minimally good life. Therefore, one should respect human rights by virtue of their instrumental or prudential value for securing the necessary conditions of human well-being.

Thomas Hobbes is one of the most prominent advocates of social contract theory (as propounded in his work *Leviathan*), although he was certainly not talking about human rights in our sense of the term. However, the interests-based approach of human rights, at least, stems from this kind of ethical reasoning. In more detail, proponents of this approach generally argue that each person has a basic and general duty to respect the rights of every other person. The basis for this duty is (certainly) not benevolence or altruism, but individual self-interest. That means that one's own basic interests require others' willingness to recognise and respect these interests, which, in turn, requires reciprocal recognition and respect of the basic interests of others. The adequate protection of each person's basic interests necessitates the establishment of a cooperative system on the national and international level.

Two vital objections should be mentioned briefly with regard to this particular approach: one, the appeal to human nature; and two, self-interest and respecting the rights of all human beings. First, history shows that appeals to human nature are controversial and fail to achieve a broad consensus among people in order to be a sound basis for any viable moral doctrine, especially when social and cultural diversity come to the fore. Although people around the world may have the same fundamental interests in order to live a minimally good life, the conditions for doing so differ significantly in different cultural settings. This goes beyond a mere specification of the general claim to satisfy the basic conditions for leading a minimally good life.

Secondly, the interests-based approach of human rights is faced with the general problem of why people should respect the interests of other less powerful people who live in distant regions of the world, given that the powerful people want to protect their own fundamental interests even at the expense of the less powerful people. That is, the appeal to self-interest cannot provide a sound basis for ensuring a universal moral community. Theoretically speaking, distance itself has no moral weight; that is, people in one's neighbourhood or people in distant countries deserve the same moral respect. However, in practice, this is different; most people usually do not (morally) consider other people who live in distant countries to the same extent. In addition, if these people are less powerful, one may think one can ignore them because they are unable to revolt. However, as one can see with regard to Hobbes, this kind of argumentation seems fallacious since one cannot be certain that they will not gain more power in the future and start to discriminate against the former elite.

The Personal Autonomy Approach to Human Rights

Alan Gewirth and the Principle of Generic Consistency

This approach attempts to justify human rights in terms of human beings' personal autonomy. In the following, I focus on the conception of Alan Gewirth, who has developed an interesting approach to how human rights can be justified (Gewirth 1978, 1982). He argues that the justification of claims to the possession of basic human rights is grounded in the capacity for rationally purposive agency. The recognition of the validity of human rights is, according to Gewirth, a logical consequence of understanding oneself as a rationally purposive agent since the possession of rights is the necessary means for rationally purposive action. Gewirth's argument is based on the general claim that all human action is rationally purposive. Every human action is done for some reason, no matter whether it is a good or a bad reason. He argues that, in rationally endorsing some end, one must logically endorse the means to that end as well.

What is required to be a rationally purposive agent? Gewirth claims that freedom and well-being are the two necessary conditions for rationally purposive action. They are also the basic requirements for being human, whereas *being human* means to possess the capacity for rationally purposive action. Therefore, each person is entitled to have access to the basic requirements. According to Gewirth, each person cannot simply will their own enjoyment of these basic requirements for rational agency *without* appropriate concern for other people. The necessary concern for others' human rights is based upon his so-called principle of generic consistency, which is a supreme principle that logically derives from the nature and structure of human agency. The principle states that each person must act in accordance with his or her own and all other persons' generic rights to freedom and well-being. A person cannot logically *will* his or her own claims to human rights without at the same time accepting the equal claims of all rationally purposive agents to freedom and well-being. In addition, Gewirth argues that there exists an *absolute* right to life possessed separately and equally by all human beings. This right to life is absolute and cannot, therefore, be overridden under any circumstances.[6] To put it in a nutshell, philosophers and others who attempt to prove the validity of human rights upon the notion of personal autonomy claim that rights are a manifestation of the exercise of personal autonomy. That means the validity of human rights is necessarily tied to the validity of personal autonomy.

One major objection against the personal autonomy approach to human rights is as follows: If the constitutive condition for the possession of human rights is said to be the capacity for acting in a rationally purposive manner, then it seems logically correct to assume that people who are incapable of meeting this criterion have no legitimate claim to human rights at all. That is, all human beings who are temporarily or permanently incapable of acting in a rationally autonomous way (e.g., children, the impaired elderly, comatose people, or people who suffer from dementia, schizophrenia, or clinical depression) cannot validly claim to be protected by human rights. This is a logical consequence that people certainly have good reasons to avoid.

Michael Boylan and the Table of Embeddedness

In his book *A Just Society* (2004), Michael Boylan offers a somewhat different version of the concept of rational agency as presented by Gewirth that might be fruitful for the justification of human rights. His approach—even though it is partially influenced by Gewirth's line of reasoning (Spence, 2009: 133–146)—seems to avoid the abovementioned pitfall, at first sight. To put it in a nutshell, both authors make the *possibility* of human action a cornerstone in their theories. Gewirth claims that human action is absolutely foundational; Boylan instead thinks that an action is not primary but instrumental, and that "the agent's desire to be good" is more foundational. Furthermore, Gewirth argues that a person has a claim right to the necessary goods of his or her agency and generalises this to all people. Boylan, however, is "involved in a claim about human nature predicated specifically and then applied individually" (Boylan, 2009, 207). But what about human rights? The preconditions of action according to Boylan "involve possession of a nested hierarchy of goods," which he calls the *Table of Embeddedness* (Boylan,

2004, 53–54). This list of goods contains basic goods, for example, goods that are absolutely necessary for human action, such as food, clothing, shelter, protection from unwarranted bodily harm, and secondary goods—goods that are necessary for effective basic action within any given society such as literacy, mathematical skills, basic human rights, etc. (For a detailed discussion on Boylan's hierarchy of moral goods, see Düwell, 2009, 71–80.) The basic goods enable, first, the biological conditions of action and second, the basic societal skills as well as the *basic human rights* that allow any effective action. In this respect, human rights have an instrumental value and seem to be justified only by their contribution to "the agent's desire to be good."

It is hard to assess and appreciate fully Boylan's approach to human rights in *A Just Society* since they are only mentioned briefly. It is possible, however, to speculate about the concept of human rights in Boylan's account at least to some extent, given their particular role in his theory. Two main points should be mentioned in the following. First, Boylan argues that each agent desires to be good by virtue of his or her human nature. This seems to presuppose that the person in question must have *the ability to desire*; the ability to desire, however, presupposes a rational and reflective agent who is able to follow his or her interests. Foetuses, babies, comatose people, the impaired elderly, etc., are unable to form a desire, since they obviously lack the capacity to do so. Hence, they are—strictly speaking—not protected by basic human rights because they are not (yet) rational and reflective agents who are able to desire to be good. On this account, Boylan fails to avoid the abovementioned pitfall.

Secondly, Boylan believes that he is able to avoid the is-ought problem. His appeal to human nature and the idea that one *must*—by virtue of "the logical predication at the species level as a medical/scientific question" (2004, 57)—provide human beings with the necessary goods for action seem to undermine his initial assumption. Why must one provide human beings with the necessary goods for action in the first place? Just because it is *logically necessary* does not itself justify a "normative must" and cannot be conceived as a solution to the problem of justification. The justification of human rights in my interpretation of Boylan is finally based on the agent's desire to be good and this is too thin for a philosophical foundation. On the other hand, it is not Boylan's goal in *A Just Society* to answer the question of the justification of human rights.

Human Rights as Rational Rights—A New Approach

In the second section, "Transition from Popular Moral Philosophy to the Metaphysic of Morals," of his famous work *Groundwork for the Metaphysic of Morals* (1785 [2002]), Kant argues that pure practical reason is not limited to the nature of human reason alone, but is the source and realm of general norms that derive from the general notion of a rational being as such (Ak 4: 408). This line of reasoning is the cornerstone of Kantian Ethics. Simply speaking, human beings fall into the category of moral beings only because they are *rational* beings (Ak 4: 425). According to Kant, the categorical imperative is the tool by which the universality of maxims can be determined. If the particular maxim can be universalised, then the action in question is permissible and, if no inclination is involved, has moral worth—for *all* rational beings!—given the action was performed solely for the sake of the duty itself. Kant's main idea that an appropriate understanding of the notion of rationality is of utmost importance for morality—moral laws are valid for every rational being (Ak 4: 412)—is certainly ingenious and intriguing. There are other parts, however, such as the role of inclinations and the rigid idea of doing the right thing only for the sake of duty itself that seem to be somewhat questionable and rather misleading (e.g., Schopenhauer). In the following, I give a brief outline of a justification of human rights depending on Kant[7] (notion of rationality) and Rawls (veil of ignorance). Here, my general claim is that one is able to derive moral rights—in particular human rights—from a proper understanding of the notion of rationality. One major distinction between Kant's approach and my conception should be mentioned right at the beginning, because it is crucial for the correct evaluation of my approach. Kant believes that the difference between *Moralität* (morality: law-abiding and for the sake of duty itself, i.e., doing the right thing because it is right) and *Legalität* (legality: law-abiding but not for the sake of duty itself) is essential for the evaluation of an action concerning its moral worth. Only actions that are performed for the sake of duty itself have moral worth according to Kant. I am not committed to this claim, however. It is sufficient that human beings follow human rights without additionally being "dedicated" to them; in this sense the notion of legality is fully adequate and people will not be overloaded by too rigid demands.

The Concept of Rationality—A Thought Experiment

Suppose a group of fully rational beings is asked to develop a general system of moral norms in order to establish a community for its members to live a minimally decent life. The rational beings are totally uninformed about their own capabilities and empirical distinguishing features in the community. That is, they have to abstract from their current situation in such a way that their existing capabilities or empirical features, such as gender, race, colour, religion, etc., will not influence them in their decision-making (veil of ignorance). In order to determine the moral norms or moral rights of the community it is necessary to disclose the basic needs of a rational being. The following culturally neutral short list contains the *basic needs* of a rational being:

1. Physical and psychological security
2. Basic material subsistence and health
   - Proper food (no malnutrition)
   - Clothing
   - Proper housing and sanitation
   - Health (access to health care and resources)
3. Personal liberty
4. Social and political participation and law
   - Moral equality, mutual recognition, and fair trial
   - Participation in communal life (no social exclusion)
   - Freedom of expression (belief, expression, association, assembly, and movement)
   - Basic education

This list of the most basic needs of a rational being is related to a small set of basic rational rights (or moral rights) that can be seen as a starting point and constraining framework for a decent community of rational beings. Rationality itself commands the fulfilment of the basic needs *on behalf of all rational persons for all rational persons.* All contraventions concerning the fulfilment of the basic needs carry the burden of proof for the particular exception. The *basic rational rights* that can be derived from the list of basic needs is as follows:

1. Rights to life and physical integrity
2. Right to material subsistence
3. Rights to health care and resources
4. Right to personal liberty
5. Rights to moral equality and mutual respect
6. Right to fair trials
7. Right to the participation in communal life
8. Right to the freedom of expression
9. Right to basic education

From Basic Rational Rights to Human Rights

Following Kant's thesis that human beings are moral beings because they are rational beings, I suggest converting the basic rational rights into human rights. How can this be done? According to Kant's line of reasoning, both lists would be identical; that is, human rights can be derived from pure reason or, in other words, from the notion of rationality itself. The vital difference between a pure Kantian version of moral norms and my own approach is that, in order to apply human rights, one has to consider the special nature of human beings (anthropology) in the process of ethical reasoning and decision-making. In other words, the *justification* of moral norms is fully based on the notion of rationality, which is the first step. The second step, which concerns the *applicability* of moral norms, must also consider the empirical nature of human beings in order to spell out what a particular rational right in terms of a human right really means. The notion of rationality and the description of the empirical nature of human beings are independent of any particular cultural influence; the idea is to provide a culturally and religiously neutral approach to the justification of human rights.

The point of the (empirical) nature of human beings is also stressed by James Griffin in his important contribution to the philosophy of human rights, *On Human Rights* (2009), where he argues that there are two fundamental grounds for human rights concerning his normative agency approach: one, personhood—each of us has a right to security of person; and two, practicalities. His idea of practicalities—which are the features of human nature and the nature of human societies—is similar to my second step, which concerns the applicability of human rights and is needed to determine the content of many human rights. Griffin argues that the practicalities "are not tied to particular times and places. They are universal, as any existence condition for rights that one has simply in virtue of being human must be. Practicalities will be empirical information about, may I say, human nature and human societies, prominently about the limits of human understanding and motivation" (Griffin, 2009, 38).

Consider the following simple case. Suppose that all rational beings in the universe have the *basic need* to proper food; from our notion of rationality, it follows that all rational beings have a *rational right* to proper food. Because we are human beings, we are concerned with *human rights,* and here the question is about the proper food *for* human beings (see Griffin's practicalities) and not for rational beings in general (method of specification). To put it in a nutshell, what a rational Martian would accept as proper food could be quite different from what a rational human being needs. Therefore, one has to take the empirical nature of human beings into account.

Sen's Capability Approach and the Rational Rights Approach to Human Rights

One might have the impression that my rational rights approach is similar to Amartya Sen's capability approach, since both accounts—broadly speaking—finally rely on the fulfilment of basic human needs concerning human rights, but this assumption would be premature. Let me briefly examine and clarify this.

In his article "Human Rights and Capabilities" (2005), Sen examines the important relationship between human rights and his notion of capabilities: many human rights, according to Sen, can be seen as rights to particular capabilities.

The basic connection between both notions is the notion of freedom(s). Human rights, according to Sen, are "rights to certain particular freedoms," while capabilities are "freedoms of a particular kind" (Sen, 2005, 152). According to Sen, there is no *final* or *fixed* list of basic human capabilities[8]; any given list of capabilities depends on a particular use concerning "different purposes . . . e.g. whether we are evaluating poverty, specifying certain basic human rights, getting a rough and ready measure of human development, and so on" (159). Finally, with regard to human rights, Sen argues:

> If the listing of capabilities must be subject to the test of public reasoning, how can we proceed in a world of differing values and disparate cultures? How can we judge the acceptability of claims to human rights and to relevant capabilities, and assess the challenges they may face? How would such a disputation—or a defence—proceed? I would argue that, like the assessment of other ethical claims, there must be some test of open and informed scrutiny, and it is to such a scrutiny that we have to look in order to proceed to a disavowal or an affirmation. The status that these ethical claims have must be ultimately dependent on their survivability in unobstructed discussion. In this sense, the viability of human rights is linked with what John Rawls has called "public reasoning" and its role in "ethical objectivity." [160]

To put it in a nutshell, I disagree with Sen that the viability of human rights is linked to public reasoning in the sense that public discourse should decide about the permissibility of the application of human rights in a given community. Human rights can (in effect only) be determined by pure reasoning alone. Additionally, human rights can be seen as a *lingua franca* or common morality (see below) that provides a *cross-cultural* moral framework for all people. Furthermore, it seems correct to believe that human beings share basic needs such as food, shelter, clothing, etc. These basic needs can be compiled in one comprehensive, final, and (almost) fixed list. Human rights can be conceived of as *objective* and *subjective* at the same time. But, what does that mean? Is this not a contradiction? The basic idea is this: Human rights *as* rational rights are *objective* in the sense that they exist independently of human beings by being commands of rationality itself. Human rights *as* human rights are *subjective* in the sense that they depend on the nature of human beings (see practicalities) and not, say, Martians, etc.

Objections

One might question the general idea of my rational rights approach by raising at least five main objections. Below, I respond to these objections and clarify the concerns, which will give me the opportunity to explain the approach in more detail.

1. What Is the Rationale Concerning the List of Basic Needs and What Is the Difference Between Needs and Basic Needs?

The abovementioned list covers the most important basic needs of a rational being. This does not mean, however, that one can be 100 percent certain that there could be no other basic need that is not yet on the list. In this respect, however, the list is *open* and not 100 percent watertight, but it is unlikely that a new basic need will suddenly emerge that has not been on the list before. The rationale for creating this list depends on the reasonableness concerning the particular basic needs, which is partly due to the fact that life itself tells us what is really valuable and of utmost importance with regard to living decently. In other words, based on empirical findings and after due deliberation, this list seems to be most appropriate to capture the most important aspects of a rational being and hence a human being. The basic needs in the list are culturally neutral and apply to all people around the world.

The fulfilment of basic needs is necessary for a human being in order to live a minimally decent life. Basic needs are mostly characterised by their inalienability and high importance. The loss of one or more basic needs would be highly detrimental for the well-being of the particular human being. Not to meet this important threshold would result in living a life below decency. Nonbasic needs, however, even though they can certainly be very important to the person in question, are characterised by the fact that they are not inalienable. People can still live a decent life without having fulfilled some of their nonbasic needs, such as drinking champagne and eating caviar and lobster on a regular basis. The fulfilment of nonbasic needs, however, makes lives richer; it gives people the possibility to live not only a minimally decent but also a good or very good life.

2. What About Nonrational Human Beings? Are They Protected by Human Rights as Well?

Even though we started by explaining how human rights can be justified by appealing to the notion of *rationality*, it is nonetheless guaranteed that *all* human beings—including nonrational human beings—are protected by human rights. As we already saw, philosophers such as Gewirth and Kant take a different view; they believe that only rational beings should be protected (Orend, 2002, 46–49). The concept of human beings having human rights is not limited by the right holder's rationality or personhood, but is due to his or her membership of the human race in the first place. This line of reasoning is faced with the objection of speciesism (limiting human rights to human beings, which is immoral). Peter Singer refers to Richard Ryder as the author who coined the term "speciesism" in the debate concerning animal rights (Singer, 1975, 17–21). However, as a matter of fact, *human* rights are made for humans only and not for animals. This does not mean in the end, however, that we are allowed to treat animals—in particular, sentient animals—in an unkind or cruel way, whenever it pleases us. Rationality itself commands that we should treat all living creatures that are sensible to pain in a decent way.[9]

With regard to, for instance, foetuses or babies, the point is not that simple. On the one hand, we do think that they should be protected because they are human beings or, in the case of viable foetuses, they do have, at least, the potential to become adult human beings, and that it should not simply be up to us to kill them. On the other hand, however, it seems difficult to justify abortion, for instance, against the background that foetuses might have a human right to life according to the proposed approach. How can one solve this difficult situation? At first sight, it seems that there is no way out. On second glance, however, one might acknowledge that there is a fairly good possibility to solve this puzzle, which has something to do with the nature of human rights in general. Some people think that human rights are absolute; others argue that they are *prima facie* rights. By claiming that human rights are *prima facie*, one is able to provide a solution for the abovementioned dilemma, since viable foetuses—according to this view—can be aborted if there are other important moral considerations that outweigh the foetus's human right to life. Certainly, good reasons should be provided, but it would seem irrational to assume that human rights are necessarily *absolute*. Additionally, morality is not only about moral rights and moral duties, but also about the moral appropriateness and moral inappropriateness of human conduct. Many ethicists seem to forget this last point all too often.

3. The Underlying Notion of Rationality Seems Too Vague.

Kant reveals some deep insights about the notion of rationality in relation to morality. The general idea of basing morality on the structure of practical reason is ingenious and, according to the question of what could justify *universal* moral norms, it is an intriguing response. However, I disagree with Kant (and Utilitarians) that all moral claims (or rights) are universal in character. According to common morality theorists, such as Tom Beauchamp and James Childress (2009), there is a hard core of *universal* moral norms (common morality), such as, "One should not kill or insult other people," or "One should not break promises." On the other hand, there are many different *community-dependent* moral norms (particular moralities), which are only valid within a given community (see, also, Walzer's idea of a globally shared *thin* moral code and a culturally dependent *thick* morality: Walzer, 1999). This picture of morality seems intuitively appropriate. My general idea is that universal moral norms are justified by an adequate understanding of a culturally neutral notion of rationality. The moral norms of the particular moralities are (rather) based on tradition, culture, religion, etc., and stand in a dialectical relation to the "common morality" (reflective equilibrium). Human rights fall under the category of common morality.

4. The Human Rights Approach—What About the Is-Ought Problem?

At first sight, it seems that the proposed approach is facing the is-ought problem—the view that an ought-claim or moral claim cannot be validly derived from any number of is-claims or nonmoral claims alone (Hume's Law).[10] At second glance, however, this is not exactly the case. Here is why: human rights are not simply derived from basic needs in the sense that they are just invented to protect the basic needs in question. Admittedly, it might look like that, and, of course, people have done so (or the like) in the past (e.g., Martha Nussbaum or proponents of the interest-based approach), but this approach is somewhat different. The line of argumentation is rather that fully rational beings would conclude that, according to the notion of rationality, both concepts—basic needs and basic rights—are two sides of a coin and deeply interwoven with each other, so that one cannot really conceive or fully grasp one concept without conceiving the other concept as well. One might still object, however, that this is an *ad hoc* argument and hence invalid. What could be a proper response to this claim? In order to answer this objection, one could make use of the analogy concerning *rights* and *duties* (see above). One distinctive feature, which is important with regard to rights and duties, concerns their relation. Rights and duties *usually*[11] stand in a *reciprocal* and *symmetrical relation* to one another. That means the concept of a right entails a corresponding duty (and vice versa) without being inexplicit or vague. Given the validity of the analogy, there is no *ad hoc* argument involved concerning basic needs and human rights because it is simply the way both concepts are naturally related to each other.

5. Why Should People Care About Other People's Basic Human Needs?

The question why one should care about the basic human needs of other people is almost similar to the widely discussed ethical question: *Why should one act morally?* The latter question has been addressed by at least three different strategies: the Golden Rule, the self-interest approach, and the idea of living a morally good life. To put it in a nutshell, the *Golden Rule* or "ethics of reciprocity" states in the positive form: "Do to others what you would like to be done to you!" and in the negative form: "Do not do to others what you would not like to be done to you!" The general idea is that people have a right to just treatment, and at the same time they are responsible to guarantee justice for other people. The *self-interest approach* claims that it is in one's own best interest—in the long run—not to be a freeloader, because the chances that one will be caught increase over time. To risk social exclusion or to be shunned by the moral community seems to be too high a price in order to only live for the moment and for one's own advantage. Therefore, it is rational, according to the proponents, to act morally and to resist those temptations that might maximise one's own utility for the moment, but could jeopardise one's own reputation for a long time. The third response is based on the notion of the *morally good life* and the concept of prudence most prominently found in ancient virtue ethics. The idea is that, in order to reach happiness (*eudemonia*), one has to act morally but not in the sense that the latter is only the means to live a happy life; rather, one has to act morally for the sake of acting morally in order to live a happy life.

The three abovementioned approaches respond to some degree to the initial question of why one should care about basic human needs, but the most straightforward answer in accordance with my own approach is the following. It is not about (simple) needs but about basic human needs, such as food, shelter, clothing, or security and liberty. For example, to deny a person his or her liberty—that is, to keep him or her in slavery—has certainly a different moral quality compared with being a freeloader and going by bus or train without a ticket occasionally. *The most basic needs of a human being should not be at the disposal of other people.* Basic human needs concern the very vulnerability of human beings. It seems impossible to provide a sound justification for violating any basic needs for one's own private affairs. The burden of proof is on people who want to violate basic human needs *or* who refrain from helping people whose basic human needs are in danger or have already been jeopardised. At the end, a person who does not care about other people's basic human needs should ask himself or herself whether he or she wants to be a moral person who deserves the same respect as everybody else in the moral community *or* to consider himself or herself as a human rights violator and thereby exclude himself or herself from the group of morally decent people.[12]

Conclusion

In this chapter I have discussed briefly four different approaches to justifying human rights: the natural rights approach, the divine rights approach, the fundamental interests approach, and the personal autonomy approach. I believe that these approaches are misleading and should be abandoned. The second part of the chapter broadly outlines and examines a novel approach to justifying human rights, which can be called the rational rights approach to human rights and is based on a modified application of Kant's notion of rationality and Rawls's idea of the veil of ignorance. The chapter deals with some important questions concerning the philosophy of human rights and provides challenging insights. Some important questions remain, however, and were simply beyond the scope of this chapter, such as *whether* human rights also apply to nonrational beings, that is, sentient animals; *how* the particular human rights and their contents can be conceived within the rational rights approach; and *what* kind of general implications and particular consequences follow from the proposed approach. It is my hope that my approach contributes to the philosophy of human rights in a way that enriches the debate.

Notes

1. Security rights: protect people against crimes such as murder, massacre, torture, and rape. Due process rights: protect people against abuses of the legal system such as imprisonment without trial, secret trials, and excessive punishments. Liberty rights: protect freedoms in areas such as belief, expression, association, assembly, and movement. Political rights: protect the liberty to participate in politics through actions such as communicating, assembling, protesting, voting, and serving in public office. Equality rights: guarantee equal citizenship, equality before the law, and nondiscrimination. Social welfare rights: require provision of education to all children and protection against severe poverty and starvation. Group rights: include protection of ethnic groups against genocide and the ownership by countries of their national territories and resources.

2. The following depiction is partly based on Andrew Fagan's entry on human rights at *The Internet Encyclopedia of Philosophy* (2005).

3. The story of *Antigone* is as follows: Oedipus had two sons, Polyneikes and Eteokles, who shared the power in the state after his departure from Thebes. After a while both brothers antagonised each other and Eteokles expelled Polyneikes. Polyneikes came back to Thebes with his army in order to become king. Both brothers died in the war and their uncle Kreon became king. Kreon issued a decree that Polyneikes should not be buried because he acted against the fatherland. Any attempt to bury him would be punishable by death. Antigone symbolically buried her brother by special funeral rites because she felt that she had to follow her own conscience instead of Kreon's immoral decree, and to obey rather the divine rights than human-made law. She was discovered by a guard and brought to the king, where she confessed the deed. Kreon sentenced her to death by being buried alive, although Antigone was promised to be the wife of Kreon's son, Haimon. Haimon bitterly complained against his father's decision and taunted him with his stubbornness. The seer Teiresias predicted death in Kreon's family and Kreon decided to spare Antigone. But it was too late: Antigone had already committed suicide in her dungeon, and Haimon did not want to stay alive

without her so he committed suicide as well. Haimon's mother, Eurydice, Kreon's wife, followed her son by virtue of her deep sorrow and also committed suicide.

4. For a detailed and thorough discussion on the idea of natural rights, see Strauss (1953).

5. The theological line of reasoning can be interpreted as follows: the Ten Commandments are crucial moral duties demanded by God from which one can infer corresponding human rights (see Perry, 2000).

6. Gewirth claims: "so that it can never be justifiably infringed and it must be fulfilled without any exceptions" (Gewirth, 1982, 92).

7. Here, I do not focus on the first part of *The Metaphysics of Morals*, in which Kant derives "natural rights" from the idea of respect for persons. Kant's natural rights are based on the *a priori* "Universal Principle of Right," which says that "any action is right if it can co-exist with everyone's freedom in accordance with a universal law, or if on its maxim the freedom of choice of each can co-exist with everyone's freedom in accordance with a universal law." The reason I do not refer to this line of reasoning is that Kant's natural rights do cover much more of morality than the term *human rights* does.

8. Sen argues:

> My scepticism is about fixing a cemented list of capabilities that is seen as being absolutely complete (nothing could be added to it) and totally fixed (it could not respond to public reasoning and to the formation of social values). I am a great believer in theory, and certainly accept that a good theory of evaluation and assessment has to bring out the relevance of what we are free to do and free to be (the capabilities in general), as opposed to the material goods we have and the commodities we can command. But I must also argue that pure theory cannot "freeze" a list of capabilities for all societies for all time to come, irrespective of what the citizens come to understand and value. That would be not only a denial of the reach of democracy, but also a misunderstanding of what pure theory can do, completely divorced from the particular social reality that any particular society faces. [2005, 158]

9. It is beyond the scope of this chapter to discuss the consequences of my approach for the moral status of animals. Even though I hold the view that sentient animals should be treated appropriately, I have strong doubts whether they are protected by *human* rights. Will Kymlicka and others, however, believe that if human rights do indeed apply to nonrational humans, then they also should be extended to sentient animals.

10. For a discussion of the plausibility of the is-ought problem, see Hume (1740 [1978]), Hare (1952), and Nowell-Smith (1954) (these provide the standard interpretation: Hume is arguing for a general *logical* principle); Searle (1964) (*social facts*

such as the institution of giving a promise seem to entail normative conclusions that can be derived from non-normative claims); Hudson (1969) (given the context of the is-ought passage, it is unfortunate to call Hume's principle "Hume's Law"); MacIntyre (1981) (facts about the *purpose* of something seem to entail normative conclusions, e.g., if something is a knife, one expects that the knife *ought* to be sharp); or Mackie (1980) ("social facts" or "purposes" are already normatively loaded; the counterexamples do not violate Hume's Law).

11. Reciprocity with regard to rights and duties, however, holds only for the core area of morality depending on rational human beings. Small children, for example, have rights but no corresponding duties. There is no reciprocity at the marginal areas of morality; only rights but no corresponding duties. However, even in the core area of morality, cases exist that are an exception to the supposed symmetrical relation, such as in the case of benevolence. Some people claim, not unconvincingly, that people have a duty to be benevolent, but the duty of benevolence does not correspond to any claim right of a person concerned. No person has a right to (the fruits of) benevolence.

12. Of course, one can care about the basic human needs of other people but still be an immoral person. It goes beyond of the scope of this chapter to discuss the many details of the general issue at stake: Is there any moral difference between people in one's own community and people who live far away, concerning the question of whether one should support them in their pursuit of having their basic human needs fulfilled?

References

Aristotle. (1995). "Nicomachean Ethics" in *The Complete Works of Aristotle II*, ed. Jonathan Barnes: 1729–1867. Princeton, NJ: Princeton University Press.

Beauchamp, Tom, and James Childress. (2009). *Principles of Biomedical Ethics*. Oxford: Oxford University Press.

Beitz, Charles. (2009). *The Idea of Human Rights*. Oxford: Oxford University Press.

Boylan, Michael. (2004). *A Just Society*. Lanham, MD, and Oxford: Rowman and Littlefield.

Boylan, Michael. (2009). "Ethics, Metaethics, Political Theory, and Policy: A Reply to My Colleagues" in *Morality and Justice. Reading Boylan's A Just Society*, ed. John-Stewart Gordon: 179–223. Lanham, MD: Rowman and Littlefield.

Düwell, Marcus. (2009). "On the Possibility of a Hierarchy of Moral Goods" in *Morality and Justice. Reading Boylan's A Just Society*, ed. John-Stewart Gordon: 71–80. Lanham, MD: Rowman and Littlefield.

Dworkin, Ronald. (1977). *Taking Rights Seriously*. Cambridge, MA: Harvard University Press.

Fagan, Andrew. (2005). "Human Rights" in *The Internet Encyclopedia of Philosophy.* Retrieved from http://www.iep.utm.edu/hum-rts/

Gewirth, Alan. (1978). *Reason and Morality.* Chicago: University of Chicago Press.

Gewirth, Alan. (1982). *Human Rights. Essays on Justification and Applications.* Chicago: University of Chicago Press.

Gewirth, Alan. (1996). *The Community of Rights.* Chicago: University of Chicago Press.

Griffin, James. (2009). *On Human Rights.* Oxford: Oxford University Press.

Hare, Richard. (1952). *The Language of Morals.* Oxford: Oxford University Press.

Hart, Herbert Lionel Adolphus. (1955). "Are There Any Natural Rights?" *Philosophical Review 64*(2): 175–191.

Hart, Herbert Lionel Adolphus. (1961). *The Concept of Law.* Oxford and New York: Oxford University Press.

Hobbes, Thomas. (1651 [1996]). *Leviathan,* ed. Richard Tuck. Cambridge: Cambridge University Press.

Hudson, W. Donald. (1969). *The Is-Ought Question.* London: MacMillan.

Hume, David. (1740 [1978]). *A Treatise of Human Nature,* ed. P. H. Nidditch. Oxford: Oxford University Press.

Kant, Immanuel. (1785 [2002]). *Groundwork for the Metaphysic of Morals,* ed. Allen Wood. New Haven, CT: Yale University Press.

Locke, John. (1688 [2005]). *Two Treatises of Government,* ed. Peter Laslett. Cambridge: Cambridge University Press.

MacIntyre, Alasdair. (1981). *After Virtue: A Study in Moral Theory.* Notre Dame, IN: University of Notre Dame Press.

Mackie, John L. (1980). *Hume's Moral Theory.* London: Routledge.

Nickel, James. (1987). *Making Sense of Human Rights.* Malden, MA, and Oxford: Blackwell.

Nowell-Smith, P. H. (1954). *Ethics.* Baltimore: Penguin Books.

Orend, Brian. (2002). *Human Rights. Concept and Context.* Ontario: Broadview Press.

Perry, Michael. (2000). *The Idea of Human Rights: Four Inquiries.* Oxford: Oxford University Press.

Rawls, John. (1993). "The Law of Peoples" in *On Human Rights. The Oxford Amnesty Lectures 1993,* ed. Stephen Shute, et al.: 41–82. New York: Basic Books.

Rorty, Richard. (1993). "Human Rights, Rationality, and Sentimentality" in *On Human Rights. The Oxford Amnesty Lectures 1993,* ed. Stephen Shute, et al.: 111–134. New York: Basic Books.

Schopenhauer, Arthur. (1840). *On the Basis of Morality.* Indianapolis and Cambridge: Hackett Publishing.

Searle, John. (1964). "How to Derive 'Ought' from 'Is.'" *Philosophical Review 73*: 43–58.

Sen, Amartya. (2005). "Human Rights and Capabilities." *Journal of Human Development 6*(2): 151–166.

Shue, Henry. (1980). *Basic Rights: Subsistence, Affluence and U.S. Foreign Policy.* Princeton, NJ: Princeton University Press.

Singer, Peter. (1975). *Animal Liberation.* London: Avon Books.

Sophocles. (2002). "Antigone" in *Sophocles: The Oedipus Cycle: Oedipus Rex, Oedipus at Colonus, Antigone*, ed. Dudley Fitts and Robert Fitzgerald. Fort Washington, PA: Harvest Books.

Spence, Edward. (2009). "Justice in *A Just Society*" in *Morality and Justice. Reading Boylan's A Just Society*, ed. John-Stewart Gordon: 133–146. Lanham, MD: Rowman and Littlefield.

Strauss, Leo. (1953). *Natural Right and History.* Chicago: University of Chicago Press.

Walzer, Michael. (1999). *Thick and Thin: Moral Argument at Home and Abroad.* Notre Dame, IN: University of Notre Dame Press.

CHAPTER THREE

When Is Ignorance Morally Objectionable?

JULIE E. KIRSCH
D'Youville College

Abstract

There are certain things that we must do or not do in order to live a morally decent life. Are there also things that we must believe or not believe in order to avoid the charge of moral indecency? With advances in technology, and the emergence of a global village, we can no longer justify our ignorance about various social injustices by appealing to a lack of accessible information about the world. If we can justify our ignorance, it is becoming more difficult to do so, and the conditions that make this possible are changing. In this essay, I will argue that a commitment to acquiring knowledge about morally significant aspects of the world is an important component of a moral life.

Key Words

ethics of belief, social justice, ignorance, morality, doxastic responsibility

---

Introduction

Morality makes certain demands upon our external lives; it requires that we act and not act in particular ways. Does morality also make demands upon our doxastic lives? As cognitive beings, do we have an obligation to seek evidence for and against certain beliefs and not others?

In what follows, I will argue that we have strong moral reasons to care about our doxastic lives as well as our external lives as agents acting in the world. In particular, I will show that a commitment to acquiring knowledge about morally significant aspects of the world is an important component of a moral life. Toward the end of the essay, I will focus upon the specific interest that we ought to take in matters of social justice and the plight of suffering people around the world.

The Moral Significance of Belief

I want to begin by considering why we might accept that our doxastic lives are morally significant. No matter what our moral views happen to be, we can make sense of the claim that it is morally wrong to cheat, steal, or commit murder. But what sense can we make of the claim that it is sometimes morally wrong to *believe*? What reasons do we have for thinking that belief, not just action, is subject to moral evaluation? W. K. Clifford (1999) attempted to answer this question in his well-known essay on the ethics of belief. In this section, I will outline one of Clifford's main arguments and defend a modified version of his position.

In *The Ethics of Belief*, Clifford states that "it is wrong always, everywhere, and for anyone, to believe anything upon insufficient evidence" (77). He offers a consequentialist argument in support of this categorical claim. According to Clifford, a person should not believe something based upon insufficient evidence because, in so doing, she risks harming humanity. Clifford outlines a number of "harms" associated with believing something based upon insufficient evidence. The most serious harm to which believing upon insufficient evidence can give rise is credulity. When we fail to insist upon evidence in support of our beliefs, we weaken our critical thinking abilities and become epistemically naive. This consequence is especially dangerous when it is spread throughout a community of believers.

Believing without sufficient evidence is also dangerous because of the close connection between belief and action. Clifford maintains that a belief is not a belief at all if it fails to influence the actions of the believer; action-guidance is built into the very concept of belief (73). Consider Clifford's example of a shipowner who sends an immigrant ship to sea even though he suspects that the ship is in need of repair. The shipowner is able to do this because he stifles his doubts about the ship and deceives himself into thinking that it is seaworthy. In this case, the shipowner's belief is dangerous because it enters into his practical deliberations about the ship and its passengers. Convinced that the ship is seaworthy, the shipowner decides to send the ship to sea and risk the lives of its passengers.

Although there is an obvious connection between belief and action in the shipowner example, we might question Clifford's claim that this is always the case. Some beliefs are too trivial or removed from our daily lives to provide us with much if any practical guidance. We might replace this strong claim about the connection between belief and action with a weaker one. Accordingly, we might say that a belief is not a belief at all unless it has the *potential* to influence the actions of the believer. But this weaker version of Clifford's claim may not be sufficient for his purposes. If it is unlikely that a given belief would reveal itself in a believer's *actual* actions, then its potential to do so may not be an adequate cause for concern. After all, everything that we do involves some risks; we only alter our conduct in light of these when they are sufficiently probable and harmful. Nevertheless, the more general point that Clifford is trying to make here is correct: our beliefs often do influence our actions. And as I shall argue later in this chapter, we should be especially concerned with those beliefs that do provide us with practical and moral guidance.

Clifford identifies a third harm associated with believing upon insufficient evidence that is important for our purposes. Given that our beliefs tend to be mutually reinforcing, any single belief can set us up for more of the same: a racist will be more willing to accept racist beliefs than a nonracist, a sexist will be more willing to accept sexist beliefs than a nonsexist, and a homophobe will be more willing to accept more homophobic beliefs than a non-homophobe. This entrenchment of belief can cause one to develop a distorted and non-representative view of the world. We can appreciate this point if we consider the role that our current beliefs play in providing us with (subjective) grounds for accepting new beliefs. If I believe without justification that all Latin American immigrants are lazy, then I may be inclined to believe that all Latin American immigrants want to exploit our country's social welfare services. Similarly, I may be inclined to believe that any individual Latin American immigrant would not be a productive worker or member of society. This is possible, or probable, because we use the beliefs that we already have in making inferences that lead to new beliefs. In this way, groundless beliefs can become infectious and cause us to accept more of the same.

Clifford makes a strong case in support of an ethics of belief. However, as I intend to show, we have good reason not to accept an unqualified version of his position. What is right about Clifford's position is his emphasis upon the role that belief plays in contributing to action. If we care about the way that people act, then we have at least indirect reasons for caring about the way that people believe. Indeed, if we hope to shape people's actions for the better, then we have grounds for starting with the beliefs that help bring these actions about. There are, however, a few concerns that we might have about Clifford's position or any ethics of belief. It is to these that we now turn.

First of all, we might doubt that an ethics of belief is possible due to the involuntary nature of belief. Although we can pass judgment upon the way that people act, we cannot pass judgment upon the way that people believe; this is because action is under our voluntary control and belief is not. In Clifford's example, he describes the shipowner as *willfully* or *deliberately* deceiving himself into believing that his ship is seaworthy. Surely the shipowner's willful attempts at self-deception do not represent the way that we ordinarily form beliefs. In many (if not most) cases, our beliefs *form themselves*, as it were, without our intervention as agents. We cannot bring ourselves to believe that the human body is immortal when we see it perish before our eyes. Similarly, we cannot convince ourselves that it is snowing outside if we experience sunshine, blue skies, and the sweltering summer heat. In these cases, and others like them, the facts of the world impose themselves upon our belief-forming processes; we form beliefs of this kind without *willing* or *doing* anything at all. As John Heil (1983) explains, we are often "passive" and "largely *at the mercy* of [our] belief-forming equipment" (357). Our beliefs "come to us unanticipated and unbidden" (357). If this is true, then there is an important action/belief asymmetry that presents a challenge to any ethics of belief.

One way of responding to this challenge is to dig in one's heels and defend a version of *doxastic voluntarism*—the view that we can, at least in certain cases, decide to believe or believe at will. However, given the nature of belief, it is difficult to see how this is possible. When a person believes that *P*, she regards *P* as true or as more likely to be true than not-*P*. If I decide to believe that *P* for practical reasons, and in the absence of epistemic reasons, then I have no grounds for believing that *P* is true. And if I have no grounds for believing that *P* is true, then it is unlikely that I will, as a matter of fact, believe that *P* is true. A person's beliefs tend to be undermined by an awareness that there are no grounds for thinking that they are true. This is not to say that it is *logically* impossible for someone to believe at will (and in full consciousness) that *P* without epistemic reasons or evidence. However, given the nature of belief and the way that our minds work, it is difficult to see how this can happen. And so, while believing at will may not be logically impossible, it may very well be humanly impossible.[1]

A philosophically less ambitious response to the claim that belief is not under our voluntary control emphasizes the indirect control that we have over our beliefs. We can admit that we have no *direct* control over our beliefs while maintaining that we do have some *indirect* control over our beliefs. I may not be able to believe that *P* at will; however, I can choose to act in various ways that make it more or less likely that I will believe that *P*. As Kieran Setiya (2008) puts it, we can "manage our beliefs" by taking "productive means" to bring them about (41). Just as a man can make himself blush by dropping his trousers, he can make himself believe that *P* through an act of hypnosis. In both cases, the man does not bring about the desired state directly or *at will*; rather, he brings it about indirectly through some productive means (41). To be sure, we generally do not get ourselves to form beliefs on the basis of hypnosis. The control that we exercise over our beliefs tends to be far more subtle than this: we read newspapers and books, we make certain friends and not others, and we question our assumptions or take them for granted.

Now, in some cases we manage our beliefs in a way that is truth-conducive and in other cases we do not. I may pursue evidence in support of a particular belief because it is a path toward truth or because it is a path toward comfort or some other desired end. To the extent that we agree with Clifford, we should say that a morally responsible believer (hereafter abbreviated as "responsible believer") always manages her beliefs in a truth-conducive way; truth should be her exclusive goal in managing her beliefs. One serious problem with this view of responsible believing is that it sets a goal that is impossible to achieve. We do not have the resources necessary to succeed in acquiring the truth in all of our epistemic endeavors. Furthermore, it implies (as Clifford insists in his essay) that we *always* believe immorally when we hold beliefs that lack epistemic justification. For this and other reasons, I am offering a modified version of Clifford's ethics of belief. In my view, truth plays an important but not exclusive role in responsible belief management. Pace Clifford, a person can sometimes have moral reasons for accepting a belief that lacks epistemic justification.

What then should we say about a responsible believer? If I am right, responsible believing is an *ideal* that we cannot reasonably expect to achieve or perfect in our ordinary lives.

As philosophers, the best that we can do is put forward a set of strategies that characterize the responsible believer. While a comprehensive account of responsible believing is beyond the scope of this chapter, I offer the following four strategies of responsible believing that should point our theoretical efforts in the right direction.

A responsible believer should:

1. *Seek and evaluate evidence for and against beliefs.* Most obviously, perhaps, a responsible believer is one who takes the time to acquire evidence for and against current and prospective beliefs. A person who forms beliefs on the basis of partial or non-representative evidence acts in an irresponsible way. Although we often acquire evidence passively, we can exercise control over our beliefs by seeking out evidence for and against a proposition. In addition to gathering new evidence, a responsible believer should evaluate the evidence that she already has in support of a belief. Among other things, she should consider whether or not the evidence that she possesses is reliable and provides adequate justification for what she believes.[2]
2. *Identify and eliminate biased belief formation.* A responsible believer should make herself aware of potential biases that threaten to influence her own thinking and believing. For example, she should consider the influence that her desires and emotions have upon her beliefs. As Alfred

Mele (2001) has shown, our desires can have a profound effect upon the way that we gather and interpret evidence relevant to a desired belief. The fact that a person would like to believe that *P* can make it more likely that he will believe that *P*. This kind of influence can set a person up for self-deception and other forms of motivationally biased belief (25–49). Various "cold" or unmotivated biases can also influence our belief-forming processes. For instance, the well-documented confirmation bias can make it more likely that a person will form beliefs that confirm rather than disconfirm a working hypothesis.[3] A responsible believer should maintain a vigilant doxastic attitude and minimize the effect that motivated and unmotivated biases have upon her beliefs.

3. *Open beliefs to interpersonal criticism and discussion.* A responsible believer should welcome criticism of and discussion about her beliefs. We often revise or rethink our beliefs in light of the feedback that we receive from others. This can happen when others both accept and reject the beliefs that we hold. In both cases, we can acquire new evidence and learn to see things from a different point of view. As Robert Audi (2008) has observed, even if this exchange of evidence or epistemic grounds does not result in new beliefs, it can enhance communication and stabilize agreement (414). We often learn as much from those who agree with us as we do from those who disagree with us.

   As I have already mentioned, these general strategies represent an ideal of responsible believing for which we should strive. Given our limited resources and finite nature, we cannot hope to perfect these strategies in our daily lives. I therefore offer a final strategy that encourages us to prioritize certain beliefs over others in our pursuit of truth.

4. *Decide which beliefs are most important and pay particular attention to them.* We can all appreciate why certain beliefs are more important than other beliefs. Some theoretical beliefs are especially important because they are foundational or interconnected to a considerable degree with other beliefs. Indeed, we can say that some true beliefs are important to acquire because they lead to a significant number of additional true beliefs. If one of our epistemological goals is to acquire as many true beliefs as possible, then we have an epistemic reason to prefer foundational truths to non-foundational truths. Still, other beliefs are important because of what they contribute to our personal and moral lives. I may have personal or moral reasons for paying particular attention to beliefs concerning the well-being of my children and spouse. In defending this strategy, we need to step outside the epistemic realm and think about belief from a broader perspective.

Before proceeding, I would like to summarize what I have tried to establish thus far. In agreement with Clifford, I have argued that we have strong consequentialist reasons to take our doxastic lives seriously. Although belief does not always lead to action, it often enough does. For this reason, we can meaningfully evaluate belief, or belief formation, from the perspective of morality. In explaining how we might go about doing this, I put forward four strategies that represent a rough ideal of responsible believing. My account differs from Clifford's in at least two important respects: One, I have suggested that we cannot hope to acquire sufficient evidence in support of all of our beliefs. And two, because of this, we must prioritize our beliefs and focus upon those that we take to be most important. To be sure, we cannot know in advance which beliefs will and will not be important. A belief that strikes me as inconsequential at one point in time might help me to save thousands of lives in the future. However, given our finite resources, we have no choice but to make informed judgments about these cases and hope for the best.

For purposes of clarification, I should emphasize that the focus of my discussion has been on morally responsible belief. My intention has not been to outline standards for epistemically responsible belief or to provide an account of epistemic justification. In my view, we have strong moral reasons to ensure that most of our beliefs are epistemically justified. However, as I have already explained, we at times have moral reasons for accepting beliefs that are not epistemically justified. While it is useful and important to evaluate beliefs from an epistemic perspective, it is not the only perspective that we can take on beliefs.

Ignorance and the Moral World

When thinking about the relative importance of our beliefs, one class of beliefs immediately comes to mind: our beliefs concerning morality. Earlier in this chapter, I commented on the fact that many trivial and abstract beliefs fail to influence our actions. This is because they tend not to enter into our practical deliberations. We certainly cannot say the same about our moral beliefs; they are defined, in part, by their role in guiding or directing action. For this reason, we have grounds for paying particular attention to moral beliefs and the processes that contribute to moral belief formation. In speaking of "moral beliefs," I do not intend to limit our concern to theoretical moral beliefs (beliefs concerning issues of normative ethics and metaethics). Instead, I am suggesting that we understand "moral beliefs" in a broad sense that includes our beliefs about various applied issues as well. Paying particular attention to these beliefs will require that we investigate questions of value and fact. After all, a person cannot make an informed judgment about the ethics of cloning unless she knows something about the science of cloning.

In explaining why our moral beliefs, and not just our actions, are morally significant, I want to focus upon moral beliefs of a particular kind. By focusing upon one narrow category of moral beliefs, we will be able to explore in detail the impact that moral beliefs in general have upon others. With these observations in view, I can then put forward specific advice about how best to evaluate our own failures and successes at responsible believing. The moral beliefs that I would like to focus upon are those concerning global suffering and justice. I hope to show that by broadening our horizons and considering moral issues on a global scale, we can develop a more comprehensive and realistic moral vision.

I want to begin by considering what Michael Boylan has said about our need to develop a personal worldview that embraces the international community. According to Boylan, each person has, at the very least, a working or uncritical worldview. A worldview is a "web of beliefs" that expresses a person's "voice" (2000, 24–25; 2004, 22). Throughout a series of works, Boylan has urged us to replace our uncritical worldviews with worldviews that respect what he calls the personal worldview imperative (PWI): "All people must develop a single comprehensive and internally coherent worldview that is good and that we strive to act out in our daily lives" (2004, 21). As the PWI states, a person's worldview must not only be good, it must also be comprehensive, internally coherent, and acted upon in our daily lives. More recently, and of particular interest for our purposes, Boylan has advanced what he calls the extended-community worldview imperative (ECWI). The extended worldview imperative states that:

> Each agent must educate himself and others as much as he is able about the peoples of the world—their access to the basic goods of agency, their essential commonly held cultural values, and their governmental and institutional structures—in order that he might create a worldview that includes those of other nations so that individually and collectively the agent might accept the duties that ensue from those peoples' legitimate rights claims, and to act accordingly within what is aspirationally possible. [2011, 23]

Both the PWI and the ECWI emphasize the intimate connection between belief and action. The PWI insists that we "strive to act out [our worldviews] in our daily lives," and the ECWI insists that we educate ourselves about the peoples of the world so that we can respect their legitimate rights claims. Among the notable differences between the two, the ECWI is more explicit than the PWI about our duty to educate ourselves. In the terminology that I introduced in the previous section, the ECWI requires that we "seek and evaluate evidence for and against beliefs." Boylan, then, recognizes the need to treat belief-formation and personal education as a problem in its own right.

In Boylan's view, we have a special obligation to educate ourselves about the peoples of the world because we cannot recognize our duties to them without this information. As he explains in his discussion of the ECWI, "Those in other countries who have legitimate rights claims are entitled to our responding via our correlative duties. Ignorance of their plight does not absolve us from our responsibility" (2011, 24). He later adds that "there is much truth in the old adage 'out of sight, out of mind.' When we are ignorant of the plight of others and when we haven't undergone the imaginative connection of the other to ourselves, then it is certainly the case that we will be less likely to be moved to action" (2011, 25). Even if we do not accept a rights-based approach to ethics, we can appreciate the force of Boylan's point. We cannot *do* what morality requires of us if we do not *know* what morality requires of us. Indeed, we can only learn what morality requires of us if we educate ourselves about morally relevant features of the world. If morality requires that we come to the aid of people living in distant parts of the world, then knowledge concerning their plight is important for us to acquire.

Personal education about these matters would also seem to be crucial from the perspective of the PWI. Recall that the PWI requires that our worldviews be comprehensive and internally coherent. Our worldviews become more comprehensive as we think about the peoples of the world and about how we should respond to their circumstances. Moreover, in gaining this new insight about the world, we may discover latent inconsistencies in our current ways of thinking. While a person's worldview may be internally coherent in a state of ignorance, it may cease to be so in a more enlightened state. In this way, personal education and responsible believing can help us satisfy the goals of the PWI. We might then view personal education and responsible believing as important background conditions in the development of a personal worldview. Alternatively, we might supplement the PWI with a reality or correspondence condition. To this end, we might insist (roughly) *that our worldviews correspond with reality and take account of morally relevant features of the world.*

It will be useful at this point to consider examples of how the acquisition of information about other peoples can prompt us to revise our moral thinking or worldviews. Suppose that a university student, Sarah, believes that we should be tolerant of other cultures; built into her worldview, then, is the value of tolerance. This appreciation of tolerance leads Sarah to accept a position of moral relativism. Sarah believes that we should not pass judgment on other cultures because there is no "truth" in ethics. Who are we to criticize the practices of cultures? As it happens, Sarah also happens to be a budding feminist. She believes that women are equal to men and is profoundly concerned with their social and economic progress in the world.

Now, after taking a few classes at university, Sarah begins to sense a certain degree of tension in her worldview. On the one hand, she believes that we should not pass judgment on other cultures; and on the other, she believes that women are equal to men and should be treated with love and respect. As she learns more about other cultures, she begins to find her inner feminist battling against her inner relativist. She is bothered by the fact that women in various cultures are subject to considerable violence and deprived of rights that are given to men. After experiencing this tension, Sarah realizes that she must modify her worldview. As she sees it, she can either abandon her feminism, or abandon her moral relativism. In the end, she abandons her moral relativism and becomes involved with organizations that promote women's rights. If Sarah had never become informed about the practices of other cultures, she would not have modified her worldview; for, she would never have felt the pressure to do so by the information that she discovered in her classes.

Someone who first learns about factory or working conditions in other parts of the world may have a similar experience. Suppose that Seth believes that we should spend as little money as possible on consumer goods. This belief follows from his commitment to thrift and "smart shopping." Soon, however, Seth learns that his consumption of cheap goods has a considerable cost of its own. He is purchasing goods that support corporate greed and the unfair treatment of workers living in distant parts of the world. Seth is able to buy goods at cheap prices by keeping people employed at low wages and in poor working conditions. This conflict of values may prompt Seth to rethink his current purchasing practices.

Both of these examples reveal the importance of possessing a worldview that corresponds to the world and responds to its morally significant features. When our worldviews fail in this regard, they risk becoming fantasies that provide us with poor moral and practical guidance. Educating ourselves about issues of global suffering and justice can help us in other ways as well. Learning to think about ethical issues on a global scale can mark a significant step in our moral development. Even if we ultimately reject this perspective on things, we can experience a kind of consciousness raising that is valuable in itself. As Boylan pointed out, our ignorance about the plight of others can cause us to think and behave as though they do not exist. When we become aware of others and their struggles, we will often think differently about ourselves. A university student who reads Peter Singer's "Famine, Affluence, and Morality" (1972) may reconsider the distinction that we ordinarily draw between matters of charity and obligation. He may also question the disproportionate concern that he gives to his own interests. Even if the essay fails to influence his behavior in a profound way, it may change the way that he interprets his behavior and explains it to others. He may indulge his interests while believing that he is behaving selfishly—chalking this up to *akrasia*. Alternatively, he may indulge his interests while believing that he is justified in so doing given his reasoned disagreement with Singer.

Thus far, I have claimed that we have grounds for paying particular attention to our moral beliefs. I have placed particular emphasis upon our beliefs concerning global suffering and justice. But just how much is enough? If responsible believing is an ideal for which we should strive, when have we done our share? Before I present my answer, I want to consider what Boylan has said about how much we should do. In presenting the ECWI, Boylan suggests that we have an obligation to educate ourselves about other peoples to the extent necessary to recognize their legitimate rights claims. *Prima facie*, this may appear to be a rather modest proposal. We should not have to educate ourselves to any great extent in order to appreciate the suffering of others—in order to grasp their legitimate rights claims. But upon closer consideration, even this may require a monumental effort on our part. If we have to educate ourselves to the extent necessary to recognize the legitimate rights claims of *each individual*, then we may find ourselves with a new full-time job. A more manageable goal, and perhaps this is what Boylan intends to say, is to educate ourselves about the peoples of the world to the extent necessary to recognize the peoples'—understood as groups, not individuals—legitimate rights claims. Even this may be too much for most of us to accomplish. After all, most people cannot name every country in the world, let alone identify their unique social struggles.

This problem of trying to determine how much is enough, or how much we ought to do, is not limited to the ethics of belief. It is a problem that any theorist must face who attributes positive duties to others. How we respond to this challenge will likely depend upon our other theoretical commitments. A utilitarian will claim that we ought to educate ourselves to the extent necessary to promote the greatest amount of happiness for the greatest number of people. A virtue ethicist will recommend that we pursue moderation in our education and follow in the path of the virtuous person. And a Kantian will claim that we have an imperfect duty to educate ourselves about the plight of others; we cannot, however, quantify how much or how little we ought to do in promoting this end. As a person whose ethical views do not fit neatly into any of these categories, I must confess that my answer will be somewhat vague. At the very least, our education about the world should provide us with a general awareness of the kinds of struggles that the peoples of the world face. At the same time, we should not educate ourselves to the point that we become inactive; that is, our education should not be so consuming that it interferes with our ability to bring about change and progress. My suspicion is that most of us do not have to worry about educating ourselves to the point of exhaustion and inactivity. We can probably do considerably more than we are currently doing in the form of education and the change and progress that it promotes.

Some readers might object to my claim that we ought to concern ourselves with these issues at all. Surely the mother or father who devotes all of his or her time to family and is unfamiliar with the global struggles of our time is a moral success, not a moral failure. Though I think there can be conditions that genuinely excuse a person from pursuing information about these matters, we need to be honest with ourselves about what they are. If the average American watches four hours of television per day, then she can certainly make time to inform herself about the moral state of our world. If the average American regularly surfs the Internet while at work, then she can visit UNICEF or Human Rights Watch between email accounts and celebrity gossip sites. Nevertheless, as I stated at the beginning of the chapter, a commitment to acquiring knowledge about morally significant aspects of the world is an *important*—not necessary or exclusive—component of a moral life. There are people whose lives make it virtually impossible for them to dedicate themselves to information acquisition of almost any kind. While there is something unfortunate about this state of affairs, it need not represent a moral failure.

One challenge that many of us face in attempting to educate ourselves about matters of global suffering and justice concerns the sheer amount of information that is available to us. Today's Americans have access to a tremendous amount of information about almost everything, from the most trivial to the most profound. Although this information overload can be beneficial in certain respects, it can also be harmful. As consumers of information, we need to know which sources to trust and which sources to ignore. Blogs and other Internet resources are not always monitored or edited by experts. Virtually anyone with an opinion can make himself heard if he has enough resolve and technical ability. If we rely heavily upon such sources, we make ourselves vulnerable to various forms of "groupthink," as Lawrence Sanger has warned (2009, 58). In explaining how this can happen, Sanger examines the Internet encyclopedia sensation that he helped to create (as cofounder), Wikipedia. Although Wikipedia presents its users with an astonishing breadth of information, it is not entirely reliable—especially concerning controversial and non-technical issues. Many articles on Wikipedia are edited or "managed" not by experts, but by persistent individuals with a great deal of time on their hands. These individuals stalk certain articles and alter what might otherwise have served as reliable sources of information (64–65).

Even well-respected information sources may approach a topic with a particular bias or ideological slant. If we are in the habit of consulting sources that reinforce what we already believe, then we may fail to acquire new information or broaden our horizons altogether. This is complicated by the fact that we often dismiss publications as "biased" or "untrustworthy" that promote points of view that we do not ourselves accept. While our judgments about the merits of various publications may sometimes be correct, we can have no guarantee that they are foolproof and immune to our own personal biases.

Conclusions

In this chapter, I have argued that there are strong consequentialist reasons for treating belief as a moral problem in its own right. The ethics of belief that I support concerns itself not with beliefs per se, but with the management of beliefs—the voluntary activities that culminate in belief. For the most part, we manage our beliefs in a moral way when we implement strategies for responsible believing, and we manage our beliefs in an immoral way when we do not. We can understand belief management through the lens of morality because it can either promote or fail to promote the ends of morality, whatever we take these to be. Although we cannot reasonably expect people to perfect the strategies of responsible believing, we can hold others and ourselves to certain broad standards of responsible believing. At times, we may be tempted to criticize others for holding individual beliefs that we take to be unwarranted and objectionable. My view accounts for these cases by pointing to the strategies of belief management that contributed to them. If a belief is unwarranted or objectionable for one reason or another, then we can be reasonably confident that the believer's behavior (in the form of belief management) is to blame.

I have been careful throughout the chapter to defend an ethics of belief that is flexible and sensitive to our priorities and limitations. Not all of our beliefs are of equal importance and any plausible ethics of belief must respect this fact. In promoting the ends of morality, we may at times be justified in believing on the basis of insufficient evidence. But in matters of belief, as in matters of action, it is not the case that anything goes. When a person's ignorance is widespread and concerns morally significant issues, then it may serve as an obstacle to a morally decent life.

Notes

1. In "Deciding to Believe," Bernard Williams (1973) offers a similar argument against believing at will. According to Williams, it is a "non-contingent fact" that we cannot believe at will. His argument depends, in part, upon the observation that belief aims at truth (148).

2. As Robert Audi (2008) has pointed out, we can envision situations in which it may not be wise to implement this strategy. If we are confident that *P*, and fear that we may be "overinfluenced," or improperly influenced, by evidence against *P*, then it may be wrong for us to pursue it (405). If situations of this kind do occur, they

will be rare exceptions to the general rule of believing on the basis of comprehensive evidence.

3. For a broad introduction to the confirmation bias, see Nickerson (1998).

References

Audi, Robert. (2008). "The Ethics of Belief: Doxastic Self-Control and Intellectual Virtue." *Synthese 161*: 403–418.

Boylan, Michael. (2000). *Basic Ethics*. Upper Saddle River, NJ: Prentice Hall.

Boylan, Michael. (2004). *A Just Society*. Lanham, MD: Rowman and Littlefield.

Boylan, Michael. (2011). "The Personal and Shared Community Worldview Imperatives" in *Morality and Global Justice*: 15–26. Boulder, CO: Westview.

Clifford, W. K. (1999). "The Ethics of Belief" in *The Ethics of Belief and Other Essays*: 70–96. Amherst, NY: Prometheus Books.

Heil, John. (1983). "Doxastic Agency." *Philosophical Studies 43*: 355–364.

Mele, Alfred. (2001). *Self-Deception Unmasked*. Princeton, NJ: Princeton University Press.

Nickerson, Raymond S. (1998). "Confirmation Bias: A Ubiquitous Phenomenon in Many Guises." *Review of General Psychology 2*: 175–220.

Sanger, Lawrence M. (2009). "The Fate of Expertise After Wikipedia." *Episteme: A Journal of Social Epistemology 6*: 52–73.

Singer, Peter. (1972). "Famine, Affluence, and Morality." *Philosophy and Public Affairs 1*: 229–243.

Setiya, Kieran. (2008). "Believing at Will." *Midwest Studies in Philosophy 32*(1): 36–52.

Williams, Bernard. (1973). "Deciding to Believe" in *Problems of the Self*: 136–151. New York, NY: Cambridge University Press.

CHAPTER FOUR

The Ethics of Otherness

WANDA TEAYS
St. Mary's College

Abstract

This article examines the effects of categorizing certain groups of people as "other" and according them a lower moral status. It is easier to justify draconian laws and policies if the boundary of us *versus* them *is solidly in place, particularly if it is global in scope. I will focus on four groups: detainees, refugees, "enemy" women, and gays. They tend to be treated as expendable, socially inferior, aberrant or alien, and undeserving. The costs of marginalization raise both ethical and human rights concerns. I will look at the linguistic, conceptual, and ethical levels and offer some recommendations.*

Key Words

otherness, detainees, refugees, enemy women, gays, human rights, justice

---

"Perhaps rationality isn't enough."

—Robert McNamara

To be "other" is to be marginalized—sometimes cast in a glaring light as the freak, the deviant, or social outcast—other times invisible, a veritable social ghost, able to come and go unseen.

As the outcast, the other is all too easily objectified and turned into an object of disdain or even brutality. Examples come to mind: detainees stacked naked in pyramids and subjected to abuse and torture; refugees running for their lives, falling off boats, or dying in deserts; enemy women sexually violated or kept by opposing forces to service soldiers; members of the underclass used as organ "donors"; lesbians and gays whose sexual orientation unleashes ostracism, discrimination, or violence. Members of these groups may be singled out, targeted for exploitation, punished simply for being *other*, and discarded when no longer of use.

When not objects of disapproval or abuse, socially inferior others are often invisible, under the radar. They have no status per se and can move about with little notice. Think of Mike Max, a character in the movie *The End of Violence*: He found refuge by taking on the guise (and job) of a gardener. He and the Latino workers who took him in managed to avoid detection simply by being too insignificant to be perceived. They were social "nobodies," irrelevant, and forgettable. This invisibility occasionally has its attractions. We see this with gays and lesbians who choose to stay in "the closet" in order to have some semblance of safety not always open to nonheterosexuals.

Being "other" means living at the boundaries of civilization, not quite making it into the realm of power and status. The harm, the collateral damage, can be momentary, but is often long-term. Excluded from the norm by policies, laws, tradition, and social standing, those who reside in this no-man's-land may be trapped for years or decades.

When inquiring into global ethics, we need to look beyond local or national boundaries and the lines drawn by tradition, culture, and religion. This inquiry necessarily encompasses human rights concerns. It also leads us into metaethics, where we must determine what is just or unjust, right or wrong—and do so without the specific guidelines of *this* place, *that* country, or *those* sets of beliefs. No one country, religion, or tradition has the upper hand when it comes to ethical dilemmas that affect all humanity.

Such an inquiry is broad—vast in scope and yet specific—where any given case is a microcosm of the whole. From each manifestation of stripping others of their moral equality, we see the significance of ethics for analysis and problem solving. It thus helps to frame the issue in terms of both theoretical and practical aspects. This we'll do by looking at three groups of "others"—refugees, detainees, and gays.

The first group is made up of those who feel compelled to leave their homeland in hopes of a better life in another country. They may lack money, skills, and resources and thus are dependent upon others to extend a helping hand. Such help is not always forthcoming. The fear is that they will take away jobs from tax-paying citizens, sap precious resources, and lower the quality of life with their strange customs and unfamiliar religious practices. Refugees thus represent a threat both to the economy and to dominant values and traditions.

The second group we will examine is detainees. They are seen as real or potential enemies of war. The threat they pose has to do with national security, as well as our own personal safety. Detainees tap into our fear of terrorist attacks, ticking bombs, and suicide "martyrs" with weapons strapped to their waists, ready to detonate at a moment's notice. They can't be trusted—*any* detainee could be the next Osama bin Laden. That very possibility separates us from them.

The last group we will look at is gays and lesbians. Their violation as others is under the skin—literally. They pose the threat that, like vampires converting the good citizens in *True Blood*, innocent heterosexuals will be "bit" and it's downhill from there. We fear their alien lifestyle and sexual differences. Also, this other could be contagious—inadvertently or intentionally causing those who are straight to join their ranks. Even worse, they might inflict their deviancy on society's most innocent—our children.

Each group threatens the status quo by their very identity as *them*, not us. Of course, each group has members who have stood out—public figures and spokespersons who have shaped the societal dialogue and brought to light key issues and concerns. However, each group has had but limited success in effecting transformation. We need to understand why that is.

The dynamics involved in labeling others "other" shows us how we sustain and deepen the divisions between people. We need to acquire greater insight into such fortifications and how they solidify social strata, moral status, and legal power. Until then, we risk continuing destructive laws and policies and putting more in place.

Individual members of these groups lie along an ethical spectrum—some are good; some are not. Granting them more legitimacy will not eliminate moral turpitude, but we can level the playing field. By moving from the realm of the abstract into the world, we can focus on the human dimension and the ethical questions and concerns that follow. With that in mind, let's look at each group to see what lessons we should learn.

Refugees

The 1951 United Nations Convention relating to the Status of Refugees classified a refugee as, "a person outside of his or her country of nationality who is unable or unwilling to return because of persecution or a well-founded fear of persecution on account of race, religion, nationality, membership in a particular social group, or political opinion." This definition has three aspects—place (outside one's own country); status (unable/unwilling to return); and justification (fear of persecution due to affiliation with a group or ideology). Any one of these three can affect a refugee's moral status.

Consider the range. There are economic refugees who seek a "better" (more financially secure) life and political or religious refugees seeking asylum. The US Department of Homeland Security recently recognized domestic violence (but not genital mutilation) as a possible basis for asylum (Preston, 2009). According to the US Committee for Refugees and Immigrants, "The United States [in 2008] accepted 48,300 refugees for resettlement and granted asylum to 23,000. Almost 93,400 asylum seekers had claims pending at the end of the year."

The response to asylum seekers is not uniformly positive—they may elicit sympathy, but are frequently seen as yet another burden on society (Cox, 2008). This resulted in an expanding use of jail-like facilities as holding pens. A *Human Rights First* report (2009) states that:

> They are held in facilities that are actual jails or are operated like jails [by the US Department of Homeland Security]. They are often brought in handcuffs and sometimes shackles to these facilities, where they wear prison uniforms, are guarded by officers in prison attire, visit with family and friends only through glass barriers, and have essentially no freedom of movement within the facilities. The cost of detaining these asylum seekers over the past six years has exceeded $300 million.

Whatever the dangers they pose to others, refugees, as a whole, face their own set of dangers. There are risks of endurance—crossing rivers, deserts, and mountaintops, as portrayed in such films as *Journey of Hope* and *Sin Nombre.* There are risks of indifference or rejection—as seen by the Thai military leaving hundreds of Burmese asylum seekers to die after setting them adrift in boats with no engines (Bell, 2009). Many who arrive are sent back. In 2008, "the U.S. Coast Guard returned nearly 1,600 Haitians and more than 3,200 Cubans it intercepted at sea as they tried to reach Florida" (US Committee for Refugees and Immigrants, 2009).

The risks, however, are not often a deterrent. For example, in the first six months of 2009, 10,000 Somalis sought refugee status in Yemen, adding to the thousands already there ("Somali Refugees," 2009). Such numbers bring health risks. Thousands of Zimbabwean refugees—many with cholera—waited for weeks in a showground to apply for asylum in South Africa (Ndlovu, 2009).

And then there is rejection. Governments spend time and money to block the flow of refugees. We saw this in the case of Tucson, Arizona, sanctuary workers brought to trial in *United States of America v. Maria Del Socorro Pardo De Aguilar* (1985). Here eleven people[1] (including two priests, a nun, and other activists) were prosecuted for assisting 3,000-plus refugees fleeing El Salvador and seeking housing across the US.

The defendants saw their work as a modern-day Underground Railroad for runaway slaves in the nineteenth century (Cohan et al., 1986). The prosecution, in contrast, thought they were usurping governmental authority to regulate immigration policy and saw the sanctuary workers "as common alien smugglers who transport aliens into the country for a fee" (Passaro and Phillips, 1986, 139). *These* coyotes, however, charged no fee for their actions.

Prosecuting attorney Donald Reno put forward a motion *in limine* that circumscribed the use of language. It was a major blow to the defense. The motion prohibited the use of the word "refugees"—only "illegal aliens" could be used during the trial (Reno, 1985, 9–10). "This ruling totally impaired the defendants' ability to present evidence related to negating the 'specific intent' element of the crime of conspiracy," notes Karen Snell, defense counsel for Maria del Socorro Pedro de Aguilar (cited in Colbert, 1987, 1315).

It helps to keep in mind the historical significance of sanctuary. The term connotes protection and refuge and is inextricably tied to religion. "The first explicit reference to a legally authorized sanctuary privilege exercised by Christian churches is in the Theodosian Code of 392. For eleven centuries, the privilege of providing sanctuary in churches was part of the English common law" (Cohan, 1986, 549). The sanctuary tradition began in the US when dissenting Pilgrims and Puritans who settled there viewed the country as a refuge (Cohan, 1986, 550). Those in other countries have also recognized sanctuary as an enduring value to society. As a concept, its application extends across species—from humans to virtually any kind of animal life.

Some recognize the moral or religious force of sanctuary, while denying its social or legal significance. The US Constitution itself says nothing about sanctuary. "In fact, the precise limits of religious freedom are not contained in the Constitution" (Passaro and Phillips, 1985, 165). The use of the term is as much caught up with dictates of conscience as with any historical roots.

Sister Marian Strohmeyer said, "I think it is incumbent upon people to help strangers, people who are fleeing for their lives in our midst. . . . [Many] people take that as their obligation, work that they are called to do" (National Council of Churches, 1986, 10). Parallels have been drawn to the (illegal) sheltering of Jews during World War II and runaway slaves (Brown, 1986, 126; Butler, 1986).

In contrast, Immigration and Naturalization Service (INS) commissioner Alan C. Nelson (1986) asserted that "it has been hundreds of years since any system included a legal concept of sanctuary or allowed sanctuary to serve as a legal defense." He insisted that, "religious affiliation or motives cannot insulate anyone from the consequences which flow from the violation of the immigration laws, anymore than from violation of other criminal or civil laws (US Department of Justice, Immigration, and Naturalization 1985, 2). Prosecutor Reno (1985) spoke of the sanctuary workers "in the underground railroad *conspiracy*" (8). This view was seconded by the Appeals Court (1989): Sanctuary workers were accused of "masterminding and running a modern-day underground railroad that smuggled Central American natives across the Mexican border with Arizona" (1).

On the other hand, the defendants saw their work as "in a very real sense a religious ministry" (*US v. Clark*, 1985, 1). Freedom of religion, they contended, affords protection both to freedom of belief and to freedom to act according to those beliefs.[2] The prosecution argued that the INA (Immigration and Nationality Act) is neutral as to religion. This was reiterated by the Court in *Church of Scientology* (1979): "Courts must remain neutral in matters of religious doctrine and practice." According to Senator Rick Santorum (2005), the idea that the government is neutral to religion goes no further back than the 1947 case of *Everson v. Board.* He says, "The term 'neutrality' does not appear in the U.S. Constitution. This doctrine is a pure invention of the Court."

Edward Cellar, one of the 1952 immigration bill's authors, insisted that, "I do not wish to center an attack on anybody except the smuggler and the [person] who tries to make money out of the misery of some of these workers. . . . Certainly we do not want to get after the good people. It is the bad at whom we aim our shafts."[3]

While not disputing the defendants' "firmly held religious beliefs," the government sought to "stem the torrent of aliens unlawfully entering the U.S. across the southern border."[4] As with a flood or infestation, the "torrent of aliens" should be stopped by any means necessary. For the Appeals Court, the "government's interest in controlling immigration outweighs appellants' purported religious interest" (*US v. Aguilar*, 1989).

The role of surveillance in this case resonates with later, post–Patriot Act methods. The US government gathered information via an undercover operation using informants who had been coyotes to infiltrate the movement. They wore recording devices into churches and religious services where meetings on sanctuary were held. "Never before," Cohan et al. (1986) note, "have prosecutions arisen from evidence obtained in this manner. There is irony and hypocrisy in the use of informants who have been commercially involved in the very smuggling activity the government accuses the Workers of committing" (599).[5]

There are a host of concerns regarding the covert and overt government operations involving political action for refugees. "These activities marked a new phase in the government's treatment of [the sanctuary movement]," Carl W. Levander reports, "not only because agents were entering churches, but also because such entries were carried out without a warrant" (1986, 208). Such tactics have been carried forward to the war on terror—for example, with FBI spies in mosques and attempts to recruit others. "Muslims are being approached by the FBI to spy on activities of Muslim congregations," reports the *Arab American News* (*"CIOM,"* 2009).

Aguilar defendant Sister Darlene Nicgorski saw a change in the government's approach: "The government's line," she remarked, "was always that refugees were here for economic reasons. Then there was a real clear shift and they linked them to people's fear, especially of terrorism" (Teays, 1987). She added that four of President Reagan's speeches used the words "sanctuary" and "terrorism" in the same paragraph. Making refugees an object of fear only intensifies their status as alien, as other.

The Tucson Sanctuary trial left many unresolved issues. Just as the "torrent" of refugees around the world has yet to be stopped, the issue of the moral status of the refugees as "others" continues to call for an ethical response. So, too, does the situation of the second group—detainees.

Detainees

As we saw with "refugees" and "aliens," a great deal of energy has been expended in manipulating language to serve certain ends. Instead of terms like "prisoner," which carries some moral force, we now have "detainees." That term is bereft of moral significance.

Detainees exist in a legal and moral limbo—held indefinitely, neither accused nor convicted of a crime. Once labeled a "detainee" and taken to a detention facility, prison, or CIA "black site," they enter a no-man's-land of complete vulnerability. Other uses of language act in consort. The terms "insurgents," "unlawful enemy combatants," "illegal combatants," and "unprivileged enemy combatants" contrast with our "lawful combatants." The division between *them* and *us* is absolutely necessary for the term "detainee" to stick. When attempting to shape policies by linguistic engineering, it is crucial that there be an opening to push through changes.

Once in place, we can turn our attention to allowable treatment. It is here that severing the moral ties to "prisoners" was a gold mine. "Detainees" are not afforded the protections of the Geneva Conventions or international treaties and ethical codes. Only "prisoners" qualify for such moral stature. The door is then opened to treating detainees as truly "other." With their moral and legal status diminished, detainees are prey to degradation, humiliation, abuse, and torture.

As "unprivileged enemy combatants," they are doomed. Once so labeled, they can be picked up anywhere in the world—even within the US—and subjected to a twenty-minute "takeout":

> Members of the Rendition Group follow a simple but standard procedure: Dressed head to toe in black, including masks, they blindfold and cut the clothes off their new captives, then administer an enema and sleeping drugs. They outfit detainees in a diaper and jumpsuit for what can be a day-long trip. Their destinations: either a detention facility operated by cooperative countries in the Middle East and Central Asia, including Afghanistan, or one of the CIA's own covert prisons—referred to in classified documents as "black sites," which at various times have been operated in eight countries, including several in Eastern Europe. [Priest, 2005]

Citizenship status provides no safeguards, as we saw with John Walker Lindh, Jose Padilla, and Yaser Hamdi. No one wants a terrorist going "scot-free" and, so, these maybe-possibly-could-be terrorist detainees are the undead. They are locked away indefinitely, with few or no rights.

Karen J. Greenberg (2008) examines "this nebulous class of persons" made up of both citizens and noncitizens. She sees the creation of a "new category of person" at the center of the reorganization of power, symbolically and legally. In "one fell swoop, the administration thus extricated the United States from the international obligations that have governed the treatment of prisoners in armed conflict since the middle of the nineteenth century." Such legal deviation was used to defend coercive interrogation techniques and redefine torture, thus allowing medieval techniques such as waterboarding (Greenberg, 2008, xi). Gender is no protection either—though far more men than women are in this category. However, women have been detained and some sexually assaulted, as the *Taguba Report* notes. And remember that the Abu Ghraib photos released to the public were censored—none showed the abuse of women and children, which even Secretary of Defense Donald Rumsfeld characterized as "blatantly sadistic" (Rumsfeld, 2004).

And mistakes do happen. One estimate is that thirty-six people have been victims of "erroneous rendition" (Priest, 2005). Two well-known examples are German citizen Khaled el-Masri and Canadian Maher Arar. After being captured, el-Masri was sent to a CIA "black site" in Afghanistan and Arar was "rendered" to Syria, a country known to use torture (a few others are Libya, Morocco, and Egypt). Both men allege horrific treatment while detained. Neither was able to seek legal remedies, because the US government successfully invoked a "state secrets" privilege.

There is a lot to be learned from President Bush's Executive Order 13440 and the various torture memos written by John Yoo, Jay Bybee, and Steven Bradbury. They reveal near-total indifference to those caught in the net of the war on terror. Not only does Bush's order specify nonadherence to the Geneva Conventions with respect to detainees, it includes a statement regarding the "basic necessities" for those subject to interrogation by the CIA. Bush deems such necessities to be adequate food and water, shelter, necessary clothing, protection from extremes of heat and cold, and essential medical care. This seems quite reasonable. But linguistic sleight of hand being highly developed, it should not be surprising that key things are not included among these basics. But first, we should note that the order for protection from extreme temperatures seemed not to carry sufficient weight—as examples abound regarding detainees who were subjected to blazing heat or hypothermia. Ex-interrogator Tony Lagouranis tells of Navy SEALs who burned detainees by holding cigarette lighters up to their legs and other SEALs who put naked detainees out on the snow or forced them to lie down so ice water could be poured over them. Meanwhile rectal thermometers were used to make sure they didn't freeze to death (Conroy, 2007).

Unfortunately, Executive Order 13440's omissions are noteworthy. Bush failed to mention the right to sleep or a bed to sleep on—leaving an opening for days-long sleep deprivation and metal platforms as "beds." For instance, Jose Padilla spent nearly two years in solitary confinement, having only a cold steel slab without a mattress, blanket, or pillow.

Bush also omitted the right to a toilet or facilities for bathing—thus permitting buckets or, worse, nothing at all, for example, in transport, interrogation sessions, and restraint chairs (used in forced feedings), when detainees had to urinate or defecate on themselves. He failed to clarify what counts as "adequate" food—leaving it open for bottles of Ensure or MREs (meals ready to eat) to be handed out, limited in supply, or used as a bargaining tool.

There is no mention either of having access to fresh air or light. There is no prohibition against the use of either complete darkness of twenty-four-hour strobe lights. Nor is it off-limits to resort to deafeningly loud music, blindfolds, hoods, earmuffs, duct tape, and other means of sensory deprivation. The barbaric use of these "enhanced interrogation methods" is now well documented.

Bush's order recognized no right to freedom of movement, such as being able to sit down. This left open forced standing, shackling, and stress positions, as well as imprisonment in cages, coffins, or containers that contort the human body. And there was no prohibition against solitary confinement—as used on Mahed Arar, Mohammed al-Qahtani, Abu Zubaydah, Moazzam Begg, Jose Padilla, Khalid Sheikh Mohammed, and Feroz Abassi. The sheer injustice here has not escaped notice. The United Nations has supported a public declaration of experts seeking to restrict the use of solitary confinement.

The list of basics also offers no protection against abusive techniques like waterboarding, or the intentional use of dogs, vermin, or insects to terrify detainees. Ex-interrogator Tony Lagouranis, for example, cites the frequent use of dogs to terrify the hooded detainees (who had no idea that the dogs were usually—though not always—on a leash).

The omissions tell us a great deal. So, too, does the convoluted use of language in both Bush's order and the various torture memos. With careful framing and sufficient legalese, the sanctioned methods might avoid being labeled "torture." The twisted precision in the memos demonstrates a coldness and depravity like something out of Dante's *Inferno.*

Slavoj Zizek (2007) refers to Khalid Shaikh Mohammed (high-profile suspect "KSM") as the "Knight of the Living Dead." He writes: "For the first time in a great many years torture was normalized—presented as something acceptable. The ethical consequences of it should worry us all." As Clayton Whitt (2009) observes:

> It's difficult to comprehend that anyone in a position of authority in America can get away with calling these practices anything *but* torture, and also hard to believe

> there's a debate taking place at all over whether or not the torture outlined in the Office of Legal Counsel memos is justifiable. However, in a survey published on April 29, the Pew Forum found that 49 percent of the U.S. public believes that torture can sometimes or often be justified. . . . The Pew Forum didn't carry out the survey using a euphemism such as "enhanced interrogation techniques" or another such watered-down phrase. Respondents were actually endorsing torture.

Of course, not all interrogators are vicious and not all detainees are abused. Far more issues have arisen around the CIA and their surrogates than the military (who set higher standards with the "Rules of War"). But the isolated facilities, the lack of protections set down by the Geneva Conventions, and the lack of public oversight or easy access by the Red Cross raise an array of ethical issues. Moreover, the fact that detainees can be held indefinitely—with no end in sight—is simply macabre. They are dead to the outside world.

With such an abysmally low moral status, their very humanity has been forsaken. This need not be a permanent state. Things can change as our moral reasoning skills are sharpened. Calling on our sense of justice and compassion for others really does matter—even if progress is in fits and starts.

The Obama administration has abandoned the use of the term "enemy combatant," supposedly to better root detention policies in legal principles. However, it has retained the right to hold a detainee indefinitely—a stance that has come under fire from human rights groups as unconstitutional and unjust (ACLU, 2009).

The issue of what is constitutional and what is just is also a central concern for our last group of others—gays and lesbians. As with the first two groups, we need to think long and hard about the "them versus us" division. This is not easy to do—a fact that makes many simply avoid the issue entirely. But we can benefit from such an analysis, as we will see.

Gays and Lesbians

Unlike refugees, members of this group need not be fleeing another country and, unlike detainees, they need not be seen as insurgents or enemies. The otherness manifested here has to do with what is thought natural, normal, and spiritually pure or clean. As a result, gays and lesbians have had to fight for equality in terms of social, moral, and legal standing.

The idea is that those who are neither natural nor normal are probably moral deviants and, thus, should not expect equal moral status or access to opportunities available to nondeviant heterosexuals. This is not without irony. Think of it: gays and lesbians are prohibited from serving in the military, though they can give blood, sell sperm and eggs, and donate organs. They cannot get legally married in most states or countries, but they can adopt children and use surrogate mothers to procreate.

On one hand, there appears to be a strong argument for at least some prohibitions gays and lesbians face—particularly if they *are* abnormal. On the other hand, most favor the equality of competent adults. Thus, the argument:

> Nothing is more fundamental to the very foundation of our constitutional government than the principle of equal protection of the laws. Article I, section 1's declaration of "inalienable" rights itself assumes every person's fundamental equality before the law, asserting that *all people* have rights that are fundamental and *inalienable*. . . . This equal protection principle is the basis of our governmental social contract and thus the bedrock foundation upon which our state Constitution is built. [*California Council of Churches,* 2008, 23]

The same-sex marriage ruling by the California Supreme Court (2008)—as well as the proposition (Prop 8) meant to strike it down—offers a window on the key issues.

Those seeking to overturn Proposition 8 (defining marriage as between only a man and a woman) drew an analogy between gays and religious minorities. They argued that, "majorities sometimes fall into patterns of distrust and discrimination against religious minorities, particularly in times of national crisis or war" (*California Council of Churches*, 2008, 30). They cite the case of Jehovah's Witnesses in the 1940s who were beaten, tarred and feathered, and even castrated in waves of violence following the ruling in *Minersville School District v. Gobitis* (1940). In *Gobitis,* the US Supreme Court upheld the expulsion of two elementary-school children for their refusal to salute the American flag in public schools.

Parallels have been drawn to same-sex marriage: "Petitioners in the marriage equality case note that in hindsight, we can clearly see that Jehovah's Witnesses and their children never really posed the threat to public order and national security that so many Americans, in a time of war, once so vividly perceived" (*California Council of Churches*, 2008, 30–31).

A great deal turns on the decision of marriage equality. The stakes are high—whomever a society permits to be legally married says a great deal about who we are as a people and what sort of values we hold dear. The mere fact of requiring the participants to be of a certain age separates one society from the next. The structure of the marriage can also reveal values and prejudices. For example, restricting marriage to a couple, as opposed to three or more, reflects both ethical and religious beliefs about what sort of union should be sanctioned.

There are also issues of asymmetry, as when societies have institutions around a bride's dowry or "bride price" but nothing comparable for grooms. There are human rights concerns with some marriage practices (such as husbands selling their wives' organs or forcing them into paid medical experimentation). And we should note—these are not simply practices limited to the United States—marriage is an institution that has carried significant weight around the globe. Yes, the stakes around marriage are high and, thus, its role with respect to homosexuals is not at all abstract or inconsequential.

Proponents argue that marriage should be as much a right for gays and lesbians as for heterosexuals. To think otherwise, they contend, is to exclude marriage from the list of *inalienable rights*. If marriage were only a right for heterosexuals, this would imply that the Constitution draws lines according to sexual orientation. Evidence does not support this view. In addition, the California Supreme Court saw sexual orientation as a "suspect classification" in the same way that race, gender, and religion are suspect bases for imposing differential treatment under the law. No more than we should prohibit marriage between those of different religions or different races should we impose a standard around gender—so saw the Court. Chief Justice George argued that "tradition alone does not justify the denial of a fundamental constitutional right" (Liptak, 2008).

And yet same-sex marriage taps into some pretty strong fears. Deeply entrenched views affirming that only male-female couples should qualify for a legal marriage can be traced back to Leviticus, where the issue of cleanliness was put under the spotlight (Chap. 18). There continues to be dispute around the interpretation of the various proscriptions (Ontario Consultants on Religious Tolerance, 2008). Nevertheless, the concept of spiritual cleanliness still has powerful repercussions—as we see with recent controversies around the Boy Scouts of America (BSA).

The BSA organization sought to exclude atheists as well as gays from becoming boy scouts. This brought about a "wave of civil-rights litigation in the 1990s when the BSA expelled seven-year-olds whose religious beliefs were not up to snuff [they did not swear to a belief in God] and barred gay scouts and leaders as neither 'morally straight' nor spiritually 'clean'" (Isaacson, 2007).

Boy Scouts of America argued that homosexuals violate "the Scout Law that a Scout be clean in word and deed" (*Boy Scouts of America v Dale*, 2000). In other words, homosexuals are apparently considered spiritually unclean. As such, they are shut out of the Boy Scouts. Does that mean they aren't clean enough to get married?

Ronald M. George, chief justice of the California Supreme Court, may help us navigate these waters. Chief Justice George, a moderate Republican, wrote the ruling on marriage equality in California (allowing same-sex marriage). He said the decision "weighed most heavily" on him—more than any previous case in his nearly seventeen years on the Supreme Court. Reading the legal arguments, he thought of a trip he had taken years ago to the American South. There he saw signs warning "No Negro" and "No Coloreds"—and these made a deep impression on him (Dolan, 2008).

Chief Justice George said, "I think there are times when doing the right thing means not playing it safe," adding, "I am very fatalistic about these things." He observed, "If you worry, always looking over your shoulders, then maybe it's time to hang up your robe." In his opinion, the fight for same-sex marriage was a civil rights case similar to the battle to ban laws against interracial marriage. The California Supreme Court moved ahead of public sentiment sixty years ago when it became the first in the country to strike down the anti-miscegenation laws—which he saw as a precedent that should be followed here (Dolan, 2008).

He argued that the basis for the decision was that, "What you are doing is applying the Constitution, the ultimate expression of the people's will." Reflecting on the matter, he said, "When is it that a court should act? When is it that a court is shirking its responsibility by not acting, and when is a court overreaching? That's a real conundrum" (Dolan, 2008).

These questions *are* conundrums. And they are ones that extend from one country to the next and across cultures around the world. But we need only look at the discrimination that gays and lesbians face—from schools to boy scouts–type organizations to prisons to politics—to know that all is not right. There is a long history of violence and prejudice perpetrated on homosexuals in acts of cruelty without national boundaries. The problem is international in scope.

That we are so afraid that they will harm our children, taint our religions, and corrupt our societies calls for reflection and action. Most abuse is at the hands of one's own family members (by birth or marriage) and *not* some random homosexual maniac. Like the "prawns" in the movie *District 9*, gays and lesbians suffer more from what we do to them than what "they" do to "us."

The truth is that refugees and detainees and gays—all these "others"—*are* us and we are them. We post distinctions to elevate our moral stature—but not without a cost. Those divisions have created far more harm than good. We have more to gain by seeing what is in common, what interests are shared, and how we can live together.

Conclusion

"Perhaps rationality is not enough," as McNamara said. These "conundrums," as Chief Justice George called them, are not solved by logic alone. That is not to say that our analytical skills should be shelved. Hardly. However, in deciding what is right or wrong, just or unjust, fair or unfair, we need to try to understand the ethical dilemmas we face against the backdrop of our values and beliefs—as well as moral principles, such as those affirming human dignity and the right to individual liberty (so long as no one else is harmed). This entails clarifying our criteria of evaluation—the "context of discovery" and the "context of justification" that Sandra Harding (1986) recommends for framing a discussion.

With the context of discovery, we should draw upon conceptual frameworks to help structure the debate around the various groups that lie at society's margins. We should also look at the ways power is manifested—who sets the rules, who calls the shots, who counts, and who doesn't. We should also examine the role of language in shaping the dialogue. As we saw in this chapter, the very terms used may even determine what count as solutions to the problems. When the inquiry is twisted—even contorted—by words like "aliens," "unprivileged enemy combatants," and "fags," we can hardly be surprised at the decisions and policies that are made. Language has been used as a wedge between people—the wider the distance, the easier to put in place discriminatory practices that result in the objectification, if not abuse, of those seen as socially, morally, or legally inferior.

It also helps to have in place some context of justification to assess our progress as we confront ethical dilemmas and societal conflicts. We need to ensure that the criteria used to sort evidence and evaluate moral claims meet our standards in terms of justice and morality. And using different frames of reference can help us see the broader issues and the repercussions of our policies and decisions.

As we saw with our three different groups of "others," shifting points of view to include those of the most disadvantaged is crucial. The fact that many people have turned their backs on refugees, detainees, and gays reminds us that we still have a lot of work to do. And yet, there are many who *have* cut the distance, who see these others as deserving of respect and dignity—and, thus, work to change the status quo. Whatever are their perceived shortcomings, they *are* still human.

Rationality really isn't enough. Fortunately we can take a wider look around—see beyond our personal interests to global ones. We can call up empathy and compassion and work in community for a more just society. With a commitment to addressing human rights concerns, we can find a better way to live with one another.

Notes

1. Namely, Rev. Anthony Clark (parish priest), Jim Corbett (Quaker), Mary K. Doan Espinoza (coordinator of religious education for Clark's church), Rev. John M. Fife (Presbyterian), Peggy Hutchinson (director of border ministry for the Tucson Metropolitan Ministry), Wendy LeWin (Unitarian Universalist), Nena McDonald (Quaker), Sister Darlene Nicgorski, Rev. Roman Dogoberto Quinones (parish priest in Sonora, Mexico), Phillip Willis-Conger (director of Tucson Ecumenical Council's task force on Central America), and Maria del Socorro Pedro de Aguilan, the primary defendant.

2. Defense cites *Founding Church of Scientology v. United States,* 409 F.2d 1146, 1156 (D.C. Circ. 1969), where it was ruled that First Amendment protection embraces not only the religious belief but also the religious action of solicitation premised on that

belief. (See *US v. Clark, et al.,* 1985, "Motion to Dismiss" page 6.) Cited as support for this claim is the ruling in *Wisconsin v. Yoder* that exercise of freedom of religion permitted the Amish to opt out of public (mandatory) education for their children.

3. As quoted in No. CR-85-008-PHX-EHC (D. Ariz., 1985), "Response to Government's Motion in Limine-Intent," page 8.

4. "Defendant Aguilar's Opposition to the Government's Motion to Preclude a Defense Based on the Free Exercise Clause," CR-85-008-PHX-EHC (D. Ariz. 1985), page 1.

5. Reportedly, ex-coyote Jesus Cruz had knowingly transported illegal aliens for profit (as noted in *United States v. Aguilar*, 1985).

References

American Civil Liberties Union (ACLU). (2009, 26 June). "Obama Administration Indefinite Detention Order Would Undermine American Values of Justice." Retrieved from www.aclu.org/safefree/detention/40051prs20090626.html

Arizona Sanctuary Defense Fund. (1985, December). Weekly Update for the Sanctuary Trial: 17–19.

Army Regulation 15-6: Final Report. (2005, 1 April). "Investigation into FBI Allegations of Detainee Abuse at Guantánamo Bay, Cuba Detention Facility." Finding #11B, Unclassified.

Bell, Thomas. (2009, 18 January). "Growing Anger at Claims Refugees Were Set Adrift 'To Die.'" *Telegraph* (UK). Retrieved from http://www.telegraph.co.uk/news/worldnews/asia/thailand/4283685

Boy Scouts of America v. Dale (99-699). (2000). 530 U.S. 640.

Brown, Robert McAfee. (1986). *Saying Yes and Saying No: On Rendering to God and Caesar.* Philadelphia: The Westminster Press.

Butler, Bates III. (1986, Summer). "Legal Issues of Sanctuary." *New Conversations: Call This Witness 'Sanctuary' 9*(1).

California Council of Churches v. Mark D. Horton, et al. (2008). Petition for Writ of Mandate or Prohibition. No. 168332.

Church of Scientology of California and Founding Church of Scientology of Washington, DC, v. James Siegelman, Flo Conway, J. B. Lippincott Company and Morris Deutsch. No. 79 Civ. 1166 (GLG). United States District Court, S. D.

"CIOM [Council of Islamic Organizations of Michigan] Says FBI Spying on Michigan Muslims." (2009, 17 April). *The Arab American News.*

Cohan, Deborah, Rachel San Kronowitz, Clara Amanda Pope, and Gloria Valencia-Weber. (1986). "Project on the Sanctuary Movement." *Harvard Civil Rights-Civil Liberties Law Review 21*(2).

Colbert, Douglas L. (1987, July). "The Motion in Limine in Politically Sensitive Cases: Silencing the Defendant at Trial." *Stanford Law Review 39*(6): 1271–1327.

Conroy, John. (2007, 2 March). "Tony Lagouranis—Confessions of a Torturer." *Chicago Reader.* Retrieved from www.chicagoreader.com/features/stories/torture/

Cox, Jonathan. (2008, 19 June). "Mind Your Language: Banning Asylum or Saving Sanctuary?" *Open Democracy.* Retrieved from http://www.opendemocracy.net/blog/migrantvoice-on-refuge/jonathan-cox/2008/06/19/mind-your-language-banning-asylum-or-saving-sanctuary

Dolan, Maura. (2008, 18 May). "California Chief Justice Says Gay Marriage Ruling Was One of His Toughest." *Los Angeles Times.*

Founding Church of Scientology v. United States. (1969). 409 F.2d 1146, 1156 (D.C. Circ. 1969).

Greenberg, Karen, ed. (2006). *The Torture Debate in America.* Cambridge: Cambridge University Press.

Harding, Sandra. (1986). *The Science Question in Feminism.* Cornell, NY: Cornell University Press.

Human Rights First Report Summary. (2009, April). "U.S. Detention of Asylum Seekers Seeking Protection, Finding Prison." *Human Rights First.* Retrieved from http://www.humanrightsfirst.org/pdf/090429-RP-hrf-asylum-detention-sum-doc.pdf.

Isaacson, Eric Alan. (2007, April). "Assaulting America's Mainstream Values: Hans Zeiger's *Get Off My Honor.*" [Book Review]. *Pierce Law Review 5*(3).

Levander, Carl W. (1986). "*En El Nombre De Dios*—The Sanctuary Movement: Development and Potential for First Amendment Protection." *West Virginia Law Review 89*(1).

Liptak, Adam. (2008, 16 May). "California Court Affirms Right to Gay Marriage." *The New York Times.*

Minersville School District v. Gobitis. (1940). 310 U.S. 586.

National Council of Churches of Christ USA, Presbyterian Church USA, Friends United Meeting, American Lutheran Church, The Commission on Social Action of Reform Judaism, The United Church of Christ, and the Department of Church in Society Division of Homeland Ministries showground Christian Church (Disciples of Christ). (1985). Amicus Curiae Brief in support of Stacey Merkt, *United States of America v. Stacey Lynn Merkt,* 764 F.2d 266, NO.84-2401.

Ndlovu, Nosimilo. (2009, 13 March). "Evicting Refugees Spreads Epidemic." *Mail & Guardian* (South Africa). Retrieved from http://www.mg.co.za/article/2009-03-13-evicting-refugees-spreads-epidemic

Nelson, Alan C., and William Sloane Coffin. (1986). "A Debate on Sanctuary." Reprinted from Newsletter on Church and State Abroad, Council on Religion and International Affairs. *New Conversations: Call This Witness 'Sanctuary' 9*(1).

Ontario Consultants on Religious Tolerance. (2008, 23 September). "Homosexuality in Leviticus 18:22." *Religious Tolerance.* Retrieved from http://www.religioustolerance.org/hom_bibh4.htm

Passaro, Geralyn, and Janet Phillips. (1986). "Sanctuary: Reconciling Immigration Policy with Humanitarianism and the First Amendment." *University of Miami Inter-American Law Review.*

Preston, Julia. (2009, 16 July). "New Policy Permits Asylum for Battered Women." *New York Times.*

Priest, Dana. (2005, 4 December). "Wrongful Imprisonment: Anatomy of a CIA Mistake." *Washington Post.*

Reno, Donald M., Jr. (1985). Government's Memorandum in Support of Motion in Limine. CR-85-008-PHX-EHC (D. Ariz. 1985).

Rumsfeld, Donald. (2004, 7 May). Testimony of Secretary of Defense Donald H. Rumsfeld Before the Senate and House Armed Services Committees. Retrieved from http://www.globalsecurity.org/military/library/congress/2004_hr/040507-rumsfeld.pdf

Santorum, Rick. (2005, 20 July). "Enter 'Neutrality.'" *National Review.* Retrieved from http://www.nationalreview.com/comment/santorum200507200827.asp

"Somali Refugees' Inflow Continues." (2009, 20 June). *Yemen Post.* Retrieved from http://www.yemenpost.net/Detail123456789.aspx?ID=3&SubID=916.

Teays, Wanda. (1987, 27 November). Phone interview (unpublished) with Sr. Darlene Nicgorski.

United Nations Conference of Plenipotentiaries on the Status of Refugees and Stateless Persons. (1951, 28 July). Convention Relating to the Status of Refugees. Office of the High Commissioner for Human Rights. Retrieved from http://www.unhchr.ch/html/menu3/b/o_c_ref.htm

United States Department of Justice, Immigration and Naturalization Service. (1985, 18 March). "Letter to the Most Reverend Manuel D. Moreno, Bishop of Tucson, the Most Reverend Thomas J. O'Brien, Bishop of Phoenix, and the Most Reverend Jerome J. Hastrich, Bishop of Gallup."

United States of America v. Father Antonio Clark, et al. (1985). "Motion to Dismiss." No. CR-85-008-PHX-EHC (D. Ariz. 1985).

United States of America v. Maria Del Socorro Pardo De Aguilar, et al. (1985). "Supplemental Memorandum on Religious Defense." No. CR-85-008-PHX-EHC (D. Ariz. 1985).

United States of America v. Maria Del Socorro Pardo De Aguilar, et al. (1985). "Defendant Aguilar's Opposition to the Government's Motion to Preclude a Defense Based on the Free Exercise Clause." No. CR-85-008-PHX-EHC (D. Ariz. 1985): 1.

United States of America v. Maria Del Socorro Pardo De Aguilar, et al. (1989, 30 March). United States Court of Appeals, 9th Circuit. 83 F.2d 662. Nos. 86-1208 to 86-1215.

United States of America v. Stacey Lynn Merkt. (1985, 18 June). United States Court of Appeals, 5th Circuit. 764 F.2d 266, No. 84-2401.

US Committee for Refugees and Immigrants. (2009). World Refugee Survey 2008. *UNHRCR*. Retrieved from http://www.unhcr.org/cgi-bin/texis/vtx/refworld

Whitt, Clayton. (2009, July/August). "Nothing Sacred: What We Talk About When We Talk About Torture." *The Humanist.*

Wisconsin v. Yoder. (1972). 406 U.S. 205, 230, 92 S.Ct. 1526, 1540, 32 L.Ed.2d 15.

Zizek, Slavoj. (2007, 24 March). "Knight of the Living Dead." *New York Times.*

PART TWO

NORMATIVE THEORIES

■ Chapter 5 Consequentialism and Global Ethics
HALLVARD LILLEHAMMER

■ Chapter 6 How to Think About Global Duties
CHRISTIAN ILLIES

PART TWO
INTRODUCTION

We are now in a position to further integrate the normative principles we have just examined (as well as other normative principles) into a more systematic approach to questions of morality and justice: these are the normative theories. In this venue, it is not our purpose to present all the major moral theories that are presently being espoused.[1] Rather, what is presented are two very popular approaches: consequentialism and deontology. To get the most out of this book, I would *not* suggest that the reader feel compelled at this stage to choose between these theories but rather to learn the strengths of each in order to apply them along with the normative principles to create a critical structure to evaluate the global applications in part three of this book.

Hallvard Lillehammer introduces the reader to consequentialism. Consequentialism is a theoretical standpoint in which the agent chooses a course of action on the basis of likely consequences maximizing what the agent sees as the most positive outcome possible. When this positive outcome is viewed in terms of *utility*, then the theory is utilitarianism. But utility can be rather narrow when it has a *pleasure* focus, which is often interpreted in global terms purely as economic development. However, when this positive outcome is more generally defined—such as in terms of goodness à la G. E. Moore—then the consequential direction becomes agathistic (good producing) in design. Lillehammer's depiction of consequentialism is of this latter emphasis where consequentialism is seen as promoting or increasing the amount of good in the world so that the right thing to do is to promote the good.

Sometimes this result comes about by presenting agents with vivid thought experiments such as Singer's shallow pond in which an agent by chance comes upon a shallow pond where another individual is drowning. The agent can save the other person with no risk to his life and only minor inconvenience (such as getting his clothes dirty). Surely, saving a life would increase the amount of good in the world. Therefore, he should do so.

Henry Sidgwick grounds his version of consequentialism upon three axioms: one, we ought to promote our own good; two, the good of any one individual is not of any more importance than the good of any other individual; three, we ought to treat like cases alike. If we follow these axioms out it would seem as if our lives would have a directional compass toward doing good to ourselves and others without partiality.

Lillehammer then examines possible problems to this model. First, there is the possibility that doing good to others might be against our own self-interest. Second, there may be problems with impartiality. Many would assess that we are properly *partial* to our friends and associates as well as to our blood relations. This is especially true when we consider the competition of needs among those to whom we are partial against those who are distant from us, whose needs compete with those to whom we are partial.

A further way to think about this problem is through the role of beneficence in ethics via the boundary conditions of *constraints* and *permissions.* Constraints put limits upon the scope of otherwise valid ethical obligations. Permissions allow for certain exceptions to be made from our otherwise valid ethical obligations. The grounds and applications of these constraints and permissions is thus a matter of great concern—that they be neither too broad nor too narrow.

Lillehammer's essay ends by examining how we are to think about *indifference.* In part one of this book, this problem was characterized as *moral motivation.* One approach to this is to class indifference as a vice of omission. However, such a characterization is complicated by failing to distinguish indifference to events to which we are accidentally connected (the drowning person in Singer's shallow pond) from those to which we are connected due to prior harms committed (such as Pogge's negative duties incurred by wealthy nations to poor ones for previous exploitative actions).

However, despite these complications, Lillehammer advocates that we embrace the consequentialist model to increase good in the world via impartially beneficial norms and institutions.

Christian Illies presents the deontological way of viewing morality and global ethics. There are three parts to Illies's essay: one, a general introduction to deontology; two, a version of deontology that is indebted to Kant and Hegel; and three, a reply to common objections raised against deontology.

First, there is the general introduction to deontology. Illies argues that deontological ethics (DE) aims at universally valid and general principles that tell rational agents how they ought to behave. This inclination toward universality (that we encountered in part one of this book) may incline many to DE. But there are possible problems as well. For example, can DE justify its fundamental principles? Does such a justification require a theistic metaphysics? These two queries give rise to four internal objections and three external objections to DE. The first two *internal* objections come from Elisabeth Anscombe: one, DE is impossible to accept if it is separated from God; and two, when we separate DE from God, then moral relativism results. These are important objections since 15 to 20 percent of the world's population are atheist, and among the theists, there are many disputes about the nature of God.

A third objection is that DE is useless in particular cases (because its focus is on generating abstract general principles). The fourth *internal* objection is that DE is too rigid whereas actual moral cases require some degree of flexibility.

These are strong objections. The three *external* objections are, first, that DE rests upon a flawed view of human nature and of communities (as per MacIntyre). A theory that is based upon a flawed anthropology is doomed to failure. Second, DE actually devalues communities, and communities are necessary for practical justice. Finally the last *external* objection is that DE is false because it is based upon a misconception of reason, which contextually changes over time.

The second major division in the essay is developed by Illies in his 2003 book on the grounds of ethical judgment. We begin with a pivotal point: in DE *right* is prior to *good.* In order to determine what is right, a special kind of argument is required: the transcendental deduction. This sort of move as practiced by Kant takes our experience in the world as a given, but then looks for necessary preconditions that might logically account for the very possibility of such experience. So where do we start on such a transcendental journey? Illies suggests that it is a notion of the good. He cites me in this regard. As we progress on this journey, we see that certain conditions are necessary in order to do good: most primary and prior is moral freedom. This structures the moral enterprise as supporting freedom in ourselves and others.

One original twist to this comes as Illies turns Hegel (often seen as a critic of Kant) into a second-tier ally. By accepting the empirical criteria of efficiency and permanence as operative in putting the more abstract principles into effect, Illies has introduced a new dimension to DE: a mode of practical judgment sharpened by experience to discover which action realizes actions' fundamental goals in the most efficient and durable way. This is also analogous to Aristotle's distinction between theoretical reason about justice (*theoretikon*) and practical decision making ability (*phronesis*). Part of this latter mode may include personal duties to keep informed, for example, my own *extended community worldview imperative* (cited here by Illies).

In the third part of this essay, Illies goes back to the possible objections raised in the first section and argues that his original two-tiered DE account satisfies the essence of each objection. For Illies, both tiers are necessary in order to use DE successfully to shape policy that can address global injustice.

Note

1. For readers who wish a broader exploration, I would suggest they turn to books designed for just this purpose such as my text *Basic Ethics, Second Edition.* Upper Saddle River, NJ: Prentice Hall, 2009.

CHAPTER FIVE

Consequentialism and Global Ethics

HALLVARD LILLEHAMMER
Cambridge University

Abstract

The consequentialist claim that right actions are those that result in the best outcome impartially considered is sometimes said to be especially illuminating for framing the basic challenges of global ethics. In this chapter, I make four observations about the consequentialist approach to global ethics. First, I show that in some of its most influential manifestations, the challenge is grounded in a substantial and controversial theory of practical reason. Second, I show how the implications of the consequentialist claim are limited by the fact that all else is never equal. Third, I argue that the consequentialist challenge retains its bite even if consequentialism is rejected as a comprehensive ethical theory. Fourth, I argue that one of the basic insights embodied in the consequentialist challenge is that a systematic attitude of complete indifference to the suffering of others is an important ethical vice.

Key Words

consequentialism, constraints, global ethics, indifference, permissions, Henry Sidgwick, Peter Singer, Peter Unger

---

> *"There is scarcely any widely spread political institution or practice—however universally condemned by current opinion—which has not been sincerely defended as conducive to human happiness on the whole."*
>
> —Henry Sidgwick, *The Elements of Politics*

The consequentialist claim that right actions are those that result in the best outcome impartially considered is sometimes said to be especially illuminating for framing the basic challenges of global ethics. If we take impartiality to mean that everyone is to count for one and no one for more than one, the consequentialist claim entails that, all else equal, we have no less reason to care about the suffering of distant strangers than about the suffering of our nearest and dearest. A number of consequentialists have drawn direct implications from this about the ethical responsibilities of individuals and institutions in contemporary society. In this chapter, I make four observations about the consequentialist approach to global ethics. First, I show that in some of its most influential manifestations, the consequentialist challenge is grounded in a theory of practical reason that seldom plays an explicit role in discussions of global ethics. Second, I show how the practical implications of the consequentialist claim are limited by the fact that all else is never equal. Thus, not only will any plausible consequentialist approach to global ethics have a self-effacing aspect, but there are also ethically relevant considerations that any consequentialist approach may struggle to account for. Third, I argue that the consequentialist challenge retains its bite even if consequentialism is rejected as a comprehensive moral theory. Fourth, I argue that one of the most important insights embodied in the consequentialist challenge is that systematic indifference to the suffering of others is an important ethical vice.

The Consequentialist Challenge

According to consequentialism, the right thing to do is to promote what is good. The idea is as attractive as it is deceptive. On the one hand, it is attractive because it is hard to deny that it is reasonable to act for the best. Surely, to prefer a lesser good to a greater is, in some sense, irrational. On the other hand, the idea is deceptive because it is hard to say precisely what acting for the best amounts to. What should we understand by 'good' or 'best'? Should we promote the good by aiming to act for the best on every individual occasion, or by following a policy that will have the best consequences only in the long run? How do we deal with the fact that we are often either unsure or ignorant about the far-reaching effects of our actions? Consequentialists themselves disagree about these and many other questions.

The consequentialist approach to global ethics is often motivated by appeals to vivid examples (see Singer, 1972; Unger, 1992). The following is a version of one of the best-known examples of this kind. Imagine that you become aware of a stranger who is drowning in a shallow pond near you. You are not the only one around, but you have good reason to believe that if you don't help then no one else will.[1] With little effort you can pull the stranger out of the pond and save his life. It may seem obvious that it would be seriously wrong of you not to. Indeed, in some countries it would be against the law for you not to. Now imagine that you become aware that another stranger is dying of dysentery in a country far away from you. You are not the only one who can help, but if you don't then no one else will. With little effort you can make a five-dollar donation to a relief fund and save his life. Perhaps it no longer seems obvious that it would be seriously wrong of you not to. Certainly, it is unlikely to be against the law for you not to. Why so? If we agree that you should care enough about the good of others to save the stranger drowning in the pond, then surely by parity of reasoning, you should care enough about the good of others to save the stranger dying of dysentery. As Singer points out, the mere fact of physical distance is not an ethically relevant difference. Nor does there seem to be a relevant difference between death by drowning and death by dysentery. And the sacrifice involved in writing a cheque for five dollars as opposed to pulling someone out of a pond can hardly be thought to make the crucial difference either. According to the consequentialist, this settles the issue. It is as wrong for you not to aid in the one case as it is in the other, all other things being equal.[2] This is a conclusion with potentially radical implications.[3] For if the consequentialist is right, many of us ought to change our lives. Given the undeniable fact of massive suffering across the globe, most people reading these words are arguably complicit in the perpetuation of an ethical atrocity. We may not often encounter a drowning stranger in a pond. Yet scores of innocent strangers die from dysentery and other trivial ailments every day in countries across the world. And most of us apparently do nothing. This, in a nutshell, is the consequentialist challenge in global ethics.

Contemporary discussions of consequentialism and global ethics have been marked by a focus on examples such as that of the shallow pond. In this literature, distinctions are drawn and analogies made between different cases about which both the consequentialist and his or her interlocutor are assumed to have a more or less firm view. One assumption in this literature is that progress can be made by making judgements about simple actual or counterfactual examples, and then employing a principle of equity to the effect that like cases be treated alike, in order to work out what to think about more complex actual cases. It is only fair to say that in practice such attempts to rely only on judgements about simple cases have a tendency to produce trenchant stand-offs. It is important to remember, therefore, that for some consequentialists the appeal to simple cases is neither the only, nor the most basic, ground for their criticism of the ethical status quo. For some of the historically most prominent consequentialists, the evidential status of judgements about simple cases depends on their derivability from basic ethical principles (plus knowledge of the relevant facts). Thus, in *The Methods of Ethics*, Henry Sidgwick argues that ethical thought is grounded in a small number of self-evident axioms of practical reason. The first of these is that we ought to promote our own good. The second is that the good of any one individual is objectively of no more importance than the good of any other (or, in Sidgwick's notorious metaphor, no individual's good is more important 'from the point of view of the Universe' than that of any other). The third is that we ought to treat like cases alike. Together, Sidgwick takes these axioms to imply a form of consequentialism. We ought to promote our own good. Yet since our own good is objectively no more important than the good of anyone else, we ought to promote the good of others as well. And in order to treat like cases alike, we have to weigh our own good against the good of others impartially, all other things being equal.[4] It follows that the rightness of our actions is fixed by what is best for the entire universe of ethically relevant beings. To claim otherwise is to claim for oneself and one's preferences a special status they do not possess. When understood along these lines, consequentialism is by definition a global ethics: the good of everyone should count for everyone, no matter their identity, location, or personal and social attachments, now or hereafter.[5] Some version of this view is also accepted by a number of contemporary consequentialists, including Peter Singer, who writes that it is 'preferable to proceed as Sidgwick did: search for undeniable fundamental axioms, [and] build up a moral theory from them' (Singer, 1974, 517; Singer, 1981). For these philosophers the question of our ethical duties to others is not only a matter of our responses to cases like the shallow pond. It is also a matter of whether these responses cohere with an ethics based on first principles. If you are to reject the consequentialist challenge, therefore, you will have to show what is wrong with those principles.

All Other Things Are Not Equal

All plausible versions of consequentialism agree that our duties to promote the good impartially in practice are limited. Part of the explanation is that other things are never equal. There are several ways in which other things not being equal affects questions in global ethics. Here I shall mention two. The first derives from all else not being equal on consequentialist terms. The second derives from all else not being equal in ways that threaten the claim of consequentialism to be a comprehensive ethical theory.

First, all plausible forms of consequentialism are partly self-effacing. It is natural to think that our effective pursuit of impartial good favours an ethical division of labour. Each individual can be liberated from the task of aiming at impartial good directly provided the framework of social interaction is so adjusted that each individual's pursuit of partial good also promotes impartial good. This indirect mechanism for the promotion of impartial good will sometimes require incentives for individuals to comply with social norms when complying is perceived to be against their individual interest. According to the consequentialist, the provision of such incentives is the ultimate rationale for social institutions such as families, communities, societies, or states (see Harrison, 2000). Thus, government is good because the instruments of state encourage individuals to pursue partial good in such a way as to benefit (or not undermine) impartial good. Furthermore, government can be good for the individual for at least two reasons. First, the existence of government can enhance the individual pursuit of partial good so long as this pursuit does not conflict with rules designed to promote impartial good. One obvious example of this is publicly recognised standards of fair trade. Second, the existence of government can enhance the individual pursuit of impartial good by embedding individual effort within a wider network of impartially beneficial institutional action, thereby reducing the cost to the individual of acting in favour of impartial good. One obvious example of this is the provision of public services paid for by taxation. The latter feature is of particular interest in global ethics. For even if it follows from consequentialism that my own good is objectively of no more importance than the good of distant strangers, it does not follow that I am wrong in practice to be more interested in my own good than in the good of distant strangers. On the contrary, this kind of ethical partiality would be licensed by consequentialism against the background of effective social institutions that promote impartial good, for example by appropriately taxing individuals who are dedicated to the promotion of partial goods and distributing the proceeds accordingly. The consequentialist complaint against existing forms of partiality is that the necessary conditions of impartially effective social institutions do not obtain, and that the actual amounts of suffering involved are so great that no appeal to the self-effacing aspects of consequentialism can excuse existing levels of indifference toward that suffering. According to this complaint, the world as we have it is not ethically well ordered enough for the self-effacing nature of consequentialism to commend our actual dispositions. We do not live in the best of all possible worlds, in which individual pursuit of partial good is guaranteed to promote the good of all. We live in an ethical disaster scenario, in which a tightening of the permissive norms of received morality is not only permissible, but ethically required.

There is second way in which all other things are not equal. This point is sometimes conceded by consequentialists when they say that their approach is meant to capture 'the morality of beneficence' (Parfit, 1982; Broome, 2004). There would be no point to this label unless there were a contrast class to which the morality of beneficence is compared. There are at last two historically prominent candidates for what falls into this contrast class. I shall refer to the first as 'the ethics of choice', to the second as 'the ethics of nature', and to both of them collectively as 'the ethics of special ties'.

The ethics of choice concerns the rights and duties that derive from voluntary agency. Thus, it is widely agreed that there are some ethical relationships we stand in to others because, and only because, we have voluntarily placed ourselves in those relationships (see Nozick, 1974). The rights and duties that derive from the ethics of choice are paradigmatically associated with interpersonal interactions, such as promises, contracts, and other forms of voluntary association. According to the ethics of choice, voluntary agency is a basic source of rights and duties, distinct from considerations of either partial or impartial good. This idea is arguably implicit in the widely shared assumption that even promises and contracts that do not promote the good ought to be given independent weight in ethical thought, all other things being equal. On this view, our duty to promote impartial good is constrained by the fact that some of our relationships with others are characterised by ties of voluntary agency that do not exist between ourselves and distant strangers. This does not entail that our duties toward others are exhausted by those that arise directly from voluntary agency. It is compatible with accepting the ethics of choice as a basic feature of ethical thought to also hold that the norms to which it gives rise ought to constrain our actions all other things being equal, in the same way as the norms arising from the ethics of beneficence.

The ethics of nature is distinguished from the ethics of choice by the fact that not all special ties arise directly from our own voluntary actions. Thus, it is widely held that we owe a distinct form of respect toward members of our family, our basic relationship with whom is not normally a result of any voluntary action on our part. Historically, it has been common to claim that we owe a special form of respect to our community, nation, or state—some of which we will normally have chosen our membership of voluntarily, and none of which may offer a prudentially attractive right of exit. On this view, our duty to promote the good impartially is constrained by the fact that some of our relationships are characterised by a tie of collective identity which does not exist between us and members of other social groups. Once more, this does not entail that our duties to others are exhausted by those that derive from the ethics of nature. If the ethics of nature gives rise to basic ethical norms it is reasonable to think that these should constrain our actions all other things being equal, just as the norms arising from the ethics of choice or beneficence.

If the ethics of special ties is a basic feature of ethical thought, our ethical relationship toward others is more complicated than the ethics of beneficence suggests. Thus, between you and any distant stranger will be a plurality of special ties, the ethical significance of which must be taken into account before we can draw definite conclusions about the nature and extent of your all-things-considered duties. This is not to say that if we take account of the ethics of special ties, it will undermine the consequentialist challenge. Indeed, the contrary is arguably the case. First, the ethics of choice may suggest that we are bound by duties of reparation toward distant strangers whose suffering is a consequence of voluntary agency in which either we, or those to whom we owe are related by special ties, have been voluntarily involved (see Barry, 1982). Second, the ethics of nature may suggest that the way we have traditionally distinguished between those we do, and those we do not, count as members of our ethical community is based on ignorance and arbitrary prejudice, such as sexism, racism, or even 'speciesism' (Singer, 1981). Third, there are ways of formulating the consequentialist challenge that undermine the force of appealing to the social complexities deriving from special ties in defence of the ethical status quo. Thus, it should be obvious that neither pulling a stranger out of a pond, nor writing a cheque for five dollars, is likely to make many readers of these words neglect their special ties to kin or country. The question is not whether all other things are equal. The question is whether enough is.

The limits imposed on the ethics of beneficence by the ethics of special ties can be divided into two kinds, which (following common usage) I shall refer to as 'constraints' and 'permissions' (see Scheffler, 1982). Constraints restrict promotion of the good as a matter of obligation, for example where the acts involved would infringe on important rights of those affected. Thus, it might be argued that it is not permissible to steal another person's property in order to give it to someone else who would benefit more from it. Some consequentialists question this view. Thus, Peter Unger suggests that it would be wrong for an employee to not steal small amounts of money from their employer and give it to charity, provided they could get away with it (Unger, 1992). However, most consequentialists stop short of making this claim on the grounds that a general respect for property rights is indirectly justifiable on consequentialist terms (Sidgwick, 1891; Hooker, 2000). On this view, the effective distribution of institutional surplus is better approached by means of a system of government taxation or the like, including incentives that favour charitable giving. Either way, the examples with which we started have no obvious implications that run foul of property rights or other important constraints. In each case, the claim is that you ought to act so as to promote the good impartially on the assumption that you can do so at little or no cost to yourself. In undertaking to do so, you do not necessarily interfere with anyone's rights, including your own.

Permissions allow failure to promote the good in restricting the range of obligation, for example, where the acts involved conflict with important personal commitments. Thus, it is widely accepted that it is permissible to distribute the fruits of one's labour primarily among family or friends, even if there are other people who would benefit more from them. To this extent, thinking in terms of permissions arguably comes closest to capturing the essence of the received view about our ethical relations to the distant needy that is the primary target of the consequentialist challenge. According to this view, we are obviously permitted to help the distant needy, and indeed it might be better if we did. Yet we have no obligation to, so long as we put the resources thereby saved to good use. Many consequentialists would agree with this claim. First, some partial values are indirectly justifiable on consequentialist terms. Second, permissions do not entail that acting to promote the good impartially is morally prohibited. The permissibility of partial concerns is consistent with the equal permissibility of impartial commitment. Other consequentialists would object that this compromise conjures a virtue out of a vice. Short of neglecting our nearest and dearest to the point of infringing on their rights, there is no rationally defensible case for the policy of promoting our own good exclusively at the cost of others, at least in cases where the cost of helping others is negligible in comparison to the benefits gained. That is the lesson Singer claims to derive from the examples with which we started. Even someone defending the centrality of permissions in ethical thought may find it hard to reject this claim. As already noted, for many people reading these words, occasionally writing a cheque for five dollars and sending it to a charity would not conflict with any serious commitment to their nearest and dearest, some of whom would even hold them in higher esteem for doing so.

There is more than one way of handling permissions and constraints as they affect the consequentialist challenge. The first we have seen at work already, namely to argue that some constraints and permissions are indirectly justifiable on consequentialist terms. On this view, constraints and permissions are strongly defeasible, in the sense that their strength and scope is a direct function of what will promote impartial good in the long run. If so, the strength and scope of permissions and constraints will vary considerably across history and across cultures, sometimes in ways that contemporary readers will find surprising or uncomfortable.[6] Furthermore, and given the extraordinary increase in our capacity to help distant strangers highlighted by Singer and others, there is no *a priori* guarantee that the permissions and constraints that apply in our actual social circumstances will commend the status quo. Finally, even if permissions and constraints understood along consequentialist lines actually do support the status quo, they will do so by displacing what for many is their most natural explanation. For as understood by the consequentialist, your duty toward your nearest and dearest is not ultimately a matter of the intimate relationship in which you stand to them, but rather a matter of how conducive such relationships are to the promotion of an impartial good with which you may struggle to stand in any meaningful personal relation (see Williams, 2006). It is partly this fact that explains why so many philosophers have failed to be convinced by consequentialism, even in its most sophisticated contemporary formulations.

The alternative way to handle permissions and constraints is to admit a plurality of basic ethical considerations, grounded in considerations of the good, choice, and nature, etc. (see Ross, 1930). This approach is incompatible with consequentialism considered as a comprehensive ethical theory. It is nevertheless important to bear in mind when evaluating the consequentialist challenge in global ethics. Consider, once more, the examples with which we began. Suppose that special ties give rise to ethical considerations that are just as basic as considerations of beneficence. Why should we think this makes a crucial difference to the consequentialist challenge? Surely, it would have to be a very important promise that would trump your duty to save someone next to you from drowning? Likewise, it would surely have to be an exceptional need of a friend that would outweigh the threat of imminent death to a distant stranger you can save at little or no cost to yourself? Even a non-consequentialist should concede that sometimes the ethics of beneficence weighs more heavily than the ethics of special ties. The gist of the consequentialist challenge therefore remains even if we reject consequentialism as a comprehensive ethical theory. Thus, even though it might be tempting to think that there are two ways to go in response to this challenge, depending on whether or not you are a consequentialist, this is a mistake. Consequentialist or not, you might go either way.

Indifference as a Vice

Whichever way we decide to handle permissions and constraints, the consequentialist challenge forces us to question how we normally decide what counts as ethically relevant. The ethics of choice apparently allows us to draw a basic distinction between those with whom we stand in voluntary relations and everything else. The ethics of nature apparently allows us to draw a basic distinction between those with whom we are biologically, socially, or otherwise continuous and everything else. The ethics of beneficence extends the domain of ethical concern to all beings in possession of whatever properties we identify as ethically relevant, whatever the relations in which we stand to them. According to those consequentialists who accept Sidgwick's axioms, our refusal to so extend the domain of ethical concern amounts to an irrational prejudice. Yet even those of us who doubt Sidgwick's axioms are faced with the challenge of defining the range of ethical concern in a way that is reflectively robust. The history of modern moral philosophy suggests that we shall only be able to do this by including among the basic features of ethical thought some version of the ethics of beneficence (see Schneewind, 2003). If so, any reflectively robust extension of our ethical beliefs will contain an aspect that is genuinely global in its reach. As already noted, it does not follow that this global aspect of ethical thought will be judged on reflection to be always, or even mostly, overriding. What does follow is that no reflectively robust extension of our ethical beliefs can permit a basic distinction between different beings, all of whom possess the ethically relevant properties, but only some of whom count as ethically significant. What the ethics of beneficence rules out as impermissible is a systematic attitude of complete indifference toward beings with whom we are not connected by special ties. Insofar as our actual attitudes toward ethically relevant beings in that category is characterised by such indifference, we are to that extent guilty of exhibiting an important ethical vice. If Singer's argument succeeds in proving anything, this is arguably it. After all, in the case of the drowning stranger, it is assumed we agree it would be seriously wrong to not help, even if the person saved is not someone to whom we are connected with any obvious special ties. In accepting this point we should also accept that the consequentialist challenge cannot be dismissed by appealing either to how all ethical theories are self-effacing; how beneficence does not exhaust ethical thought; how all individual action is embedded in a complicated causal nexus of collective historical agency; how little we often know about the distant consequences of our actions; or how the ethical status of what we do is partly a function of the ethical status of past, present, or future actions of others over which we have no control, and so on. True, these are serious difficulties we must face once we have decided to treat the suffering of others as something that matters.[7] They do not, however, show that we are right to treat that suffering as a matter of indifference if, as in the examples with which we started, we can actually do something about it at little or no cost to ourselves.

It might be tempting to classify indifference as a vice of omission, in virtue of the fact that it seems to consist in a passive failure to respond to ethically relevant facts. This appearance is importantly misleading. There are at least two ways of being indifferent, only one of which is classifiable as a simple omission. This is the kind of indifference manifested by an agent who fails to intervene in a causal process with which he or she is at best accidentally connected. Singer's example of the drowning stranger can be read as presenting an opportunity for indifference of this kind. Thus, we can imagine that the agent in question is confronted with the results of a natural accident, such as a sheet of ice breaking at the sound of thunder. A second way of being indifferent is to not intervene in a causal process in which one is intentionally entwined. With some adjustment, Singer's example of the drowning stranger can also be read as presenting an opportunity for indifference of this kind. Thus, we can imagine the drowning stranger to be trapped in a pool of water accidentally released from the community septic tank. In this case, failure to help is less obviously a simple omission, insofar as the threat facing the stranger is one in the causes of which the agent is in some way intentionally involved. As has frequently been pointed out, many of the opportunities for indifference presented by the consequentialist challenge are (inevitably much more complex) versions of the latter kind (see Pogge, 2007). Thus, if the causes of world poverty include the economic relations between rich and poor countries that sustain our own standard of living, the vulnerability of many innocent strangers to death from poverty-related causes is partly conditioned by a nexus of social relations in which each of us is intentionally entwined. The consequentialist challenge to those of us who belong in the privileged category is then as follows. If we do not propose to act to directly address the avoidable suffering produced by the causal nexus in which we are intentionally entwined, what else do we propose to either think, say, or do (as family members, friends, colleagues, volunteers, shareholders, taxpayers, institutional representatives, voting citizens, etc.) in order to respond to what the ethics of beneficence classifies as ethically significant suffering? If the answer is 'Nothing', then the indifference exhibited is better described as a vice of 'complicity' rather than a vice of 'omission'.

In this respect, Singer's way of presenting the consequentialist challenge is less than helpful. True, considered as one-off opportunities to display or acquire ethical virtue, his examples may awaken us from our indifferent slumbers. Yet the practical significance of Singer's discussion is that these are not rare or isolated cases, but persistent features of our social reality. Given this fact, it is impossible to draw any sensible practical conclusions without further consideration of prevailing norms and social institutions as they actually apply in concrete historical circumstances. A consequentialist approach to these questions would obviously take as its ultimate criterion the overall tendency of such norms and institutions to promote impartial good (see Sidgwick, 1891). It is therefore reasonable to think that a consequentialist approach to global ethics should encourage individuals to act so as to promote the development of impartially beneficial norms and institutions. Quite apart from writing a cheque for five dollars, this is something that any enfranchised member of a democratic state has a legally protected right to do. In exercising this right, it falls upon individuals to make difficult judgements about which, among the available alternatives, propose reasonable ways of handling the fact of massive human suffering in a global context in which people are related to each other not only *qua* individuals, but also *qua* members of the social entities of which they are a part. Thus, it is incumbent on us to reflect, in light of available evidence, on which part of the ethical burden is better placed on centralised systems of aid and development funded through tax receipts, donations, and the like, and which part is better placed in the hands of private individuals. It is also incumbent on us to reflect on the extent to which different alternative practices are more or less effective in the prevention of suffering and injustice than other available alternatives (see Pogge, 1997; Ayittey, 2005). In some cases, this will be a Herculean task. Either way, a systematic attitude of indifference is indefensible, both on consequentialist and non-consequentialist grounds. Even this modest conclusion is practically significant in the context of the widespread moral and political apathy seen in many contemporary societies. If so, there is a good case after all for returning to Singer's example of the shallow pond, in all its naive simplicity.

Notes

1. The significance of this assumption is as follows. If there are other people present who would act in your place, then your assistance is not required in order to secure the relevant good. So you are arguably permitted to not make the effort (or at least not as much effort). On the other hand, if other people present would not act in your place, then your assistance is actually required to obtain the relevant good. Singer argues that the latter scenario is analogous to our actual situation with respect to massive amounts of actual human suffering. His claim is that in this case, given that the cost of helping is small, we are required to do so, even if in some possible scenario where others were more generous, we might not be. This claim conflicts with other consequentialist views, some of which claim that our duties are fixed by what would secure the relevant goods in a possible scenario where all, or most, people were more generous (see Hooker, 2000). The shallow pond example clearly brings out what is at stake in adopting this (less demanding) version of consequentialism. It also brings out how different versions of consequentialism will give different answers to the questions of who should help, how often, and how much. In this chapter, I shall bracket these important questions by assuming that the consequentialist would answer: 'More than most of us actually do'.

2. This way of formulating the challenge is sometimes faced with the objection that there is an ethical difference between cases where we are faced with the possibility of helping one or more identified individuals on the one hand, and cases where we are faced with the possibility of helping one or more nonidentified individuals on the other. Whereas the shallow pond case clearly falls into the first category, our actual situation with respect to distant strangers normally falls into the second. It might therefore be thought that Singer's argument trades on an ambiguity with respect to how we are related to the distant stranger, on one reading of which we are obliged to help and on the other reading not (or at least not obviously). On reflection, however, this objection can be seen to overshoot its target. True, there may be no reason to save the life of one nonidentified individual as opposed to another, all other things being equal. It does not follow that there is no reason to save the life of any one of these individuals at all. I shall return to the ethical significance of all other things not being equal below.

3. In the final chapter of his *Living High and Letting Die*, Peter Unger stops short of this conclusion by proposing a 'contextualist' semantics for ethical terms, according to which the radical conclusions implied by consequentialism are correctly as-

sertible only in the context of philosophy seminar rooms and the like. I shall ignore this complication below. Singer's discussions of this topic make no use of this kind of sophisticated semantic casuistry.

4. Three caveats about Sidgwick: One, Sidgwick was a classical utilitarian, in the sense that he identified the good with pleasure, or happiness. This part of his theory does not, however, follow from his three self-evident axioms; two, Sidgwick worried that there might be an irreducible conflict between two of his axioms in the sense that the rationality of moving from egoism to impartial beneficence requires a metaphysical guarantee of prudential reward for altruistic sacrifice, if not in this life then after (see Schultz, 2004). This problem does not prevent Sidgwick (or his contemporary followers) from applying his theory to global ethics as if this conflict has a resolution in favour of impartial beneficence; three, Sidgwick was aware that all else is not equal with respect to the ability of individuals to successfully promote the good directly and on their own. This partly explains his defence of what has later come to be known as 'Government House Utilitarianism' (see Williams, 1973). I shall return to this third caveat below.

5. There are particular difficulties attaching to our ethical relations to future generations, the population and identity of which is in part determined by how existing individuals act in the present. I shall bracket these issues here. For further discussion, see, for example, Mulgan (2006).

6. Thus, contemporary readers are likely to be taken aback by Sidgwick's descriptions, in *The Elements of Politics*, of native inhabitants of European colonies as 'savages' of 'inferior race', who 'though not uncivilized, are markedly inferior in civilization to the conquerors', whose dominion of the colonised territories should 'not be hampered by pedantic adhesion to the forms of civilised judicial procedure' (Sidgwick 1891, Pt. I, Ch.XV, Sect. 4; Ch. XVIII, Sect. 7–8). The issue here is not that contemporary consequentialists are guilty of the same prejudices as Sidgwick. It is rather that the application of ethical theory in practice leaves hostages to historical fortune that armchair moral philosophy gives no easy handle on. It is therefore unsurprising if serious doubts remain about the idea of consequentialism as a realistic guide to politics even among those of us who take the consequentialist challenge seriously.

7. For discussion of some these complications in the context of a radical critique of the individualist assumptions embedded in contemporary moral philosophy, see Geuss (2005).

References

Ayittey, G. B. N. (2005). *Africa Unchained.* New York: Palgrave Macmillan.

Barry, B. (1982). "Humanity and Justice in Global Perspective" in *NOMOS XXIV: Ethics, Economics and the Law,* ed. J. R. Pennock and J. W. Chapman: 219–252.

Broome, J. (2004). *Weighing Lives.* Oxford: Oxford University Press.

Geuss, R. (2005). *Outside Ethics*. Princeton: Princeton University Press.

Harrison, R. (2000). "Government Is Good for You." *Proceedings of the Aristotelian Society 100*: 159–173.

Hooker, B. (2000). *Ideal Code, Real World*. Oxford: Oxford University Press.

Mulgan, T. (2006). *Future People*. Oxford: Oxford University Press.

Nozick, R. (1974). *Anarchy, State and Utopia*. New York: Basic Books.

Parfit, D. (1982). "Future Generations: Further Problems." *Philosophy and Public Affairs 11*: 113–172.

Pogge, T. (1997). "Migration and Poverty" in *Citizenship and Exclusion*, ed. Veit Bader: 12–27. London: Macmillan.

Pogge, T. (2007). *World Poverty and Human Rights, Second Edition*. Cambridge: Polity Press.

Ross, W. D. (1930). *The Good and the Right*. Oxford: Oxford University Press.

Scheffler, S. (1982). *The Rejection of Consequentialism*. Oxford: Oxford University Press.

Schneewind, J., ed. (2003). *Moral Philosophy from Montaigne to Kant*. Cambridge: Cambridge University Press.

Schultz, B. (2004). *Henry Sidgwick*. Cambridge: Cambridge University Press.

Sidgwick, H. (1891). *The Elements of Politics*. London: Macmillan.

Sidgwick, H. (1907). *The Methods of Ethics, Seventh Edition*. London: Macmillan.

Singer, P. (1972). "Famine, Affluence and Morality." *Philosophy and Public Affairs 1*: 229–243.

Singer, P. (1974). "Sidgwick and Reflective Equilibrium." *The Monist 58*: 490–517.

Singer, P. (1981). *The Expanding Circle*. Oxford: Oxford University Press.

Unger, P. (1992). *Living High and Letting Die*. Oxford: Oxford University Press.

Williams, B. (1973). "A Critique of Utilitarianism" in *Utilitarianism: For and Against*, ed. J. J. C. Smart and B. Williams: 77–150. Cambridge: Cambridge University Press.

Williams, B. (2006). "The Human Prejudice" in *Philosophy as a Humanistic Discipline*, ed. A. W. Moore: 135–152. Princeton: Princeton University Press.

CHAPTER SIX

How to Think About Global Duties

CHRISTIAN ILLIES
University of Bamberg[1]

Abstract

This chapter argues for deontological ethics (DE) as a sound basis for global duties. A transcendental argument is outlined. It starts by taking the stance of asking for some moral good with universal authority (here called the 'moral stance'). It is reasoned that for any such notion, it would also have to be regarded as morally good to promote this moral good. Promoting the good, however, is only possible if we are free to do so. Consequently, if one takes the moral stance, then a fundamental demand follows, namely to protect and promote the freedom of all human beings to act morally (called 'moral freedom'). The demand can be expanded to include all things necessary to support this freedom. A further argument is added as to why we have to aim at efficient and long-term realisations of what is morally demanded. This constitutes a second (empirical) level for DE and bridges the duty-teleological divide. It is then shown why an ethical theory of this type can withstand common criticisms against deontological ethics. It provides a reflectively robust basis for global duties, including duties toward future generations and the environment.

Key Words

deontological ethics, transcendental argument, justification, 'moral freedom', concrete realisation of abstract demands, consequences, global duties to future generations, environmental duties

---

Author's note: This chapter is dedicated to Reinhard Zintl.

Deontological Ethics (DE) and Global Duties

The Aim of This Chapter

'Deontological ethics' or 'deontological theories' aim at universally valid and general principles that tell rational agents how they ought to behave. These ethical theories are centrally about the rightness of types of action; they often speak about general duties to act in a certain way (*deon* means 'duty') and about corresponding rights of the recipient to be treated accordingly. The principles are not derived from a prior notion of good, as John Rawls (1971) emphasises in his definition: 'deontological theories are defined as non-teleological ones'.

Can an ethical theory without a rich notion of good ever succeed? It is often objected that the entire idea of a principle-based morality is too abstract to do justice to the particulars of the world and, more so, missing the point of what morality is all about. Without a notion of the good, moral theories seem to become formalistic and empty. The aim of this chapter is to reject this and other criticisms and to show that DE is an apt basis for global duties.

This chapter is divided into three sections. This first section introduces deontological theories in general and briefly describes their appeal. It will also list commonly raised objections against them. In the second section, a version of deontological ethics that is indebted to Kant and Hegel will be introduced. The task of the third section is to show that this version of DE can withstand the prior mentioned objections.

The Attraction of DE

Why should we turn to DE at all? What is its possible attraction? Enlightenment philosophers faced two major challenges, and deontological ethics can be seen as an attempt to answer both: One the one hand, the sixteenth, seventeenth, and eighteenth centuries had given rise to many conflicts between diverse cultures and religious traditions, all of them having diverging ideas of the good—and hence making different moral claims. Here a universally accepted, at least acceptable normative orientation was much desired. On the other hand, due to the diversification of Christianity and the decline of religion, the problem of justification became more prominent. Neither religion nor cultural tradition could do the job. This challenge was intensified through the high standards for a successful justification as having been set up by Descartes. Consequently, philosophers tried to ground morality on something whose authority should be universally acceptable. Immanuel Kant, for example, based it upon human freedom or our rational nature as something to be found with—and, as he hoped, acknowledged by—all human beings.

Problems like economic oppression; social, political, and legal abuse; religious and racial conflicts; and wars are even more pressing today than they were two hundred years ago. Solving these problems requires concerted action, and in some cases, like climate change, only a united effort of the whole world, of all nations and individuals, will do. But we are still confronted with a melange of different cultures, and their moral systems are often mutually incompatible. Thus a universally acceptable orientation should be as attractive today as it was then; we urgently need guidelines (like human rights) with binding authority to direct our activities, to protect people, and to make our world a better place. It is here that we find the strongest attraction of DE. As a context-independent ethical theory, its scope is universal. It aims at nothing less than moral demands or rules for all rational agents, and thus for all nations. Without some such rules on the global level, there is little hope for our world to survive.

The Apparent Shortfalls of DE

But can deontological ethics live up to this high ambition? A fundamental objection is DE's apparent *failure to justify universal principles.* There are different methodologies employed in the tradition of DE (contractualist, intuitionist, transcendental, etc.), and all of them have been criticised for not succeeding with their central ambition. To give just one example: Natural law theories, like the ones by John Locke or Samuel Pufendorf, have been accused of being grounded upon a rich metaphysics that will not be accepted outside a theistic tradition.[2]

Are modern deontological ethics even 'harmful', as Elisabeth Anscombe (1958) has argued? Her argument comes in two steps. First, she states that the idea of universal principles or rules becomes an *impossible conception* if separated from the idea that God is the legislator. There simply cannot be any moral *laws* (be it of nature or of reason) without a divine *law-giver.* We might rephrase Anscombe's critique as follows: Even if some set of moral principles turned out to be the identified law, we can still ask *why we should obey it.* The possibility of this question might be turned against the very possibility of any justification of moral laws (or deontological principles). If moral principles could be justified *as* moral laws, then the answer is obvious and the open question trivial. But since the why-question can always be asked, the moral law cannot be what it claims to be, namely a law (in the normative sense of *law*). Here the second step follows: if one continues to use these impossible concepts, the project fails in its efforts and cannot persuade anyone—and moral relativism seems the most likely conclusion (and its cousins: emotivism and utilitarianism). This makes modern deontological theories so *harmful* (Richard Rorty, the 'fallen' former deontologist, seems to prove her case). Anscombe suggests a rather archaic manner of solving these philosophical problems: 'The notions of "moral obligation", "the moral ought", and "duty" are best put on the Index.'

Another, and quite old objection is that deontological principles are *useless for particular cases*; they are empty or at least too general to tell the agent what to do in concrete situations. G. W. F. Hegel (1821) has already raised this objection against Kant when he talks about an 'empty formalism'; it is the only point where Arthur Schopenhauer agrees with his worst philosophical enemy—and even John Stuart Mill (1863) joins in: 'When [Kant] begins to deduce from this precept any of the actual duties of morality, he fails almost grotesquely.'

Rather the opposite objection is held by others who consider deontological principles as being *too rigid*.[3] In particular the ethics of Kant has been accused of offering an inflexible moral code that is insensitive to the particular situation, to exceptions, and to conflicting norms. Very much like Procrustes, who adjusted his guests to their bed in an often lethal manner (his name means 'he who stretches'), deontologists are suspected to adjust situations rigidly in the Procrustean bed of their principles.

The just-mentioned criticisms all claim that DE is doomed to fail if judged by its own standards by not achieving its aim—namely a well-justified set of norms that serves as a useful compass for particular situations. Another type of criticism is based upon standards that are external to DE.

It argues that DE is based upon a distorted and even dangerous view of what *human existence* and the social sphere are. Even if DE could provide a justification of substantial, useful, and context-sensitive principles, so this criticism goes, it would not be enough for ethics because they are not about the true good of human existence. Most prominently, virtue ethicists have argued that DE is based upon a *deficient, impoverished anthropology* that abstracts from all that human life is ultimately about. Alasdair MacIntyre (1981) has stated that this deficiency makes deontological principles pointless: 'All [deontological theories] reject any teleological view of human nature, any view of man as having an essence which defines his true end.'[4] The underlying anthropology of DE, at least in diverse contractual versions, is seen to be that of a selfish preference-maximiser—that is, a self-interested rational being who interacts with others in order to get as much as possible out of it.

Further, DE seems (consequently) to lead to a distorted notion of *communities*. It is objected that the social sphere appears to be reduced to functional interactions between self-interested rational entities. The intrinsic value of communities, as much as their true importance for us, is not recognised. See again MacIntyre's remarks: For Robert Nozick and John Rawls 'A society is composed of individuals, each with his or her own interests, who then have to come together and formulate common rules of life. . . . Individuals are thus in both accounts primary and society secondary, and the identification of individual interests is prior to, and independent of, the construction of any moral or social bonds between them' (1981). This (alleged) fundamental misconception and devaluation of communities has also fatal consequences for the political practice, as several authors have stressed. Charles Taylor and Michael Sandel (1984) conclude that the deontological approach—for them, mainly in the form of modern liberalism—has distorted our society and has led to an increasing loss of public engagement and to the general moral fragmentation of modern life.

More radical is the allegation that the idea of a rational (timeless) foundation must fail because it is based upon a *misconception of reason.* There is not one reason (neither in the sense of a human faculty nor as a timeless argument), it has been objected, but a plurality of reasons, differing from culture to culture and over time within the same culture. Therefore, any reasoning will remain contextual; it can never reach universal validity. To be sure, humans are able to distance themselves partly from their situation, but it is a self-deception to think that they could ever distance themselves completely and reach a view—or argument—from nowhere (to use Thomas Nagel's (1986) famous expression). Michael Sandel (1984) stresses this inescapable contextuality of reason: 'As a self-interpreting being, I am able to reflect on my history and in this sense to distance myself from it, but the distance is always precarious and provisional, the point of reflection never finally secured outside the history itself.' In contrast to the deontological aspirations, we should see human insights as embedded in a particular, historically local framework.

In brief, DE will have to prove that it can live up to its own aspirations and that it provides substantial orientation for action on a global level. It will also have to show that it is based upon a plausible anthropology and social vision, and not upon a biased concept of reason.

Outline of a Deontological Ethics

Respect for Human Freedom as a Primary Deontological Demand

The definition of DE, namely that its notion of right is not derived from a prior notion of good, leaves the source of normativity open. The term DE can therefore be used as for very different ethical theories: John Locke's theory of individual rights, Kant's categorical imperative, Rawls's contractualism, and the Decalogue of the Torah are all deontological in this sense.[5] It is therefore not very productive to investigate whether deontological ethics *in general* can withstand the objections mentioned above. We need to look at a specific DE—and the most promising type seems to me the transcendental version in the Kantian tradition.

Faced with the problem of justification in the context of his theoretical philosophy, Kant developed a new methodology, the 'transcendental deduction'—or *transcendental argument,* as we call it today. Roughly speaking, such an argument goes as follows: We start with some *x* that we take for granted—for example, that we have experience—and look for a necessary condition *y* of this *x* being possible. If there is some *y*, like that all experience is in time, and if it is a necessary condition (because we cannot imagine any experience that is not in time), then we can regard a judgement *that* y *is the case* as being justified (at least as much justified as *x*).[6] By the time of the *Grundlegung der Metaphysik der Sitten*, Kant aims at expanding his new methodology to ethics; he wants to justify the categorical imperative transcendentally. The third part of the *Grundlegung* documents his attempts—but it also documents his failure, mainly because he cannot identify a firm starting point *x* for practical reason.[7]

Let us be more optimistic about the methodology that Kant has introduced.[8] What could be a starting point for a transcendental argument in ethics? The one I want to use is simply that *we have a notion of good and bad.* Thereby, we leave it open what the form or content of this notion is; we merely begin with a general positive or negative evaluation of some kind, so that this *x* could be accepted by the different ethical systems, by virtue ethicists as much as utilitarians, deontologists, and hedonists alike. They all regard and appreciate some things (actions, states of affairs, habits, consequences, etc.) as good (positive, advisable, recommended, etc.). Michael Boylan goes as far as calling it a 'fundamental assumption' of all agency that 'all people, by nature, desire to be good' (Boylan 2004, 1–2). This, however, would imply that all agents have some, possibly implicit notion of the good.

What does it mean to call something good? Whatever content we give to the notion, it seems obvious that the good *x* (state of affairs, action, duty, etc.) should be supported or realised. To give a few examples: A deontological theory of duties spells out what should be done. Also, consequentialist theories conclude from their notion of good (e.g., general happiness or preference satisfaction) that we should bring this good state about by acting appropriately. Virtue ethicists will agree that it is good to have or develop certain virtues. We can spell this out quite generally as a conceptual truth about goodness: calling something good means that it is *good* (or even demanded) *to have an active pro-attitude toward it.* If someone denies this, then she seems not to understand 'good' properly. (And, obviously, the inverse can be said about our notion of 'bad'.) To be sure, that does not imply that all possible ways of supporting something good are themselves good or recommended; it is only in general good to have this active pro-attitude—if it is not directed against another good at the same time. Concrete cases still demand concrete considerations, and whether a *specific* realisation of this pro-attitude can rightly be judged as good will depend on the circumstances (for example, whether an action is violating some other good).

Starting from some notion of good, we have deduced a positive evaluation of a practical pro-attitude toward this good. We can now ask the transcendental question: What is the necessary condition for the possibility of having an active practical pro-attitude? Well, that there are beings with the ability to have this pro-attitude. The existence of pro-attitudes without someone having them is unimaginable. There cannot be a smile without someone smiling (the Cheshire Cat's smile in *Alice in Wonderland* being the only exception), and there cannot be an active pro-attitude without *someone* having this attitude. We can be even more specific: As far as we know, the only being with active pro-attitudes toward the good is the human being who acts intentionally. And the necessary condition for any active pro-attitude is not merely the existence of human beings, but also that they are capable of having this attitude—that human beings *can* do this. Further, the most important requirement for this capability is our freedom to act.

Here the argument has come to its completion: We began with an analytic truth, namely that if there is something good, then it is good that the good is supported, and if the capability to do so is a necessary requirement for this support, then it is *also good* that human beings have the capability and exercise it. We have then made a transcendental move toward the goodness of freedom, *qua* being the necessary condition *y* for *x* being possible (*x* means 'having an active pro-attitude toward the good'). Thus human freedom to support the good is itself good. Let us call this *y* 'moral freedom'. We can now formulate the result as a fundamental moral principle of action (that comes close to Kant's man-as-an-end formula of the categorical imperative):

1. *Exercise and promote moral freedom!* This demand is directed to the way we deal with ourselves and with others. For each of us, it means that we should realise our freedom, and we should do it in a manner that supports the freedom of others so that they can do the same. Thus, whatever we hold to be morally good or valuable, we are also transcendentally committed to acknowledge the goodness of moral freedom and to enlarge its realm.

What is expressed as an absolute demand ('absolute' in the sense of being basic to all ethics) or fundamental duty can also be formulated as a *right* on the side of all (potentially free) agents: the duty correlates with rights of the recipients. Everyone has a right to be respected and supported in her moral freedom, hence in her ability to act freely in ways that realise some good. In this way, the outlined argument can be used as a justification of human rights as to be found in the declaration of human rights (indeed, most of them are pointing to the conditions necessary for humans to commit free action). We can therefore state:

2. *Everyone has a fundamental right for his or her moral freedom to be respected and supported.* Obviously, supporting the freedom of ourselves or others never guarantees that this freedom will be used in the morally right, namely freedom-supportive, way. If we liberate others, we also enable them to use their newly

gained freedom in a destructive way. But this risk is inevitable; without human freedom, no moral good could be realised—but with freedom, humans are also capable of immoral behaviour. This simply is the necessary ambivalence given with the delicate good freedom.

One might object that the resulting principle is not in accordance with the definition of DE given above, namely that its demands are not derived from a *prior* notion of good. Yet contrary to this objection, the suggested transcendental reasoning is not starting with any particular idea of the good in order to derive norms—it begins with *any* notion of good that someone happens to have (including duties or rights), so long as it is a universal one. The first time the argument makes an explicit statement about what is good is when it spells out what we must (morally) care about and support if we want to make any rational moral judgement. That is why it can be characterised as a deontological ethical approach.

Taking the 'Moral Stance'

There are two possible objections at this point. The first: Is the resulting demand directed toward *everyone*? Why does it not suffice to respect the moral freedom of a few, namely of a number sufficient to allow morality to be possible? Against this, it can be argued that any limitation of the group of people whose moral freedom is supported is also a limitation of the potential realisation of the good. We do not know in advance whose moral freedom will be required to make some good possible. A full realisation of the good demands to presuppose a wide range of the principle so that it includes all possible instances of moral freedom, and therefore all human agents. This follows if the starting point is a *universal* notion of good (as we find it with rational ethical theories). If, however, the starting point is limited (for example, when we take our nation or religion as the good to begin with), then will we have a limited group of addresses: to support the value of my nation, I merely need the freedom of my co-patriots.

Let us therefore specify the beginning of our argument: We must start from a universal idea of the moral good, or from the search for some such idea. This does not mean putting a high burden on the starting point, because this simply is the way in which we normally define 'moral' goodness anyway: In contrast to other (personal, collective) goods, a moral good is normally defined as something that *everyone* should respect in a comparable situation. (It follows, for example, from what Henry Sidgwick calls a self-evident axiom of practical reason—namely, that we ought to treat like cases alike.) The transcendental argument runs therefore as follows: Everyone who takes a 'moral stance' (as we might call the search for a universal moral good) is committed to accepting Number 1 toward everyone.

Does the outlined transcendental argument work? A second objection can be raised in a nihilist fashion by questioning the moral stance *tout court*. Why should we take this stance and assume that there could be anything that we can judge 'morally good'? Friedrich Nietzsche would surely dismiss the moral stance as a common deception; according to him, an honest approach would find merely a universal will to power. Apparent ideas of a moral good are but clever disguises of egoism. And, admittedly, the outlined argument does not address (let alone refute) Nietzschean scepticism; it remains *internal* to ethical reflection.

However, that is enough for our purpose, namely to show that deontological ethics is reflectively robust and attractive in comparison with alternative ethical systems; and that it provides a rational answer to everyone asking for a moral (universal) good. The point is not to secure DE against radical scepticism; this would demand a much more elaborated argument (for example, by showing that we are inevitably committed to taking the moral stance).[9] We can therefore bracket radical scepticism by setting the starting point in a hypothetical form:

3. *If we look for moral orientation (take the moral stance), then we must recognise the fundamental duty to exercise our own and promote others' moral freedom.*[10]
Although expressed in a conditional, Number 3 is still a categorical imperative or duty according to Kant's terminology. The demand does not depend on anything we wish or desire, or even on something we inevitably want as human beings (many do not seem to care too much), but remains *categorical* for someone taking the moral stance by asking for some universally binding idea of moral goodness—and thus for practical reason, as Kant would put it. (We can therefore even follow Kant by calling the demand an inherent 'fact of reason'.)

Efficiency and Permanence

Let us go a step further. We have already mentioned Hegel's suspicion that the categorical imperative amounts to an empty formalism. Yet it is worth looking at a further point that Hegel makes. Morality as understood by Kant is too abstract, he objects. Moral judgements are about ideal states that should be realised in a 'concrete' way. Therefore, we need a rich notion of *Sittlichkeit*, as Hegel calls it, rather than abstract morality. Hegel goes so far to see it as a form of *evil* to think that it suffices 'to will the abstract good' without willing its concrete embodiment.[11] Even if we do not follow this hellish condemnation of Kant's endeavour, we must accept the truth in Hegel's objection: morality is about concrete acting in the world. This can be specified further. We have seen above that it is a conceptual truth that it is good to have an active pro-attitude toward the good—thus to realise the good. This insight has been utilised earlier to argue for the fundamental demand to promote freedom as a necessary condition for any realisation of the good. However, we can take this conceptual truth to come even closer to Hegel's demand for *Sittlichkeit* by deducing two requirements from it: One, the good ought to be realised *efficiently*, and two, it should be done in an *enduring way*. Both requirements are important for a full realisation of the good (whatever it might be); only then will the realisation be independent from the unreliable caprices of individual human beings. Let us look at the argument in some more detail:

A. We have argued above that if there is something right, then we should realise (sustain, protect, etc.) it in relevant situations. Of two actions, we should always choose the one that contributes to this realisation rather than the one that does not. The difference, however, is often not sharp but comes in degrees. We can therefore go a step further: When we compare two actions, it is likely that one contributes more, and the other less toward the realisation or support of the good. In such a situation, there is at least a *prima facie* reason to go for the action that supports the good more—it is a fuller realisation of the demanded active pro-attitude.

   If we accept that the consequences of an action are morally relevant (if we reject pure intentionalism), then we can conclude that if there are reasons to support, promote, etc. some good in a situation, then it is better if the good is supported, etc. more rather than less efficiently.

B. The second requirement can be formulated in parallel terms: if there are reasons to support, etc. some good in a situation, then it is better if it is supported more rather than less permanently. This follows from the timeless nature of transcendental justifications as a rational enterprise; reasons are (by their very nature) valid independently from time and place. If there is a reason why *z* should be done, then this will set a demand for everyone and independently from a particular time—the demand is applicable as long as (and whenever) there is a relevant situation. Thus, if a relevant situation is long-lasting, then a long-lasting realisation of *z* is (morally) preferable over a short-term realisation. To give an example: Since it is good to save a child from drowning in a pond, we should jump into the water to pull it out when we find a child in such a situation. And if this danger is permanent—the playground, for example, is next to the pond—then we ought to build a fence as the most effective (see above) and long-term realisation of the demanded help. Similarly, if we want to protect the natural environment, for example the rain forest, it will be better to do it in a more stable manner. If the World Wildlife Foundation buys parts of the rain forest in order to protect it, then this is, *ceteris paribus*, better than renting it for the same purpose, and much better than merely paying someone for not

> knocking down trees. The good demands a stable manifestation in time which makes it independent from chance and whims.

We can summarise the two requirements in the form of a further categorical imperative:

4. If we look for moral orientation (take the moral stance), then we must recognise the fundamental duty to exercise our own and promote others' moral freedom as efficiently and as permanently as possible.[12]

Levels of Ethical Enquiry

How can we take Number 4 seriously? As it stands, it is a general imperative, but we cannot apply it in general; each application is a specific act in a concrete context. The demand provides orientation, but what it means to support moral freedom in a given situation efficiently will depend on the context. We need empirical knowledge to find out whose freedom is in need of protection or what forces and facts make people unfree—and an investigation of the best ways to develop their freedom. There will be general patterns that can serve as a rule of thumb: Obviously, the ability to act freely will always require some basic goods like food, water and shelter. Without them, freedom can hardly be exercised. Thus, some goods simply have to be provided to all agents. For a more long-term promotion of moral freedom, however, education and economic independence will be more crucial; they widen the range of possible actions and thus the freedom of choice. Often individual cases will be rather difficult to judge. For instance, does it help to financially support poor people in a politically highly unstable situation, or will the money be misused? And even if it does help, will it really help them to become more independent and morally free in the long term?

Transcendental deontological ethics requires a mixed methodology. We need transcendental reflections to justify fundamental imperatives. But in order to gain (derived) demands for concrete situations, empirical insights have to be added to these imperatives. Otherwise, we could not apply these timeless and general demands to the empirical world. On this subordinate level, neither can decisions be made with the direct employment of the basic imperatives nor can we find an ethical algorithm. Already Aristotle (1894) wrote that the practical wise man needs to know both, what is good or valuable, namely eternal invariable ends, and how to achieve the good in this world. Aristotle saw the first task as being done by contemplation, the second by deliberation (*phronesis*).[13] Kant, too, was well aware of this need to bring a priori principles down to earth and talks about the need to employ 'a power of judgement sharpened by experience'.[14] With other words: DE requires transcendental reflection and empirical investigations as sources of insight, and deliberation to bridge between the two and come to concrete conclusions.

What follows with regards to the two Hegelian requirements? To satisfy them is part of the deliberation on the empirically informed level. Here, we use the power of judgement sharpened by experience to find out what the best action is—and the best action is the one that realises the fundamental imperative in the most efficient and durable way. How do we realise the promotion of freedom efficiently and in a durable way, given human beings as we are and given the world that we live in? Possible ways are habituation of supportive behaviour on the individual level—and, most importantly, institutionalisation on the level of society and between nations. An example for habituation is the cultivation of one's willingness to help by developing a corresponding virtue, an example for an institutionalisation is a good university system or strong international institutions like the UN that guarantee global respect for basic human rights.

Deontological ethics comes, as we might put it, in at least two levels. We have a fundamental set of norms, namely the deontological principles. If we express it in Kant's terminology, we can also call them 'categorically' demanding in that they are uncircumventable; their rightness does not depend on (and is not deduced from) any prior good. On a higher level, we find empirically informed demands or concrete rights. And this empirical level comes with different degrees of generality. We might, for example, distinguish more or less basic sets of demands, correlated with different rights (and mirrored by the distinction between negative and positive rights). Basic rights include the absence of anything that harms human life, and include those things that people necessarily need to survive. Accordingly, we can formulate demands like 'Do not harm others!' or 'Help starving people!' Less basic, but still important are demands (and corresponding rights) about proper education, economic independence, etc. Besides various degrees of generality, the different circumstances of each situation will have to be taken into account; they lead to specific realisations of the same demand (or right). 'Donate money to UNICEF!' might be the appropriate demand in one situation; 'Break your bread and give it to your neighbour' in another.

It is important to note that, according to this line of argument, the deliberative process *itself* is morally demanded: if the moral principles tell us what to do and tell us to do it in the best possible way, then we are morally obliged to actively search for this way in particular. Moreover, if we apply the arguments given above to this demand for deliberation, we need efficient and enduring ways of deliberation—and this means we need to develop our own abilities, talents, and our sensitivity toward the situation and needs of others on a global level. And we have to accumulate knowledge about others and their situation. In his transcendental argumentation, Michael Boylan (2011) introduces an 'extended-community worldview imperative' of self-education that stresses this obligation: we must study different peoples, their worldviews, and the particular conditions of free agency so that we can support every agent (or as we might say, his or her moral freedom) in the best possible way.

General Conclusion

More generally, the suggested perspective allows us to overcome the sharp contrast between the deontological-teleological as much as the deontological-consequentialist divide. Although the outline version of DE remains in the liberal tradition, it includes elements of teleological *and* deontological theories: at the heart of the transcendentally founded demand to support moral freedom stands an idea of the good, namely moral freedom. This mellows the contrast between deontological and teleological approaches that John Rawls stresses so strongly. Further, consequentialist considerations find their place in the transcendental version of DE: it has been argued that there is an obligation to act so that the effects are maximised—thus in full awareness of the consequences of our doings. All of this does not put the different types of ethical theories on an equal footing, but it shows that they can be synthesised. Based upon a transcendentally founded imperative, we find a *telos,* namely a notion of the good at the heart of the fundamental moral demand, and this demand points toward a consequence-sensitive engagement with the world.

The Attraction of Deontological Ethics

Justified Principles with Universal Authority

How does the outline DE compare with one of its main rivals, with consequentialism—and in particular with the utilitarian version thereof? After all, utilitarianism has been seen by many as the most promising basis for global ethics. It seems to offer a basis for moral rules that are not committed to any religion or metaphysics; it simply begins with something like an empirical fact, namely the preferences of human beings and their general interest in their being satisfied. Further, by focussing on the suffering of human beings, utilitarian consequentialism has an immediate plausibility when applied to many problems of global scale. The pains and misery of starving people, the profound unhappiness of so many under compulsion and in situations where not even the most basic human rights are respected—this suffering cries for clear moral answers. Utilitarianism presents an immediate orientation; we should act in such a way that we do not create more pains, that suffering ends, and that as many people as possible can live their own self-determined life in which they do what they want to do. No doubt, this is an appealing vision of a better world.

However, if we look more into detail, utilitarianism's attraction fades away. Let us just point out three far-reaching problems of the utilitarian approach. First, it cannot justify the universal inclusion of everyone into the moral picture (let alone future generations—see below). To be sure, already Mill's classic formulation is aiming at *everyone's* happiness. But he cannot offer any justification for his universal aspiration. Mill as much as his followers do not provide an argument.[15] To care for everyone's happiness or interests remains a mere axiom that finds no further grounding in the theory. In particular, if morality is built upon individual preferences (by utilitarianism, they are regarded as the source of normativity), it is entirely unclear what to say to someone who simply fails to have 'concern for everyone' as her preference. If utilitarianism answers by pointing to the axiom and by stating that she *should* have this universal concern, then preferences are no longer the last point of reference; they are replaced by the axiom, in which case utilitarianism is no longer based upon an empirical foundation but upon a mere postulate.[16] A second problem is also linked to the preferences: it is highly implausible to demand concern for all preferences people happen to have—we all know that some preferences are rather wicked or evil. Humans are different from what utilitarianism wants them to be. We find cultures, including their women, who accept female circumcision. We know of people who believe that they must kill for the sake of God. And what about someone who cares only for herself and not about others? Or someone who does not care about morality at all? To ground an ethics on all given 'human preferences and interests' is ultimately self-defeating for an ethical theory. But to select 'good' preferences is also defeating for utilitarianism because it presupposes *prior* criteria for this selection. These criteria would need a different ethical theory. A third problem of utilitarianism is its lack of any strong notion of human rights. Ultimately, morality is regarded as a trading-off process between different interests; and there are no fundamental limits to this exercise. Human rights are only part of the game—and there is no strong utilitarian reason to care for someone who simply accepts his miserable fate. It is here that the apparent plausibility of utilitarianism in face of the world's suffering finally vanishes: We find often no clear, at least no convincing, answers to global problems.

Is it any better with the outlined version of DE? Does everyone have to accept it? Let us turn to the above-mentioned objections. Someone might want to argue that the transcendental argument shows at most that some principle has been justified *according to a certain understanding of reason*. But there is no reason, and can be no reasons, to accept the *universal* validity of the resulting principle. The justification apparently remains within the limits of a type of Western rationality that is characterised by classical, bivalent logic. Good for 'Enlightened' Kantians in their grey study-rooms, but useless for the verdant colour of a pluralistic world?

To refute this objection requires much more space than this chapter allows for; all we can do is to point in an argumentative direction. The privileged status of Enlightenment-Reason, as we might call it, results from the impossibility of *denying* this status in a consistent way.[17] Why? Any attempt to raise scepticism about Enlightenment-Reason is itself making use of this reason because it is expressed in a form that is reasonable according to the standards of Enlightenment-Reason. Otherwise it would be incomprehensible. Thus the sceptic *affirms by what she does* (namely when she raises her doubts in a rational objection) the very validity of Enlightenment-Reason that she denies expressively at the same time. Following the terminology of speech-act theory, we could say that the sceptic is 'performatively' inconsistent. Enlightenment-Reason simply *is* the manner in which we argue, even if we argue about, or reject, types of reason in general.

More so, sceptics of Enlightenment-Reason are often making claims to universal validity in practice. For example, many sociologists, postmodernists, and feminist thinkers state that there are no shared ideas or principles in all cultures and conclude that there is no privileged form of reason. This claim is not only committed to the standards of Enlightenment-Reason (it is, for example, meant to be true and not at the same time false), but the claim is aspiring to universal validity ('It is a misconception of reason to regard Western reason as having a privileged role' is seen as correct or true). Many postmodernists do exactly what they claim to be impossible. To be sure, there is the jungle of different cultures with various notions of reason and reasons, but that is a sociological fact, not itself an argument. In the moment someone raises scepticism about Enlightenment-Reason's role on the basis of this fact, she is going to the study-room of Enlightenment-Reason reason—and is therefore performatively inconsistent.

Again, we have a transcendental argument: Enlightenment-Reason is the necessary performative condition for any act of reasoning, including any rational scepticism about Enlightenment-Reason.[18] Scepticism of Enlightenment-Reason is *either* not expressed in a rational way (and then we need not take it seriously) *or* it is rationally expressed and then performatively inconsistent. A rational critique of Enlightenment-Reason is therefore self-defeating and thus false. But if the universal validity of Enlightenment-Reason cannot consistently be refuted, then it must be right. Enlightenment-Reason is unique and the form of reasoning that transcends all contexts—thus the best (and only) possible basis for a global ethics.

What about Anscombe's concern? Is the resulting list of demands not irrational by being based upon a chimerical notion, namely an (impossible) law without a law-giver? Well, it all depends on what we understand under 'law'. If it is *defined* as something given by a law-giver, then Anscombe's critique is correct but begging the question. Why should it be the only possible and thus adequate definition of 'law'? Alternative understandings (or definitions) make sense. We can think of laws of nature, where law is a generalization that describes recurring facts or events and is based on *empirical observations*. Although they were originally seen as God-given, their current use makes them independent of any divine origin. There is no reason why this should be inconsistent. Closer to the example of moral laws come the laws of logic. They are fundamental rules, which collectively prescribe how a *rational mind* must *think* (for example, it should not contradict itself). Their force rests on it being irrational to break any of these laws of logic; we can acknowledge their authority without assuming that they are God-given—they are rather self-imposed by reason. The authority of transcendentally justified principles can be seen as similar. According to the deontologist view, the prize for ignoring the principles would be to act against reason—thus their authority is based upon our willingness to be consistent rational beings (and this willingness itself is rational and not a mere desire). And that we should avoid the inconsistency is the answer to Anscombe's open question, why we should obey these moral principles in the first place. For reason, the demand for rational consistency has a self-evident authority.

Admittedly, the willingness to be rationally consistent is not extremely strong in all cases. Some people believe that to strive for consistency is a limiting or false ideal, and many people have a more strongly developed will-to-power, *libido*, or egoism. But this is a problem every moral theory faces. Not everyone wants to be good at the praxis he is engaged in, he might not care about virtues, and although many want to be happy, only few see the greatest amount of happiness for the greatest amount of people as their primary goal. Any ethical theory has to consider possible incentives, and any moral education will have to foster these incentives. Here, the troubles of transcendental DE are not any bigger than the ones of other ethical theories; it does not claim to provide a motivational bulwark against the weakness of the will. As Robert Nozick (1981) rightly remarks: 'The motivational force of the argument . . . can be no stronger than the motivation to avoid the particular inconsistency specified by the argument.' However, DE does claim to provide an intellectual bulwark against relativism by offering a justification of some moral rules. Since Elisabeth Anscombe was worried about moral relativism, she should have supported DE's ambitions.

Abstract Demands and Particular Cases

What about the criticisms with regards to the content? Are the resulting imperatives and rights Numbers 1 through 4 empty? No. The demand to promote human freedom provides a clear direction. To be sure, it gives a general orientation that will have to be concretised through deliberation in different circumstances. But by bringing together the knowledge of both, of what is good in general and how to achieve it in particular, in a deliberative process, DE proves to be useful for concrete cases. Moral norms are applied to (yet not altered in the light of) particular situations, and those norms are chosen that promise to achieve the (morally) best outcome. Thus, reality is not 'stretched' to fit into a Procrustean bed of moral principles; rather, norms are embedded into contexts (and here the metaphor ends because these norms should, of course, not seduce us to sleep but stir us to act).

The process of deliberation leaves enough space for the particulars of a situation, and also for changes and developments through time. Again, this follows from the two Hegelian requirements mentioned above: the best way to promote freedom will have to be modified in different contexts, since the peculiar forms of compulsion will always be different. In a slave-owner-society like North America around 1750, the most important moral demand was to abolish slavery, while today to strive for better health care, schooling, and the protection of the environment is (or should be) centrally placed on the moral agenda of the US and most nation-states. Also, our understanding of what freedom requires and how it is limited has become much more profound—think about the many things we know about manipulation, for example through advertisements. The way we make the moral demands concrete must always be based upon the best knowledge we have at any time. Obviously, this adjustment also includes the risk of error. (In the seventies, for example, some people thought that the best way to make people peace-loving and thus peaceful was to take recreational drugs and to bring up children in an antiauthoritarian manner.) And the more empirical knowledge is needed for a particular situation, the more likely it is that we will make mistakes. We will have to accept these risks because there is no rational alternative to using the best knowledge we have. We cannot shelter behind general principles or duties, they cannot 'decide for us', as Onora O'Neill (1987) rightly remarks.

Freedom is the true end that has been demonstrated above, but the argument could be applied to discover further necessary conditions for any practical pro-attitude toward any good. The development of our capacity to understand situations and to find out what is right or wrong might be regarded as another true end since it is also necessary for realising the good, at least in an efficient and permanent manner. And all ends that we can justify transcendentally are universal; they are the ends of all rational beings alike. However, transcendental DE does not provide (directly) a rich set of individual human goals that are specific for individuals, groups, or communities.

The objection of an impoverished anthropology still seeks an answer. Does the suggested transcendental DE abstract from what our life essentially is all about, from our 'true ends'? But against what MacIntyre (1981) suspects, the deontological principle is compatible with a teleological view of man, though a rather different one from the one MacIntyre holds. The DE implies that we know at least one 'true end' of human existence, namely the realisation of freedom in a moral way, which means having a practical pro-attitude toward the good. The principle presupposes that humans are capable of exercising this freedom (that is why the freedom was seen as a condition for the realisation of the good) and demands its promotion, and everyone who values anything at all will also have to acknowledge the value of his or her freedom. *Qua* being rational we find, by self-reflection, an end in us, and all human beings share the potential to realise this end. Neither is this result naively presupposed (as some utilitarians do when they assume a general preference to care for everyone) nor based upon some essentialist intuitions (as Neo-Aristotelians seem to have). We could call it a 'transcendental essentialism'—the ontological status of this teleology is that it is not deduced from empirical knowledge of any kind, but from transcendental reasoning. It is justified through a controllable method: no rational being who takes the moral stance can deny this end without a 'pain of self-contradiction' (to use a phrase by Alan Gewirth).[19] Certainly, such a method is better apt to make a *truth*-claim than the mere reference to a commonly shared praxis or to cultural or legal traditions. But it is also aware of its epistemic limits—someone who is not willing to take the moral stance will not find compelling reasons to accept this moral *telos* (which does not imply that we should not treat him differently; he still has the potential to moral freedom and thus a right to be treated accordingly). And there is a second epistemic limit to be mentioned: there can be more individual *teloi* than moral freedom. When it comes to human flourishing, people will have to look at themselves in a way that goes beyond their essential moral *telos*. This, however, is beyond the outlined transcendental investigation into global duties.

It should be added that DE remains of importance for individuals and their specific ends in an indirect manner—that is, for those things that individuals evaluate highly: the morally demanded freedom cannot be executed or promoted in an abstract fashion; promoting freedom necessarily means to get engaged in a concrete situation as a concrete individual. A dedicated teacher, for example, will promote the freedom of others primarily through education. The teacher's *specific* end will be to teach well or to be a good teacher, but if he reflects about this occupation and its contribution to the universal moral good, he will see teaching as his individual way to do so, namely, by promoting understanding, providing knowledge, or strengthening other abilities. Obviously, he will not always see it in this light. For him it might seem that his end is merely being a good teacher, period. But if he thinks more profoundly about *why* his particular end should be regarded as good, even as *truly* good, then transcendental reasoning will lead him to the universal ends of all rational beings.[20]

What about communities? Is DE able to grant them an intrinsic value or do they have to be regarded as mere functional spheres of interactions between individuals without 'any moral or social bonds between them'? This is not the only alternative according to DE. Communities will not be regarded as good *tout court*, simply by virtue of being a community, but only insofar (and to the extent that) they are places to realise moral freedom. A community that does not further moral freedom will be regarded as having no moral value. More so, to erect and uphold moral communities is itself a *moral demand* for two reasons: First, if a community has developed societal forms and institutions that secure and promote the freedom of its members (like good schools), then it is a particularly efficient and permanent way to do what is morally demanded. Second, humans can develop and realise their specific ends only within communities. To become a teacher, for example, presupposes schools or at least an environment in which teaching is possible. That is true for most professions, but also for other ends people might have, like helping the poor, caring for someone beloved, playing an instrument in an orchestra, gardening, or riding horses.[21] Most of the things that are essential for us either need a social world (like some division of labour) or are only possible in communities. It is probably an empirical truth that we can only become and live as moral human beings through and within communities that nourish and support us. Thus, even for the outlined transcendental DE, communities are of high moral importance, but only instrumentally so.[22] We are obliged to support our particular communities as the place where moral freedom can become concrete in a more permanent way.[23]

Global Duties and the Future of Our World

But communities are not the last word—and that is why we are also obliged to go beyond them. Many moral challenges of today's world are global and require transcultural, joint efforts and strong international institutions. We must keep in mind that there is a fundamental demand to respect and support *all* human beings, whatever community or nation they belong to. Therefore, we must think and act globally as the most efficient ways to realise and guarantee the moral freedom of everyone. And we are justified and obliged to do so because the source of normativity transcends the social or legal structure of the community we happen to live in. We live in a world of excessive, global suffering in which not even the basic needs of billions of humans are satisfied—and we have the global duty to help people efficiently and permanently to overcome their misery and become free agents who are capable of moral engagement.

More so, this demand is also relevant for the way our actions affect future generations. Hans Jonas has argued powerfully that today's technological possibilities are far-reaching so that they trouble the earth as a whole and its future. Our doings will influence and alter the conditions of life for generations to come. According to Jonas, this leads to two important concerns that traditional ethical theories have simply ignored, namely the rights of future generations and care for the environment. Ethics must answer to this challenge. Jonas argues that this requires adding a temporal dimension to traditional ethics. We must be worried about the long-term consequences of our actions for the future of humanity and thus not only for existing human beings, but for those to come and even for the possibility of them to come. It culminates in a new 'Imperative of Responsibility' that Jonas puts at the heart of his ethical theory: 'Act so that the effects of your action are compatible with the permanence of genuine human life.'[24] The permanence of genuine human life is currently at risk, but to preserve it should be ranked much higher than all other values, goods, or aims that we might have.

Hans Jonas's own justification of the Imperative of Responsibility is rather controversial; it is based upon a set of intuitions about an underlying teleological structure of reality.[25] Many traditional ethical theories, including utilitarianism and contractualism, face enormous difficulties when they want to include the future, because they take *existing* human beings and their preferences or their free consent as the ultimate source of normativity. We find a much better justification for Jonas's imperative with the outlined transcendental argumentation. It does not take concrete existing human beings and their freedom as the starting point, but demands to support free human agency as a condition for any moral goodness. This condition is currently fulfilled by supporting all agents that are alive (that is why the duty is addressed to everyone), and it is fulfilled in the long term by making future moral freedom possible. Obviously, the 'permanence of genuine human life' is essential for this future moral freedom. (If there are no more human agents, there will be no concrete moral acts—morality can no longer be realised.) And if we take 'genuine' human life to refer to all that is required for moral freedom, the future-directed imperative includes a profound concern for the environment as being essential for the world to remain habitable for humans. Whether or not nature has an intrinsic value cannot be answered by the outlined argument, but it offers a reflectively robust foundation for global duties toward everyone's (moral) freedom *and* toward the environment as a necessary condition for current and future human life.

Notes

1. An earlier (2007) version of this chapter has been published as "Étreindre le monde entre des bras transcendantaux. Les promesses de l'éthique déontologique" in *Sujet moral et communauté*, ed. D. Müller, M. Sherwin, N. Maillard, C. S. Titus: 112–133. Fribourg: Academic Press. The argument delivered in Section II has found its

first formulation in: C. Illies. (2008). "Why Should We Help the Poor? Philosophy and Poverty" in *International Public Health Policy and Ethics*, ed. M. Boylan: 143–156. Berlin: Springer. I am grateful to Matthew Maguire and Reinhard Zintl for commenting on an earlier version of this chapter.

2. The (normative) natural law was seen as some equivalent to the well-established laws of natural science; its tradition, however, is older than modern natural science. See: Mark Murphy. (2002). "The Natural Law Tradition in Ethics" in *The Stanford Encyclopedia of Philosophy,* Winter Edition, ed. Edward N. Zalta. Retrieved from http://plato.stanford.edu/archives/win2002/entries/natural-law-ethics/

3. The two points of critique are, of course, in a tension. Either empty or rigid—after all, what would it mean that deontological ethics demands rigidly 'nothing'?

4. MacIntyre expands his criticism by saying that the enlightenment project is doomed to fail because it presupposes for its applicability the very teleological anthropology that it rejects.

5. See also William K. Frankena's (1973) definition: 'Deontological theories . . . assert that there are other considerations that may make an action or rule right or obligatory besides the goodness or badness of its consequences—certain features of the act itself other than the value it brings into existence, for example, the fact that it keeps a promise, is just, or is commanded by God or by the state' (15).

6. It should be added that transcendental arguments are faced with several problems. For example: How do we find out whether something is a necessary condition for the possibility of something else? And what can serve as a self-evident starting point? (Already Fichte supposed that Kant is presupposing too much.) A more modern objection reads: Even if we can demonstrate transcendentally that we must *think* that something is a certain way, how can we be sure that it *is* like that—maybe the way we must think has nothing to do with how things really are. In the current debate, this point has been made famously by Barry Stroud (but was discussed earlier by Hegel).

7. In his later work, Kant gives up his transcendental aspirations in ethics. See *Kritik der praktischen Vernunft*, page 46 (in Kant's *Werke* [1968], Akademie Ausgabe Vol. 4, Berlin: de Gruyter). We find a 'total reversal of positions' (Ameriks, 1982, 211). From now on, Kant considers the categorical imperative as a *Faktum der Vernunft.* Whatever that exactly means (maybe an appeal to intuition; see L. W. Beck (1960, 166 ff.), it is certainly no longer a transcendental argument.

8. In recent years, several authors have tried to offer a transcendental justification of first principles; Alan Gewirth's, Onora O'Neill's, or Christine Korsgaard's Ethics are examples of this endeavour.

9. See for example: Alan Gewirth (1970, 107–118).

10. This comes close to Kant's second formula of the categorical imperative: Act in such a way that you always treat humanity whether in your own person or in the

person of any other never simply as a means but always at the same time as an end! *Grundlegung*, 429 (Kant's *Werke* [1968], Akademie Ausgabe Vol. 4, Berlin: de Gruyter).

11. G. W. F. Hegel (1821), *Grundlinien*, 269. The only objection might be raised by pure ethical intentionalists (though there are hardly any around). But their concerns can be disregarded, because they are not consistent: it seems that intentionalism is driven by itself to go beyond mere intentions. At least it is hard to reject that an *intention* 'to be good and to realise the good in a concrete situation' is preferable over an *intention* merely 'to be good'.

12. This comes close to Kant's second formula of the categorical imperative: Act in such a way that you always treat humanity whether in your own person or in the person of any other never simply as a means but always at the same time as an end! *Grundlegung*, 429 (Kant's *Werke* [1968], Akademie Ausgabe Vol. 4, Berlin: de Gruyter).

13. See *Nichomachean Ethics*, 1140a. For Aristotle, *phronesis* is a virtue. According to some interpretations, *phronesis* for Aristotle involves the ability to *determine* the good—and not merely the ability to decide how to realize or achieve the good. We can leave it open, what exactly the view of Aristotle was. At least for the suggested DE, determining the good is not the task of deliberation but of transcendental reflection.

14. *Grundlegung der Metaphysik der Sitten* (in Kant's *Werke* [1968], Akademie Ausgabe Vol. 4, Berlin: de Gruyter: 389. In the second *Critique* he calls it the 'faculty of practical judgement' (Kant's *Werke* [1968], Akademie Ausgabe Vol. 4, Berlin: de Gruyter: 67).

15. There is an obvious naturalistic fallacy in Mills's *Utilitarianism*, Chapter 4, that has often been pointed out.

16. It should be noted that the moral stance is not an axiom in this sense. It does not serve as a substantial presupposition from which an ethical system is deduced, but is the framework of practical reason from within which the question for the moral good is asked. Utilitarianism cannot be reconstructed in a similar fashion; it does *not* follow from the moral stance that we should take the preferences that human beings happen to have as the source of normativity.

17. I avoid the often-used term 'Western reason' because it is missing the point: the claim of Enlightenment Reason is exactly *not* to be local (Western, etc.) but universal.

18. See the typology of transcendental arguments in Chapter 2 of Illies (2003).

19. Alan Gewirth (1978, 26–27). Gewirth, however, develops a different transcendental argument on the basis of action theory.

20. It is noteworthy that this does not diminish the value of the specific ends to see them as concretisations of universal ends. After all, specific, concrete ends are *the only way* for the universal ends to become real. As we have learned from Hegel, the highest realisation of the abstract ideas is that they become *concrete*. Thereby the

suggested DE leaves it open for the individual to discover the best concretisation in his situation, that is the specific ends of his life, based upon his talents, capacities, or profession, upon the time and place where he lives and the community he belongs to. There is no dichotomy between genuine individual ends and universal ones (from which the individual ends derive their value). There *can* also be a sharp contrast, namely when the specific ends are not in accordance with the universal ones. It is here that DE shows its second advantage over many rival theories. It provides not only better-justified ends, but has also a strong *critical* potential: specific ends will have to be checked against universal ones. We can investigate, for example, whether the teacher furthers his pupils' freedom or indoctrinates them (as it might be in a fundamentalist school). Contrary to utilitarianism, we do not need to accept his preferences as they are, and contrary to MacIntyre and others, we can criticise him even when he acts in accordance with his community. For DE, specific human ends (and what individuals, groups with a shared practice, or communities think about them) are *not* the last word in moral matters.

21. Obviously, not *everyone* is in the privileged position of philosophers, teachers, and others to be able to regard her job also as a specific end of her life.

22. See A. MacIntyre's *After Virtue*, where MacIntyre writes that communities' 'primary bond is a shared understanding both of the good for man and of the good for that community and where individuals identify their primary interests with reference to those goods' (1981, 250).

23. The above-mentioned diagnosis that our society gets distorted and faces an increasing loss of public engagement might (sadly) be true. There are surely many reasons for this, and one might be that people no longer grant any authority to communities. Yet this ethology, even if correct, does not provide by itself a strong reason to postulate the revival of the bonds of community; at most we can conclude that it would be *desirable* if communities could retain their traditional role. Desirability might give rise to pragmatic advice, but it is certainly not sufficient a reason to grant communities any intrinsic value.

24. See: Jonas, Hans. (1984). *The Imperative of Responsibility*. Chicago: University of Chicago Press.

25. See C. Illies, 1999, 97–119.

References

Ameriks, K. (1982). *Kant's Theory of Mind*. Oxford: Oxford University Press.

Anscombe, Elizabeth. (1958). "Modern Moral Philosophy." *Philosophy 33*(124): 1–19.

Aristotle. (1894). *Nichomachean Ethics*, ed. I. Bywater. Oxford: Oxford University Press.

Beck, Lewis White. (1960). *A Commentary on Kant's* Critique of Practical Reason. Chicago: University of Chicago Press.

Boylan, Michael. (2004). *A Just Society*. Lanham, MD: Rowman and Littlefield.

Boylan, Michael, ed. (2008). *International Public Health Policy and Ethics*. Dordrecht: Springer.

Boylan, Michael. (2011). *Morality and Global Justice: Justifications and Applications*. Boulder, CO: Westview.

Frankena, William K. (1973). *Ethics, Second Edition*. Englewood Cliffs, NJ: Prentice Hall.

Gewirth, Alan. (1970). "Must One Play the Moral Language Game?" *American Philosophical Quarterly* 7(2): 107–118.

Gewirth, Alan. (1978). *Reason and Morality*. Chicago: University of Chicago Press.

Hans, Jonas. (1984). *The Imperative of Responsibility*. Chicago: University of Chicago Press.

Hegel, G. W. F. (1821). *Grundlinien der Philosophie des Rechts* in: *Werke* Vol. 7, Frankfurt: Suhrkamp.

Illies, Christian. (1999). "Das gute Leben. Die Theorie des Organischen als Zentrum der Ethik bei Hans Jonas." *Jahrbuch f. Philosophie des Forschungsinstituts f. Philosophie Hannover 10*: 97–119.

Illies, Christian. (2003). *The Grounds of Ethical Judgement*. Oxford: Oxford University Press.

Kant, Immanuel. (1968). *Kant's Werke* Vol. 5. Berlin: de Gruyter.

MacIntyre, Alasdair. (1981). *After Virtue*. London; Duckworth.

Mill, John Stuart. (1863). *Utilitarianism*, ed. M. Warnock. London: Meridian Books.

Nagel, Thomas. (1986). *The View from Nowhere*. Oxford: Oxford University Press.

Nozick, Robert. (1981). *Philosophical Explanations*. Oxford: Oxford University Press.

O'Neill, Onora. (1987). "Abstraction, Idealization and Ideology in Ethics" in *Moral Philosophy and Contemporary Problems*, ed. J. D. G. Evans: 55–71. Cambridge: Cambridge University Press.

Rawls, John. (1971). *A Theory of Justice*. Cambridge, MA: Harvard University Press.

Sandel, Michael. (1984). "The Procedural Republic and the Unencumbered Self." *Political Theory 12*: 81–96.

PART THREE

NORMATIVE APPLICATIONS

Poverty and the Global Economy

- Chapter 7 Collective Responsibility and Global Poverty
  SEUMAS MILLER
- Chapter 8 Building Wealth with Conditional Cash Transfers
  MICHAEL BOYLAN
- Chapter 9 Ethics and Global Finance
  KLAUS STEIGLEDER
- Chapter 10 Global Business and Global Justice
  NIEN-HÊ HSIEH

PART THREE: Poverty and the Global Economy
INTRODUCTION

In Part Three of this volume we move to normative applications. These are specific problem areas: poverty and the global economy; global health; religion; war; and gender, identity, and family. In each subsection, specific global problems are addressed and various suggestions are brought forward for progress. I hope that these essays stimulate discussion and debate on the pros and cons of the problem assessment and the various solutions being touted.

Seumas Miller begins the first subsection. Miller makes use of distinctions he made in his 2010 book on the moral foundations of social institutions. Miller's first key distinction is between actions in which one acts at a particular time in history to bring about a positive effect and those in which one acts in concert with others in an effort carried through an institution over time. An example of the first case is Singer's shallow pond. But these sorts of cases are more rare. Generally, helping is in the context of an ongoing problem (the second type), for example, giving twenty dollars to Oxfam. In this latter instance, one donation at one point in history will *not* solve any single problem. Rather, what one does by making the donation is to link into a social welfare institution that is acting over time. One joins her money with that of others in a collective effort: collective action in response to collective responsibility.

To get a better handle upon responsibility, Miller contrasts individual responsibility and collective responsibility. There are four modes of responsibility. In the first case there is natural responsibility in which a particular agent intends to do *x* and carries it out. Second is when a person fulfills a role in an institution. The individual's obligation follows from being in that role. Then there is the case in which one's institutional role includes the ability to govern the actions of subordinates. In this third sense, one's institutional-role duty extends to making sure others act according to institutional ends. Finally, when the responsibility in question has moral significance, then the responsibility transforms into *moral responsibility*.

Collective responsibility involves joint action through the institution. The individual actors connect to the collective end and their individual actions contribute proportionally to that end. Thus all agents act naturally in a collective project. Because of one's chosen institutional role, each actor has a *joint institutional obligation* to fulfill the given end. This joint obligation creates a collective institutional responsibility. When the end in question has moral significance, then the collective responsibility becomes *moral.*

Positive duties can be met via collective responsibility and the ensuing collective action. Miller cites an example of a group of bushwalkers who come upon an injured hiker. Without help, the injured hiker will die. No single bushwalker can help the injured hiker alone, but together they can get the hiker to a hospital for care without risk or undue inconvenience. This example represents a case of collective moral responsibility and the ensuing collective action.

The next question that Miller addresses is how positive collective responsibility arises—especially in a global context in which we are often separated from those in need. His answer is a needs-based rights approach that has been presented by David Wiggins. This is very similar to the *interest-based* approach to rights discussed in Part One. When more important needs are not being fulfilled in the world—such as extreme poverty—then a moral right ensues that creates collective moral responsibility that is to be addressed by international welfare institutions (and other international institutions that exist to provide other goods such as education and civil protection).

Now one can view the motivation question either from a positive or negative duty standpoint. The positive duty standpoint says that legitimate human needs incur collective responsibility (via positive rights) and all of us via our roles in international institutions (including the role of financial contributor) have a positive duty to provide the goods that are lacking. The other position sets out that we have special negative duties to those we harm in order to make the victims whole again. These are called negative duties.

Miller thinks that neither positive nor negative duties tell the entire tale. Both are incomplete, but positive duties are a little easier to assess (since one merely has to demonstrate need), whereas with negative duties one must assess both need and blame: it's a steeper path to climb. In the end, Miller believes that his institutional standpoint when pointed to the world will replace the provincial national perspective and offer a realistic mechanism to think about and make progress toward lessening world poverty.

The second article is also about lessening poverty. It originated from my work at the Center for American Progress (a Washington, D.C., policy think tank) on the economic mobility project that is an ongoing project of the Pew Center, the Brookings Institution, and others. The perspective aims toward the more wealthy countries of the world that have their own poor populations despite their aggregate affluence (though the strategy could work anywhere there is adequate money for human capital investment). I take for my example the United States.

The basic strategy is the conditional cash transfer. A conditional cash transfer is a payment made widely in a society, and the payment comes with strings attached. It is my contention that these strings will help direct peoples' behavior toward successful life strategies within that society—such as getting an adequate education, starting a business, sustaining a family crisis, buying a home, etc. These steps in life are essential to obtaining economic mobility. Economic mobility is the ability of a person to move up or down in the quartiles of wage earners in the society. In this instance the focus is upon the lower two quartiles of income distribution. This policy is designed to help them rise. The essential heart of this policy is the creation of personal wealth. *Wealth* is to be understood as reserve money that can be used at critical life moments to take advantage of opportunity or to weather adversity. Wealth makes it considerably easier for individuals to gain positive economic mobility.

Now one thing must be perfectly clear: there will always be people in the lowest quartile of income distributions. This is the nature of statistics. So there is a secondary sense of economic mobility and that is the opportunity to possess the basic goods necessary for human action (which I set out in a hierarchical order in my Table of Embeddedness). If everyone possessed levels one and two basic goods and level-one secondary goods, then for me the economic mobility problem has been solved in that society: everyone has the tools necessary to gain what they may by a theory of progressive deserts.

The way we should think about conditional cash transfers is not as "handouts" to the least advantaged. This essay describes this process as an *investment* in human capital. This investment can pay off for a society in increased wages and salaries (as the World War II GI Education Bill proved). The basic intuition behind this policy is that many people are held back from achieving a part of their nation's prosperity because at pivotal junctures they do not possess a backup fund (wealth) that can protect them against adversity and enable them to seize opportunity. Because it is so important that this personal wealth fund stay intact until one of these two events occurs, there is highly restricted access to this money (so that it is never considered as an income device to be wasted in pursuit of transitory pleasures).

This policy is very controversial, but it seeks to be another strategy of equal opportunity that operates under the assumption that much of what is achieved by many is due to undeserved preferment. The personal wealth fund is intended to be one step in the opposite direction.

The third article in this section is from Klaus Steigleder on the role of macroethics as a tool to help maintain efficient financial markets. Traditionally, financial ethics has concentrated upon micro- and meso-level economic events. In these cases the role of individual behavior is highlighted. Steigleder contends that this has been the role of traditional business ethics. However, Steigleder argues that macroethics possesses a cognitive and normative priority over micro- or meso-ethical approaches. This is because macroethics deals with appraisals of, one, the fundamental tasks of the financial market; two, the systemic structures and interrelations of the economy; and three, the existing regulative framework. The guiding principle behind such appraisals is the establishment of a *permanently sustainable financial market.* Such a market is of primary moral import. Steigleder uses "financial market" to mean all financial markets and institutions within a given economy. It is shorthand for the systemic financial structure within any economy. The moral principle behind this imperative is that a well-functioning financial market contributes to self-fulfilling agency (that is the goal of all prospective purposive agents on earth). Thus, the more properly sustainable these markets become, the more individuals are helped along with their fundamental life quest. The ability to fulfill this quest is also a key feature of real operative human rights.

Steigleder makes it clear that he distances himself from others who have made similar appeals from a more laissez-faire approach. Regulations have a real place in the operation of financial markets for Steigleder. The goal is to find which sorts of regulations will help the financial market fulfill its essential mission of prudently building wealth for people everywhere. This is why Steigleder emphasizes the permanence and sustainability of the financial market. When wild speculation is the name of the game, the level of risk rises and the time horizon is very short—this is far from permanent or sustainable. When permanence and sustainability are factored in as an essential characteristic that is not to be compromised, then the wild cyclic nature of capitalism can be leveled off.

In order to fulfill this task, macroethics steps in alongside efficiency considerations to point to what limitations of risk and speculation might obtain. The result of this in the policy sphere yields sustainability. Such an approach combines normative and economic expertise to define and carry out specific tasks within the larger systemic structure so that "the financial market *in its entirety* must be permanently efficient and the coexistence of sustainable efficient financial markets of individual national economies on the level of the global economy has to be ensured." In this regard Steigleder recognizes the dynamic nature of individual economies and the interconnectedness of local economies to the global economy. In this respect the moral imperative is international in its scope.

Since markets don't regulate themselves (contrary to what the laissez-faire folks contend), and because they are inherently unstable, the regulatory environment will be an ongoing process. Profound regulations are needed both to *promote* efficiency and to *prevent* disasters. To do this, one must be constantly looking at both the ends and their associated means at each juncture. Often, the most comprehensive approach (the full-scope moral norms) are not practically possible to effect; in that event more limited (restricted-scope moral norms) should be put into place. In either event, the beneficiaries will be the citizens of that state and by extension (because the economies of the world are interconnected), people everywhere will be assisted in their individual quests toward self-fulfilling human agency.

The last essay in this section is from Nien-hê Hsieh. The essay begins with a challenging problem: one, the justice approach is generally directed at nations toward their own citizens; and two, theories of corporate responsibility generally do not address issues of justice in evaluating the ground of corporate social duty. Nien-hê Hsieh seeks to rethink these two positions and find a way to combine them.

The universe of exploration begins with multinational enterprises (MNEs), which are enterprises headquartered in one country that control one or more enterprises based in other countries—in this case within developing economies (poor countries). These MNEs are major players in the day-to-day operation of how much of the world lives. It is therefore important to ascertain what, if any, duties fall upon this particular subset of MNEs and the manner in which they should respond.

Nien-hê Hsieh begins with the Rawlsian perspective that justice is best pursued within the confines of a nation and is first understood as being satisfied through procedural justice within the context of just institutions that follow Rawls's two principles of justice: One, each person has an equal right to a fully adequate scheme of equal basic liberties that is compatible with a similar scheme of liberties for all. Two, social and economic inequalities are to satisfy two conditions. First, they must be attached to offices and positions open to all under the conditions of fair equality of opportunity; and second, they must be to the greatest benefit of the least advantaged members of society (Rawls, 1993, 291).

The basic strategy is this: the original position, a thought experiment, plays out a constitutional convention with restrictions on personal interests (the veil of ignorance). From the original position, principles of justice would be chosen (Rawls's two principles) and these would structure social institutions such that these institutions would produce justice within the society.

Nien-hê Hsieh creates his argument upon: one, an examination of MNEs vis-à-vis whether they have a responsibility to the developing nations in which they do business, and if they do whether it is simply a negative duty (to correct harms the company had caused) or the more robust positive duty (to act on behalf of the people of the country who lack the basic goods of agency); two, an evaluation of the arguments grounding social responsibility; three, an assessment of the claim that MNEs have positive duties; and four, an examination of how the justice approach makes a difference.

In the first point Nien-hê Hsieh turns to Henry Shue's notion of three sorts of negative duties. This is interpreted via Thomas Donaldson's understanding of agenthood by corporations. This is a key problem in business ethics since corporations are in some ways artificial persons. As such they are both *like* and *unlike* persons.[1] Donaldson suggests that corporations are something like limited moral agents who have a responsibility to the societies in which they do business where their intervention has caused harm. Onora O'Neill describes this ontological problem in terms of primary and secondary agency. If businesses are only secondary agents, their responsibility is limited.

For Nien-hê Hsieh the emphasis upon negative duties and the prevention of future harms are explored. This has been the approach of Thomas Pogge in dealing with these issues and is very influential here. The goal here is well-ordered societies via social institutions that lead the way to just societies (see Seumas Miller on this very issue). This balances various fiduciary duties to stockholders with a quasi-environmental impact statement of the company upon some other society. This sort of analysis conflates O'Neill's primary and secondary agents. It is the introduction of justice as a factor that does this. Following Donaldson, Nien-hê Hsieh contends that MNEs' constitutive aims are consistent with negative duties but are not committed to positive duties. Duties to rescue are grounded in justice. But the justice relation involves both the corporation and the recipients. Valid claims at this level must be grounded in ethical principles and not simply in a company's ability to pay—the deep pockets mentality.

In the end Nien-hê Hsieh has advocated for what he contends is a practical blueprint for what we might expect from multinational enterprises: accepting the environmental impact of their operations by responding to these ensuing negative duties to support national institutions based upon principles of justice so that developing societies might be transformed for the better.

Note

1. For a discussion of this, see Michael Boylan, ed. (2001). *Business Ethics*. Upper Saddle River, NJ: Prentice Hall.

Reference

Rawls, John. (1993). *Political Liberalism*. New York: Cambridge University Press.

CHAPTER SEVEN

Collective Responsibility and Global Poverty

SEUMAS MILLER
Charles Sturt University/
Australian National University/
Delft University of Technology

Abstract

In this chapter I outline my individualist, teleological (normative) account of social institutions and apply it to welfare institutions or, at least, to one kind of welfare institution, namely international institutions concerned with global poverty. I do so in the context of the assumption that, speaking generally, basic needs, for example for food, clean water, shelter, medicines, etc. are, and ought to be, provided for by nonwelfare institutions, notably by business organizations operating in competitive markets. Nevertheless, given the manifest and ongoing failure on the part of such organizations, including in relation to global poverty, there is a need for welfare institutions. In addition, as will become evident below, there is a need to redesign markets and market-based organizations so that they are better able to provide for basic needs.

Key Words

global poverty, social responsibility of business, international institutions for poverty relief

---

Global Poverty and the Moral Obligations of the Affluent

According to Peter Singer (relying on the World Bank figures), there are approximately one billion people in the world living in absolute poverty, and of the affluent persons in the world, each has an individual moral obligation to assist (Singer, 2007; Pogge, 2008, 2).[1]

Moreover, it is a very strong individual moral obligation; it has the same strength as the moral obligation that I have to save a drowning child in a pond adjacent to me if I can (Singer, 1972). Further, it is a very demanding individual obligation in that my obligation is to give and keep giving to the threshold point at which either the great harm to others has been averted or the cost to me of giving is no longer comparatively insignificant. So even if I have given away most of my income to, say, Oxfam, I still have a moral obligation to continue giving, if my (by now) very modest income is, nevertheless, significantly above what is required to meet my basic needs. Comparatively speaking, the cost to me of giving an additional amount of my very modest income is insignificant compared to the harm thereby averted, for example, saving one more starving child's life. I do not dispute the existence of a moral obligation on the part of the affluent to assist those living in absolute poverty; indeed, I believe that there is such an obligation. However, I do dispute the nature of the obligation (as expressed in the analogy with saving the drowning child) as well as Singer's view of its demandingness. (For arguments against its demandingness, in particular, see Cullity, 2004.)

Let us consider the nature of the moral obligation to assist those currently living in absolute poverty (mainly in the so-called developing world). I argue below that the obligation in question is not an individual obligation per se, but rather a collective moral responsibility, albeit collective responsibility is a species of individual moral responsibility—namely, joint moral responsibility. The collective moral responsibility in question is grounded in the aggregate needs-based rights of those living in absolute poverty. But let us first get clarity on Singer's analogy.

What is the analogy between giving to the needy and saving the drowning child supposed to be? In the case of the drowning child, I have a one-off, individual moral obligation to save the child. This is in part because my action is a necessary and a sufficient condition for the child's life to be saved; my single action, and my single action alone, will save the child. Do I have the same moral obligation to give, say, twenty dollars to Oxfam today as I have to save the drowning child?

Surely this cannot be correct, because if I make a one-off payment to Oxfam, I do not know that it will save any additional person; a large organization such as Oxfam with a budget in the hundreds of millions does not adjust its budgets and delivery schedules to the needy on the basis of twenty-dollar increments. Moreover, even if my twenty dollars were to be earmarked for an additional child with, say, malnutrition (supposing this is my arrangement with Oxfam), it will not necessarily save the child's life in the manner that I save the life of the drowning child. Children in absolute poverty typically face a range of ongoing threats to their life, and my twenty dollars might only slightly prolong the child's life; the immediate threat from malnutrition is averted today only to have some disease, such as malaria, kill the child tomorrow. The implicit background assumption in the case of the drowning child is that the child when saved from drowning will return to a very different default state from the one facing the child in absolute poverty; specifically, the child saved from drowning will return to a situation in which she has adequate food and shelter, clean water, health care, and so on.

Moreover, even if the twenty dollars were to be earmarked for a particular child, and even if that child's life were to be saved for the long term because short-term malnutrition was the only threat to her life (perhaps malnutrition was the consequence of a one-off, disastrous crop failure), it was not *I* who saved her life; rather, I provided the money that enabled someone else to save her, for instance, the aid worker who fed the child over the requisite time period or the health worker who administered the vaccine or what have you. So it was the aid worker who saved the child, albeit my twenty dollars paid for the food; so I am much more like the donor who paid for the life jacket that is thrown to the drowning child rather than I am like the passerby who actually saves the drowning child.

Finally, many, if not most, of those living in absolute poverty are not infants, and the problem they confront is not an individualized problem that each confronts alone, as is the case with the drowning child. Rather, they are capable adults confronting a problem (or set of interrelated problems) as a collective. Consequently, unlike the drowning child scenario, the solution does not lie in, so to speak, rescuing each adult person one by one. Rather it involves creating the conditions under which they can collectively act to assist themselves.

So unlike in the drowning child case, my action of giving twenty dollars to Oxfam is not sufficient to save anyone's life (not for a short time, and certainly not for a long time); the actions of many other people are required—including those of the needy themselves—and required over a long period of time. Nor (again, unlike the drowning child case) is my one-off action necessary, because it is almost certainly the case that the same number of lives will be saved (for a long period of time) whether or not I give my twenty dollars. Indeed, it is far from probable that I will save even one life for a short period of time; certainly in most cases I do not *know* that my giving twenty dollars today is a necessary condition for someone's life being saved (for either a short time or for a long time).

I conclude that the proposed analogy between saving the needy and saving the drowning child is defective in three fundamental respects. First, unlike saving the drowning child—which requires an individual person to perform an individual action in accordance with his or her *individual* moral obligation—saving the billion in absolute poverty is to be understood as a situation calling for collective, interdependent action on the part of many (perhaps millions, certainly thousands) in accordance with their *collective* moral responsibility to do so. Second, again unlike saving the drowning child, saving the billion in absolute poverty is a long-term project requiring a series of actions performed over a period of years on the part of each (or at least most) of the relevant persons; it is not a matter of a one-off action, even a one-off collective action. In short, there is a collective moral responsibility to save the billion in absolute poverty by means of long-term, collective action—indeed, institutional action (Shue, 1996, Chap. 5; Miller, 2010, Chap. 1). Third—and again unlike the drowning child scenario—the actions required to save the billion in absolute poverty are principally, though by no means exclusively, the collective actions of the billion themselves; so the collective moral responsibility (or responsibilities) is in large part the collective responsibility that the billion (or various sub-cohorts thereof) have toward one another.

Collective Moral Responsibility

Let me now outline my account of the key moral concept in play here, namely, collective responsibility (Miller, 2006). We need first to distinguish some different senses of responsibility. Sometimes to say that someone is responsible for an action is to say that the person had a reason, or reasons, to perform some action, then formed an intention to perform that action (or not to perform it), and finally acted (or refrained from acting) on that intention, and did so on the basis of that reason(s). Note that an important category of reasons for actions are ends, goals, or purposes; an agent's reason for performing an action is often that the action realizes a goal the agent has. Moreover, it is assumed that in the course of all this, the agent brought about or caused the action, at least in the sense that the mental state or states that constituted his reason for performing the action was causally efficacious (in the right way), and that his resulting intention was causally efficacious (in the right way).

I will dub this sense of being responsible for an action "natural responsibility." It is this sense of being responsible that I will be working with in this chapter: intentionally performing an action and doing so for a reason.

On other occasions what is meant by the term "being responsible for an action" is that the person in question occupies a certain institutional role, and that the occupant of that role is the person who has the institutionally determined duty to decide what is to be done in relation to certain matters. For example, the welfare officer has the responsibility to ensure that the correct payments are made to welfare recipients, irrespective of whether or not he does so, or even contemplates doing so.

A third sense of "being responsible" for an action, is a species of our second sense. If the matters in respect of which the occupant of an institutional role has an institutionally determined duty to decide what is to be done include ordering other agents to perform, or not to perform, certain actions, then the occupant of the role is responsible for those actions performed by those other agents. We say of such a person that he is responsible for the actions of other persons in virtue of being the person in authority over them.

The fourth sense of responsibility is in fact the sense that we are principally concerned with here, namely, moral responsibility. Roughly speaking, an agent is held to be morally responsible for an action if the agent was responsible for that action in one of our first three senses of responsible, and that action is morally significant.

An action can be morally significant in a number of ways. The action could be intrinsically morally wrong, as in the case of a rights violation. Or the action might have moral significance by virtue of the end that it was performed to serve, or the outcome that it actually had (and that could have foreseeably been avoided by the agent).

We can now make the following preliminary claim concerning moral responsibility:

1. If an agent is responsible for an action (or a relevant outcome) in the first, second, or third senses of being responsible, and the action is morally significant, then—other things being equal—the agent is morally responsible for that action, and—other things being equal—can reasonably attract moral praise or blame and (possibly) punishment or reward for performing the action (and/or for its outcome).

Here the "other things being equal" clauses are intended to be cashed out as follows. The first occurrence arises by virtue of the possibility that the agent is not a moral agent and, therefore, cannot be held morally responsible, as in the case of, for example, a psychopath. The second occurrence arises by virtue of the possibility that the agent might have a justification or excuse for performing the action, as in the case of, for example, the agent having been coerced.

Having distinguished four senses of responsibility, including moral responsibility, let me now turn directly to collective responsibility.

As is the case with individual responsibility, we can distinguish four senses of collective responsibility. In the first instance I will do so in relation to joint actions.

Agents who perform a joint action are responsible for that action in the first sense of collective responsibility. Accordingly, to say that they are collectively responsible for the action is just to say that they performed the joint action. That is, they each had a collective end, each intentionally performed their contributory action, and each did so because each believed the other would perform his contributory action, and that therefore the collective end would be realized.

Here it is important to note that each agent is individually (naturally) responsible for performing his contributory action, and responsible by virtue of the fact that he intentionally performed this action, and the action was not intentionally performed by anyone else. Of course the other agents (or agent) *believe* that he is performing, or is going to perform, the contributory action in question. But mere possession of such a belief is not sufficient for the ascription of responsibility to *the believer* for performing the individual action in question. So what are the agents *collectively* (naturally) responsible for? The agents are *collectively* (naturally) responsible for the realization of the (collective) *end* which results from their contributory actions. Consider two agents jointly lifting large sacks of grain onto a truck. Each is individually (naturally) responsible for lifting his side of a sack, and the two agents are collectively (naturally) responsible for bringing it about that the sack is situated on the truck.

Again, if the occupants of an institutional role (or roles) have an institutionally determined obligation to perform some joint action, then those individuals are collectively responsible for its performance, in our second sense of collective responsibility. Here there is a *joint* institutional obligation to realize the collective end of the joint action in question. In addition, there is a set of derived *individual* obligations; each of the participating individuals has an individual obligation to perform his/her contributory action. (The derivation of these individual obligations relies on the fact that if each performs his/her contributory action, then it is probable that the collective end will be realized.)

There is a third sense of collective responsibility that might be thought to correspond to the third sense of individual responsibility. The third sense of individual responsibility concerns those in authority. Suppose the members of the cabinet of country A (consisting of the prime minister and the cabinet ministers) collectively decide to exercise their institutionally determined right to reduce their aid to developing countries in the light of the global recession and reduced government income. The cabinet is collectively responsible for this policy change.

There are a couple of things to keep in mind here. First, the notion of responsibility in question here is, at least in the first instance, institutional—as opposed to moral—responsibility.

Second, the "decisions" of committees, as opposed to the individual decisions of the members of committees, need to be analyzed in terms of the notion of a joint institutional mechanism (Miller, 2010, Chap. 2). So the "decision" of the cabinet can be analyzed as follows. At one level each member of the cabinet voted for or against the policy; let us assume that some voted in the affirmative, and others in the negative. But at another level each member of the cabinet agreed to abide by the outcome of the vote; each voted having as a collective end that the outcome with a majority of the votes in its favor would be pursued. Accordingly, the members of the cabinet were jointly institutionally responsible for the policy change—that is, the cabinet was collectively institutionally responsible for the change.

What of the fourth sense of collective responsibility, collective *moral* responsibility? Collective moral responsibility is a species of joint responsibility. Accordingly, each agent is individually morally responsible, but conditionally on the others being individually morally responsible; there is interdependence in respect of moral responsibility. This account of collective moral responsibility arises naturally out of the account of joint actions. It also parallels the account given of individual moral responsibility.

Thus we can make our second claim about moral responsibility:

2. If agents are collectively responsible for an outcome—the realization of a collective end (or some further foreseeably avoidable outcome thereof)—in the first or second or third senses of collective responsibility, and if the outcome in question is morally significant, then—other things being equal—the agents are collectively morally responsible for that outcome, and—other things being equal—can reasonably attract moral praise or blame and (possibly) punishment or reward for bringing it about.

As was the case in the earlier definition, the "other things being equal" clauses are intended to be cashed out as follows. The first occurrence arises by virtue of the possibility that the agent is not a moral agent and, therefore, cannot be held morally responsible. The second occurrence arises by virtue of the possibility that the agent might have a justification or excuse for performing the action.

Social Institutions and Collective Responsibility

Having provided ourselves with an account of collective moral responsibility, we need now to explore the relationship between collective responsibility and social institutions.

It is generally accepted that an individual should help others—at least where she is the only one able to do so, the harm facing those others is serious and imminent, and the cost of providing assistance is relatively small. The same holds true of groups: there are collective responsibilities on the part of members of societies to one another, salient subgroups and, more generally, those who happen to be particularly well-placed to assist, whether or not they themselves belong to the needy group. Consider the following scenario. A group of bushwalkers comes across another bushwalker who has fallen and broken his leg. Without assistance, the bushwalker will die of exposure. No single member of the group could carry the injured person to safety, but if they act jointly, they can do so without risk to themselves, or indeed any great inconvenience. It seems that, given their awareness of the near certainty of the death of the injured bushwalker if they do not intervene, the members of the group have a collective moral responsibility to do so.

So the need of groups for various forms of assistance that can only be adequately rendered by other groups generates collective responsibilities on the part of groups that can assist to do so. Moreover, such responsibilities exist even where the harm is prospective rather than imminent. Of course, in many cases, the fact that a potential harm to others is temporally distant is relevant to whether or not we are the ones who have a duty to assist them in avoiding it, since there will be time for others who are better equipped to assist or for those who can do so at a lower cost to intervene. But there is no reason for holding that whether or not we have a duty to assist can depend on the temporal proximity of the harm, in itself.

Where such collective responsibilities to assist can most effectively be discharged by establishing institutions and institutional roles whose institutional duties consist of providing such aid, such as firefighters and fire brigades, doctors and hospitals, welfare workers and welfare agencies, and so on, then members of the group who have the collective responsibility have a derivative responsibility to establish and support such institutions.

Further, members of a given group may have collective moral responsibilities toward the membership of that very group, that is, the group of which they are members. Assume that there is a high probability of a disease, say, tuberculosis, taking the life of some very small percentage of Australia's population, but that with respect to any individual Australian the risk is close to zero. In this situation all or most Australians have a collective moral responsibility to prevent TB, and that responsibility can be discharged at minimal cost and inconvenience to any individual Australian. However, from the perspective of narrow individual self-interest, each Australian would not contribute. In the first place, given the almost zero possibility of harm to his or her self-interest, each does not have an incentive to contribute to the prevention of TB. And in the second place, even if such a cooperative scheme existed, self-interest would dictate that each putative participant free ride. We conclude that the health care provision in question is undertaken in large part as a consequence of a perceived collective moral responsibility, and might initially take the form of local volunteer health care services. In due course, a division of labor tends to evolve, and the institution of professional medical practitioners is established to discharge the collective moral responsibility to avoid the harms caused by diseases such as TB (Alexandra and Miller, 2009).

The (collective) duty to assist may, then, in certain cases, imply the duty to establish and support institutions to achieve the object of the duty. Once such institutions with their specialized role holders are in place, it may be that we generally have no further duty to assist within the area of the institutions' operations. Indeed, it may be that generally we should not even *try* to assist, given our relative lack of expertise and the likelihood that we will get in the way of the role holders. Still, on occasions when no role holder is available to assist and we possess relevant capacities, etc., the individual or collective duty becomes reanimated. Moreover, we may have an ongoing duty to ensure that these institutions remain in place.

Once institutions and their constitutive roles have been established on some adequate moral basis, such as the duty to aid, then those who undertake these roles necessarily put themselves under obligations of various kinds—obligations that attach to, and are in part constitutive of, those roles. To understand the specific content of professional role morality, then, we need to examine the purposes—to meet the aggregated health care needs, in the case of the health care professions—which the various professions have been formed to serve, and the way in which professional roles must be constructed in order to achieve those purposes. Of course, one only comes to have a professional role through voluntary action, but the morality that comes with that role is not itself ultimately grounded on the individual's choice.

Needs-Based Rights

In the previous section, I outlined the relationship between collective moral responsibility and, in particular, social institutions that have as their collective end the satisfaction of some need. In this section I elaborate on the notion of a need. Here I make use of the work of David Wiggins (1991).

Each member of a community has individual needs for food, water, shelter, and the like, and a derived set of needs-based human rights. However, it is only when a certain threshold of aggregate need (or, for example, aggregated rights violations) exists that the establishment of an institution takes place; agribusinesses or welfare institutions, for example, are not established because a single person's need for food has not been realized. As discussed above, when such a threshold of unmet aggregate need exists, there is a collective moral responsibility to engage in joint activity to fulfill the aggregate need in question. Accordingly, a cooperative enterprise is, or ought to be, embarked on that has as a collective end the provision of goods to the needy many by means of the joint activity of the participants in the enterprise; that is, an institution producing a collective good has been, or ought to be, established.

There is a threefold distinction to be made between the desired, the desirable, and the needed; something can be desired without being desirable, and desirable without being needed. Here I stress the importance of the distinction between needs and desires. As David Wiggins (1991) argues, needs are not simply a class of strong desires. If I desire to have *x* and *x* is *y*, then I do not necessarily desire to have *y*. Assume, for example, that *x* is a glass of water and *y* is a glass of H_2O, but I do not know that water is H_2O. Now consider needs. If I need *x* (water) and *x* is *y* (water is H_2O), then I need *y* (H_2O). Unlike *desire, need* is not an intentional verb, and, unlike desires, what I need depends on the way the world objectively is, as opposed to how I think it is (Wiggins, 1991, 6). As Wiggins also points out (9), categorical needs, such as for food, should not be confused with, and are not reducible to, mere instrumental needs: for example, I need two dollars (as a means to buying an ice cream). Merely instrumental needs are not categorical needs, nor are they in the service of categorical needs; rather, instrumental needs are simply the means to realize desires.

An important feature of a categorical need of a person is that it must be fulfilled, if harm to the person is to be avoided (Wiggins, 1991, 9). This noncontingent connection between needs and harms is in part reflective of the fact that many needs and, specifically, basic human needs, are relative to constitutive properties of human beings. Being the kind of organisms that we are, human beings need, for example, a flow of oxygen; indeed, we cannot survive without it. Importantly, human needs are relative to human well-being—relative, that is, not simply to human survival, but to human flourishing. This is not to say that any condition that contributes to human flourishing is a need. But it is to say that unless certain human needs are met—including some needs that are not strictly necessary for survival—humans cannot flourish; children, for example, need to be reared in a relatively safe and caring environment if they are not to suffer long-term psychological harm.

The noncontingent relation between needs and harms and, more specifically, the relativity of human needs to human flourishing implies that needs, or at least human needs, are ethico-normative in character (Wiggins, 1991, 11). Hence to fulfill someone's human need is *pro tanto* a good thing to do, and to deprive someone of their human need is *pro tanto* a bad thing to do. Indeed, under certain conditions human needs generate moral rights and correlative moral obligations. Whether or not a human need generates a moral right to the thing needed will depend on the extent of the harm suffered if the need is not fulfilled, the existence of someone who could meet the need and do so at little cost to him- or herself, and so on. Moreover, not all needs that morally ought to be fulfilled are such that the person or persons with the need have a moral right that it be fulfilled. In short, some categorical needs generate moral rights, but others do not. However, all categorical needs are such that they morally ought to be met, if this is possible and at a relatively small cost.

Needs are relative to circumstance (Wiggins, 1991, 11), albeit some needs, such as for water, are relative to unalterable or invariable circumstances, although this is not so in the case of other needs, such as the need for a dentist. Finally, some, but by no means all, needs generate moral rights and obligations. Suppose I have a need for food and water but am unable to provide for these needs of mine. If so, perhaps I have a right that you provide me with food and water, if you are able to do so at little cost to yourself. On the other hand, if I have a need for friendship, it does not follow that I have a right to your friendship, even supposing that you could provide it at little cost to yourself.

The Moral Foundations of Social Institutions

I have argued, in effect, that there is a collective moral responsibility to assist the one billion living in absolute poverty, and that this responsibility is a responsibility to establish and maintain appropriate social institutions that is grounded in the aggregate needs-based moral rights of the billion human beings in question. I now want to extend this account of the moral foundations of welfare institutions to enable it to apply to nonwelfare institutions. By doing so, I reveal the continuity that obtains between welfare institutions and other social institutions.

On my teleological account, social institutions exist to serve various collective ends that are also collective goods, such as needs (welfare institutions, agribusinesses, etc.), security (police services), the acquisition, transmission, and dissemination of knowledge (universities), etc. The extent to which actual institutions fail to serve these collective ends is the extent to which they are in need of redesign or renovation.

Elsewhere I have provided a detailed account of the general normative character of social institutions based on an individualist, teleological model, according to which social institutions have a multifaceted normative dimension with multiple sources (Miller, 2010, Chap. 2). These sources include ones that are logically prior to institutions, such as basic human needs and (institutionally prior) human rights, such as the rights to life, to freedom, and not to be tortured.

The normative character of social institutions includes the collective goods that they produce, the moral constraints on their activities, and a variety of *institutional* moral rights and duties (as opposed to moral rights and duties that are logically prior to institutions, that is, natural rights and duties). Such institutional moral rights and duties include ones that are derived from institutionally produced collective goods and, indeed, that are constitutive of specific institutional roles, such as the rights and duties of a welfare officer, fireman, doctor, or banker. They also include more broad-based institutional (moral) rights and duties that are dependent on community-wide institutional arrangements, such as the duty to obey the law in the jurisdiction in which one resides, the duty to assist the national defense effort of one's country in time of war, the right of access to paid employment in an economy in which one participates, the right to own land in some territory, and the right to freely buy and sell goods in an economy in which one participates.

These moral rights and duties are institutionally relative in the following sense. Even if they are in part based on an institutionally prior human right (e.g., a basic human need, the right to freedom), their precise content, stringency, context of application (jurisdiction, national territory, particular economy), and so on can be determined only by reference to the institutional arrangements in which they exist and, specifically, in the light of their contribution to the collective good(s) provided by those institutional arrangements.

On this account, collective ends are collective goods by virtue of their possession of the following three properties: one, they are produced, maintained, or renewed by means of the *joint activity* of members of organizations, for example, schools, hospitals, welfare organizations, agribusinesses, electricity providers, police services—that is, by institutional role occupants; two, they are *available to the whole community*, for example, clean drinking water, clean environment, basic foodstuffs, electricity, banking services, education, health, safety, and security; and three, they *ought* to be produced (or maintained or renewed) and made available to the whole community because they are desirable (as opposed to merely desired) and such that the members of the community have an *(institutional) joint moral right* to them.

Note that my notion of a collective good, as defined, is different from standard notions of so-called public goods deployed by economists[2] and others, for example, in respect of a good's being jointly produced and having an explicitly normative character as the object of a joint moral right.

More importantly, note that the communities in question are relative to the *context of application*. However the context of application is not necessarily the economy, jurisdiction, or territory bounded by the nation-state. It could, for example, be the global economy (in the case of trade or of capital markets) or the international community (in the case of international law).

Many, if not most, social institutions are in large part grounded in one or another of the following basic human needs, rights, or desirable (as opposed to merely desired) goods: food, water, and shelter (economic institutions that produce basic foodstuffs, medicines, houses, etc., and welfare institutions); the right to personal physical security (police organizations); the acquisition, transmission, and dissemination of knowledge and understanding (universities); the storage, retrieval, and communication of knowledge (institutions in part constituted by information and communication technology); and the organization, maintenance, and direction of other institutions (government).

On my teleological, normative account (roughly speaking) the university has as its fundamental collective end the acquisition, transmission, and dissemination of knowledge, whereas police organizations have as their fundamental collective end the protection of the human and other moral rights (including institutional moral rights) of members of the community. Again, the traditional professions have a range of specific collective ends, for example, the administration of justice (lawyers). The collective end of each of these institutions is a collective good: a jointly produced good that is, and ought to be, produced and made available to the whole community because it is a desirable good and one to which the members of the community have a joint moral right.

By contrast with these social institutions, business corporations and markets in general do not have ethico-normative purposes (collective goods, in the above sense) that are *internal* to them. Rather they should be understood in instrumentalist terms, for example, as an institutional means for the production of desired (but not necessarily desirable) goods. Accordingly, a business organization in a competitive market is not deficient *qua* institution merely because it produces candy rather than basic foodstuffs; obviously, many business organizations operating in competitive markets produce material goods and services that are desired but not needed, or otherwise desirable—and they should continue to do so. Nevertheless, there are moral and other value-driven purposes that should give direction to the design and operation of at least some markets and business organizations. Specifically, there are collective goods, for instance, aggregated needs-based rights to basic foodstuffs, clean water, clean air, clothing, housing, medicines, that markets and business organizations ought to produce as a matter of priority.

In addition, business organizations operating in competitive markets—including organizations that produce only desired (as opposed to desirable) goods—provide jobs; in doing so they fulfill a moral right, namely, the right to paid work. In contemporary societies there is a (derived) moral right (and corresponding moral obligation) to work for a wage—that is, a right to a job (some job or other)—because (other things being equal) without a job one cannot provide for one's basic needs and one cannot contribute to the production, maintenance, and renewal of collective goods, such as via taxes. In short, although business organizations in competitive markets per se do not serve inherently valuable collective ends that are internal to them, they do have enormous instrumental value. Accordingly, they are available to serve value-driven, including moral, purposes and should be made to do so by way of regulation, incentive structures, and the like, as required.

Duty to Aid or Duty Not to Harm?

Thomas Pogge has sought to reframe the moral problem of global poverty as it has been presented by Singer and others. Pogge (2008) has argued, in effect, that our obligations (duties, in his terminology)—the collective obligations of the governments and citizens of the world's rich countries—to the world's poorest are not principally positive obligations to assist, but rather negative obligations not to harm. He holds that we in the rich countries are violating our negative obligations not to harm, and that if we desisted from these violations, then the plight of the world's poorest would be substantially eliminated (26).

Elsewhere (Miller, 2010, Chap. 7) I have discussed Pogge's empirical claim and found it to be overstated. (This is not to say that there is not a considerable degree of truth in it, for example, when Western governments support the corrupt dictators of resource-rich African countries who are lining their own pockets by stealing from their own citizens.) Accordingly, in my view the problem of world poverty should neither be framed exclusively as a duty to aid—and, therefore, as a positive rights issue (Singer's account)—nor as a massive negative rights violation (Pogge's account). Both moral perspectives on the problem are legitimate, but each is only partially correct.

Moreover, there is a degree of conceptual unclarity surrounding the notions of positive and negative rights in play here; this affects the truth/falsity of the empirical claim by virtue of the unclarity that now attaches to the meaning of that claim. It is this issue that I want to consider in what remains of this article.

Firstly, it is often assumed that negative rights violations are especially egregious rights violations, whereas this is not the case with positive rights violations. Moreover, this difference in stringency is indicated by the fact that in general respect for negative rights, but not positive rights, is justifiably enforced. However, this strong contrast is unwarranted. For negative rights are not necessarily justifiably enforceable, and some positive rights are justifiably enforceable. If, to use a variation on one of Pogge's examples, you promise to water my potted plant while I am on holidays but fail to do so, you have violated my negative right not to be harmed by the making of false promises. But this is a violation of a relatively trivial right. It would be absurd to equate this violation with, for example, failing to assist the drowning child, to return to Peter Singer's example; and the idea that you should be charged with the offense of, say, harmful breach of a potted plant promise and locked up, or otherwise suffer the coercive imposition of some punishment or compensation, is likewise absurd. On the other hand, it is far from absurd to enforce many positive rights; indeed, the imposition of legally enforceable taxes to pay (in part) for welfare is a well-established enforcement of a positive right.

In relation to certain institutional moral rights and concomitant duties in particular, it is far from clear that positive rights have less moral strength than negative ones. Elsewhere (Miller, 2007), I have argued that certain positive rights, such as human rights to basic food or medicines, once institutionalized, generate *justifiably enforceable* institutional moral rights. Thus if a corrupt government is refusing to provide available medicines to its disease-afflicted, dying citizens, then, other things being equal, the latter may well be justified in using force to appropriate the needed medicines, if there are no nonviolent options available.

It might be suggested that such institutionalized moral rights are in reality negative rights. But this is not so. The suggestion, for example, that the harm consequent on a failure to keep a promise is an infringement of a negative right because the promisor has created an expectation that the promised action will be performed is not relevant here. For as we saw above, institutional duties are not based on promises or expectations; rather, they are based on collective moral responsibilities that are, in the types of case in question, in turn based on aggregated needs-based rights, that is, positive human rights.

Above I suggested that the moral problem of world poverty should not be framed exclusively in terms of a duty to aid or an obligation to refrain from negative rights violations, although both perspectives are partially correct. In closing I want to suggest a third—and additional—perspective.

Recall that by my lights the collective moral responsibilities that underpin social institutions are relativized to what I referred to as contexts of application. Importantly, contexts of application are not necessarily economies, jurisdictions, or territories bounded by, and defined in terms of, the nation-state. Rather, the limits of contexts of application are typically drawn largely on the basis of the extent and density of the web of economic, political, or communicative, etc. interaction and interdependence between the participants in question. Thus in the case of the ongoing, intensive, and extensive economic relations between large corporations, including international banks, the context of application is now the global economy. The Global Financial Crisis has underscored this point in a quite dramatic fashion. Again, the web of international political interaction and interdependence has global rather than merely national or bilateral or even regional boundaries, and hence the international community of nation-states comprises the context of application of much international policymaking and associated law-making (notably, in the case of the increasing amount of international law). The recent UN climate change negotiations have underscored this point, as no doubt will future climate negotiations.

The point to be extracted from this is that the nation-state (and its sub-elements) is no longer necessarily always the most appropriate unit for the purpose of determining the limits of collective responsibilities and, thereby, the reach of the social institutions established on the basis of those responsibilities. To be sure the citizens of a given nation-state have a collective responsibility to provide for the needs of all their own citizenry and, therefore, to establish economic and other institutions that enable these needs to be provided for. However, the extent and density of economic interaction and interdependence between citizens of diverse nation-states is now such that the participants have collective responsibilities to participants who are not necessarily members of their own nation-states and, as a consequence, to establish or, more likely, redesign and reshape global institutions to address the needs of those participants and, in particular, of the billion living in absolute poverty. This is not really aid, at least as it is conventionally understood. Nor is it necessarily desisting from harming others, at least in any straightforward sense. Rather it is reshaping global institutions so that *all* participants cooperate and, where appropriate, compete in accordance with laws, rules, and norms that respect rights, fairness, etc. and in a manner that ensures that the collective goods that are the raison d'être for these institutions are in fact provided to those that have a joint right to them: *all* participants.

Notes

1. Much of the material in this section and in the last three sections constitutes an abridged version of parts of Miller (2010, Chap. 7).

2. Economists typically define public goods as being nonrival and nonexcludable. If a good is nonrival, then my enjoyment of it does not prevent or diminish the possibility of your enjoyment of it; for example, a street sign is nonrival because my using it to find my way has no effect on your likewise using it. Again, a good is nonexcludable if it is such that if anyone is enjoying the good, then no one can be prevented from enjoying it, for instance, national defense.

References

Alexandra, Andrew, and Seumas Miller. (2009). "Ethical Theory, 'Common Morality' and Professional Obligations." *Theoretical Medicine and Bioethics 30*(1): 69–80.

Cullity, Garrett. (2004). *The Moral Demands of Affluence.* Oxford: Oxford University Press.

Griffin, James. (2008). *On Human Rights.* Oxford: Oxford University Press.

Miller, Seumas. (2006). "Collective Moral Responsibility: An Individualist Account" in *Midwest Studies in Philosophy* vol. XXX, ed. Peter A. French: 176–193.

Miller, Seumas. (2007). "Civilian Immunity, Forcing the Choice and Collective Responsibility" in *Civilian Immunity*, ed. Igor Primoratz: 137–166. Oxford: Oxford University Press.

Miller, Seumas. (2010). *The Moral Foundations of Social Institutions.* New York: Cambridge University Press.

Pogge, Thomas. (2008). *World Poverty and Human Rights, Second Edition.* Cambridge: Polity Press.

Shue, Henry. (1996). *Basic Rights, Second Edition.* Princeton: Princeton University Press.

Singer, Peter. (1972). "Famine, Affluence and Morality." *Philosophy and Public Affairs 1*: 229–243.

Singer, Peter. (2007). *The 2007 Uehiro Lectures* (unpublished). Oxford: Oxford University.

Wiggins, David. (1991). "Claims of Need" in *Needs, Values, Truth: Essays in the Philosophy of Value, Second Edition*, ed. David Wiggins. Oxford: Blackwell.

CHAPTER EIGHT

Building Wealth with Conditional Cash Transfers

MICHAEL BOYLAN
Marymount University

Abstract

This chapter first examines the role of wealth within the context of a progressive theory of deserts. It then offers a policy suggestion for building wealth among the poor in any nation that can afford the conditional cash transfers. The driving force of the policy rests upon conditional cash transfers that give money to its citizens tied to performance measures such as education, community service (including military service), and good choices in life. It is suggested that this approach can stimulate economic mobility within countries that can afford such measures.

Key Words

conditional cash transfer, baby bonds, wealth acquisition, economic mobility, poverty

---

It is an aspirational dream among most people on earth—especially among the poor—that they might be touched by a miracle that would transform their miserable plight into an opportunity to work in a job that has a brighter future. Such a destiny might elevate the individual to a higher economic plane whereby his or her basic needs *and more* might be satisfied. This narrative drives the imaginations of many. For example, in the United States it is called the American Dream. One part of the American Dream is to be able to move up economically in one generation in order to be able to attain a fair share of the tremendous affluence that is the United States in the twenty-first century. However, for the most part, the facts do not match the dream—even in the richest country on earth! Economic mobility, the movement upward or downward between classes (measured here in quartiles), is a complicated dynamic to understand. There are many competing antecedents that may contribute to why any given individual rises or falls economically in his or her lifetime. One of the most important factors in this may be called individual deserts. Let's take a moment to explore how we deserve anything.

Progressive Desert Theory

Some would contend that any individual deserves some outcome *x* whenever he or she performs the actions that are functionally related to the acquisition of *x*. This may be called the *pure outcomes* perspective. Those who fail to achieve the established norms, as such, do not deserve the outcome reward. For example, individuals who do not make college admission, professional school admission, or hiring in desirable jobs do not merit it (on the pure outcomes model). They are losers in the competition of life. They *deserve* to fail. Those promoting this position often say that merit[1] must be based upon past actions and not upon some sort of social, utopian goal. Who do you want holding the scalpel (in the case of medical school admissions)—a person whose actions have shown his excellence or some other individual that acquired her position based upon some sort of legalistic quota? For simplicity's sake, let us label this pure outcomes position as merit$_1$ (m$_1$).

Proponents of progressive desert-based criteria agree that merit should be based upon past actions. However, how are these past actions measured? M$_1$ asserts that they are interested in outcomes achieved: actual work performed to judge an individual's merit. However, it seems to some advocating the progressive position that this is not the case. Really what m$_1$ wants to assert is that some sort of outcomes positioning on the majority population's grid marks work performed. This is not necessarily indicative of merit.

In order to explain this, let us examine the argument via the model of the puzzle-maker.[2] In this thought experiment, any given period of life (a subcategory of life—such as preparing for one's life profession as an orthopedic surgeon—or the whole of one's life) can be thought of as putting together a puzzle. Now anyone who has worked at puzzle-making knows the early stages of puzzle creation are the hardest. One has to assemble the border and then organize the thematic and color combinations in a general, holistic fashion. This is very time consuming. Most aspiring puzzle-makers fail during this stage.

As one progresses in the puzzle-making process, things become easier. The final 10 percent is really a breeze. Now, what if life were really like puzzle-making?[3] Some people enter life with very little if any of the puzzle completed for them. In these situations, most fail. Others are given a 40 percent, 60 percent, or even an 80 percent completed puzzle. This dynamic means that those individuals must only complete the rest (the easy part). Now, let us try to compare two individuals at the extremes. Person A was given only 10 percent of her puzzle at birth and when she finished high school she had completed 50 percent of the puzzle (the hardest part). She is up against Person B, who was given an 80 percent completed puzzle at birth (via various advantages that accrue from family wealth, tutors, freedom from having to work an extra job to help support the family, high-priced lawyers should the child become involved in a compromising situation, etc.). B had a calm and supportive domestic life, two hard-working, supportive parents, comfortable income, and a biological makeup that was free from chemical imbalanced mental afflictions. With so much oversight and environmental and natural advantages, it's no wonder that B went from 80 percent to 87.5 percent in his precollege years. However, when evaluating the two candidates, which one really *did* more?

FIGURE 8.1. Merit Measured by the Puzzle-Making Thought Experiment

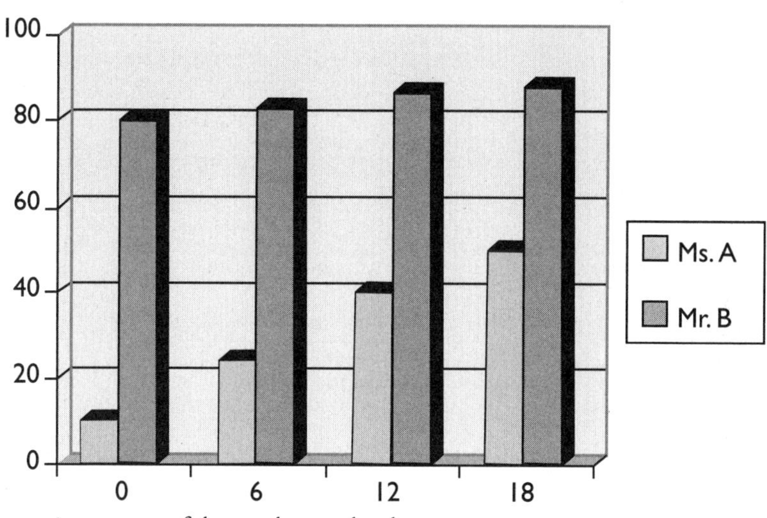

y axis = percent of the puzzle completed
x axis = age of Ms. A and Mr. B

Looking at Figure 8.1, the m_1 group would say Mr. B did more based upon functional outcomes achieved. They would point to the differential between 50 percent and 87.5 percent on society's grid. However, this author would demur; broadly construed, Ms. A has demonstrated greater merit because she went from

10 percent to 50 percent. This indicates that by her own actions alone she accomplished 40 percent—the hardest part of the puzzle. Whereas B, by his own actions, only achieved 7.5 percent (a rather easier part of the puzzle).

Obviously, this is a case at the extremes. However, it is put forth to make an abstract point about merit. Some people have natural advantages of environment and family wealth that can include some or all of the following when it comes to the ability to enter a college, professional school, or profession:

- Adequate food, clothing, shelter, and protection from unwarranted bodily harm
- Basic educational opportunity
- Being treated with dignity and love for who you are
- A nurturing home environment
- Parental models for patterning behavior (that the society views positively)
- Freedom from disabling disease whether it be mental or physical
- Inside connections affecting admission to universities and to the professions
- Affluence (family income)
- Family wealth

Obviously, this list could go on and on. But when Mr. B speaks with hubris about how he has become a partner in the accounting firm, it may be important to know that Mr. B's father is the senior partner in the firm and got B his job in the first place (and has been holding B's hand all his life). This is the life of preferment that allows parents to present to their children, ceteris paribus, a puzzle that is 80 percent complete. All the child has to do is not screw up too badly and he's set for life.

This preferment list need not merely include socioeconomic factors. Race and gender are also factors. For example, in a profession that is not representative of society's diversity, one will (by definition) find an overrepresentation of the majority power group. Let it be assumed that this overrepresented group is comprised of white males. And let it further be assumed that unreflective members of that group, without actual malice, simply imagine that the typical member of said profession is a white male. In this case, a clique is created that seeks its own continuation (as all cliques do). Thus, the practitioners of the profession put up barriers that create "old boys club" expectations that have the effect of excluding all others outside of that model. If such assumptions are correct, then on the puzzle-maker example, being a white male (in the United States) seeking to enter that profession is to possess (whether one seeks it or not) a preferment: a significant part of the puzzle completed for him. It is the position of this essay to claim that this is *not* success by merit; it is success by unmerited preferment.

The progressive deserts model (m_2) assumes a more complicated description of deserving *x*. It assumes that the graph extension in Figure 8.1 will most probably (in time) show Ms. A surpassing Mr. B, ceteris paribus. However, all things are never equal. Continued preferment over time occurs through the vehicle of wealth. It will be the assumption of this essay that social wealth analysis supports policies to stimulate supportive advancement conditions in lower economic quartiles, and that *wealth* will do more for allowing merited economic mobility than policies aimed at income creation alone.

Why Wealth?

Positive economic mobility occurs when people move upward in their ability to obtain the goods that are necessary and desirable to actualize one's vision of the good. I set these goods out in a hierarchical order that I've termed the *Table of Embeddedness.* 'Embeddedness' refers to how necessary a good is to committing action. I argue that purposive action toward one's vision of the good is what is most primary about being human and thus incurs a general duty against the society to provide as many of the basic goods as possible (subject to a society's ability to provide such goods).[4]

The goal in poverty reduction is to provide first level-one basic goods to everyone in every society and then to proceed from there. The perfect end-state would be when every person has all basic goods and level-one secondary goods (the acquisition of level-two and level-three secondary goods is up to each individual given the possession of the more embedded goods of agency).

What gets in the way of people realizing this goal? The complete answer is probably beyond us all. But one way to think of this is to make the lowest economic quartile of society comfortable (meaning that they have at least the basic goods and possibly all the level-one secondary goods). When this point is reached, the mission is accomplished. But how do we get there?

It is still an open question about how to encourage economic mobility. A study by the Brookings Institution that focuses upon the United States suggests a number of possible factors such as intergenerational connection, race, gender, education, immigration, and wealth (Isaacs, Sawhill, and Haskins, 2008). These are not all separate, insular causes. A recent paper at the Center for American Progress discusses wealth in relation to many of these other factors (particularly race) with an aim to show how important wealth can be (Conley and Glauber, 2008). These studies follow within a tradition that has been examining economic mobility over the past several years. On the one hand, there are studies that show the importance of setting some conditions on the allocation of resources in order to change behavior. These are called conditional cash transfers and have proven very effective in

TABLE 8.1. Table of Embeddedness

Basic Goods

Level One: *Most Deeply Embedded* (that which is absolutely necessary for human action):

- Food, clean water, sanitation, clothing, shelter, protection from unwarranted bodily harm (including basic health care)

Level Two: *Deeply Embedded* (that which is necessary for effective basic action within any given society):

- Literacy in the language of the country
- Basic mathematical skills
- Other fundamental skills necessary to be an effective agent in that country (in the United States, some computer literacy is necessary)
- Some familiarity with the culture and history of the country in which one lives
- The assurance that those one interacts with are not lying to promote their own interests
- The assurance that those one interacts with will recognize one's human dignity (as per above) and not exploit one as a means only
- Basic human rights such as those listed in the U.S. Bill of Rights and the United Nations Universal Declaration of Human Rights

Secondary Goods

Level One: *Life Enhancing*: Medium to High-Medium on Embeddedness

- Basic societal respect
- Equal opportunity to compete for the prudential goods of society
- Ability to pursue a life plan according to the personal worldview imperative

(continues)

TABLE 8.1. Table of Embeddedness *(continued)*

Level Two: *Useful*: Medium to Low-Medium Embeddedness

- Ability to utilize one's real and portable property in the manner she chooses
- Ability to gain from and exploit the consequences of one's labor regardless of starting point
- Ability to pursue goods that are generally owned by most citizens (in the United States today, a telephone, television, and automobile would fit into this class)

Level Three: *Luxurious*: Low Embeddedness

- Ability to pursue goods that are pleasant even though they are far removed from action and from the expectations of most citizens within a given country (in the United States today, a European vacation would fit into this class)
- Ability to exert one's will so that she might extract a disproportionate share of society's resources for her own use

NOTE: *Embedded* in this context means the relative fundamental nature of the good for action. A more deeply embedded good is one that is more primary to action.

Mexico, Brazil, and other developing countries (Cuesta, 2007; Das et al., 2005; Janvry and Sandoulet, 2006; O'Brien, 2007). On the other hand, some of these same studies show that even without conditions some real benefits result. The disparity of wealth is well documented (Kerwin and Hurst, 2003; Keister and Deeb-Sosa, 2001). Others indicate incremental wealth enhancement—albeit at a very slow pace (Carasso et al., 2008; Sawhill and Morton, 2007) but status quo wealth enhancement is not nearly enough. This is because the governmental initiatives have favored some and slighted others—such as women and African Americans in the United States (Conley and Glauber, 2008). Also, it is often the case around the world (and even in some cases in the United States) that (when possible) the wealthy often deny basic goods, such as clean water, to the poor—even when it doesn't affect their own interests (Boylan, 2008a).

In the midst of these studies, we need a fresh perspective. Let's start at the beginning. So what is wealth and how might it function to facilitate economic mobility? First of all, let's define wealth as *liquid assets that are held in reserve for important situations in life—such as overcoming an emergency (health or any other unexpected life event), starting a business, continuing one's education, and buying a house.*[5] Having access to wealth can be critical to one's ability to move up in income and one's ability to obtain the basic goods of agency (along with level-one secondary goods). The possession of these goods goes a long way to enabling the individual to lead a happy and productive life—they are necessary but not sufficient to this end.[6] It is certainly possible that a person might possess all the necessary goods of agency but yet fail to use them effectively to achieve his or her goals. And on the flip side, there will always be (*pace* W. E. B. Du Bois, 1903) a group of people who are able to achieve their goals despite their lacking many essential goods of agency. However, when we deal with large statistical groups, we must set our policy sights on what will work (for the most part). It will be the assumption of this essay that the widespread creation of wealth will do just that.

Let us be perfectly clear what our objectives are. They are not to eliminate the lower statistical categories of wage earners. Obviously there will always be people in all the four quartiles. This is just a statistical sorting device. What is important is that within all those categories people are provided with an acceptable floor of goods for agency that will allow them the opportunity to take their best shot at completing as much of the puzzle of life as possible.

Let me end this section with two anecdotes that are illustrative of the importance that access to wealth can give. In the first example, there was a man I knew who was a medic in Vietnam. Let's call him Jon (not his real name). He longed to be a physician. He used a much weaker Vietnam GI Education Bill (compared to the World War II bill) to attend an excellent community college and took courses that might transfer to a four-year institution and prepare him for medical school. He got more As than Bs. He was accepted to the University of Maryland. Then the snag occurred. His father was dying and had medical bills that exceeded the bare-bones medical plan his employer provided (a plumbing contractor). Jon had to take two jobs so that his father could get cancer treatment. It dragged on for three years. His father died. Jon got married. He ditched one job (delivering the *Washington Post*) and concentrated on the more lucrative job of selling insurance to the poverty community—often called "debit insurance." I don't know if Jon could have cut it to become a physician (his life dream). But I do know that had he had a personal wealth account, he would have been able to give it a decent shot (due to its covering specified life emergencies and additional schooling).

The second case I want to cite is a poor second-generation legal immigrant family living in the United States (Maryland). The family lived in the same apartment building that my research assistant lives in. My research assistant told me that the family (a Latino household where both parents worked full-time at jobs at or below the minimum wage) was required in their rental lease to maintain utilities—stove and refrigerator—at the current level or replace them upon system failure beyond repair. When the refrigerator stopped working in the summer of 2008, they could not afford the nine hundred dollars to buy a new one (it could not be repaired). They couldn't afford it. This meant that the family of working parents had to go out on the street. This wouldn't have happened if my policy of personal wealth accounts had been in effect.[7]

These two anecdotes from my personal experience are illustrative of how having a personal wealth fund can make a positive difference in peoples' lives. Whether it be for approved emergencies, continuing education, starting a business, or buying a house, a personal wealth fund can be crucial in realizing one's personal goals and aspirations.

Personal Wealth Funds

The policy proposal that this essay recommends is the establishment of personal wealth funds in all the countries of the world that can afford them. These funds have as their aim the creation of individual wealth accounts to facilitate upward mobility by providing a small measure of wealth to all sectors of society. With this assurance, the model of merit (m_2) will reward personal initiative and hard work by offering a small measure of financial backup to those who are generally left without any significant level of personal financial support. It would move the Ms. As of this world from a 10 percent starting point to something closer to 25 percent. This difference can be pivotal.

Because most of my readers (I assume) are from wealthier countries, I will sketch out the details of this plan as if it were set in the United States. If the proposed policy seems plausible here, then it is my conjecture that it will be equally applicable to all other countries that can afford conditional cash transfers.

A few key points are necessary to understand the intent of conditional cash transfers. First, it is inefficient to pay people for what they already do in their economic class. For example, in the United States (and probably in most countries), the highest economic class graduates their children from high school (secondary education) in high numbers. Thus, it is not efficient or fair to pay them to do what they are already doing. Second, all benchmarks have some availability to all on the basis of a direct grant to the personal wealth fund or as a tax deduction (for those who are already performing in this positive social manner). Third, unlike other plans of this sort, these funds are not intended to pay for undergraduate college expenses. These should be funded separately. The funds in this program are there for the long term and cannot be touched before age twenty-five.

Now, let me present the outline of the plan, followed by its costs and its anticipated effects.

An Outline of the Plan (As Activated in the US)

1. At birth every child who is a US citizen in the lower three quartiles of income (as measured by tax returns) will receive $5,000 to be deposited in a special account keyed to their social security number. (It will occur automatically when the social security number is assigned at birth.) The highest quartile will be given the opportunity to make a tax-deductible contribution on behalf of their child into the same fund (roughly costing the government $1,300).[8] Let this account be titled *the personal wealth fund.*
2. The account of deposit will be in the Federal Government's F fund (established for government employees' retirement: 6.01 percent ten-year average with almost no downside potential).[9] Funds deposited grow on a tax-free basis and at their historic average will double every twelve years.
3. Upon successful graduation from high school, the lower two quartiles will receive $1,000 as a deposit in their personal wealth fund.[10] The upper two quartiles will receive a tax deduction for $1,000 if their parents or a relative wishes to make a deposit into their personal wealth fund.
4. Upon successful completion of two years of college (sixty semester credits) at either a community or a four-year college, each student's personal wealth fund will be increased by $2,000 (all quartiles).
5. Upon successful completion of a year of national service (defined by Congress), each individual will receive $4,000 per year as a deposit in his or her personal wealth fund (a maximum of two years)—all quartiles.
6. Upon attaining the age of twenty-five, an individual may make withdrawals from his or her personal wealth fund for specified purposes—such as starting a business, buying a house, continuing schooling, or overcoming an emergency (health or any other unexpected life event).[11] Unused monies will continue to accrue tax-free and may be used as supplemental retirement income according to ERISA guidelines (57.5 as the earliest withdrawal date and 70 as the latest date to start).

What This Plan Will Do

As mentioned above, in the context of the puzzle-maker thought experiment, the earlier parts of puzzle creation are the hardest. There are many times where one might be tempted to quit the struggle to succeed in one's society because of significant challenges. Knowing that one has a wealth fund awaiting oneself at age twenty-five will be a strong incentive to meet those challenges and to prevail. The added bonuses will act as conditional cash transfers that have proven effective in influencing conduct (Cuesta, 2007; Das et al., 2005; Janvry and Sandoulet, 2006; O'Brien, 2007). It will also engender a connectedness to the society that created the fund in the first place and instill a sensibility to the common good—so lacking in these past decades of libertarian individualism and rampant greed.

The expectation will be made clear that participants should use this money to actualize themselves according to their highest aspirations. This will help the individual and the society. And because it clearly recognizes the positive role of the community in their lives, we will no longer be espousing a rhetoric that "government is bad" or "taxation is robbing individuals of what they garnered all by themselves" or that "giving a helping hand is abhorrent to all who worship freedom." This program can revolutionize and revitalize the progressive spirit of a nation. This will reinvigorate the common body of knowledge and the shared community worldview away from fragmented cultural wars to common purposes so important in national personal and economic development (Boylan, 2004, Chapter 5).

Last, the personal wealth fund initiative will be a step toward offering real meritocracy—the rewarding of individuals in society for what they do and accomplish themselves without preferment (Boylan, 2007). This will offer hope and opportunity to those who currently see ever-widening gaps between the "haves and the have-nots."

Costs of the Plan

Using the current figures of people residing in the various economic quartiles in the United States (our sample exemplar), the baby bond component will cost around $12 billion (see appendix). The extra incentives will cost around $7.7 billion (delayed eighteen years if the *initialization model* is chosen and immediately if the *youth population model* is chosen).[12] It is this author's conjecture the latter model would work best.

This initial outlay of money has projected human capital investment offsets. This will be greatest in the baby bond generation. That fruition will take around twenty-five years—much like the payoff of the initial World War II GI Bill in the United States that cost $50 billion in inflation-adjusted dollars and netted the economy $350 billion in increased economic growth due to greater tax revenue (because of better jobs) and greater consumer consumption (Humes, 2006). This is a seven-fold return on investment. I have assumed a rather more modest human capital return in my model based upon, one, the value of education in job earnings (that pays off through consumer spending and higher tax revenues); and two, the value of community service (that pays off through more efficient social programs which conditional cash transfers engender). My estimate using these criteria is that we will receive a 150 percent return on investment in inflation-adjusted dollars in twenty-five years. The break-even point will be about twenty years for the initialization method and fifteen years if the youth population model is chosen. Thus, the program will be self-sustaining within a short time period. The human capital investment makes financial as well as humanitarian sense.

If this approach were to become widespread around the world, it is this author's conjecture that *wealth* would constitute a key component in stimulating economic mobility. Income alone is not enough. To be able to transition to higher economic levels, one needs a backup for emergencies and a stake to go forward. Since the society benefits from such a human capital investment, they should do so on strictly prudential motives. But because this plan also is morally justified on the basis of progressive deserts, it is not an optional strategy for the reduction of poverty through the opportunity of economic mobility but an obligation for all societies that can afford to implement it (ought implies can).

Other Versions of the Plan

The plan outlined above is tailored for the United States. However, as cited earlier, conditional cash transfers have been tried all over the world with varying degrees of success. Obviously a country would be constrained by an *ought implies can* caveat. Many countries are so poor that they cannot implement basic services much less create a wealth fund. For these countries, I would suggest a more modest version of the personal wealth fund (perhaps a turnkey version could be established by the United Nations through the International Monetary Fund). In order to fill the gap of areas with corrupt regimes, I would suggest that the funds be held in sovereign banks outside of those countries. Various mechanisms exist for this via the boom phenomenon of micro-lending. Thus, avenues exist already to insure that funds aren't stolen from the poor. All that is necessary is access to a cell phone—available at the writing of this essay to two-thirds of the world directly and over 80 percent indirectly.

Conclusion

This essay has argued for the pivotal role of wealth in the promotion of economic mobility and the economic betterment of lower quartile individuals (as measured by the Table of Embeddedness). The policy that is advocated to this end in the sample case of the United States is the creation of a personal wealth initiative that will transfer wealth to individuals at birth and make further conditional inputs dependent upon the completion of certain benchmarks: finishing high school, finishing two years of college, and completing one or two years of national service (other benchmarks may be set for different countries according to the shared community worldview of that country). These payments are also conditional vis-à-vis what they may be used for: starting a business, buying a house, continuing schooling, or overcoming an emergency (health or any other specified unexpected life event). Since conditional cash transfers are more successful than unconditional cash transfers, it is the conjecture of this writer that the personal wealth fund initiative will do much toward meeting its projected goals. Some may contend that in difficult economic times such expenditure is uncalled for or impossible. But it is this writer's opinion that it is precisely in difficult times that such targeted human capital investments will best aid the society toward economic resurgence (along with its stated social justice aims). This is a progressive program, needed for every country in the world to implement within their political system to assist their own citizens as soon as possible according to their means. One might imagine, if these programs are successful, that the International Monetary Fund might assist countries with fewer resources so that they, too, might be able to fuel a powerful flame that could shine as a beacon to those around the world who seek the reduction of poverty everywhere through economic mobility.

Appendix: Calculation Assumptions for the United States (Sample Group)

A. Ten-year mean numbers of births per quartile of income (source: US Census Bureau—rounded to the nearest thousand).
   Lowest ($0–19,999): 833,000
   Second Lowest ($20,000–$29,999): 559,000
   Second Highest ($30,000–$49,000): 799,000
   Highest ($50,000+): 1,4003,000
B. Ten-year mean population extended for both the *youth population model* and the *initialization model* for numbers expecting benefits for high school, college, and national service.
C. Percentage assumption for utilization of the high school graduation benefit (lower two quartiles) = 85 percent
D. Percentage assumption for utilization of the two-year college benefit (all quartiles) = 50 percent
E. Percentage assumption for utilization of national service benefit (all quartiles): One year = 25 percent; Two years = 12.5 percent
F. Human capital appreciation in twenty-five years (the first year that funds are available to recipients) = 150 percent (less than the 700 percent thirty-year return on the WWII GI Bill). Figure is based upon higher high school graduation rates and a greater number completing

two years of college. These lead to better jobs that contribute to consumer spending and contribute more in taxes. The national service leads an intangible stability and citizenship component that will lead to more successful adults.

Notes

1. The reader should note that "merit" (often referred to in the literature of philosophy as "deserts") refers to a theory of what agents can justifiably claim on the basis of their achievements; a further expansion of this argument can be found in Michael Boylan (2004, Chap. 7).

2. By "puzzle-maker" we mean the person who puts a puzzle together, not one who manufactures it.

3. Often this discussion is based upon a racing track metaphor. The problem with this metaphorical model is that it is one-dimensional. It is this author's conjecture that deserts is more complicated than that—thus the multidimensional puzzle-maker model (Boylan, 2004, Chap. 7).

4. My argument for this comes from Boylan (2004, 15–16):

   1. Before anything else, all people desire to act in order to be good—Fact
   2. Whatever all people desire before anything else is natural to that species—Fact
   3. Desiring to act is natural to *homo sapiens*—1, 2
   4. People value what is natural to them—Assertion
   5. What people value they wish to protect—Assertion
   6. All people wish to protect their ability to act beyond all else—1, 3, 4, 5
   7. The strongest interpersonal "oughts" are expressed via our highest value systems: religion, morality, and aesthetics—Assertion
   8. All people must agree, upon pain of logical contradiction, that what is natural and desirable to them individually is natural and desirable to everyone collectively and individually—Assertion
   9. Everyone must seek personal protection for her own ability to act via religion, morality, and/or aesthetics—6, 7
   10. Everyone upon pain of logical contradiction must admit that all other humans will seek personal protection of their ability to act via religion, morality, and/or aesthetics—8, 9
   11. All people must agree, upon pain of logical contradiction, that because the attribution of the Basic Goods of agency are predicated generally, it is inconsistent to assert idiosyncratic preferences—Fact
   12. Goods that are claimed through generic predication apply equally to each agent and everyone has a stake in their protection—10, 11
   13. Rights and duties are correlative—Assertion

14. Everyone has at least a moral right to the Basic Goods of Agency and others in the society have a duty to provide those goods to all—12, 13

5. There may be others, but this essay will focus upon these categories as pivotal.

6. Personal self-fulfillment is obviously a nuanced topic. For a discussion of some of the key issues involved in self-fulfillment in the context of the goods of agency, see Boylan (2008b, Part 3).

7. Of course, we need to have an administrative layer to decide what constitutes an "emergency." For example, an emergency to someone at the verge of poverty will not be an emergency to someone else. The discretion of this can be folded into our existing welfare system.

8. I will guess that 50 percent of people will take advantage of this opportunity in the upper quartile. Lower participation rates will make the total cost lower.

9. Source: http://www.tsp.gov/rates/monthly-history.html

10. The reason for limiting this to the lower two quartiles is that the upper two quartiles already have high graduation rates. Paying for something that that group will already perform without the program is inefficient. This is connected to the conditional cash transfer concept.

11. In order for this to be practical, there needs to be a listing of acceptable family emergencies and an appeal process for those events that seem to fall between the cracks.

12. In the initialization model we choose a starting time—say 2010. Everyone born then and afterward would benefit. If the youth population model is chosen, then we begin with the entire under-twenty-one population but without the initial baby bond. Thus, they would be eligible for high school, college, and national service stipends.

References

Boylan, Michael. (2004). *A Just Society*. Lanham, MD: Rowman and Littlefield.

Boylan, Michael. (2007). "Meritocracy" in *Encyclopedia of Business, Ethics, and Society*, ed. Robert W. Kolb. Thousand Oaks, CA: Sage.

Boylan, Michael. (2008a). "Clean Water" in *International Public Health Policy and Ethics*, ed. Michael Boylan: 273–288. Dordrecht: Springer.

Boylan, Michael. (2008b). *The Good, the True, and the Beautiful*. London: Continuum.

Carasso, Adam, Gillian Reynolds, and C. Eugene Steurle. (2008). "How Much Does the Federal Government Spend to Promote Economic Mobility and for Whom?" The Economic Mobility Project, The Pew Charitable Trusts.

Conley, Dalton, and Rebecca Glauber. (2008). "Wealth Mobility and the Volatility in Black and White." Washington, DC: The Center for American Progress.

Cuesta, José. (2007). "Field Report on More Ambitious Conditional Cash Transfers, Social Protection and Permanent Reduction of Poverty." *Journal of International Development 19*: 1016–1019.

Das, Jishnu, Quy-Toan Do, and Berk Ozler. (2005). "Reassessing Conditional Cash Transfer Programs." *The World Bank Research Observer 20*(1): 57–80.

Du Bois, W. E. B. (1903). *The Souls of Black Folk.* New York: Blue Heron.

Humes, Edward. (2006). *Over Here.* New York: Harcourt.

Isaacs, Julia, Isabel V. Sawhill, and Ron Haskins. (2008). *Getting Ahead or Losing Ground: Economic Mobility in America.* Washington, DC: Brookings Institution.

de Janvry, Alain, and Elisabeth Sandoulet. (2006). "Making Conditional Cash Transfer Programs More Efficient: Designing for Maximum Effect of the Conditionality." *The World Bank Economic Review 20*(1): 1–29.

Keister, Lisa, and Natalia Deeb-Sosa. (2001). "Are Baby Boomers Richer Than Their Parents? Intergenerational Patterns of Wealth Ownership in the United States." *Journal of Marriage and the Family 63*(2): 569–579.

Kerwin, Kofi Charles, and Erik Hurst. (2003). "The Correlation of Wealth Across Generations." *Journal of Political Economy.*

O'Brien, Rourke L. (2007, June 17). "Investing Your Way out of Poverty." *New York Times*: A9.

Sawhill, Isabel V., and John E. Morton. (2007). *Getting Ahead: Economic and Social Mobility in America.* Washington, DC: Urban Institute Press.

CHAPTER NINE

Ethics and Global Finance

KLAUS STEIGLEDER
University of Bochum, Germany

Abstract

Hitherto, the focus of financial ethics has been mainly on questions concerning the micro- and meso-level of economic interaction, questions that are predominantly discussed in the field of "business ethics." The business ethicist discusses normative issues arising from commercial activities from a microethical viewpoint. This chapter, on the contrary, intends to stress the importance of financial macroethics. It will be argued that the guiding principle of financial macroethics ought to be that it is of the utmost moral importance to ensure the sustainable efficiency of the financial market. From this perspective, the criterion for the normative analysis of global finance—as well as of each financial market, institution, and instrument—has to be whether it is compatible with the sustainable efficiency of the financial market of each national economy. All fundamental normative orientations and tasks of the macroethics of financial markets derive from this principle, some of which will be discussed in this essay.

Key Words

efficiency, finance, financial regulation, full scope/restricted scope norms, macroethics, rights, risk

---

There is a tendency to discuss questions of political, social, and global ethics and especially of economic ethics, as if it were only a matter of good will to set things right. But the normal motivations of human beings have to be taken into account as a given fact. The collective behavior in society and the economy follows laws that cannot be changed and these laws limit what is possible to achieve. The economy is not simply malleable according to the precepts of the ethicist or other well-meaning individuals. Certain ends cannot be realized at all, and others might be achievable only indirectly or partially or at great costs. The effects of institutional changes are often difficult to anticipate. Often we do not know what the right policies are.

Unlike the disciplines of macroeconomics and microeconomics, where the microfoundations of the macroeconomic phenomena and processes are sought, there is a cognitive and normative priority of macroethics over microethics in economic ethics and financial ethics. From a macroethical perspective, economic ethics is concerned with the appraisal of the fundamental tasks, of the systemic structures and interrelations of the economy, and the evaluation of existing regulations. Furthermore, macroethics assesses the feasibility or need for the implementation of further measures of governance concerning the economy as a whole. In contrast, microethics deals with the normative analysis of individual economic institutions and individual contexts of actions.[1]

It is striking to see that thus far, in the field of financial ethics, macroethical approaches are relatively rare (see Van Liedekerke et al., 2000; Emunds, 2003). This may be due to the dominance of business ethics (as distinguished from economic ethics) in the English-speaking world. Business ethics, as a subdiscipline of economic microethics, usually does not question the existing economic macrostructures, under which businesses operate and compete. Therefore, the business ethicist ignores macroethical considerations. Most of the existing literature on ethics and finance falls within the domain of business ethics (see Boatright, 2008).

In the following, I will draw the outlines of a macroethical approach to ethics and finance. For this purpose I will portray, explain, and argue in favor of what I consider to be a guiding principle of financial ethics. While this principle may look unbearably affirmative at first sight, I aim to show that it can serve as an adequate measure of critique of the actual conditions of financial markets and of the actual workings of financial institutions and instruments, and the actual effects financial institutions and instruments have. This principle is therefore apt to establish a macroethical approach to ethics and finance.

A Guiding Principle of Financial Ethics

The principle that should guide any reflection on ethics of financial markets is the following: A sustainably efficient financial market is of the utmost moral importance. Hence, there is a fundamental moral obligation to provide for a sustainably efficient financial market, to create and protect the preconditions for such a market.

Before I elucidate this principle and its normative implications and shield it from possible misunderstandings, I would like to indicate first how I will try to justify it. I will elaborate this justification in more detail in the following section.

I assume that a sustainably well-functioning market economy is a necessary condition for the effective and lasting protection of the fundamental moral rights of the citizens living on the territory of a state. A sustainably efficient financial market is in turn a necessary condition for a developed and well-functioning market economy. Thus, the moral importance of a sustainably efficient financial market and the resulting moral obligations relating to the financial market derive from the fundamental moral rights of human beings.

By "*the* financial market" I refer to the multitude of financial markets and of the financial institutions existing in a single closed or open economy. Thus, the term "the financial market" does not refer to the global financial market (the global flows of foreign capital and the global operations of foreign financial institutions into countries abroad). Each national economy (or the people living therein) has the same right to a sustainably efficient financial market. This right entails at least a negative duty of states and individual market players (including firms and institutions) to see to it that the financial markets of other national economies do not suffer damage or are disrupted in their development by the workings of their economies or by their actions. A global financial market must be evaluated according to the degree to which it fosters or harms the sustainable efficiency of the financial markets of each country.

The term "efficiency of the financial market" is to be understood in a broad sense, and should be defined in accordance with the tasks of the financial market. The purpose of financial markets consists above all in providing capital for the most productive utilization, and to make sure that capital is available where and when it is needed the most. A further task is to ensure national and international monetary transactions and to provide stable prices and exchange rates. Thus, an "efficient financial market" is a market that operates *as efficiently as possible*: a market that fulfills its main tasks to the highest possible extent. The most important task of a financial market is to contribute to a well-functioning, productive, and sustainable economy. To attain efficient financial markets that are able to fulfill their tasks, the diversification into the various financial markets, financial institutions, and financial instruments is a necessity. Still, the efficiency of an individual market, (type of) institution, or instrument does not guarantee the efficiency of the financial market as a whole. On the contrary, the individual markets, institutions, or instruments can even be detrimental to it. In such a case, there is a moral obligation to take countermeasures and, if necessary, to forgo certain markets, institutions, or instruments (to ban them). On the other hand, the efficiency of the financial market may be improved by the development of new markets, institutions, or instruments.

A financial market that fulfills its tasks is not identical with a largely unregulated, autonomous market. Insofar as regulations are necessary or conducive to the fulfillment of its tasks, a sustainably efficient financial market is a market that is regulated in accordance with its tasks.

The Justification of the Principle

In the following I will presuppose that every agent possesses equal moral claim rights to the necessary *preconditions* of self-fulfilling agency.[2] These rights comprise rights to individual goods such as life and physical and psychic integrity. Moreover, moral claim rights pertain to common and public goods, such as the conservation of natural resources or the provision of institutions that secure the conditions of a peaceful coexistence. These institutions must assure that the rights of (individual) agents are protected, and that these agents will be free to pursue their projects, provided they respect the rights of others. The institutions also need to make sure that individuals will receive assistance if their fundamental rights are threatened, they are not able to help themselves, and they can be helped "at no comparable costs" (Gewirth, 1978).[3] These institutions comprise the state, which must be a welfare state based on a democratic constitution (for a detailed elaboration of this precondition see the important, but neglected, Chapter 5 of Gewirth, 1978), but they include the economy and its basic framework as well.

My claim is that, given adequate basic conditions, a well-functioning market economy has the greatest potential—more than any other economic system that we know thus far—to contribute essentially to the permanent provision of the necessary preconditions for self-fulfilling agency. A market economy is able to make such a contribution first and foremost because it can render widespread and lasting prosperity. On the one hand, such wealth contributes directly to the protection of the fundamental rights of the individual agents. On the other hand, only sustained wealth provides the government with the opportunity to effectively protect the rights of the inhabitants of the state. Finally, market economies have the potential to render the liberty to develop and pursue one's projects.

This is not meant to advocate markets with as little regulation as possible. Nor do I assert that a market economy will automatically lead to the morally best results. By moral standards a market economy is certainly not an ideal system. The economic behavior of individual actors is mostly driven by self-interest and the desire to make profits. It is governed by exchange values and not by moral values (O'Neill, 1998, 5). Thus, there is at least an immanent tendency to exploit others in horrendous ways. Nor can it be denied that, in a globalized economy, it is increasingly difficult to curb the behavior of the players on global markets. But we have to ask ourselves what the alternatives to a market economy would be, and whether these alternatives would not cause even greater harm and generate considerably less benefits. Humans and the world they live in and create are far from ideal and certainly never will be. However, my proposition is, that from a moral point of view a (well-regulated) market economy, even if it does not yield ideal results, is the best economic system we know thus far. Therefore, a functioning, productive, and sustainable market economy is of the utmost moral importance. Because such an economy is in need of regulations, but cannot be planned, governments possess only a limited command over that on which their abilities and the abilities of the governed are highly dependent. Questions of social and global justice are, therefore, on the whole not independent from questions of efficiency. Policies that are meant to correct injustices and to bring about just conditions may turn out to be counterproductive, because they have negative or even deleterious consequences for the economy.

A sustainably efficient financial market is morally relevant, insofar as it is an indispensable part of a well-functioning, productive, and sustainable market economy. This is not to say that the development of financial markets is an indispensable prerequisite for the development of a market economy, or that it is pressing or urgent to include the developing countries in the financial globalization (see the critical remarks of Rodrik and Subramanian, 2009, 123–124). But the moral relevance of sustainably efficient financial markets arises not only from their potential contribution to the functioning of developed market economies, but also from the extremely adverse effects financial crises or the breakdown of financial markets have on the (global) economy and therefore on the protection of human rights.

Basic Normative Orientations of Financial Macroethics

Assuming the justification of the principle was successful, does it not follow from the principle that we do not really need a macro*ethics* of financial markets? For, if efficiency ensures moral rightness, we appear to need economical, not moral expertise, and economics, at least in the field of financial markets, seems unexpectedly to have been restored as a "moral science."

However, the principle does not say that efficiency ensures moral rightness, but that sustainably efficient financial markets are of the utmost moral importance. As already indicated, the principle implies a fundamental norm for the ethics of international and global financial markets, namely the prohibition to impair the financial market or the financial system of a foreign economy. Each state has the obligation to provide for the effective protection of the rights of its inhabitants. Economic wealth, a well-functioning economy, and a sustainably efficient financial market are essential prerequisites for the realization of this end. But as there is an equal right to a sustainably efficient financial market, the efforts aimed at the development of domestic financial markets are not to be pursued at the expense of the efficiency of foreign financial markets. Not surprisingly, as a moral principle, the principle not only stresses the moral importance of efficiency, but also restricts efficiency by the demands of justice.

However, the question of how individual economies and individual players on the financial markets can be limited in their pursuit of efficiency or gain poses a central problem for financial ethics. Moreover, as the current financial crisis demonstrates, it has to be taken into account that the disruptions and dysfunctions of the financial markets of powerful national economies have global impacts. This is due to the global financial market and the existing interdependencies between different national economies. Thus, the prevention of such (local) disruptions and dysfunctions has an importance beyond the directly affected economy, and therefore receives additional moral relevance.

As such, ethics possesses no economic expertise. The ethicist who inquires the macroethics of financial markets is therefore at risk to dabble in economics and to proclaim annoying or even dangerous nonsense. (Though the appalled economists may perhaps humbly be reminded how numerous are the dabblers on normative ethics in their own guild.) Nevertheless, an attempt must be made to combine normative and economic expertise. Moral norms represent mixed judgments, in which evaluative or deontic and factual contents are combined. With reference to financial markets, the goal of ethics is to specify tasks of research and highlight their urgency. Furthermore, it has to name deficits in our understanding; scrutinize and, if necessary, reject pretensions; and try to provide specific normative evaluations and proposals. Ideally, financial macroethics will be a cooperative undertaking in twofold respects: on the one hand, considerable efforts and different approaches will be undertaken and discussed within the field of ethics itself. On the other hand, there will be an exchange and collaboration between economically interested ethicists and normatively interested economists.

A characteristic feature of the macroethics of financial markets is that, on the level of social structures, it postulates a normative priority of the system: the financial market *in its entirety* must be sustainably efficient and the coexistence of sustainably efficient financial markets of individual national economies on the level of the global economy has to be ensured. Each individual financial market, institution, and instrument, each rule and regulation that guides the markets and institutions, must be assessed according to whether it is conducive to—or at least compatible with—the sustainable efficiency of the financial market. It is an imperative of financial ethics that financial crises must be avoided and that a global financial crisis such as the crisis of 2007–2009 must never be allowed to occur again.

To this end, it is important to conceive of the financial market as a dynamic system, the behavior of which cannot simply be described as the sum of the behavior of its parts, but which interacts with its parts and is therefore able to determine the behavior of its parts. Accordingly, it is a hallmark of financial markets that positive or negative feedback mechanisms may reinforce themselves and that sudden slumps or reversals of trend are always possible. The normative priority to ensure the permanent stability of the system in its entirety does not only require attentiveness to the dangers for the system which may arise from some of its parts. It also requires our vigilance with respect to the dangers which may arise from the (potentially positive) interaction of its parts. The neglect of this point is now seen as a grave shortcoming of the previous regulations of financial markets (see FSA, 2009; Brunnermeier et al., 2009).

The depiction of the dynamics of financial markets as outlined in this essay contradicts the theory of endogenously efficient financial markets, which dominated both economics and politics until the current financial crisis. According to this theory, prices reflect all information available on the financial market, and changes in prices are the result of new (and therefore unpredictable) information. The market itself is perceived as the best available instrument to test financial innovations. If these innovations are able to persist in the market, they contribute to its efficiency. Regulatory interventions concerning the market are overbearing, since they follow the presumption to possess a higher amount of knowledge than that which is already available on the market. Interventions are seen as being not only superfluous, but even harmful. Thus, to deregulate is tantamount to the removal of disruptive and destabilizing influences on the financial market, which is most efficient when left alone. Financial crises, according to this analysis, are the result of external shocks.

While the so-called efficient market hypothesis[4] is certainly not overcome yet, no longer does only a small minority oppose it. In the wake of the financial crisis, it is no longer seen as outright absurd to argue that financial markets are inherently unstable and exposed to the dangers of endogenous negative developments (see Minsky, 1982; Cooper, 2008). From this point of view, the rational behavior of individuals can lead to irrational behavior ("irrational exuberances") of the market, and even cause its breakdown.

Thus, to arrive at an appropriate evaluation of the financial market is highly relevant with respect to the proposed guiding principle for financial ethics and its consequences. If the efficient market hypothesis was correct, a well-functioning financial market would be a largely unregulated market, and ethics would have to support the economists in their critique of regulations. But if, on the contrary, the financial market is inherently unstable and can behave irrationally or is merely "imperfectly efficient" (Smithers, 2009, 4, 67–79), then profound interventions and regulations will be needed to secure the moral requirement of sustainable efficiency of the financial market.

It follows that to arrive at an appropriate theory of the financial market is of the utmost moral and social importance. The ethics of financial markets cannot provide such a theory, but it should urge for extensive efforts to be made for the development of such a theory. Moreover, financial ethics can contribute to unmask the ideological roots of proposals. Since all knowledge is fallible, there is no guarantee for us to arrive at a definite, unquestionable theory of the financial market. It is therefore essential, to be sensible of the limitations of theories, to remain open to alternative approaches, and to examine theories thoroughly, scrutinizing their line of argument and their verification. Besides, it is important to pursue research on the financial markets from different disciplinary perspectives both via an economic approach (here, a closer connection of finance and macroeconomics may be called for) and from other fields of research (e.g., from the perspectives of history, political science, and jurisprudence). Due to their relevance for societal and political decision-making, the subject-specific as well as the interdisciplinary insights and discussions must be made accessible to the wider public in a repeated process of translation. Furthermore, more general education in economics and finance is needed.

There is growing support for the proposition that the financial market is in need of extensive and profound regulations. But the macroethical approach is confronted with several problems here. A first question is how extensive the regulations can be, and how extensive they should be. The answer to this question depends on the handling of two different kinds of problems involved here. First of all, it has to be evaluated whether the prevention of financial crises or the promotion of the efficiency of the financial market is more urgent. At least in theory, it is conceivable to regulate the financial market to such an extent that it will be substantially constrained in its functionality. Under these conditions, the occurrence of financial crises would be almost impossible. On the other hand, one may be willing to restrict the financial market less in its functionality and to accept in return a higher risk for the occurrence of financial crises. I will return to this problem in the following section.

Another problem is to estimate what the chances for the implementation of possible regulations are, and to evaluate how effective they will be. Regulations are subject to a "boundary problem" (Goodhart, 2008): by subjecting a domain to rules, they demarcate it from other domains not comprised by the rules. Rules for depository institutions do not comprise non-depository institutions. Rules for the financial market of one country leave the financial markets of other countries untouched. Since regulations restrict the freedom of action and the opportunities to make profits, they provide incentives to avoid the regulations by entering unregulated domains. In part, financial innovations are developed exactly for this purpose: to allow market players to circumvent regulatory restrictions. Thus, regulations may be ineffective or even counterproductive, because they stimulate avoidance strategies, that give rise to new and unknown systemic risks, which may be greater than the original risks intended to be contained. In face of global financial markets, transnational regulations are important. However, the implementation of transnational regulations is difficult, since international agreements often only reflect the smallest common denominator and therefore fall short of what is necessary.

Again, we have to bear in mind that the financial market is not malleable according to our wishes. However, this fact does not exonerate the macroethics of financial markets from its tasks, but, if anything, confronts it with some special challenges. First of all, we must distinguish between what can be achieved in principle and what—given the normal motivations of human beings, the laws of collective behavior, and of the mechanisms governing markets—is either unattainable or could only be achieved by using disproportionate or morally unacceptable means. This distinction possesses a heuristic relevance, because it can prevent the ethicist from fantasizing about an ideal world, or developing utopian claims. To make this distinction is in fact more difficult than it may appear at first sight. For what cannot be achieved directly can perhaps be achieved indirectly, and what cannot be realized completely can perhaps be realized approximately.

This leads to a second fundamental distinction. As regards what can be achieved in principle, we must distinguish between the ends and the means to achieve these ends. On many occasions, means that are feasible in principle for the implementation of certain feasible goals cannot be applied due to lack of political will. A regulatory authority may decline to take the necessary measures, a government may refrain from establishing a required regulatory authority or from endowing it with the requisite competences, or there may be no willingness in the international community to accept binding transnational regulations. We must therefore distinguish between two different kinds of moral norms. On the one hand, there are norms that formulate which ends ought to be realized and which means ought to be applied in principle, in order to achieve the respective ends. I propose to call these norms *full scope norms*. On the other hand, there are norms that formulate what ought to be done, if essential elements of that which ought to be normatively binding are not realized. I propose to call these norms *restricted scope norms*. The distinction between full scope (FS) norms and restricted scope (RS) norms is pertinent if, despite the absent implementation of norms, there remains relevant room for maneuver. With reference to financial markets, this is the case, for instance, if required transnational regulations cannot be implemented at present, but national regulations may nonetheless achieve certain desired effects. These regulations will probably be different in many respects from a situation where international regulations were in place. Certain precautionary measures may be necessary; certain rules must perhaps be construed more strictly. Other regulations may have to be renounced, because they would be ineffective or counterproductive under the conditions of global markets.

Thus, it is possible that the demands of RS norms are different from those of FS norms. RS norms do not abrogate FS norms. On the contrary, they are justified by the same normative considerations that justify the corresponding FS norms. It is necessary to fall back on RS norms if addressees of FS norms are unable to realize the respective requirements alone and cannot persuade other addressees to cooperate. Ideally, FS norms would be obeyed (as is the case for any valid norm), but it would be very misleading to call them "ideal norms." The task of FS norms is not to draw an alternative draft to the existing financial markets or the economy. They refer to the given conditions; they are derived from the existing financial markets and the actual economic, social, and political circumstances. FS norms attempt to explicate which norms are valid for—and which moral rules must be obeyed on—the existing financial markets, and which alterations in their design and regulation are necessary for this purpose. Thus, the objective of FS norms is to serve as real norms, in the sense that they are binding norms for their addressees.

Consequently, the macroethics of financial markets must try to establish both the FS and the RS norms as dynamically (responsive to alterations) and as comprehensively as possible. Even if FS norms are not obeyed, they remain relevant. They draw attention to the deficits of the basic conditions of global financial markets; they allow for insights into the severity of those deficits and call for change. But, the efficiency of financial markets provided, they do not only possess a critical function, but also, at least in part, a justifying function. In this regard, they emphasize the fundamental moral relevance of a sustainably efficient financial market and the importance of its fundamental structures and functions. Accordingly, FS norms comprise both imperatives of preservation and imperatives of change.

Fundamental Tasks of Financial Macroethics

The preceding remarks on the imperatives of preservation are not meant to convey the impression that the present financial markets were only in need of minor adjustments. The present financial crisis, which according to Adair Turner is "arguably the greatest crisis in the history of financial capitalism" (FSA, 2009, 5), points to fundamental structural problems of the financial market.[5] Thus, it can be assumed that fundamental alterations of its structures will be necessary. At any rate, the task of financial macroethics is to highlight these problems and to contribute to their solution. The distinction between FS and RS norms makes way for the requisite considerations. These considerations should first and foremost aim at the development of FS norms, and are therefore not yet burdened by the problems which make the development of RS norms necessary.

The increasing liberalization of financial markets and the simultaneous financial globalization are accompanied by an increase of financial crises. In the past, these crises affected above all the developing countries, but were not confined to them. It is safe to assume that the increased instability of the financial markets is a consequence of their liberalization in the context of globalization (see Wolf, 2008, 28–57). Because the prevention of financial crises is a highly important moral objective, it is necessary to gain a deeper understanding of the correlation between liberalization and instability. In addition to this, the question of whether certain structural developments ought to be reversed has to be pursued in as unprejudiced a manner as possible. This question is particularly urgent, because the financial crisis of 2007–2009 led to a dramatic increase of budget deficits around the globe, so that the ability to respond adequately to further crises may be limited in the future (see Kay, 2010).

An important task in this context is to pursue a transformation of the existing incentive structures, in order to be able to handle problems of "moral hazard" effectively. These arise whenever those who run risks are the beneficiaries of the positive outcomes, but need not bear (to a sufficient extent) the negative consequences. On a limited scale this is the case when deposits are insured and depositors can therefore allocate their deposits to banks which are able to offer more attractive terms due to riskier business concepts. On a broader scale, moral hazard problems occur whenever institutions can be sure that due to their size the government will not let them go bankrupt, because the damage for the whole economy would be too catastrophic ("too big to fail" or "too connected to fail"). Moral hazard problems also occur when the compensation system is designed in such a way that taking huge risks is rewarded and negative outcomes are not (adequately) punished.

It follows from this that it must be examined how and when institutions become "too big to fail," and whether these institutions ought to be split up and downsized. Furthermore, research has to be done on the question of whether it is possible to formulate rules for the permissible market power of individual firms and to establish control instruments with the task of preventing institutions from becoming too big. Perhaps such measures would do more harm than good. And it may well be that less invasive and equally—or sufficiently—effective measures exist. Ethics is as such not competent to decide this. But ethics can emphasize that it is morally obligatory to solve these questions in as unbiased and comprehensive a manner as possible. And if it turns out that such invasive measures are necessary, then this will result in the appropriate FS norms. There is reason to assume that an adequate and unbiased debate on this issue is missing so far.

Another question in this context is whether to limit deposit insurance and the function of the central bank as "lender of last resort" to depository banks which are strictly limited in their tasks and permissible activities ("narrow banking," see Kay, 2009). This would not imply that the activities of other financial intermediaries were not subjected to comprehensive regulations. But these financial intermediaries would not be protected by official arrangements. Such proposals must likewise be discussed openly.

It is important to note that the objective of the (possibly radical) structural reforms and redemptions of previous liberalization of the financial market cannot be the restitution of the status quo ante. This would certainly be neither possible nor desirable. A restitution of the status quo ante is not possible, because the current conditions of the world economy are different from the conditions that existed, say, fifty years ago. It is not desirable, because there may be several financial innovations which could contribute to the end of a sustainably efficient financial market. Thus, the diagnosis that a return to the status quo ante is not possible should not be used as a pretext for not even discussing radical structural reforms.

One of the most fundamental tasks of financial macroethics is to develop criteria for the evaluation of systemic risks, and to develop (moral) norms that define how to deal with systemic risks. In this context, risks are to be understood in a broad sense. The term "risk" here refers both to possible (negative) events to which probabilities can be assigned (risks in a narrow sense), and to possible (negative) events to which no probabilities can be assigned ("uncertainty").[6] The task of evaluating systemic financial risks is further complicated by the fact that an ethics of risks, which could clarify the criteria of how to deal with risks in a responsible and just manner, is still a desideratum of research.

On the one hand, this is the case because of the difficult epistemological questions about how probabilities are to be understood. These difficulties complicate the understanding of risks, which must precede the normative investigations. On the other hand, the main theories of normative ethics—utilitarian and rights-based theories—seem to quickly reach their respective limits with regard to the fundamental questions of the ethics of risks (see Hansson, 2003). Utilitarianism seems to be unable to contribute anything relevant to the important question of how risks are to be distributed. In contrast, rights-based theories seem to have to take up the absurd position that it must be prohibited from the outset to expose other persons to *any* risks. For if it is forbidden to harm another person, it seems likewise to be impermissible to expose her to the risk of being harmed. A solution to this problem could be found by first of all distinguishing different kinds of probabilities, and, in correlation to this, different kinds of risks. Secondly, it would be necessary to develop differentiated criteria for the moral acceptability of risks (see the important suggestions of Hansson, 2003). The task of a moral evaluation of systemic financial risks is also confronted with the difficulty that a normative analysis of financial market risks seems to be almost inexistent thus far. If ethics is concerned with specific risks at all, it does so almost exclusively with relation to risks concerning the use of technology.

In the above, the problem was mentioned whether the prevention of dangers (the prevention of systemic risks) or the promotion of the functionality of the financial market is more urgent. This problem refers to the difficult normative question of whether, with reference to financial markets, there are certain negative events ("catastrophes") that must not be risked and ought to be prevented if possible. But maybe the alternative between the promotion of functionality and the prevention of dangers to the financial market is too abstract and therefore misleading. For it insinuates that with increasing risk and complexity, financial markets become more efficient. But the evaluation of alternatives, some of which are difficult to assess from a normative viewpoint, can often be circumvented by looking at specific instruments, institutions, and markets. If, for instance, we look at structured or derivative financial instruments, it can be inferred that their utility for the financial markets (as distinguished from the utility for those who trade these instruments) is often at least questionable, while the systemic risks related herewith are clearly existent. But if the systemic *utility* is not, at the very least, as certain as the systemic *risk*, then a real problem of weighing potential utility and potential harm will not emerge. Financial macroethics calls for such detailed considerations and analyses. Interestingly enough, utilitarian and rights-based approaches will probably complement each other in the normative evaluation of systemic financial risks.

The increase in efficiency, which seems to be evident for simple derivative financial instruments, is not ensured for more complex instruments, such as derivatives of derivatives. The financial crisis of 2007–2009 made obvious some blatant deficits in risk management. These deficits were highlighted not only by the neglect of systemic risks, but also by unwarranted assumptions in the estimation and calculations of risks, for instance, the illusion of being able to make reliable estimations and calculations of probabilities. In the macroethical analysis of financial market risks, epistemological considerations have to be combined with genuinely normative questions. In addition, it has to be taken into account that the financial markets have become increasingly self-referential, which is indicated by the "disproportionate growth of financial sector debt" in relation to household and corporate debt (FSA, 2009, 19). This fact supports doubts that the increase of systemic risk does not correspond with the benefits for the economy.

Finally, two more important tasks of financial macroethics shall be mentioned. In contrast to the efficient market hypothesis, there is growing consent that it is possible to identify bubbles on the financial markets at an early stage, and that it would be a task of the central bank to take countermeasures not only during recession phases but also during overheated boom phases. Again, it is outside the remit of financial macroethics to decide these questions, but it has the task of calling for their unbiased analysis.

A further task of financial macroethics concerns the relevance and impact of financial globalization for the developing countries. There is little doubt that for developing countries, to open up their financial markets entails great dangers.

The debate is rather concerned with the question, whether there is a realistic chance for these dangers to be prevented by a set of institutional measures. Frederic S. Mishkin has described the requisite measures and preconditions in detail (2006, 2009). Against this, Dani Rodrik and Arvind Subramanian (2009) have objected that it is neither necessary for the development of the poor countries to open up their financial markets nor realistic to assume that the protective measures can be established. This debate hints at the important question of how the developing countries can be protected from negative effects of the financial globalization, and what the rich countries ought to do, in order to make sure that they do not contribute any longer to the financial crises of the developing countries.

This sketch of the tasks of financial macroethics does not claim to be complete. The aim of this chapter is to clarify the importance of its tasks. The goal was not to undermine the importance of questions concerning financial microethics, but I wanted to show that there is a real need for financial macroethics. Financial microethics probably has to be integrated into financial macroethics. But these are questions which cannot be discussed here.[7]

Notes

1. There is a certain parallel to the distinction between micro-prudential and macro-prudential regulations of financial markets, which I can only mention here (for the distinction, see Crockett, 2000). Suffice it to say that the current discussion of different macro-prudential regulations or regulatory regimes is of the utmost importance for financial macroethics.

2. I follow Gewirth (1978) in the sketch of these rights and of the corresponding institutional requirements. But I suppose that other theories of human rights will arrive at similar results. At this point however, I have to leave open the question of whether and how the rights can be justified.

3. I suppose that the rights of individuals include negative as well as positive rights. The rights bring about corresponding duties to forbearance and duties to assistance. In this context, I cannot elaborate on this point in more detail.

4. For the delineation and critique of the hypothesis see Shiller (2005, 177–194).

5. Turner clarifies though: "This does not mean that the economic recession which many countries in the world now face will be anything like as bad as that of 1929–33. The crisis of the early 1930s was made worse by policy responses which can be—and are being—avoided today" (FSA, 2009, 5).

6. The distinction between risk and uncertainty was introduced by Knight (1921 [2006], 19–20).

7. I would like to thank Patrick Schulte for his support and helpful suggestions for the translation of this essay.

References

Boatright, John R. (2008). *Ethics in Finance, Second Edition.* Malden, MA: Blackwell.

Brunnermeier, Markus, Andrew Crockett, Charles Goodhart, Avinash D. Persaud, and Hyun Shin. (2009). *The Fundamental Principles of Financial Regulation.* Geneva Reports on the World Economy 11. London: Centre for Economic Policy Research.

Cooper, George. (2008). *The Origin of Financial Crises: Central Banks, Credit Bubbles and the Efficient Market Fallacy.* New York: Vintage Books.

Crockett, Andrew. (2000, 21 September). "Marrying the Micro-and Macro-prudential Dimensions of Financial Stability." *BIS Speeches.*

Emunds, Bernhard. (2003). "The Integration of Developing Countries into International Financial Markets: Remarks from the Perspective of an Economic Ethics." *Business Ethics Quarterly 13*(3): 337–359.

Financial Services Authority. (2009). *The Turner Review: A Regulatory Response to the Global Banking Crisis.* London: FSA.

Gewirth, Alan. (1978). *Reason and Morality.* Chicago: University of Chicago Press.

Goodhart, Charles. (2008, October). "The Boundary Problem in Financial Regulation." *National Institute Economic Review 206.*

Hansson, Sven Ove. (2003). "Ethical Criteria of Risk Acceptance." *Erkenntnis 59*: 291–309.

Kay, John. (2009). *Narrow Banking: The Reform of Banking Regulation.* London: Centre for the Study of Financial Innovation.

Kay, John. (2010, January 6). "Unfettered Finance Has Been the Cause of All Our Crises." *Financial Times.*

Knight, Frank. (1921 [2006]). *Risk, Uncertainty and Profit.* Mineola, NY: Dover Publications.

Minsky, Hyman P. (1982). *Can "It" Happen Again? Essays on Instability and Finance.* Armonk, NY: M. E. Sharpe.

Mishkin, Frederic S. (2006). *The Next Great Globalization: How Disadvantaged Nations Can Harness Their Financial Systems to Get Rich.* Princeton: Princeton University Press.

Mishkin, Frederic S. (2009). "Why We Shouldn't Turn Our Backs on Financial Globalization." *IMF Staff Papers 56*(1): 139–170.

O'Neill, John. (1998). *The Market: Ethics, Knowledge and Politics.* London: Routledge.

Rodrik, Dani, and Arvind Subramanian. (2009). "Why Did Financial Globalization Disappoint?" *IMF Staff Papers 56*(1): 112–138.

Shiller, Robert J. (2005). *Irrational Exuberance, Second Edition.* Princeton: Princeton University Press.

Smithers, Andrew. (2009). *Wall Street Revalued: Imperfect Markets and Inept Central Bankers.* Chichester, UK: John Wiley & Sons.

Van Liederkerke, Luc, Jef Van Gerwen, and Danny Cassimon, ed. (2000). *Explorations in Financial Ethics.* Leuven: Peters.

Wolf, Martin. (2008). *Fixing Global Finance.* Baltimore: Johns Hopkins University Press.

CHAPTER TEN

Global Business and Global Justice

NIEN-HÊ HSIEH
The University of Pennsylvania

Abstract

Multinational enterprises (MNEs) represent important actors in the global economy. Yet from the perspective of global justice, relatively little has been said about what is required of them. On the one hand, theories of global justice tend to focus on the responsibilities of states and societies or the individual members of states and societies. On the other hand, theories of corporate responsibility tend not to make reference to theories of justice in examining the responsibilities of business enterprises. This chapter aims to close this gap in the literature by evaluating the plausibility of answers that may be given, from the perspective of justice, to one of the most challenging questions regarding the responsibilities of MNEs. That question is whether there is a moral responsibility on the part of MNEs headquartered in developed economies to help improve the situation of citizens in developing economies, even if this comes at some expense to long-run profitability.

Key Words

capacity building, corporate social responsibility, global health, global justice, global poverty, human rights, multinational enterprises

---

Author's note: I thank Michael Boylan for helpful comments and for support and encouragement in writing this chapter. I also thank the Harvard University Program in Ethics and Health for providing a hospitable environment in which to write this chapter. All errors remain my own.

Multinational enterprises (MNEs) represent an important class of actors in the global economy.[1] For example, exports by foreign affiliates of MNEs are estimated to account for about a third of total world exports of goods and services (UNCTAD, 2009, xxi). Depending on the basis for comparison, MNEs comprise anywhere from twenty-nine to over fifty of the world's top hundred economic entities.[2] And, for developing economies, foreign direct investment (FDI) has become the most important source of external finance and is roughly twice as large as official development aid (OECD, 2008, 2).[3]

Because of their size and global reach, commentators argue that MNEs possess not only market power, but also bargaining power in the area of policy-making and the ability to avoid many national regulations and policies (Navaretti and Venables, 2006, 1). Accordingly, it is not surprising that much has been written about the moral responsibilities of MNEs, especially with regard to MNEs headquartered in developed economies that operate in developing economies.[4] Relative to developed economies, regulatory standards are often less stringent in developing economies, and there are fewer resources to monitor and enforce compliance with those standards. Under such conditions, parties affected by the activities of MNEs—including workers, customers, and local residents—may be at increased risk of harm, thereby prompting questions about what standard of treatment they are owed beyond what is legally required of MNEs.[5] It also is difficult to ignore both the extent to which basic needs remain unmet in many of these economies and the opportunities that exist for MNEs to meet those needs.[6] In addition, many of the MNEs operating in developing economies are headquartered in Western nations,[7] raising concerns about the appropriateness of applying Western standards to non-Western contexts and about the universality of ethical standards more generally.[8]

In this chapter, I explore ways in which our thinking about the responsibilities of MNEs can be furthered by locating questions about the responsibilities of MNEs within broader debates about global justice. The literature that concerns the responsibilities of MNEs, and the literature on corporate responsibility more generally, tends not to make reference to theories of justice.[9] At the same time, the literature on global justice tends to focus on the responsibilities of states and societies or the individual members of states and societies. Given the role of MNEs in the global economy and given the general interest in questions about their responsibilities, it seems natural to inquire further about the responsibilities of MNEs from the perspective of justice.

To engage in this inquiry, I focus on what I take to be one of the most challenging questions regarding the responsibilities of MNEs and evaluate the plausibility of answers that may be given to that question on the basis of a justice-based approach. Briefly, by a justice-based approach, I have in mind an approach that specifies a set of fundamental human rights that apply equally to people, and that takes institutions to be central to its analysis—meaning that institutional arrangements, and not just individual behavior, are subjected to normative evaluation.[10] Adopting such an approach, the question on which I focus is this: Is there a moral responsibility on the part of MNEs headquartered in developed economies to help improve the situation of citizens in developing economies, even if this comes at some expense to the long-run profitability of the MNE?

For purposes of this chapter, what counts as an improvement in the situation of citizens in developing economies is to be understood broadly. For purposes of this chapter, the situation of citizens can be said to have improved if there is an increase in their well-being or an expansion in their exercise of basic freedoms or rights. The chapter takes an expansive view of what is the appropriate conception of well-being or what are the relevant freedoms or rights. For example, the chapter leaves open whether improvement in well-being should be measured in terms of the income, commodities, or capabilities that people enjoy. Furthermore, improvements in the situation of citizens should be understood to include changes to their broader social, economic, legal, and political environment so long as these changes are consistent with bringing institutional arrangements closer to meeting the requirements of justice. For example, insofar as widespread official corruption is inconsistent with the requirements of justice, efforts on the part of MNEs to combat official corruption should be understood to count as an improvement in the situation of citizens. The aim is to be as inclusive as possible with regard to the ways in which MNEs are able to improve the lives of citizens.

The chapter is organized as follows. In the first section, I set the stage by outlining the widely held view that MNEs do not have a general responsibility to improve the situation of citizens in developing economies. On this view, MNEs have a negative duty not to engage in violations of human rights and at most, a responsibility to provide assistance for reasons of rescue or beneficence. This section helps to highlight what is distinctive about a justice-based approach to questions about the responsibilities of MNEs. In the second section, I evaluate arguments that ground a responsibility to improve the situation of citizens of developing economies in a negative duty not to harm others by violating human rights. In the third section, I discuss challenges to accounts that assign to MNEs a positive duty to improve the situation of citizens in developing economies. The fourth section concludes with a discussion of the promise of a justice-based approach.

MNEs and the Provision of Assistance

At the time of this writing, sub-Saharan Africa continues to bear the brunt of the global disease burden of HIV/AIDS. In 2008, sub-Saharan Africa accounted for 68 percent of new HIV infections among adults, 91 percent of new HIV infections among children, and 72 percent of AIDS-related deaths in the world (UNAIDS,

2009, 21). In Botswana, Burkina Faso, and Swaziland, prevalence rates for HIV exceeded 25 percent of the adult population (UNAIDS, 2009, 15). The burden on the population in sub-Saharan Africa is great. For example, in Swaziland between 1990 and 2007, life expectancy fell by half to thirty-seven years, and in 2008, more than 14.1 million children lost one or both parents to AIDS in sub-Saharan Africa (UNAIDS, 2009, 21).

Greater and earlier use of antiretroviral drugs in treating HIV would help to reduce the high rates of mortality associated with HIV in sub-Saharan Africa.[11] Greater access to these drugs, however, is limited in part by their price and by levels of poverty in sub-Saharan Africa. One way to characterize this lack of access is with reference to human rights. To say a right is "human" is to mean that it applies universally to all individuals, that it is not limited to any one particular domain of human activity, and that it overrides other normative considerations, including institutional rules or social norms (Campbell, 2004, 12). Consider now Article 25 and Article 28 of the Universal Declaration of Human Rights.[12] According to Article 25, "Everyone has the right to a standard of living adequate for the health and well-being of himself and of his family, including food, clothing, housing and medical care," and according to Article 28, "Everyone is entitled to a social and international order in which the rights and freedoms set forth in this Declaration can be fully realized" (United Nations, 1948). In the context of the lack of access to antiretroviral drugs, patients in sub-Saharan Africa can be said to be deprived in the full exercise of their human rights.

The pharmaceutical companies that have developed the drugs used in antiretroviral therapy are in a position to help aid the people who are deprived in their enjoyment of their rights. One way open to them is to donate these drugs to nongovernmental organizations and the governments of sub-Saharan African countries or to provide them at cost. Another is to avoid the cost of production altogether by allowing for their production by companies that manufacture generic drugs (Gathii, 2005). The question arises as to whether global pharmaceutical companies have a general responsibility to help aid the persons in sub-Saharan Africa who are said to be deprived in the exercise of their rights.

According to a widely held view, pharmaceutical companies have no such general responsibility.[13] Thomas Donaldson (1989) puts forward one version of this view by making use of Henry Shue's highly influential typology of duties (1996).[14] Shue distinguishes three duties in relation to a person's enjoyment of a right (1996, 60). They are duties:

I. To avoid depriving
II. To protect from deprivation
    1. By enforcing duty (I)

   2. By designing institutions that avoid the creation of strong incentives to violate duty (I)
III. To aid the deprived
   1. Who are one's special responsibility
   2. Who are victims of social failures in the performance of duties (I), (II-1), (II-2)
   3. Who are the victims of natural disasters

Under this typology, a general responsibility on the part of MNEs to help improve the situation of citizens in sub-Saharan Africa qualifies as a type (III-2) duty. Donaldson considers a range of rights—ranging from the right to freedom of physical movement to the right to subsistence—and concludes that whereas a duty of type (I) applies to MNEs with respect to all rights and a duty of type (II) applies to MNEs with respect to most rights, a duty of type (III-2) does not apply to MNEs. The "profit-making corporation," he writes, "is designed to achieve an economic mission and as a moral actor possesses an exceedingly narrow personality" (1989, 84). Hence it is inappropriate, he concludes, to hold MNEs to duties of type (III-2).

Donaldson's account is instructive because it draws upon two widely held intuitions that inform much of the debate about the responsibilities of MNEs and business enterprises more generally. The first concerns the status of MNEs as a limited moral agent. The intuition is that because MNEs are artificial persons, many of the duties that apply to natural persons do not apply to them. This is not to say that no moral duties apply to MNEs. As Melissa Lane (2005) notes, even though MNEs are not natural persons, the responsibilities of the natural persons who represent MNEs can carry over to MNEs. For example, because no one is morally permitted to enslave another person, no one could morally act for an MNE to enslave a person, and hence no MNE can permissibly enslave a person (Lane, 2005, 238). On many accounts of corporate responsibility, duties of type (I) and (II) apply more readily to natural persons in part because they require agents to refrain from certain actions (e.g., causing harm) rather than to make positive contributions to advance the interests of others. Accordingly, the limited moral agency of MNEs supports the view that MNEs have duties of type (I) and (II), but not duties of type (III-2).

The second intuition on which Donaldson's account draws concerns the purpose of for-profit business enterprises. Even if one does not subscribe to the view that the sole purpose of business enterprises is to maximize returns for shareholders,[15] there is reason to hold that profit-making commercial activity ought to be a priority for business enterprises, including MNEs. One way to characterize this priority is in terms of the fiduciary duty owed by managers to shareholders.

Another way to characterize it is with reference to a societal division of labor. For-profit business enterprises have a specific role that is distinct from the roles of other kinds of organizations in civil society and from the role of the state. Either way, it seems that primary responsibility to improve the situation of people who are deprived in the exercise of their rights, even if there is no expense to the business enterprise, falls outside the proper scope of purpose for MNEs. To use a distinction drawn by Onora O'Neill, on this view, MNEs are not "primary agents of justice"—agents that have "capacities to determine how principles of justice are to be institutionalised within a certain domain"—but rather "secondary agents of justice"—agents "thought to contribute to justice mainly by meeting the demands of primary agents, most evidently by conforming to any legal requirements they establish" (2001, 189).

From this it seems to follow that the more limited one's conception of the moral agency of MNEs and the more limited one's conception of their purpose, the more reason one has to reject the view that MNEs have a general responsibility to improve the situation of citizens living in the developing economies. At the same time, adopting limited conceptions of the moral agency of MNEs and their purpose need not rule out altogether a responsibility on the part of pharmaceutical companies to address the HIV/AIDS crisis in sub-Saharan Africa.

It has been argued, for example, that pharmaceutical companies have a responsibility to help improve the situation of persons suffering from HIV/AIDS in sub-Saharan Africa on the basis of a principle of rescue (Dunfee, 2006; Hsieh, 2005, 2006). T. M. Scanlon (1998) provides one formulation of the principle: "If you are presented with a situation in which you can prevent something very bad from happening, or alleviate someone's dire plight, by making only a slight (or even moderate) sacrifice, then it would be wrong not to do so" (224). He notes that the "cases in which it would most clearly be wrong not to give aid . . . are cases in which those in need of aid are in dire straits: their lives are immediately threatened, for example" (224). The basic argument is that HIV/AIDS poses an immediate threat to the people in sub-Saharan Africa and because the sacrifice to pharmaceutical companies to aid them is minimal, it would be wrong for pharmaceutical companies not to provide aid—say in the form of drug donations. The sacrifice is considered to be minimal because the recipients of the drugs were not in a position to purchase the drugs in the first place so that by donating the drugs, pharmaceutical companies do not forgo any profits or revenues needed to cover the initial costs of research and development (Hsieh, 2005, 383).[16]

This argument is compatible with limited conceptions of the moral agency of MNEs and their purpose. In the case of moral agency, even if we deny that a duty of rescue attaches to the MNE itself, one may argue that the managers of MNEs are under a duty to direct resources under their control to engage in rescue.[17] With respect to corporate purpose, the principle of rescue is rather limited in the demands that it makes upon the provider of rescue. In the context of the life of an individual, the principle of rescue does not require her to give up her personal pursuits to become a full-time provider of assistance. It is only when confronted with a situation in which she can engage in rescue in the course of her normal activity that the duty applies to her. Analogously, when applied to the context of MNEs, the principle of rescue does not require for-profit corporations to become full-time providers of assistance.

At the same time, these features of the rescue-based argument reveal just how limited it may be. Central to the rescue-based approach is the immediacy of the threat. The classic case involves saving a person from certain, immediate death—say, for example, from drowning in a pond. The case can be made, however, that the situation facing people in sub-Saharan Africa lacks this immediacy. It is true that people will suffer certain harm if they never receive the antiretroviral drugs, but it does not follow that if the pharmaceutical companies do not provide the drugs, the people will suffer this harm. There are other agents and organizations that very well may come to their aid—for example, by purchasing the drugs and then donating them. Hence, even if one accepts that the principle of rescue applies to pharmaceutical companies, the instances in which it grounds a responsibility to improve the situation of persons in developing economies may be rather limited.

In short, a claim to assistance under the rescue-based approach lacks the scope and force associated with a claim to assistance grounded in a justice-based approach. By a "justice-based" approach, I have in mind an approach that has two main features. First, the provision of assistance is not merely a matter of charity or beneficence. Instead, the approach grounds claims of assistance with reference to human rights or what is required under some theory of global distributive justice.[18] As noted above, human rights are universal and overriding in their moral importance. In contrast to a rescue-based approach, deprivation in their exercise calls for rectification even if the deprivation is not immediately life threatening. In this manner, a claim to assistance on grounds of human rights is more demanding in what it requires of those who are responsible for rectifying the deprivation. Second, a justice-based approach takes both domestic and global institutions to be central to its analysis. On the one hand, institutional arrangements, and not just individual behavior, are subject to normative evaluation. On the other hand, evaluations of individual behavior are to be made by keeping in mind the ways in which individuals act against background institutions and in the light of what justice requires of these background institutions.[19]

Avoiding and Preventing Harm

In this section, I turn to evaluate a line of argument that aims to avoid some of the challenges noted above in grounding a general responsibility on the part of

MNEs to improve the situation of citizens in developing economies. This line of argument aims to ground such a responsibility in a duty not to harm. As suggested by the discussion in the previous section, it is widely held that even if MNEs do not have duties of type (III-2), they nonetheless are under a duty not to harm others by depriving them in the enjoyment of their rights. The main challenge for this line of argument is to make the case that not improving the situation of citizens of developing economies constitutes a kind of harm on the part of MNEs.

It will help to begin by considering the most sustained version of this line of argument as applied to the responsibilities of citizens of wealthy nations in regards to global poverty (Pogge, 2005, 2007, 2008; cf. Boylan, 2011). According to Thomas Pogge, the social institutions that structure global economic transactions are "the most important causal determinants of the incidence and depth of poverty" for three reasons (2007, 26). First, relative to individual or corporate activity, even small changes in institutional arrangements can have a significant impact on economic distribution. Second, in contrast to individual or corporate activity, the impact of institutional arrangements is easier to assess in part because of their greater visibility. Third, institutional reforms are easier to achieve and sustain than morally correct conduct on the part of individuals and corporations (2007, 26–29). Pogge then argues that much of the poverty and resulting mortality in the world today can be avoided foreseeably through relatively small changes in the institutions that structure global economic activity. He interprets this to mean that the current institutional order causes excess deaths rather than simply fails to prevent them (2007, 39). In this manner, citizens of wealthy nations, who are involved in shaping and maintaining this institutional order, are said to be harming the global poor and, as a result, to have a responsibility to work toward eliminating severe global poverty.

An argument of this form can be brought to bear on the case of pharmaceutical companies and the antiretroviral drugs for treating HIV/AIDS in sub-Saharan Africa. As part of his account, Pogge uses the intellectual property rights regime to illustrate the way in which the current institutional order harms citizens of developing economies (2007, 37; cf. Boylan, 2008). Because the intellectual property rights regime grants a monopoly to the developer of a new drug, pharmaceutical companies have strong incentives to develop drugs for developed economy markets. Furthermore, drugs are priced in such a way that they are not affordable for developing economy markets. Insofar as they support the existing intellectual property rights regime, pharmaceutical companies are harming the poor on Pogge's account. In turn, one way to avoid this harm is to donate the antiretroviral drugs used in the treatment of HIV or to relax enforcement of the intellectual property rights to allow for the manufacture of generic versions of these drugs.

In response to this line of argument, Richard Miller (2009) questions the claim that maintaining the current institutional order harms the poor in a way that would ground a general responsibility to alleviate global poverty. Specifically, he raises the question about what counts as the morally relevant alternative against which to judge the poor as being worse off under the existing institutional order. One possible alternative is an institutional order that citizens of wealthy nations could support and would be more favorable to the poor. The concern that Miller raises with taking this as the alternative is that it requires a prior moral account for why the citizens of wealthy nations ought to support this alternative institutional order (2009, 158–159). The need for such an account in turn removes the initial intuitive appeal of grounding the responsibility to assist the global poor in a duty not to cause harm. What this discussion suggests is that if an argument along these lines is to be developed for MNEs, it needs to emphasize activities on the part of MNEs that plausibly can be said to cause harm to citizens of developing economies.

One way in which normal economic activity can adversely affect a person is if it involves negative externalities. If there are negative externalities in the context of economic activity, some individuals are not fully compensated for the costs that they bear. Some individuals may not receive any benefit at all yet still bear costs. These individuals are harmed; they are made worse-off as a result of economic activity. One of the most frequently cited examples in the context of an MNE's activities is environmental pollution.[20]

In an account that I have advanced elsewhere (Hsieh, 2009), I argue that what helps to make permissible such potentially harmful activity is if a society is "well-ordered" (Rawls, 1999).[21] Well-ordered societies have social institutions that display three important features. First, a well-ordered society secures human rights for all members of the society. Accordingly, all members of a well-ordered society enjoy protection against the most basic and severe harms that may arise in the course of economic activity. Second, well-ordered societies have a system of law that is able to impose duties and obligations on all people within the territory of the society. Those subject to potential harm can be protected, for example, through environmental regulations that are effectively enforced. Third, members of well-ordered societies have the capacity to influence legislation and seek redress. In order to provide adequate protection and means for redress, it is crucial that all of these mechanisms function independently of the economic system. After all, it is the lack of market-based mechanisms to avoid such harms that gives rise to the problem in the first place. Note also that this lack of market-based mechanisms is what makes it difficult for MNEs to mitigate the harms on their own in the context of economic activity.

If the institutional features of well-ordered societies help to make permissible potentially harmful economic activity, the absence of those institutions in developing economies should raise serious doubts about the permissibility of an MNE's activities. MNEs have the capacity to engage in activities with serious potential for negative externalities. In many cases, MNEs possess a great deal of economic power even relative to the governments of the countries in which they operate. Furthermore, not only do individual citizens lack power relative to MNEs, they also lack the most basic means of protection in an absolute sense. For example, one of the most basic means of protection is to be able to exit from a potentially harmful situation. There is reason to doubt that this is a realistic option for most members of developing economies. On the basis of these points, I conclude in Hsieh (2009) that MNEs have a responsibility to help promote the institutions associated with well-ordered societies on the grounds that they ought to avoid doing harm.

In many ways, the above account can be seen as an argument for a responsibility along the lines of a type (II-2) duty in Shue's account (1996)—that is, a duty to design institutions that avoid the creation of strong incentives to violate a duty not to deprive others in the enjoyment of their basic rights. It should be noted, however, that the conclusion advanced in Hsieh (2009) may be read as not grounding a duty, strictly speaking. It may be said that all the argument shows is that a precondition for MNEs to meet their duties is that they generate the institutions associated with well-ordered societies. There is no duty to generate every precondition to meeting one's duties. For example, suppose that an MNE is not able to generate the institutions associated with a well-ordered society. When there are harms that result from this MNE's activities, this may be in violation of the MNE's duty not to cause harm. Because ought implies can, it seems incorrect to hold that the MNE had a duty to have generated the institutions associated with well-ordered societies.[22]

The two accounts discussed in this section aim to ground a general responsibility to improve the situation of citizens in developing economies in a duty not to deprive them in the exercise of their rights and not to cause harm more generally. As suggested by the discussion in this section, however, there are limits to these accounts. This prompts revisiting the intuition that motivates this line of argument—namely, that positive duties to promote justice or to aid persons deprived in the exercise of their rights do not apply directly to MNEs.

Furthering Justice

In this section, I discuss some challenges for accounts that aim to defend a positive duty on the part of MNEs to improve the situation of citizens in developing economies for reasons of justice that are independent of causing harm or a risk of harming them. Specifically, I highlight three challenges. The first concerns the moral agency of MNEs given their status as artificial persons. The second is that the responsibility does not fall on MNEs simply by default—that is, because there is no good reason not to assign them such a responsibility. The third is that the account of responsibility does not rely solely on the ability of MNEs to improve the situation of citizens in developing economies.

In the initial discussion about the moral agency of MNEs, the point was made that many commentators hold the view that because MNEs are artificial persons, the duties that apply to natural persons do not apply readily to MNEs. Indeed, some commentators hold that it is mistaken to talk about there being any moral responsibilities on the part of MNEs at all. In response, the point was raised that the responsibilities of the natural persons who represent MNEs can carry over to MNEs (Lane, 2005, 238). For example, because it is wrong to violate the rights of another person, no one could morally act for an MNE to violate the rights of another person, and hence no MNE can permissibly violate the rights of others.

There is reason to doubt that the same argument applies for a positive duty to provide assistance to citizens in developing economies. Suppose that the people who represent MNEs have a responsibility, as natural persons, to provide assistance to citizens of developing economies on the grounds of justice. To say they have such a responsibility is to hold that they have a responsibility to devote some share of what they own to the citizens of developing economies. The people who represent MNEs, however, do not own the resources of the MNE. Accordingly, the responsibility to provide assistance to citizens in developing economies need not carry over to MNEs in the same manner as negative duties that apply to the people representing MNEs. In turn, the first challenge is to account for the responsibility on the part of MNEs to improve the situation of citizens of developing economies in a way that does not assume that MNEs are natural persons and that acknowledges their status as for-profit business enterprises.

This brings us to the second challenge. Recall the distinction drawn by O'Neill (2001) between primary and secondary agents of justice. According to O'Neill, under "ideal conditions"—that is, when states are able to bring about and maintain justice—MNEs are best understood as secondary agents of justice. However, under "non-ideal conditions" in which states are weak and lack the means to bring about justice, according to O'Neill, "any simple division between primary and secondary agents of justice blurs" (2001, 201). "Justice," she continues, "has to be built by a diversity of agents and agencies," and MNEs, according to O'Neill, are among those agents (2001, 201).[23]

O'Neill makes her case by arguing against the objection that MNEs have constitutive aims that prevent them from serving as primary agents of justice (2001, 200). She writes, "For example, [MNEs] have often been criticised for using their considerable ranges of capabilities to get away with injustice: for dumping hazardous wastes in states too weak to achieve effective environmental protection; for avoiding taxation by placing headquarters in banana republics; for avoiding safety legislation by registering vessels under 'flags of convenience' or by placing dangerous production processes in areas without effective worker protection legislation" (O'Neill, 2001, 200). She continues, "If the critics who point to these failings really believed that [MNEs] cannot but maximise profits, these objections would be pointless; in fact, they assume (more accurately) that major [MNEs] can choose among a range of policies and actions" (O'Neill, 2001, 200). O'Neill concludes there is nothing constitutive about the aims of MNEs that prevents them from acting as primary agents of justice.

In response to O'Neill's account, the following point may be raised. O'Neill's argument rests on claims of injustice that can be characterized with reference to a negative duty not to harm others by violating their rights. However, even if we recognize that the constitutive aims of MNEs are consistent with negative duties not to infringe upon the rights of others, it does not follow that their constitutive aims are consistent with positive duties to assist people who are deprived in the exercise of their rights or to promote just institutions. As discussed above, the view advanced by Donaldson (1989) and others is precisely that MNEs have responsibilities not to deprive others in the exercise of their rights, but do not have responsibilities to assist those who are deprived in the exercise of their rights. For an account such as O'Neill's to provide a robust alternative, there must be good reason to assign a responsibility to MNEs to help improve the situation for citizens in developing economies, and not just the absence of a reason not to do so.

James Griffin (2004) aims to provide just such a reason for assigning a responsibility to MNEs to help citizens in developing economies. Surveying the HIV/AIDS crisis in sub-Saharan Africa, Griffin notes that pharmaceutical companies are positioned to increase access to the antiretroviral drugs used in the treatment of HIV given that they hold the patents to these drugs. In turn, he writes, "as pharmaceutical firms can now decide life and death, and as there is a human right to life, these firms are in a special moral position" (Griffin, 2004, 43). This special moral position involves providing assistance to the victims of HIV/AIDS who are deprived in the exercise of their right to life.

Griffin's account highlights what I take to be a third challenge facing accounts that aim to ground a responsibility on the part of MNEs to assist people deprived in the exercise of their rights or to promote just institutions. This challenge is that the account does not rely solely on the ability of MNEs to improve the situation of persons in developing economies as the basis for having such a responsibility. The point is not to deny that MNEs have a duty—say, of rescue—to act in ways that assist persons who are deprived in the exercise of their rights. Rather, the point is to distinguish a justice-based approach from accounts grounded in considerations of rescue or beneficence. If the claim is that MNEs have a responsibility to provide such assistance or to help promote justice, then this responsibility needs to be grounded in considerations of justice.[24]

Earlier in the chapter, a distinction between a justice-based account and an account grounded in beneficence was drawn in terms of the greater level and scope of assistance likely to be demanded by a justice-based account. This difference, however, is not the only relevant distinction that may be drawn between the two kinds of accounts. Another important distinction concerns the relationship between the recipients of assistance and MNEs. If an MNE has a responsibility to assist people solely because of its ability to provide assistance, then the recipients of assistance have no special claim against it in virtue of their interaction with the MNE or in virtue of the distinctive status of MNEs in the global economy. There is nothing particularly distinctive about their claim to have been wronged by MNEs when MNEs fail to alleviate the deprivation of their rights or when MNEs fail to promote justice more generally. In a sense, they are passive recipients of assistance without any special attention paid to the nature of their claim against MNEs. In contrast, I take it that a justice-based account of the responsibilities of MNEs aims to capture the intuition that citizens in developing economies are wronged in a distinctive manner in such cases. The intuition is that they suffer an injustice and that this injustice gives them a special claim to press. Accordingly, the third challenge for justice-based accounts is to ground the MNE's responsibility to provide assistance in features about the MNE that relate not only to its ability to provide assistance.[25]

Conclusion

The aim of this chapter has been to explore ways in which our thinking about the moral responsibilities of MNEs can be furthered by locating questions about the responsibilities of MNEs within broader debates about global justice. As a way to focus this inquiry, I evaluated accounts that take a justice-based approach to address one of the most challenging questions about the responsibilities of MNEs—namely, whether there is there a moral responsibility on the part of MNEs headquartered in developed economies to help improve the situation of citizens in developing economies, even if this comes at some expense to long-run profitability. In the light of this analysis, I close with three points relating to the promise of developing a justice-based approach to this question and to the more general issue of the responsibilities of MNEs.

The first point is a call for further examination of what justice demands of individuals in their roles as shareholders and employees of MNEs. Negative duties that apply to natural persons are thought to carry over to MNEs by way of their representatives, but there are reasons to doubt that positive duties that apply to individuals transfer in a similar manner given issues of ownership in MNEs. It may be the case, however, that occupying the position of a shareholder or an employee gives rise to additional responsibilities that carry over to

MNEs. For example, perhaps it is the case that when individuals engage in a collective endeavor that achieves more than the sum of their individual efforts, then there are good reasons for individuals to discharge their responsibilities through the endeavor.[26] Inquiry along these lines has the potential to further our understanding about the extent to which the limited moral agency of MNEs limits their responsibilities to improve the situation of citizens in developing economies. Inquiry along these lines also may help to address the challenges faced by justice-based accounts that aim to ground a responsibility to provide assistance in considerations beyond the ability of MNEs to provide assistance.

Second, if there is a responsibility on the part of MNEs to improve the situation of citizens of developing economies, there is much to recommend that MNEs work to strengthen host country institutions rather than engage in the direct provision of assistance to citizens. The reasoning is as follows. In the preceding section, the point was made that part of what justice-based accounts aim to capture is the intuition that citizens in developing economies are wronged in a distinctive manner when they are deprived in the exercise of their rights. They suffer an injustice that gives them a special claim to press for assistance. Normally, the appropriate target of such a claim is the state of which the individuals are citizens. In the case of an MNE, however, citizens of developing economies may see themselves in a different relationship. They may see themselves as recipients of corporate philanthropy, even if an MNE has a responsibility to improve their situation on grounds of justice. If so, this undermines one of the primary aims of a justice-based account. Working to strengthen the host country institutions, rather than engaging in the direct provision of assistance, helps to avoid this problem.[27]

The third point is this. Justice-based accounts have a strong claim to being able to capture the intuition that MNEs have responsibilities toward citizens of developing economies in virtue of MNEs' role in the global economy and MNEs' interaction with them, and not just by default. At the same time, accounts grounded in other considerations can lay claim to capturing this intuition. These include, for example, accounts grounded in prohibitions against exploitation or in considerations of fairness regarding the allocation of benefits and burdens from economic transactions. In focusing on a justice-based approach to the responsibilities of MNEs, I do not mean to suggest that these alternative accounts lack merit. Rather the point is this. If justice is the "first virtue of social institutions," as John Rawls claims (1971, 3), then trying to understand better what role MNEs have in promoting justice is a good place to start.

Notes

1. A multinational enterprise (MNE) is an enterprise headquartered in one country (often referred to as the "parent enterprise") that controls the activities of one or

more enterprises that are based in other countries (often referred to as "affiliate enterprises"). Control is usually exercised through the ownership of a significant share of equity in the foreign affiliate. A common threshold for control is ownership of 10 percent or more of the ordinary shares or voting power in the foreign affiliate. An important feature of MNEs is that MNEs have a decision-making structure that allows for a common strategy and a coherent set of policies among the parent and affiliate enterprises (UNCTAD, 2010). See also OECD (2010) for more detail.

2. In the case of countries, GDP is taken as the measure of their economic size. If the revenue of MNEs is used as a measure of their size, then MNEs comprise roughly half of the hundred largest economic entities in the world. However, as De Grauwe and Camerman (2003) point out, GDP is the sum of the value added by each producer, which is not the same as the sum of the revenue of these producers. Aggregating the revenue of producers is likely to involve counting more than once the value added by producers. Accordingly, the authors argue that counting the revenue of MNEs overstates their relative size. Following the authors' method of calculating the value added by MNEs, one estimate places twenty-nine MNEs within the top hundred economic entities in the world (UNCTAD, 2002).

3. Foreign direct investment (FDI) is an investment in an enterprise in another country with the objective of establishing a "lasting interest" in that country. The lasting interest implies "a long-term relationship" between the investor and the enterprise and "a significant degree of influence" by the investor on the management of the enterprise. Direct or indirect ownership of 10 percent or more of the voting power of an enterprise is taken as evidence of such a relationship (OECD, 2010, 17). As Navaretti and Venables (2006) note, because MNEs must undertake FDI to "create, acquire or expand a foreign subsidiary," FDI is a useful measure of MNE activity (3). See also World Bank (2010) for more detail.

4. For two earlier treatments, see Donaldson (1989) and De George (1993). For a more recent survey of the literature on corporate responsibility, see Crane, McWilliams, Matten, Moon, and Siegel (2008).

5. One issue that has attracted much attention concerns the working conditions for laborers in footwear and apparel manufacturing. For one discussion, see Hartman, Arnold, and Wokutch (2003).

6. For cases that illustrate ways in which MNEs are able to help meet global needs, see Hartman and Werhane (2009).

7. In 2008, over 80 percent of FDI originated from developed economies (UNCTAD, 2009, 364). Developed economies are defined by UNCTAD to include Bermuda, Canada, USA, Israel, Japan, Australia, New Zealand, Austria, Belgium, Bulgaria, Cyprus, Czech Republic, Denmark, Estonia, Finland, France, Germany, Greece, Hungary, Iceland, Ireland, Italy, Latvia, Lithuania, Luxembourg, the Netherlands, Norway, Poland, Portugal, Romania, Slovakia, Slovenia, Spain, Sweden, and the United Kingdom (UNCTAD, 2009, xiv).

8. For a recent discussion of this issue as it applies to MNEs, see Michaelson (2010).

9. For a survey of the main theories of corporate responsibility, see Melé (2008). For a survey of ways to ground questions about corporate responsibility in a liberal egalitarian theory of justice, see Hsieh (2008).

10. Of course there is some disagreement on whether institutions or group behavior should lead the way in promoting justice. John Rawls is a champion of the former (1971, 1999). For examples of the contrary view see Sen (2009, Chap. 2) and Boylan (2004, Chap. 8).

11. In high-income countries, for example, the rate of excess mortality among the HIV-infected population relative to the HIV-uninfected population declined by 85 percent with the introduction of highly active antiretroviral therapy (UNAIDS, 2009, 16). See also Ford, Mills, and Calmy (2009).

12. For purposes of this chapter, human rights are understood as moral rights rather than as legal rights grounded in international conventions. The Universal Declaration of Human Rights is introduced simply as one example of a list of specific rights.

13. As an illustration of the general acceptance of this view, consider the report to the United Nations Human Rights Council from the Special Representative of the Secretary-General (Ruggie, 2008). In this report, Ruggie concludes that although MNEs may be in a position to aid persons who are deprived from exercising basic human rights, it would be mistaken to remove this responsibility from states and assign it to MNEs (4). Instead, the appropriate responsibility for MNEs is to respect rights, by which Ruggie means, "not to infringe on the rights of others—put simply, to do no harm" (9). For another account on the limited human rights responsibilities of MNEs see Sorell (2004).

14. On the influence of Shue's account, see Pogge (2009, 125).

15. For the classic statement of this view, commonly referred to as "shareholder primacy," see Friedman (1970). A more recent statement of this view can be found in Sternberg (2000). For a review of the literature that compares this view to other prominent accounts of corporate purpose and responsibility, see Melé (2008).

16. The major potential cost to pharmaceutical companies under this scheme is the risk that the medicines provided in sub-Saharan Africa are resold in developed economy markets at a discounted price. For a discussion of this specific issue and for an argument to structure the pharmaceutical industry under a cooperative, rather than a competitive, model see Boylan (2008). Boylan argues that the cooperative model would help to address the concern with the resale of medicines (2008, 39–40) and the lack of access to medicines more generally.

17. Lane (2005) argues, for example, that a person's position as a representative of a business enterprise may give her access to information or certain capabilities that

give rise to new responsibilities. These responsibilities in turn fall back on the business enterprise.

18. For purposes of this chapter, I do not defend any one particular theory of global distributive justice. However, the account does rule out theories that do not recognize a rights-based approach, such as straightforwardly consequentialist accounts. The chapter also assumes that welfare rights can be counted as human rights. On this latter debate, see Ashford (2009).

19. For purposes of this chapter, I assume that justice requires respect for human rights. Beitz (2001), for example, argues that respect for human rights is a necessary condition for the minimal legitimacy of any state.

20. This paragraph and what follows draw from Hsieh (2009).

21. In his account, Rawls distinguishes between two classes of well-ordered societies: *liberal peoples* and *decent peoples.* Liberal peoples share "a reasonably just constitutional democratic government that serves their fundamental interests; citizens united by what Mill called 'common sympathies'; and finally, a moral nature" (Rawls, 1999, 23). *Decent peoples* are nonliberal. One type of decent peoples is what Rawls calls a *decent hierarchical people.* Such a society is nonaggressive and meets three additional criteria: first, it secures human rights for all members of the society; second, it has a system of law that is able to impose duties and obligations on all people with the territory of the society; and third, those who administer the legal system understand the law to be guided by a common good idea of justice (Rawls, 1999, 64–67). Rawls specifies human rights to include "the right to life (to the means of subsistence and security); to liberty (to freedom from slavery, serfdom, and forced occupation, and to a sufficient measure of liberty of conscience to ensure freedom of religion and thought); to property (personal property); and to formal equality as expressed by the rules of natural justice (that is, similar cases be treated similarly)" (Rawls, 1999, 65). This discussion draws from Hsieh (2009).

22. I thank Nir Eyal for raising this point in personal communication about Hsieh (2009). For other objections to the account raised in Hsieh (2009), see Michaelson (2010) and Wettstein (2010).

23. The discussion of O'Neill (2001) draws from Hsieh (2009).

24. Sorell (2004) makes a similar point (139–140).

25. In his discussion of the responsibility of pharmaceutical companies with respect to the HIV/AIDS crisis in sub-Saharan Africa, James Griffin alludes to two other considerations: the benefit that pharmaceutical companies derive from the existing economic regime and the idea that prices above a certain amount are no longer "decent" (2004, 43).

26. For an initial attempt to examine this line of argument see Hsieh (2004). For a related suggestion along these lines with regard to the responsibilities of consumers in developed economies toward workers in developing economies, see Young (2004).

27. To be certain, such an approach introduces new difficulties, including determining the most effective means for MNEs to strengthen host country institutions and the limits to involvement by MNEs in host country institutions. In Hsieh (2009), I take up some of these issues.

References

Ashford, Elizabeth. (2009). "The Alleged Dichotomy Between Positive and Negative Rights and Duties" in *Global Basic Rights*, ed. Charles Beitz and Robert Goodin: 92–112. Oxford: Oxford University Press.

Beitz, Charles. (2001). "Human Rights as a Common Concern." *American Political Science Review 95*(2): 269–282.

Boylan, Michael. (2004). *A Just Society*. Lanham, MD: Rowman and Littlefield.

Boylan, Michael. (2008). "Medical Pharmaceuticals and Distributive Justice." *Cambridge Quarterly of Healthcare Ethics 17*(1): 32–46.

Boylan, Michael. (2011). *Morality and Global Justice*. Boulder, CO: Westview.

Campbell, Thomas. (2004). "Moral Dimensions of Human Rights" in *Human Rights and the Moral Responsibilities of Corporate and Public Sector Organizations*, ed. Thomas Campbell and Seumas Miller: 11–30. Dordecht: Kluwer Academic Publishers.

Crane, Andrew, Abagail McWilliams, Dirk Matten, Jeremy Moon, and Donald Siegel, ed. (2008). *The Oxford Handbook of Corporate Social Responsibility*. Oxford: Oxford University Press.

De George, Richard. (1993). *Competing with Integrity in International Business*. New York: Oxford University Press.

De Grauwe, Paul, and Filip Camerman. (2003). "Are Multinationals Really Bigger Than Nations?" *World Economics 4*(2): 23–37.

Donaldson, Thomas. (1989). *The Ethics of International Business*. New York: Oxford University Press.

Dunfee, Thomas W. (2006, April). "Do Firms with Unique Competencies for Rescuing Victims of Human Catastrophes Have Special Obligations? Corporate Responsibility and the AIDS Catastrophe in Sub-Saharan Africa." *Business Ethics Quarterly, 16*(2): 185–210.

Ford, Nathan, Edward Mills, and Alexandra Calmy. (2009). "Rationing Antiretroviral Therapy in Africa: Treating Too Few, Too Late." *New England Journal of Medicine 360*(18): 1808–1810.

Friedman, Milton. (1970, 13 September). "The Social Responsibility of Business Is to Increase Its Profits." *The New York Times Magazine*: 32.

Gathii, James. (2005). "Third World Perspectives on Global Pharmaceutical Access" in *Ethics and the Pharmaceutical Industry in the 21st Century*, ed. Michael Santoro and Thomas Gorrie: 336–351. New York: Cambridge University Press.

Griffin, James. (2004). "Human Rights: Whose Duties?" in *Human Rights and the Moral Responsibilities of Corporate and Public Sector Organizations*, ed. Thomas Campbell and Seumas Miller: 31–44. Dordecht: Kluwer Academic Publishers.

Hartman, Laura, Denis Arnold, and Richard Wokutch. (2003). *Rising Above Sweatshops: Innovative Approaches to Global Labor Challenges*. Westport, CT: Praeger.

Hartman, Laura, and Patricia Werhane, ed. (2009). *The Global Corporation: Sustainable, Effective and Ethical Practices: A Case Book*. New York: Routledge.

Hsieh, Nien-hê. (2004). "The Obligations of Transnational Corporations: Rawlsian Justice and the Duty of Assistance." *Business Ethics Quarterly 14*(4): 643–661.

Hsieh, Nien-hê. (2005). "Property Rights in Crisis: Managers and Rescue" in *Ethics and the Pharmaceutical Industry in the 21st Century*, ed. Michael Santoro and Thomas Gorrie: 379–385. New York: Cambridge University Press.

Hsieh, Nien-hê. (2006). "Voluntary Codes of Conduct for Multinational Corporations: Coordinating Duties of Rescue and Justice." *Business Ethics Quarterly 16*(2): 119–135.

Hsieh, Nien-hê. (2008). "The Normative Study of Business Organizations: A Rawlsian Approach" in *Normative Theory and Business Ethics*, ed. Jeffery Smith: 93–117. Lanham, MD: Rowman and Littlefield.

Hsieh, Nien-hê. (2009). "Does Global Business Have a Responsibility to Promote Just Institutions?" *Business Ethics Quarterly 19*(2): 251–273.

Lane, Melissa. (2004). "Autonomy as a Central Human Right and Its Implications for the Moral Responsibilities of Corporations" in *Human Rights and the Moral Responsibilities of Corporate and Public Sector Organizations*, ed. Thomas Campbell and Seumas Miller: 145–163. Dordecht: Kluwer Academic Publishers.

Lane, Melissa. (2005). "The Moral Dimension of Corporate Responsibility" in *Global Responsibilities*, ed. Andrew Kuper. New York: Routledge.

Melé, Dominic. (2008). "Corporate Social Responsibility Theories" in *The Oxford Handbook of Corporate Social Responsibility*, ed. Andrew Crane, Abagail McWilliams, Dirk Matten, Jeremy Moon, and Donald Siegel: 47–82. Oxford: Oxford University Press.

Michaelson, Christopher. (2010). "Revisiting the Global Business Ethics Question." *Business Ethics Quarterly 20*(2): 237–251.

Miller, Richard. (2009). "Global Power and Economic Justice" in *Global Basic Rights*, ed. Charles Beitz and Robert Goodin: 156–180. Oxford: Oxford University Press.

Navaretti, Giorgio, and Anthony Venables. (2006). *Multinational Firms in the World Economy*. Princeton, NJ: Princeton University Press.

OECD. (2008, July). "The Social Impact of Foreign Direct Investment." *Policy Brief*. Paris: Organisation for Economic Co-operation and Development.

OECD. (2010). *OECD Benchmark Definition of Foreign Direct Investment, Fourth Edition*. Paris: Organisation for Economic Co-operation and Development.

O'Neill, Onora. (2001). "Agents of Justice" in *Global Justice*, ed. Thomas Pogge: 188–203. Oxford: Blackwell.

Pogge, Thomas. (2005). "Severe Poverty as a Violation of Negative Duties." *Ethics and International Affairs 19*(1): 55–83.

Pogge, Thomas. (2007). "Severe Poverty as a Human Rights Violation" in *Freedom from Poverty as a Human Right*, ed. Thomas Pogge: 11–54. New York: Oxford University Press.

Pogge, Thomas. (2008). *World Poverty and Human Rights, Second Edition.* Cambridge: Polity.

Pogge, Thomas. (2009). "Shue on Rights and Duties" in *Global Basic Rights*, ed. Charles Beitz and Robert Goodin: 113–130. Oxford: Oxford University Press.

Rawls, John. (1971). *A Theory of Justice*. Cambridge, MA: Harvard University Press.

Rawls, John. (1999). *The Law of Peoples*. Cambridge, MA: Harvard University Press.

Ruggie, John. (2008). "Promotion and Protection of All Human Rights, Civil, Political, Economic, Social and Cultural Rights, Including the Right to Development." Report to the United Nations Human Rights Council.

Scanlon, T. M. (1998). *What We Owe to Each Other.* Cambridge, MA: Harvard University Press.

Sen, Amartya. (2009). *The Idea of Justice*. Cambridge, MA: Harvard University Press.

Shue, Henry. (1996). *Basic Rights: Subsistence, Affluence, and U.S. Foreign Policy, Second Edition.* Princeton, NJ: Princeton University Press.

Sorell, Thomas. (2004). "Business and Human Rights" in *Human Rights and the Moral Responsibilities of Corporate and Public Sector Organizations*, ed. Thomas Campbell and Seumas Miller: 1129–1144. Dordecht: Kluwer Academic Publishers.

Sternberg, Elaine. (2000). *Just Business: Business Ethics in Action, Second Edition.* Oxford: Oxford University Press.

United Nations. (1948). Universal Declaration of Human Rights.

UNAIDS. (2009). *AIDS Epidemic Update*. Geneva: Joint United Nations Programme on HIV/AIDS (UNAIDS) and World Health Organization.

UNCTAD. (2002). "Are Transnationals Bigger than Countries?" Press Release. Geneva: United Nations Conference on Trade and Development.

UNCTAD. (2009). World Investment Report. New York: United Nations Publications.

UNCTAD. (2010). "Transnational Corporations." Retrieved from www.unctad.org

Wettstein, Florian. (2010). "For Better or Worse: Corporate Social Responsibility Beyond 'Do No Harm.'" *Business Ethics Quarterly 20*(2): 275–283.

World Bank. (2010). *Global Development Finance: External Debt of Developing Countries*. Washington, DC: The World Bank.

Young, Iris Marion. (2004). "Responsibility and Global Labor Justice." *Journal of Political Philosophy 12*(4): 365–388.

PART THREE

NORMATIVE APPLICATIONS

Global Health

■ Chapter 11 Global Health Justice
MICHAEL J. SELGELID

■ Chapter 12 Access to Life-Saving Medicines
DORIS SCHROEDER, THOMAS POGGE, AND PETER SINGER

PART THREE: Global Health
INTRODUCTION

One important way that we are globally connected, most would agree, is through global health. The two essays in this section highlight issues in global justice from the perspective of health. We begin with a broad essay that makes use of normative principles and a normative theory. Michael J. Selgelid's essay is centered around the problem of moral motivation (compare to Part One). The motivation is about funding for health care in developing nations around the world—particularly infectious diseases. Selgelid divides his comments to appeals from moral and prudential arguments.

The essay begins with the first of three ethical reasons for funding of global health care (particularly of the least advantaged). Selgelid cites Norman Daniels to support a policy that removes health care from the private marketplace. This is because the maintenance of health is a human right (see Part One). This is justified from Daniels's perspective because disease interferes with human functioning and thus reduces the opportunities of the sick. Equal opportunity is a crucial tenet of Norman Daniels and John Rawls (whose theories condition Selgelid's approach); thus, justice demands funding for health care around the world.

Now it is true that Rawls was more nationally oriented in his exposition, but some of his students such as Daniels and Thomas Pogge believe that Rawls's own account requires him to expand the vision of justice globally. Selgelid concurs. The policy emphasis is to aim one's resources to assist the worst-off in the world. Thus, the direction of policy should be upon expanding funding for global health beginning with the worst-off.

Health care is not only a human right, but it is also justified by desert theory. Those who are least advantaged are so (for the most part) due to circumstances beyond their control. Desert theory suggests that we do not penalize individuals for that which is beyond their control. This constitutes a second reason for funding global health care for those who lack this essential good due to conditions not in their control (compare to my version of progressive desert theory in the last section).

The second major ethical support comes from an ethical theory, utilitarianism (a form of consequentialism). On the one hand, Selgelid sees this as a clear winner:

there are substantial benefits to be achieved at a very small price. However, as we saw in Lillehammer's article, there is the issue of partiality and impartiality. If it is rational to show partiality to family, friends, and those in proximity (your city, state, and nation), then this could destroy the motivation for global health care. To respond, Selgelid cites Peter Singer's shallow pond and the small amount of sacrifice that is being asked.

The last ethical argument comes from libertarianism, another normative theory. Selgelid asserts that there is a difference between oppressive conditions caused by bad luck and those caused by injustice. As Seumas Miller argued (à la Pogge), the latter instance constitutes a negative duty. Since libertarians only recognize the duty not to harm (and if such harm could be shown by the wealthy countries against the impoverished countries), then a negative duty would ensue to fund global health care. Selgelid cites examples of such historical injustices.

The prudential (self-interested) arguments begin with our own health (wherever we live). The most immanent would be public health epidemics. The H1N1 virus (at the writing of this book) has not proved to be the killer that the post-WWI flu epidemic proved to be—but that may change. Tuberculosis was once thought to be a forgotten infectious disease, but now new strains that are immune to all treatments present themselves and threaten the health of us all. No matter how much a society wants to separate itself from its underclass (the *other*), infectious disease has a way of making all people *count as one*.

A second prudential argument for funding global health care is economically oriented. When there are significant numbers of the population subject to infectious disease, such as HIV/AIDS, then the large numbers of fatalities in that region of the world will have an economic impact that is felt by all.

The third prudential argument concerns global security. Selgelid is a part of an international global security organization operating out of Australian National University so he has "on the ground" expertise here. This twist to the argument is that pandemics and other biological situations destabilize nation-states and their international region. Social and political instability threatens global security (a goal we all share).

In the end Selgelid argues that we should fund global health initiatives based both upon moral and prudential concerns.

In Doris Schroeder, Thomas Pogge, and Peter Singer's article a more narrow issue is addressed: access to life-saving medicines. The chapter begins with some startling statistics: 75 percent of all under-five-years-old deaths occurred in only eighteen countries in the world, and one third of the world's population does not have access to life-saving medicines today—as a result 10 million lives are lost prematurely each year! To understand the dimensions of this catastrophic problem we must turn first to the legal right to health care. Some states, such as Germany, have national laws that guarantee access to health insurance. Others like Britain have a state-run delivery system. From the international perspective, the United Nations Universal Declaration of Human Rights affirms the human right to health care.

The United Nations and other negotiated treaties provide a legal basis for: (a) the various world governments' obligation to their citizens in this regard, and (b) governmental obligations for international assistance to other nations. Legal activists within a particular country can make use of these legal documents to gain a greater commitment to health care at home and abroad.

However, despite these aspirational promises of providing life-saving medications to the poor of the world, the reality falls woefully short (10 million lives short). One of the culprits here are intellectual property rights (IPRs). IPRs were created to foster research and development. It is thought that unless you provide a legally protected monopoly to the creator of a movie, toy, or pharmaceutical, the incentive for innovation will be very small. But the downside to IPRs is that their monopoly status leads to excessive pricing. In the case of pharmaceuticals, the losers are those most at risk: the poor of the world who cannot afford these life-saving drugs.

But the patent treaties themselves often cite social needs as a parallel concern that should be addressed even as intellectual property is recognized and protected. This bifurcation comes from the two sorts of social rules: (a) natural rules based on God, innate intuition, or the structure of reason, and (b) rules that are conventionally set up for social purposes. An example of the first type is the rule not to murder. Traffic rules are an example of the second type. Which sort of rule are IPRs? There are some arguments that support either approach. Clearly, the pharmaceutical companies would want to argue that they are natural rights (because this would make their claims stronger). But even if IPRs are natural, there can be a conflict between natural rights: for example, the natural right of a company to have a monopoly on a drug for a period of time versus the natural right of poor people not to be killed by diseases for which there is a pharmaceutical cure. Even natural rights advocates such as Aquinas and Locke support the right to life over excess property claims.

In order to address this dilemma, treaties have been signed by many nations. The two most relevant here are the Trade-Related Aspects of Intellectual Property Rights Agreement (TRIPS) and various Free Trade Agreements (FTAs). Before TRIPS and FTAs, poorer countries ignored patent protections and created cheap generic versions of drugs for their own use and for export to other poor countries. This had the following result: (a) it increased access to drugs among the poor, but (b) it gave large pharmaceutical companies little incentive to do research and development on drugs that uniquely affect poor populations. TRIPS and FTAs are meant to reverse this because when the poor countries sign on to these agreements they also agree to respect intellectual property and stop manufacturing generics of protected drugs. But this also results in lack of access to these protected drugs.

In order to facilitate this approach and solve the access problem, the authors support a policy called the Health Impact Fund. This international fund would pay pharmaceutical companies, for up to ten years, a supplemental fee in return for assurances that the pharmaceutical companies sell their drugs at the lowest possible price. The taxpayers of the world would support the fund progressively. The authors contend that this system would both increase drug access and encourage companies to engage in research and development for drugs uniquely affecting the poor. The choice of traditional marketing or marketing under the Health Impact Fund would be made by the pharmaceutical companies separately for each drug they bring to market.

Schroeder, Pogge, and Singer believe that the Health Impact Fund would be a significant step forward toward recognizing both intellectual property rights and the legitimate rights claim that all people can rightly make toward access to life-saving drugs.

CHAPTER ELEVEN

Global Health Justice

MICHAEL J. SELGELID
Centre for Applied Philosophy and Public Ethics (CAPPE)
The Australian National University

Abstract

This paper examines cumulative ethical and self-interested reasons why wealthy developed nations should be motivated to do more to improve health care in developing countries. Egalitarian and human rights reasons why wealthy nations should do more to improve global health are that doing so would (1) promote equality of opportunity, (2) improve the situation of the worst-off, (3) promote basic human rights, and (4) reduce undeserved inequalities in well-being. Utilitarian reasons for improving global health are that this would (5) promote the greater good of humankind, and (6) achieve enormous benefits while requiring only small sacrifices. Libertarian reasons are that this would (7) amend historical injustices, and (8) meet the obligation to amend injustices that developed world countries have contributed to. Self-interested reasons why wealthy nations should do more to improve global health are that doing so

---

Author's note: I thank Elisa Garcia Pinar for assistance producing Figure 11.1. This chapter was initially presented at a workshop on Poverty and Medicine at the Centre for Applied Philosophy and Public Ethics (CAPPE) at the University of Melbourne in January 2006. For reading that initial draft and providing constructive feedback, I thank all the workshop participants, including Tom Campbell, Leonardo de Castro, Sachin Chaturvedi, Margaret Coady, Tony Coady, Tom Faunce, John Funder, David Henry, Keith Horton, Barry Jones, Thomas Pogge, Peter Singer, and Janna Thompson. I likewise thank Thaddeus Metz and Daniel Star for reading the paper and providing valuable comments. An earlier version of this chapter was published as "Improving Global Health: Counting Reasons Why." *Developing World Bioethics* 8(2): 115–125. I thank Wiley-Blackwell for permission to reprint this material here. The essay was improved thanks to useful suggestions provided by three anonymous reviewers for *Developing World Bioethics*. Any remaining errors are my own.

would (9) reduce the threat of infectious diseases to developed countries, (10) promote developed countries' economic interests, and (11) promote global security.

Key Words

global public health, infectious disease, health rights, AIDS, tuberculosis, antimicrobial resistance, security

---

Given the current health care situation in developing countries and the wide recognition that financial assistance from wealthy developed nations is needed to improve the situation, the question of why wealthy developed nations should be motivated to do more to improve health in developing countries is paramount. This chapter argues that compatible cumulative moral (egalitarian, utilitarian, and libertarian) and self-interested reasons add up to make an overwhelmingly powerful case that increased developed world funding of developing world health is called for.[1]

The Case for Funding

Ethical Reasons

Egalitarian and Human Rights Reasons

1. Equality of Opportunity

To date, perhaps the best developed ethical argument for treating health care as a special kind of good has been that provided by Norman Daniels (1985, 2007). We should remove health care from free-market mechanisms and recognize a right to at least a minimal basic package of health care, according to Daniels, because of the importance of health to justice. Adopting a Rawlsian framework, Daniels holds (the not especially controversial claim) that equality of opportunity is a key component of justice. Heath care is, therefore, according to Daniels, especially important to justice because disease interferes with human functioning and thereby reduces the opportunities of those who are sick. Since equality of opportunity is crucial to justice, so is health care. A just society should thus ensure that provisions are made to restore individuals to the level of functioning they would have enjoyed if they were healthy.

A weakness of this argument when applied to the global scene is that Rawls's *A Theory of Justice* (1971), on which Daniels depends, is meant to apply to the institutions of domestic society rather than internationally. In his discussion of international justice, furthermore, Rawls (1999) explicitly denies that his domestic principles of justice apply globally. International justice, according to Rawls, does not require one country to ensure that equality of opportunity is realized in other countries. As others have argued, however, Rawls's denial that his domestic theory of justice applies internationally is inconsistent with what he says in *A Theory of Justice* (Moellendorf, 2002; Pogge, 2002). Given the amount of direct and indirect interaction between noncompatriots in today's globalized world—and thus the de facto international sharing of social institutions—it is reasonable to think that local demands of justice should apply worldwide. Theory aside, this will appeal to many as a commonsense precept. We have identified at least one reason for improving health in developing countries: the importance of equality of opportunity.

2. Improving the Situation of Those Who Are Worst-off

A second reason for being ethically concerned about the health care situation in developing countries also appeals to Rawls's *A Theory of Justice*. Despite Daniels's particular application of Rawls's equality of opportunity principle to the context of health care, the general spirit of Rawls is that justice requires that the situation of the worst-off members of society be improved as much as possible. For anyone who shares the general intuition that justice is promoted by improvement of the situation of the worst-off members of society, and for anyone who believes that this aspect of justice applies globally, improvement of health care in developing countries should appear to be an appropriate social goal. The sick and poor in sub-Saharan Africa are, by any measure, clearly among the worst-off members of global society, and increased provision of health care is one of the things most needed to improve their situation.

Both here and in my argument above (and in my arguments below), I should note that I am not relying on any particular theory of justice. My point is simply that central tenets of Rawls's *A Theory of Justice* embody intuitions that many of us will share—that justice is promoted by, among other things, increasing equality of opportunity and by improving the situation of those who are worst-off. (Again, despite Rawls's denial that his principles of justice for domestic justice apply worldwide, there are both commonsense and theoretical reasons for thinking that they should, as cosmopolitans such as Pogge and Moellendorf have argued.) This is not to say that most of us do or should think that these goals should have priority over all others or that we must always do whatever it takes to maximize equality of opportunity or to improve the situation of the worst-off members of society. Promotion of equality of opportunity and improvement of the situation of the worst-off members of (global) society are two goals among many that should be taken into consideration, which is not to say that there are no countervailing reasons for not taking action.

3. The Universal Human Right to Have One's Basic Needs Met

Additional support for the claim that more should be done to improve the health care situation in developing countries lies in the widely shared idea that human beings have a universal right to have their most basic needs met—and the recognition that health care and things like shelter, clothing, housing, food, and clean water count as basic human needs (Griffin, 2008; Boylan, 2004). While philosophical justification for this kind of right is beyond the scope of this paper, the idea that such a right obtains is reflected by the existence of universal health care systems in every industrialized nation except the United States. The idea that all human beings share such rights is furthermore enshrined by authoritative international documents such as the Universal Declaration of Human Rights (1999), which claims in Article 25, "Everyone has the right to a standard of living adequate for the health and well-being of himself and his family, including food, clothing, and medical care" and that, "Every individual and every organ of society . . . shall strive . . . by progressive measures, national and international, to secure [its] universal and effective recognition." The aim to promote respect of the human right to have one's most basic needs (including health care) met, as required by the Universal Declaration of Human Rights, provides a third reason why wealthy world countries should act to improve global health.

If it is legitimate that foreign policy measures are taken by one country with the aim of improving respect for human rights in other countries, and if it is legitimate for one country to spend enormous sums of money with the explicit aim of promoting human rights in other countries, then it is legitimate for wealthy developed nations to act to improve health care in developing countries. If wealthy developed nations deny that improvement of global health could justify large-scale expenditure, then they will look hypocritical when they spend huge sums of money—and sacrifice the lives of their own citizens—engaging in overseas military adventures under the guise of human rights promotion, especially when the Universal Declaration is appealed to for justification. If such denials are made, then this kind of military action will look like self-serving interference in the business of other countries and foreign policy reputations will be damaged (Pogge, 2002).

4. Desert

The final egalitarian reason for ethical concern about the health care situation in developing countries appeals to commonsense intuitions about desert. We generally think that it is unfair or unjust when there are wide disparities between peoples' level of well-being when the disparities in question do not reflect differences in desert. A situation where some people live incredibly wonderful lives while others suffer horribly—if the former did nothing to deserve their high quality lives and the latter did nothing to deserve their misfortune—should be considered a paradigm example of injustice (Rawls, 1971; Boylan, 2004). This is unfair, we think, and it would be unjust for social institutions to maintain such undeserved inequalities. The contrast between the situation of those of us living luxurious healthy lives in wealthy countries and the situation of the brutally poor and sick in developing countries, however, is exactly like this. Despite the fact that some suffer from AIDS as a result of their own (informed) careless sexual or drug-injecting behavior, examination of the complex social, political, and economic dynamics of AIDS, tuberculosis, malaria, and other infectious diseases (many of which are transmissible by casual contact) reveals that most who suffer from such diseases in developing countries are the victims of bad lack or—as I will argue below—deep injustice. The fact that millions who suffer and die from infectious diseases in developing countries are innocent people who do not deserve their dire fate is a fourth reason for doing more to improve their condition.[2]

Utilitarian Reasons

5. The Greatest Good for Humankind

Utilitarianism is the view that individuals should act—and social policy should be directed—to maximally promote human well-being. When choosing our actions or deciding how to allocate resources, according to utilitarianism, we should aim for the greatest total human benefit, while each person's benefit is weighted equally. When deciding how to use resources, therefore, utilitarian individuals and governments should aim to achieve the greatest possible payoff in terms of overall positive impact on human lives. Given that a one-dollar course of antimalarial treatment, a ten-dollar or twenty-dollar course of tuberculosis medication, or even a hundred-dollar yearly course of AIDS medication can each make all the difference between life and death—and enable prevention of huge amounts of horrendous suffering—these would appear to be among the very best uses that can be made of such sums of money in terms of positive impact on human lives, especially in comparison with the frivolous ways such sums are routinely spent in wealthy countries.

A fifth reason to dedicate more funds to improving the health of the poor is that this would arguably lead to the best overall outcome in terms of human well-being. Utilitarianism is, of course, a controversial (or some would say discredited) view; and most would, upon reflection anyway, deny that utilitarian aims should always take absolute priority over other legitimate social goals such as the promotion of equality and liberty. The goals to promote equality or liberty can sometimes conflict with—and sometimes outweigh in importance—the goal to maximally promote utility (aggregate well-being). Most will nonetheless agree that promotion of the greater good in terms of human well-being provides *a* reason for taking one action rather than another, even if other potentially overriding legitimate social aims must also be taken into consideration. The fact that promotion of developing world health would promote the greater good of humankind should thus be recognized as a reason for wealthy nations to devote more funds toward such purposes even by those who (arguably rightly) deny that utilitarian thinking should completely determine ethical action or social policy. Utilitarianism is perhaps wrong to place absolute weight on the importance of maximizing utility, but it rightly identifies at least one thing that matters from the standpoint of social policy: the greater good of (global) society.

6. Big Benefit, Small Sacrifice

One common objection to utilitarianism (which need not conflict with my point above that the fact that an action would promote the greater good impartially considered provides *a* reason for doing it) has to do with the apparently unrealistic—and overdemanding—impartiality it requires. Rather than thinking that we should give equal weight to the impact our actions or social policies have on everyone everywhere in the world when deciding what to do from an ethical perspective, we think it is morally appropriate to give special consideration to our own well-being and the well-being of friends, family members, and others to whom we stand in special relationships, such as our fellow countrymen. A more realistic moral perspective, according to Scheffler (1992), is one that aims to strikes a balance between partial commitments to benefit those with whom we are more intimately involved and impartial commitments to benefit strangers. Be that as it may, according to Peter Singer (1993, 2002), it would be wrong to fail to prevent great harm to strangers when the action required would involve only a minor sacrifice. If stopping to save an unknown child from drowning would dirty my shoes, wet my socks, make me miss the bus, or require similar inconveniences that would make me less happy than continuing on my way, I am ethically obliged to make such small sacrifices in order to avoid the much greater harm that would result if the child were allowed to drown. For those who share this sentiment, and I imagine this will be almost everyone, a sixth reason to improve the health care status quo is that only a minor sacrifice would be required by those of us living in wealthy developed nations in order to achieve tremendous benefits in terms of reduced suffering and saved lives. Dramatic improvement of global health would require only a tiny fraction of wealthy world resources. That the investment required is truly minor is well illustrated by Jeffrey Sachs (2005, 204–205):

> The [Commission on Macroeconomics and Health] concluded that donor aid [to invest in health] ought to rise from around $6 billion per year [in 2001] to $27 billion per year (by 2007). With combined GNP of the donor countries equal to

around $25 trillion dollars as of 2001, the commission was advocating an annual investment of around one thousandth of rich-world income. The commission showed, on the best epidemiological evidence, that such an investment could avert eight million deaths per year.

Libertarian Reasons—Human Rights Revisited

7. Restorative Justice

In response to what was said above about the apparent injustice of social institutions that maintain undeserved inequalities—the fourth reason—some will object that, first, a distinction should be made between misfortune (or bad luck) and injustice, and second, justice does not require equality when those worse-off suffer as a result of the former rather than the latter. They may go on to conclude that, third, even if it is not the sufferers' own fault that (because of sexual promiscuity and so on) AIDS and other infectious diseases are so prevalent in developing countries, this is simply a matter of misfortune (or bad luck) rather than injustice, concluding that justice does not require beneficent action toward those disfavored by the natural lottery. Although it may be true that there is an unlucky geographical *component* to plausible explanations of increased prevalence of infectious diseases in Africa and other tropical climates (Diamond, 1998), this argument should be rejected. Examination of the historical, social, political, and economic causes of AIDS in Africa reveals that the epidemic is largely rooted in injustice (Barnett and Whiteside, 2002). One reason that AIDS is so common in Africa is the fact that African people suffer grinding poverty—and extreme poverty promotes infectious disease for numerous reasons.

Why are African countries so poor to begin with? A long history of slavery, colonialism, racism, oppression, exploitation, cold war manipulation, militarization, conscription, protectionist trade policies, and so on provides important parts of the explanation (Benatar, 1998; Hunter, 2003). AIDS prevalence in Africa is further explained by widespread corruption and bad local governance, as evidenced by the apathy of the South African government toward AIDS for so many years. As the wealthiest African country, South Africa should have been better able than its African neighbors to control HIV/AIDS. It famously failed to do so, however, and is now home to more people living with HIV than any other country in the world. One reason for this was President Mbecki's tragic (and mysteriously motivated) long-term denial that AIDS is caused by HIV. Another is that the poverty and shambles in which apartheid left this country made it difficult for the new democratic government to deal with the epidemic while faced with so many other pressing problems providing housing, education, clean water, and so on to a population that was systematically deprived for decades (Whiteside and Sunter, 2000). The extent of AIDS in South Africa is partly a legacy of apartheid.

It is true that sexual practices in countries like South Africa partly explain AIDS prevalence there. The frequent employment of prostitutes by miners is one good example of this. The extent of prostitution in such countries, however, is itself rooted in poverty and inequality (which are in turn rooted in injustice); and the way in which the mining industry de facto mandates migration and separation of workers from families is itself open to critique from the standpoint of justice, as is well illustrated in Randall Packard's *White Plague, Black Labour* (1989). Anyone who is familiar with the complex social, political, and economic causes of AIDS (and other infectious diseases, such as TB) in southern Africa would be hard pressed to claim that the majority of those infected have themselves to blame.

To make long stories short, insofar as numerous historical injustices—and human rights abuses—are causes of prevalent poverty and social disruption in Africa, and insofar as poverty and social disruption are central causes of the infectious disease problem there, the health care status quo in Africa is rooted in injustice rather than mere misfortune. My assumption is that it is reasonable to believe that this provides additional reason for wealthy countries to act even if they are (or were) not themselves perpetrators in regard to the rights violations in question, just as they have reasons to act to prevent rights violations from being committed in other countries at present. The intuition is that while justice calls for—according to my fourth reason, in rejection of the second point three paragraphs above—reducing undeserved inequalities, the imperative to reduce inequalities is strongest when those who are worst-off suffer the fate they do because of historical rights violations, whether or not those in a position to aid, or their predecessors, were themselves guilty of the rights violations in question. It is plausible to hold that this is a morally relevant difference that may appeal even to some libertarians (given their concern with rights and restorative justice).

Whether or not libertarians agree, many (others) will share the intuition that the imperative to reduce undeserved inequalities is greater when those worst-off are (direct or indirect) victims of injustice, even if *they* are not *our* victims. For those who share this intuition, we have identified an additional reason for action (whether or not this should be considered a libertarian reason). Though I reject the second point above, the astute reader will notice that the reason in question implies something similar. It is not that inequalities resulting from bad luck do not matter from the standpoint of international justice, it is that inequalities resulting from human rights violations matter even more. The latter are matters of *restorative justice*, while the former are not.

Some will deny that one group has duties to help another group that has suffered injustices that the former group is not itself responsible for; and I admit that my assumption is debatable (at least from a libertarian standpoint). At the very least, however, there is good reason to reject an often heard supposed reason for not increasing aid—that it is, at best, bad luck or, at worst, their own fault that these people are sick and poor to begin with.

8. We Bear Responsibility

The fact that wealthy developed nations themselves bear significant responsibility for the plight of developing nations provides an eighth reason why the former should act to ameliorate poverty and the health care situation in the latter. One point is simply that the current wealth enjoyed by those of us living in developed countries is partly a result of the long-term exploitation of developing countries' human and natural resources—because we have directly or indirectly received goods and services at lower costs in virtue of the exploitation in question. Because the benefits we enjoy are products of injustice, rather than things we deserve, the onus is on us to make amends with those who suffer as a result—even if it was not us, as opposed to our predecessors, who were responsible for the exploitation in question.

Our responsibility for the poverty—and thus health—status quo in developing countries, however, runs much deeper. As argued by Pogge, we are directly implicated in the plight of the poor insofar as we respect a supposed right of illegitimate rulers to sell the natural resources of, and to incur debts in the name of, the developing world countries they rule. While we enjoy economic benefits as a result of such practices, our complicit behavior in the former case is really no different from buying stolen goods at reduced prices. In domestic society this is illegal, so why should it be permitted internationally? In both cases, furthermore, we encourage predatory authoritarian military leaders to stage coups and oppress their citizens by providing tremendous financial incentives for them to do so (Pogge, 2002).

Insofar as undemocratic bad governance, corruption and poverty are both causes of bad health in developing countries and the result of unjust social arrangements supported by wealthy world countries, wealthy world countries are themselves largely responsible for the health care status quo in the developing world. The fact that wealthy countries are partly the cause of the problem provides the eighth reason they should try harder to fix it.

Self-Interested Reasons

Health

9. Our Own Health Is Threatened

If infectious diseases are allowed to run rampant in developing world countries, then this has consequences for health worldwide. One implication of the current high prevalence rates of HIV/AIDS and other infectious diseases in poor countries is that everyone everywhere is subject to greater risk of infection than would otherwise be the case. This is partly due to a phenomenon known as *the acceleration effect*: "As the rate of HIV in the general population rises, the same patterns of sexual risk result in more new infections simply because the chances of encountering an infected partner become higher" (UNAIDS, 1999). A consequence of contemporary globalized trade and travel is that the acceleration effect has greater implications across, as well as within, national borders. While behavior modification may essentially eliminate risk of infection with HIV, the acceleration effect also applies to other infectious diseases such as tuberculosis, which is contractible via more casual contact. Increased prevalence of HIV, meanwhile, increases the prevalence of tuberculosis and other infectious diseases because those who suffer from AIDS are generally more prone to infection in virtue of the fact that their immune systems are weakened. That the rise of HIV/AIDS has increased developing world prevalence of tuberculosis in particular is a well-known fact.

As prevalence rates of HIV/AIDS increase, we are all thus more likely, other things being equal, to become infected with HIV and other infectious diseases such as tuberculosis. The magnitude of increased risk, on the other hand, warrants further study. Given the complexities and uncertainties involved, it would be exceedingly difficult to mathematically model such increased risks with a high degree of certainty. A prudential precautionary principle, in the meantime, advises that we do what we can to minimize prevalence rates of dangerous infectious diseases like HIV/AIDS everywhere we can.[3] The long-term danger of HIV/AIDS (and other infectious diseases) to global health should not be underestimated, as they have been in the past. While the World Bank/WHO projected in 1996 that "HIV/AIDS deaths would peak in 2006 with 1.7 million deaths," this number was "already exceeded . . . in 1998" (National Intelligence Council, 2000). The point is that, just like the emergence of HIV/AIDS in the first place—and the recent emergence of other diseases like Ebola, SARS, West Nile Virus, H5N1 bird flu, H1N1 swine flu, and many others—these things are hard to predict.

A related alarming health risk posed by the current health care situation in developing countries is the increasing emergence and spread of drug-resistant disease. An important cause of drug resistance is the failure of patients to complete a full course of therapy. When patients fail to complete therapy because they cannot afford to do so, as commonly occurs in developing countries (Farmer, 2003), this increases chances that drug-resistant strains of disease—which are more difficult, more expensive, or perhaps impossible to treat—will emerge and spread. Drug-resistant strains of disease, like infectious diseases in general, show no respect for international borders. The fact that so many people in developing countries lack complete access to treatment thus poses health care risks to us all, rich and poor alike.

The danger of drug resistance is perhaps most dramatically revealed by the recent emergence of "extensively" drug-resistant tuberculosis—XDR-TB. Resistant to both first- and second-line medications, these strains of tuberculosis are often considered to be virtually untreatable. In the context of TB, therefore, it is as though we have already returned to a situation analogous to the preantibiotic era. While the burden of TB is most heavily shouldered by developing countries, implications for rich countries are illustrated by a 2007 incident where a patient suspected of infection with XDR-TB was subjected to the first imposition of federal quarantine restrictions in the United States since 1963.

A ninth reason for wealthy developed nations to do more to improve the health care situation in developing countries is that the health care situation in developing countries threatens global health in general. Poverty and the state of health care in developing countries provide ideal conditions for infectious diseases to emerge, thrive, and spread (Garrett, 1995, 2000). A self-interested aim to protect health at home in developed countries provides reason for dedicating more resources to the improvement of health—and thus also living conditions—abroad.

Economics

10. Economic Self-Interest

Rather than merely causing suffering and death, infectious diseases have a devastating impact on developing world economies. Illness implies at least periodic inability to work, for example, and a shift in spending away from durable goods to things like health care and funerals. Because AIDS primarily affects people in their prime, "dependency ratios" in heavily affected countries increase as populations are skewed toward disproportionately large numbers of less economically productive elderly persons and children in need of financial support. Businesses are threatened due to absenteeism, a general loss of worker productivity, and the need to invest in the training of new workers when experienced, skilled employees become disabled and die. Companies' sales decline when consumers die or shift spending to health-related goods and services. Companies' expenses increase to the extent that they hold responsibility for employee health care provision or face higher employee insurance costs. As teachers die and are hard to replace, the education—and thus future economic productivity of—younger generations is jeopardized. Diseases like malaria, meanwhile, leave many young survivors with learning disabilities. The bottom line is that AIDS, malaria, and other infectious diseases have a drastic negative impact on the economies of households, industries, and developing world countries as a whole. AIDS in particular has already brought numerous sub-Saharan societies to the verge of economic collapse.

This all, of course, has negative implications for the wealthy world insofar as wealthy world companies have invested in overseas business projects that are threatened. Wealthy world companies also suffer opportunity costs insofar as it would have been profitable for them to invest in more overseas projects if it were not for the fact that the viability of such investments would be threatend by

AIDS. Wealthy world economies in general would, furthermore, benefit from the more robust trade in goods and services that would be possible if individuals, corporations, and governments abroad were in a better position to buy the goods we sell and if they were better able to efficiently produce more goods that we need or would want to buy. It is easy to recognize numerous reasons why dysfunction in one part of the global economy has negative implications for the global economy as a whole—just as economic dysfunction in one part of the domestic economy has negative implications for the domestic economy as a whole. US president George W. Bush is himself on the record saying that we should help poor nations "because having strong and stable nations in the world is in our own best interests. . . . Strong partners export their products, not their problems. . . . Conquering poverty creates new customers" (Allen, 2001). One need not be a human rights supporter or egalitarian to advocate global health improvement. The tenth reason why wealthy developed nations should do more to improve the health care situation in developing countries is that there are straightforward self-interested economic reasons for doing so.

Global Security

11. Disease Promotes Instability and Threatens Security

Rather than merely posing global health and economic threats, it is widely acknowledged that AIDS and other infectious diseases threaten global security. Historical studies have shown that among the best indicators of things like revolutionary war, civil war, genocide, and other major social upheavals are things like high infant mortality rate, low life expectancy, decreasing life expectancy, partial democratic transition, and economic collapse (NIC, 2000; Sachs, 2005)—the very factors that are highly salient in sub-Saharan Africa at present, largely as result of AIDS. Historical studies and the obvious links between economic collapse and social instability aside, it is easy to recognize why stability and security are threatened in Africa as a result of AIDS. Exceedingly high prevalence rates in the military and police, for example, imply weakened security forces. Because increased death and disability of workers applies to employees of government as well as industry, furthermore, governments, just like businesses, are less able to function properly. As millions of young people are, in the meantime, orphaned or otherwise deprived of education and socialization, they are more prone to bitter resentment and "radicalization" by militant groups (NIC, 2000). When developing world societies collapse as a result, this has implications for developed countries with interests in affected regions.

The eleventh reason to do more to improve the health care situation in developing countries is that we have self-interested security reasons for doing so. The threat to wealthy world security interests is well illustrated by the NIC's sobering claims in its 2000 report on *The Global Infectious Disease Threat and Its Implications for the United States*:

> Infectious diseases will pose a rising global health threat and will complicate US and global security over the next 20 years. These diseases will endanger US citizens at home and abroad, threaten US armed forces deployed overseas, and exacerbate social and political instability in key countries and regions in which the United States has significant interests. [NIC, 2000, 6]

> Infectious diseases are likely to slow socioeconomic development in developing and former communist countries and regions of interest to the United States. This will challenge democratic development and transitions and possibly contribute to humanitarian emergencies and military conflicts to which the United States may need to respond. [NIC, 2000, 2]

Again, one need not be a left-wing activist to think that more should be done to address the infectious disease problem in developing countries. Wealthy world interests in global security—including the aim to protect the health of troops stationed overseas and aims to avoid the killing and monetary expense of war—provide our final reason for improving global heath.

Conclusion

Without claiming to be exhaustive, this paper has enumerated eleven reasons why wealthy developed nations should be motivated to do more[4] to improve the health care situation in developing countries. Wealthy nations should dedicate more funds to improving global health because doing so would (1) promote equality of opportunity, (2) improve the situation of the worst-off members of (global) society, (3) promote respect of the human right to have one's most basic needs (including health care) met, (4) reduce undeserved inequalities in well-being, (5) promote the greater good of humankind, (6) achieve enormous benefits while requiring only small sacrifices, (7) amend historical injustices, (8) meet the obligation to amend injustices that developed world countries have themselves benefited from and contributed to, (9) reduce the threat of infectious diseases to developed countries themselves, (10) promote developed countries' own economic interests, *and* (11) promote global (including developed countries' own) security, as shown in Figure 11.1.

Although I have not claimed that any one of these reasons is itself sufficient to justify increased funding, these eleven reasons all count, and together they add up to make an overwhelmingly powerful case for change. Because there are so many strong reasons for doing more to improve global health, the cumulative argument will likely convince even those who doubt the plausibility of one, two, or even a few of the reasons I have given.

Rather than depending on any particular philosophical framework, the reasons enumerated are each in line with commonsense morality and ordinary beliefs and values. Though I have appealed to philosophical theory at various places in this paper, I have not (fully) adopted any of the theories considered. To

Figure 11.1. Summary Box

Why should wealthy developed nations be motivated to do more to improve the health care situation in developing countries?		
MORAL REASONS	EGALITARIAN	1. Promote equality of opportunity. 2. Improve the situation of the worst-off members of society. 3. Promote respect of the human right to have health care needs met. 4. Reduce undeserved inequalities in well-being.
	UTILITARIAN	5. Promote the overall good of humankind. 6. Achieve enormous benefits while requiring only small sacrifices.
	LIBERTARIAN	7. Amend historical injustices. 8. Meet the obligation to amend injustices that developed countries have themselves benefited from and contributed to.
SELF-INTERESTED REASONS		9. Reduce the threat of infectious diseases to developed countries themselves. 10. Promote developed countries' own economic interests. 11. Promote global (including developed countries' own) security.

the contrary, I have merely indicated where they highlight ordinary values that most of us will share. While ethical theories often place extreme weight on the particular values they emphasize, I do not attach (and I expect that most readers would not attach) extreme weight to the values in question.

There are two ways to think about the parts of this argument which appeal to ethical theory. On the one hand, one might say that I have shown that (in the context of global health) there is convergence—or an overlapping consensus—among mainstream philosophical theories. Whether one is an egalitarian, utilitarian, or libertarian, that is, one should agree that wealthy countries should do more to improve health in developing countries. Based on the arguments above, it appears that all of these theoretical perspectives should point in the same direction. This is the style of argument put forward by Thomas Pogge (2002) regarding global poverty reduction more generally.

On the other hand, we might think that the mainstream strands of political theory (egalitarianism, utilitarianism, and libertarianism) are each incorrect—because they (usually) each place extreme weight on the values they emphasize. Utilitarians, for example, only value liberty and equality insofar as they are instrumental in the promotion of utility. Libertarians are (except for the prevention of "direct harm") unwilling to sacrifice liberty for the sake of utility and equality promotion. And Rawlsian egalitarianism implies that we must make the worst-off better off even if this would entail enormous costs in terms of utility. I imagine, however, that most ordinary people and policy makers would reject each of these views. Most of us think that equality, utility, and liberty are each legitimate social aims and that we should try, whenever possible, to promote all three at the same time—and that in cases of conflict we must try to strike a balance between them rather than giving absolute priority (or such heavy weight) to any one of these values in particular. The irony regarding the overlapping consensus interpretation of the arguments above is that this might mean an overlapping consensus of incorrect views (that are overly extreme with regard to the values they emphasize). Who cares if three incorrect theoretical perspectives all point in the same direction? The point is that libertarians would not give much weight to the utilitarian and egalitarian considerations; utilitarians would not give much weight (except in an instrumental sense) to equality and liberty; and Rawlsian egalitarians would not give much weight to utility in particular. But most of us presumably think that all three of these values (i.e., utility, equality, and liberty) should be given serious weight when making policy. The second, and preferable, interpretation of the arguments of this paper is therefore *pluralistic*. On this interpretation, each of the reasons put forward is taken to really matter. The idea that each really matters is not fully captured when we say that we should improve global health because there is an overlapping consensus of (arguably incorrect) theories that says we should do so.

My final hypothesis is that those resistant to the case for improving global health will primarily appeal, implicitly or explicitly, to the idea that coercive taxation for redistributive purposes would violate the right or liberty of an individual to keep her hard-earned income. The idea that this reason not to improve global health should outweigh the whole combination of rights and values embodied in the eleven reasons enumerated above, however, seems implausibly extreme, morally repugnant, and perhaps imprudent. The right or liberty of an individual to keep her hard-earned income matters, but most would agree that this right or liberty gets outweighed by other rights and liberties, utility and equality (and national self-interest) when the stakes are sufficiently high.

If one objects that rather than the generation of funding through taxation, we should rely on voluntary donations to solve the problem of the health care situation in developing countries, then it suffices to reply that experience and the global health care status quo reveal that voluntary donations have been inadequate to deal with the problem. If this mode of funding has not worked until now, then why believe that it will suddenly and reliably work in the future—especially given the collective action problems involved? In any case, why should we wait given that the current situation is already catastrophic?

If the three self-interested reasons combined are themselves sufficient to make the case for change—and I admit that this is an empirical question—then the failure to do more to improve global health would be especially tragic. We should not, however, act on self-interest alone. Everyone should agree that ethics matter too. History will judge our action—or lack thereof.

Notes

1. The argument is directed at wealthy states—and their citizens (who would need to provide political support for, and the tax funds required by, the policies in question).

2. I am not arguing that this reason is decisive all by itself. Caveats provided in discussion of the first two reasons—for example, that these are two goals among many that should be taken into consideration, which is not to say that there are no countervailing reasons for not taking action—apply to these last two reasons as well. I will avoid always repeating these caveats in what follows. Throughout this paper I am merely appealing to what I claim to be widely shared intuitions about the things that matter from the standpoint of ethics and justice (and later self-interest) without attaching any particular (or extreme) weight to the importance of the individual considerations I am enumerating.

3. Though the precautionary principle is controversial, its force is strongest in cases like this where reduction of risk entails only relatively minor cost.

4. Throughout, I have implicitly assumed that "doing more" requires funding.

References

Allen, Mike. (2001). "Bush Targets Reduction of Global Poverty." *Washington Post.* Retrieved from http://www.washingtonpost.com/ac2/wp-dyn/A10219-2001 Jul17?language=printer

Barnett, Tony, and Alan Whitside. (2002). *AIDS in the Twenty-First Century: Disease and Globalization.* New York: Palgrave MacMillan.

Benatar, Solomon. (1998). "Global Disparities in Health and Human Rights: A Critical Commentary." *American Journal of Public Health 88*: 295–300.

Boylan, Michael. (2004). *A Just Society.* Lanham, MD, and Oxford: Rowman and Littlefield.

Daniels, Norman. (1985). *Just Health Care.* New York: Cambridge University Press.

Daniels, Norman. (2007). *Just Health: Meeting Health Needs Fairly.* New York: Cambridge University Press.

Diamond, Jared. (1998). *Guns, Germs, and Steel: The Fates of Human Societies.* New York: W. W. Norton.

Farmer, Paul. (2003). *Pathologies of Power: Health, Human Rights, and the New War on the Poor.* Berkeley: University of California Press.

Garrett, Laurie. (1995). *The Coming Plague: Newly Emerging Diseases in a World Out of Balance.* New York: Penguin.

Garrett, Laurie. (2000). *Betrayal of Trust: The Collapse of Global Public Health.* New York: Hyperion.

Griffin, James. (2008). *On Human Rights.* Oxford: Oxford University Press.

Hunter, Susan. (2003). *Black Death: AIDS in Africa.* New York: Palgrave MacMillan.

Moellendorf, Darrel. (2002). *Cosmopolitan Justice.* Boulder, CO: Westview.

National Intelligence Council. (2000). *The Global Infectious Disease Threat and Its Implications for the United States, National Intelligence Estimate, NIE 99-17D.* Washington, DC: NIC.

Packard, Randall. (1989). *White Plague, Black Labor: Tuberculosis and the Political Economy of Health and Disease in South Africa.* Berkeley: University of California Press.

Pogge, Thomas. (2002). *World Poverty and Human Rights.* Cambridge, UK: Polity Press.

Rawls, John. (1971). *A Theory of Justice.* Cambridge, MA: Harvard University Press.

Rawls, John. (1999). *The Law of Peoples.* Cambridge, MA: Harvard University Press.

Sachs, Jeffrey. (2005). *The End of Poverty: How We Can Make It Happen in Our Lifetime.* London: Penguin.

Scheffler, Samuel. (1992). *Human Morality.* New York: Oxford University Press.

Singer, Peter. (1993). *Practical Ethics.* New York: Cambridge University Press.

Singer, Peter. (2002). *One World: The Ethics of Globalization.* Melbourne: The Text Publishing Company.

UNAIDS. (1999). *Report on the Global HIV/AIDS Epidemic.* Retrieved from www.unaids.org

United Nations. (1999). Universal Declaration of Human Rights, approved and proclaimed by the General Assembly of the United Nations on 10 December 1948, as Resolution 217 A (III).

Whiteside, Alan, and Clem Sunter. (2000). *AIDS: The Challenge for South Africa.* Cape Town: Human and Rousseau and Tafelberg.

CHAPTER TWELVE

Access to Life-Saving Medicines

DORIS SCHROEDER, THOMAS POGGE, AND PETER SINGER
University of Central Lancashire, Yale University, and Princeton University

Abstract

The right to the enjoyment of the highest attainable standard of health has been recognized for more than half a century by various international instruments, most prominently the Universal Declaration of Human Rights. Yet, health outcomes such as adult and infant mortality rates show that it has not yet been achieved in major parts of the world.

One of the main obstacles to realizing the universal right to health is that almost 2 billion people lack access to life-saving medicines. This chapter has two aims: one, to assess whether intellectual property rights of innovators can trump the right to health of the poor, and two, if not, whether a feasible reform plan to the intellectual property rights system could align the interests of innovators and the poor.

Key Words

human right to health, global justice, intellectual property rights, health impact fund

---

Authors' note: The research leading to these results has received funding from the European Community's Seventh Framework Programme under grant agreement 217665. We are grateful to Cathy Lennon for assistance with the manuscript and to Michael Boylan and Julie Cook Lucas for comments on an earlier draft.

Mortality is an immovable fact of life. Human beings die. They die from numerous causes and at all ages. Since the dawn of humanity, poets and philosophers have pondered and physicians have tried to deter and postpone death. The simplest pronouncement on death is almost two and a half millennia old. "When death is not, we are, and when death is, we are not." Hence, according to Epicurus (341–270 BCE), we should not fear death (1925, Section 125). However, what we should fear and fight in the twenty-first century is avoidable, premature death. Though the fact of death is immovable, its timing for many is not.

Mortality statistics form an essential part of the World Health Organization (WHO) assessment of the well-being of populations. In particular the under-five mortality rate and the adult mortality rate (fifteen to sixty) give statisticians and policy-makers important information on the health status of societies.

In 2008, 75 percent of all under-five deaths occurred in only eighteen countries. And nearly one third occurred in only two countries: India (21 percent) and Nigeria (12 percent) (You, Wardlaw, Salama, and Jones, 2009).

Looking at further WHO statistics, 16 percent of young parents in Afghanistan, Sierra Leone, and Liberia lost their child before the age of five in 2006. In the same year, only 0.3 percent of parents lost their under-five-year-old in Finland, Italy, and Singapore. Adult mortality during the same period was highest in Zimbabwe followed by Lesotho, Swaziland, and Zambia. In Zimbabwe, only 25 percent of the population was expected to live beyond the age of sixty. At the other end of the scale, more than 90 percent of the population were expected to reach sixty and beyond in thirty-six countries ranging from Iceland, Kuwait, and Singapore to Germany, Chile, and Costa Rica (World Health Organization Statistical Information System, 2010).

The reasons for premature mortality are manifold. We are here interested in one of them: lack of access to life-saving medicines.[1] According to Anand Grover (2009):

> Access to medicines forms an indispensable part of the right to health. . . . Nearly 2 billion people lack access to essential medicines. Improving access to medicines could save 10 million lives a year, 4 million in Africa and South East Asia. The inability of populations to access medicines is partly due to high costs. . . . TRIPS [Trade-Related Aspects of Intellectual Property Rights Agreement] and FTAs [Free Trade Agreements] have had an adverse impact on prices and availability of medicines, making it difficult for countries to comply with their obligations to respect, protect, and fulfil the right to health. [6, 7, 28]

Anand Grover is the UN Special Rapporteur on the right of everyone to the enjoyment of the highest attainable standard of physical and mental health. In the above, he has captured the topic of our chapter succinctly. One third of the world's population does not have access to life-saving medicines today. As a result, 10 million lives are lost prematurely each year. These lives could be saved if access to life-saving medicines were assured. One reason why such access cannot be assured is because high drug prices facilitated through the current intellectual property rights (IPR) system make it impossible for some countries to discharge their obligation to respect, protect, and fulfill the right to health.

In this chapter, we shall

- Describe the legal basis for the human right to health.
- Outline the main purpose of IPRs.
- Assess whether the rights of innovators to intellectual property protection trump the human right to health.
- Summarize an amendment to the current IPR system, which would balance strong incentives for innovation with providing access to life-saving medicines to the poor.

Right to Health: Legal Instruments

Exactly what legal rights are and how they can be distinguished from moral rights is a contested question within philosophy.[2] The question becomes even more complex when one refers to international legal rights. For the purpose of this chapter, we shall assume with Joseph Raz (1984) that persons have rights by virtue of having interests that are sufficient reason to impose duties on others. For instance, the interest to life generates both the right to life and the duty on others to refrain from unprovoked violent attack. Those rights are then enshrined in the legislation of a particular entity (e.g., a nation-state) and become legal rights agreed upon by the representatives of this particular entity. One would call the philosophical basis of such agreements contractarianism (mutual agreement between those governed through legitimate representatives).

An example: Germany has a so-called *Sozialgesetzbuch* (social law book), which assures every citizen of social insurance. This insurance in turn guarantees universal access to health services (*Sozialgesetzbuch*, 1975, Art 4(2)). Enforcement of social rights is secured through the so-called *Sozialgerichte* (social courts), which exist at the local, regional, and national levels. Simplified, whenever a court of law is available to enforce a right (to ensure the compliance of the duty holder), one can speak of a legally binding right. If health insurance in Germany were refused to any citizen,[3] one could enforce one's access to insurance through the courts.

At the international level, the situation is more complex because it is less clear who the equivalent legitimate decision-makers and duty-bearers are and how rights could be enforced. For instance, in December 1948, the governments of the world came together to assert that each human being

> has the right to a standard of living adequate for the health and well-being of himself and of his family, including food, clothing, housing and medical care and necessary social services, and the right to security in the event of unemployment, sickness, disability, widowhood, old age or other lack of livelihood in circumstances beyond his control. [Universal Declaration of Human Rights, 1948, Article 25(1)]

Article 25(1) of the Universal Declaration of Human Rights affirms the human right to health. The formulation reads almost identically, in substance, to Article 4(2) of the German social law book. Yet, where would one go to enforce such a right? In other words, how are international rights, agreed on by far-away politicians at the UN General Assembly, enforced? There are two main possibilities: implementing legislation adopted and enforced at the national level, and judicial activism.[4]

An important link to national legislation for the Universal Declaration of Human Rights is the International Covenant on Economic, Social and Cultural Rights. This multilateral treaty—adopted by the United Nations General Assembly in 1966—commits state parties to work toward the granting of economic, social, and cultural rights domestically. Article 12 of the treaty covers the right to health and a comment on its implementation explains:

> Health is a fundamental human right indispensable for the exercise of other human rights. Every human being is entitled to the enjoyment of the highest attainable standard of health conducive to living a life in dignity. The realization of the right to health may be pursued through numerous, complementary approaches, such as the formulation of health policies, or the implementation of health programmes developed by the World Health Organization (WHO), or the adoption of specific legal instruments. Moreover, the right to health includes certain components, which are legally enforceable. [United Nations Committee on Economic, Social and Cultural Rights, 2000: E/C.12/2000/4. (General Comments) General Comment No.14]

Signatories to the International Covenant on Economic, Social and Cultural Rights are therefore legally bound to strive toward securing the highest attainable standard of health for the citizens within their borders. And they do so by instituting equivalent rights and enforcement mechanisms within a nation-state. In this regard, the German social law book achieves German compliance with the International Covenant on Economic, Social and Cultural Rights.

The second possibility (if national legal avenues are not promising) is more recent and has been referred to as judicial activism (Abramovich and Pautassi, 2008). With increasing frequency, human rights activists are mounting legal campaigns in both developing and developed countries to force governments to keep their promises on the right to health (Langford and Nolan, 2006). One of the best-known examples is *Cruz Bermudez et al. v the Ministerio de Sanidad,* which was decided by the Venezuelan Supreme Court in 1999. Cases are also being brought to national courts—typically at the Supreme Court or Constitutional Court level—or to regional organizations. A prominent example of the latter was *SERAC v. Nigeria* (*Social and Economic Rights Action Center and the Center for Economic and Social Rights v. Nigeria,* 2001), which was decided by the African Commission for Human and People's Rights in 2001.

The action in *Cruz Bermudez et al. v the Ministerio de Sanidad* was brought by 170 people living in Venezuela with HIV/AIDS. They argued that their right to health was violated by the government's failure to provide antiretroviral drugs. The Supreme Court accepted part of the claim and ordered the Ministry

> to provide anti-retrovirals, medications necessary for treating opportunistic infections and diagnostic testing, free of charge for all Venezuelan citizens and residents. The Ministry was also ordered to develop the policies and programs necessary for affected patients' treatment and assistance, and make the reallocation of the budget necessary to carry out the Court's decision. [*Cruz Bermudez et al. v. Ministerio de Sanidad y Asistencia Social,* 1999]

A later analysis published in the *Lancet* listed the above case as one of fifty-nine successful cases where "access to essential medicines as part of the fulfilment of the right to health [was] . . . enforced through the courts." Successful cases were defined as those that led to "new, continued, or expanded access to one or more essential medicines for an individual or group" (Hogerzeil, Samson, Casanovas, and Rahmani-Ocora, 2006).

The action in *SERAC v. Nigeria* was brought by an NGO, the Social and Economic Rights Action Center (SERAC). They claimed that the Ogoni People's right to health was violated by the Nigerian government, who allowed the contamination of their immediate environment by the state-owned Nigerian National Petroleum Company. In 2001, the African Commission for Human and People's Rights found Nigeria guilty of violating the right to health of the Ogoni People and asked the government to stop all current violations, compensate victims, and conduct an independent investigation into human rights abuses (*SERAC v. Nigeria,* 2001).

As a result of the judgment, the Nigerian government established "the Niger Delta Development Commission to address the environmental and other social related problems in the Niger Delta area and other oil producing areas of Nigeria" and a Judicial Commission of Inquiry "to investigate the issues of human rights violations" (African Commission on Human and Peoples' Rights, 2003, 31–34). The case has been hailed as "a giant stride towards the protection and promotion of economic, social and cultural rights of Africans" (Nwobike, 2005), although the exact impact from the establishment of the two commissions is not yet fully known.

These examples and the above short discussion have only scratched the surface of the complex and intriguing field of jurisprudence and the varied discussions one can have on legal rights. For the purpose of this chapter, they have to suffice. Importantly, the right to health has been enshrined in a variety of legal instruments, as Table 12.1 shows.

TABLE 12.1. Legal Instruments: Right to Health

Government obligations toward its own citizens:	**Government obligations for international assistance:**
Universal Declaration of Human Rights, Art. 25(1)	Declaration of Alma-Ata, Art. II
International Covenant on Economic, Social and Cultural Rights, Art. 12	UN Committee on Economic, Social and Cultural Rights E/C.12/2000/4, General Comment No. 14
Convention on the Elimination of All Forms of Discrimination Against Women, Art. 12	Millennium Development Goals 4, 5, and 6
Convention on the Rights of the Child, Art. 24(1–3)	Convention on the Rights of the Child, Art. 24(4)

Whilst some legal instruments, such as the above-cited International Covenant on Economic, Social and Cultural Rights, refer only to domestic duties, others describe international duties. In 1978, for instance, the Declaration of Alma-Ata requested international assistance for developing countries in order to achieve progress in providing access to health services. In particular it notes in Article II, "The existing gross inequality in the health status of the people particularly between developed and developing countries as well as within countries is politically, socially and economically unacceptable and is, therefore, of common concern to all countries."

Even though one may be skeptical about the power of declarations without obvious enforcement mechanisms, reading this declaration more than three decades later is particularly depressing, as Article X expresses the hope that "an acceptable level of health for all the people of the world by the year 2000 can be attained through a fuller and better use of the world's resources, a considerable part of which is now spent on armaments and military conflicts."

The fact that 10 million human beings die prematurely and unnecessarily each year because they do not have access to life-saving medicines shows clearly that states are unwilling or unable to fulfill their human rights duties. As Anand Grover noted above, the TRIPS regime is partly responsible for the inability of governments to discharge their human rights obligations. Given the grave ill that the TRIPS regime is partly responsible for, one needs to ask whether the rights of innovators to intellectual property protection trump the human right to health. To do so, we need to examine the purpose of IPRs first.

The Purpose of Intellectual Property Rights

For most of human history, private property was connected to tangible entities such as land, buildings, or goods. In more recent times, however, intangible creations of the mind or the intellect have increasingly been accepted as private property. This is no matter of public perception, but of strict legal protection. Today, not only land and other tangible items are protected through laws, but also a variety of so-called intellectual property items.

From novels to practical ideas such as LED Christmas lights or new drugs for the treatment of Alzheimer's disease, intellectual property rights are today firmly protected by national and international legislation. What this means in practice is that the originator of an idea applies for state protection through, for instance, a patent. Once obtained, the patent allows its holder to stop others from using the idea for a specified time—unless they pay a mutually agreed license fee. Table 12.2 shows standard types of intellectual property as protected through national and international legislation.

States decided to adopt binding and enforceable legislation on intellectual property rights because it provides incentives to innovators by enabling them to charge high markups on their products. Without such legislation, it is assumed, we would have fewer drugs, fewer books, fewer operas, and fewer dishwasher or Christmas lights innovations. Only because the costs of research and development (R&D) can be recouped throughout the monopoly interval are innovations cost-effective. Or as economists phrase it: "The economic purpose of patents is . . . to bar entry of copy products for the term of the patent, to provide the innovator firm with an opportunity to price above the marginal cost and thereby recoup R&D expense, in order to preserve incentives for future R&D" (Danzon and Towse, 2003, 185).

TABLE 12.2. Types of Intellectual Property

Type	Description	Example
Trademark	Typically a logo, word, or phrase to distinguish one's product from another's	Mercedes Benz star
Design	Typically a shape or pattern, which gives one's product its unique appearance	Airport massage chair of a certain design
Copyright	Typically original material in the arts, media, or computer programming	André Brink's novels
Patent	Typically a product, substance, method, or process which is newly invented and useful	Miele cutlery drawer
Plant breeder rights	New varieties of plants	New plant variety that is not eligible for a patent
Geographic indication	Protected link between a product and its local territory	Champagne
Trade secrets	Information one does not want to become public knowledge, usually protected through confidentiality agreements	The recipe for Coca-Cola
Circuit layout rights	Typically layout for computer chips	Computer chips

"Monopoly pricing powers?" one may ask skeptically. "Aren't they normally suppressed by other state laws?" Indeed, most market economies have legal systems in place to avoid the formation of commercial monopolies. So-called competition law, or antitrust law in the United States of America (US), is designed specifically to stop commercial enterprises from reaching a position that enables them to set monopoly prices. Yet, the same outcome is not only tolerated by states when it comes to patent holders, but is actively promoted.

The reason most market economies have institutionalized competition law is that monopolies tend to lead to excessive pricing, which harms consumers. Without pressure from competitors, unreasonable or predatory prices can be set, in particular if consumers cannot easily forego the transaction. Though one may do without luxury items such as skis or plasma screens, some items such as food, schoolbooks, blankets, pharmaceuticals, etc. are essential for human well-being. High prices will therefore be paid if necessary, leaving poorer consumers without access to these essential goods. This leads to market inefficiencies, which economists call deadweight losses. "Deadweight loss occurs when people are excluded from using the good even though their willingness to pay are [sic] higher than the marginal cost" (Scotcher, 2004, 36). Competition law is therefore a protective mechanism against market inefficiencies, which are harmful to consumers, in particular those with low purchasing power.

Why then are consumers not protected against monopoly pricing by, for instance, pharmaceutical patent holders? Above we quoted Anand Grover, who noted that the high drug prices facilitated through TRIPS are partly responsible for 10 million deaths per year due to lack of access to life-saving medicines. Why are patents then deemed to be compatible with competition law? This apparent conflict would only make sense if the profits of the pharmaceutical industry were not the main purpose of patents and some higher good outweighed the disadvantages of granting monopoly pricing powers. That this is indeed the case can best be shown through a major IPR treaty or, in the case of the US, constitutional law.

In 1970 the Patent Cooperation Treaty was opened for signatures. Today, it covers 142 countries (World Intellectual Property Organization, 1970). In its preamble, the signatories laid out the main reasons for granting monopoly powers to innovators through patent rights, as follows:

1. to make a contribution to the progress of science and technology,
2. to facilitate and accelerate access by the public to the technical information contained in documents describing new inventions,
3. to foster and accelerate the economic development of developing countries . . . by providing easily accessible information on the availability of technological solutions applicable to their special needs and by facilitating access to the ever expanding volume of modern technology (Patent Cooperation Treaty, 1970).

The first reason—the progress of science and technology—is mirrored in the US constitution, which gives Congress the power "to promote the progress of science and useful arts, by securing for limited times to authors and inventors the exclusive right to their respective writings and discoveries" (United States Constitution, Section 8)—in other words, to institute patent rights.

The main purpose of patent rights is therefore expressed as the progress of science, which is given priority over the protection of consumers. The reason why science is deemed to progress through patent rights is twofold. Firstly, if innovators can expect to recoup R&D costs within the monopoly interval, they are much more likely to take on the burden of innovation. A figure which is often quoted to illustrate this burden is $800 million USD to bring a pharmaceutical product to market (Tobinick, 2009). As a result of thus encouraging innovation, more drugs, more consumer products, and more scientific knowledge will become available. Secondly, as the innovator needs to disclose publicly the details of the invention in return for patent rights, other innovators can benefit from the discovery in at least two ways: one, by not investing funds in a research effort that has already been completed, and two, by being able to copy the invention using the details disclosed to patent offices after the monopoly interval has expired.

The latter refers to point two of the Patent Cooperation Treaty, namely "to facilitate and accelerate access by the public to the technical information contained in documents describing new inventions."

Point three within the Patent Cooperation Treaty makes reference to the special needs of developing countries, in particular the need to access modern technology to support development. It may strike some as surprising that the needs of developing countries were listed in support of patent rights in the most prominent early patent treaty, which has the support of 142 countries. In the area of pharmaceutical innovation, patent rights are frequently seen as opposed to the interests of developing countries. According to statistics from the World Intellectual Property Rights Organization (WIPO, 2008), the US and Japan obtained more than 50 percent of all patents worldwide in 2006. During the same period, ten countries (Japan, US, South Korea, Germany, China, France, Russia, UK, Netherlands, and Switzerland) held 88 percent of all patents granted. Although the recent success of China in terms of patent applications shows that former developing countries can develop the know-how to make use of the patent system, other developing countries lack the resources and skills to follow suit. And as we have seen at the start, an estimated 2 billion people lack access to life-saving medicines, including those priced out of their reach due to patent protection.

It is indeed a more realistic assessment of the current situation to note that patent rights on pharmaceuticals are problematic rather than beneficial for most developing countries. This was shown, for instance, by Lee Branstetter (2004), who surveyed the empirical evidence on increased innovation through patent rights in developing countries. He found that patent rights do not strengthen local innovators but instead promote further the success of pharmaceutical companies in the North. It is in recognition of this situation that a World Trade Organization (WTO) Ministerial Conference decided in 2001 that the right to protect public health and promote access to medicines for all takes priority over the right of innovators to be rewarded with monopoly price controls. The Doha Declaration on the TRIPS Agreement and Public Health declares that patent rights "should not prevent Members from taking measures to protect public health" (WTO, 2001), thereby prioritizing public health concerns over innovator reward.

Based on the above, we can therefore establish the aspirational purpose of patent rights as follows: to promote the progress of science by rewarding innovators with the power to block the market entry of copied products for a limited period, which effectively gives them monopoly pricing opportunities to recoup R&D costs, and by requiring the disclosure of the invention through the innovator, with the proviso applicable to the pharmaceutical sector that the protection of public health and access to medicines for all takes precedence over patent holders' rights to charge monopoly prices.

As one can see from the above, the provision of incentives through monopoly pricing powers for innovators is not the main goal of the IPR system. The main goal is the progress of science achieved through the tool of patents and other protective mechanisms. Even if one ignored the Doha Declaration, one could therefore not argue from a policy perspective that the legally binding International Covenant on Economic, Social and Cultural Rights and its protection of the human right to health can be trumped by IPR protection for innovators. This would be the case only if either the progress of science were more important than the human right to health or if IPRs were themselves human rights.

In the following, we shall refute the claim that IPRs are human rights and also look at rights-based rather than policy-based arguments in favor of monopoly pricing powers for innovators.

Intellectual Property and Natural Rights

Two Types of Social Rules

Social rules may be understood in two main ways: they may reflect ultimate moral requirements, whether set down by God or our innate moral sense, or dictated by reason; or they may be understood as serving a social purpose within human society.

The constitutional rights of individuals are typically understood in the first way, reflecting, as John Rawls says, a person's "inviolability founded on justice which even the welfare of society as a whole cannot override" (Rawls, 1999, 3). The inviolability of these rights applies across the globe and across time, and they are often referred to as natural rights (Brown, 1960). The right not to be killed, suitably circumscribed (to allow for self-defense, for instance), is considered such a right (Finnis, 1980, 281). Traffic rules, on the other hand, are typically understood in the second way, in terms of their social utility as facilitators of efficient travel. Such social rules are taken to be open to thoughtful revision in order to preserve or enhance their usefulness under changing conditions. By contrast, rules expressing natural-law requirements are considered outside the power of societies to change.

With regard to some social rules, their categorization into one of these two categories is contested. Thus, some argue that the social rule against torture is based on expediency and may therefore be revised or abolished in changed circumstances, whereas others present this rule as founded on a natural right (Brecher, 2007).

The social rules that create and define property rights are subject to similar contention: Some assume that such rights should be designed to promote the common good, specified as economic efficiency, for instance, or poverty avoidance (Rawls, 1999). Others, following John Locke, regard legal property rights as implementing preexisting natural rights to acquire things and to dispose of them as one pleases (Nozick, 1974). The two disputant groups may entirely agree on what the rules should be and yet disagree sharply on their justification.

Are Intellectual Property Rights Natural Rights?

The same disagreement as outlined on the topics of torture or property rights exists with regard to IPRs. Some hold that IPRs should be shaped with an eye to the common good, striking the optimal balance between encouraging innovations and ensuring easy access to them. Others believe that innovators have a natural right to control the use of their innovation. This dispute was in evidence in the 1990s when affluent states successfully pressured less developed states to accept TRIPS, which required them to legislate for very extensive IPRs.

Some argued that adopting US-style IPRs would benefit poor countries by making them more innovative. Others argued that poor countries were morally required to adopt extensive IPRs in order to suppress the natural-law crimes of "theft," "piracy," and "counterfeiting" that were being committed by copycat manufacturers within their jurisdictions.[5]

Which position is more defensible? Should IPRs be designed with social utility in mind or help realize creators' natural rights? One can offer three arguments against the latter, natural-law understanding of IPRs.

Firstly, IPRs can be shaped in myriad ways, each specifying differently their mode of acquisition, scope, or duration. The most controversial debate in this context surrounds so-called patents on life. Although patents on complex living organisms, for example, pigs (Jentzsch, 2006), are regularly granted in the US, the Canadian Supreme Court ruled that higher life forms cannot be patented within their jurisdiction. Hence, the famous OncoMouse, patented in the US by Harvard University applicants, does not fall under patent protection in Canada (Canadian

Environmental Law Association). Interestingly, the European Patent Office (EPO) rejected Harvard's patent application for the OncoMouse at first, but then decided to grant the patent arguing that benefits to humanity outweighed the harm to the mice (Irwin, 1995). This means that the EPO granted the patent on grounds of social utility rather than potential natural rights of creators. The dispute is ongoing, given that the German Green Party together with a large group of organizations are currently lobbying the European Parliament to prohibit patents on higher life forms in Europe (Institute of Science in Society, 2009).

Here, it is also important to remember that patents on life were regarded as incompatible with US patent law in 1971, when the first case was considered. The now legendary Chakrabarty application (Ananda Chakrabarty had produced a genetically engineered bacteria that could clean oil spills) was first rejected by the US Patent and Trademark Office. On appeal, the patent was granted by the Court of Customs and Patent Appeals by a three to two majority. On a second appeal by the US Patent and Trademark Office to the US Supreme Court, the patent was finally granted with a five to four majority. It is clear that opinions were split almost down the middle on this issue even in the US. As Jeremy Rifkin has put it, this one case "laid the all-important legal groundwork for the privatization and commodification of the genetic commons" (Rifkin, 1998, 43). It is certainly not obvious that patents on life are a natural right of inventors as the above disagreement at the supreme court level in several countries shows.

Secondly, like ordinary property rights, IPRs often clash with other important natural rights, such as the right to life. One of the best examples of this tension can be found in the area of access to life-saving medication, the topic of this chapter. As medicines under patent protection are priced under monopoly conditions, their invariably high markups make them unaffordable to poor patients. Given that IPR systems provide opportunities to stop generic producers from offering cheap copies of new drugs, no alternative sources of drug supply will be available to the poor, hence conflicting with—in the worst scenario—their right to life. The question, simply put, is whether the creator of a life-saving medicine should have the legal authority to deny this medicine to those who cannot afford the profit-maximizing monopoly markup. (We shall return to this topic below.)

Thirdly, IPRs are not compatible with the very natural-law understanding of property rights adduced to support them. By asserting an IPR in an innovation, the innovator claims not merely rights to the products made from his or her own materials, but also new property rights over materials owned by others who lose their freedom to convert their materials into the same products. Such a deprivation of freedom conflicts with the natural-law understanding of property rights in material items, which render owners immune to unilateral expropriation by others. If the rights one has to use one's own material property cannot be diminished by others without the owner's consent, then there can be no IPRs—that is, no restrictions an innovator can unilaterally impose on what others are allowed to do with their own property.

An example (Wynberg and Chennells, 2009, 89–124): in 1995, the South African Council for Scientific and Industrial Research (CSIR) obtained a patent concerning the appetite suppressant properties of a Kalahari succulent, the Hoodia. Efforts at developing commercial products from the succulent are directed at the antiobesity market. Since then patents have been obtained in the US, the UK, Continental Europe, and Japan. Given the patent, the CSIR (or its sublicensees) can stop competitors from bringing to market antiobesity products based on the Hoodia. This means that impoverished communities in Namibia, for instance, or local farmers, are unable to use the Hoodia growing in their own territories for commercial gain as slimming products. As this is essentially the only viable commercial opportunity involving this succulent, it renders the plant worthless in terms of livelihoods. As a result, the property right in the physical plant and with it the right to do with it as one pleases (to sell it for a specific purpose) has been taken away from physical owners in favor of intellectual property rights.[6] One can see here that the common natural-law understanding of physical property rights—far from showing the way to an analogous natural-law understanding of IPRs—actually provides natural-law grounds against IPRs.

The above three points throw sufficient doubt on the claim that creators have natural rights to the protection of their intellectual property. It is indeed unlikely that IPRs can be justified on natural-law grounds. However, before we shall move on to the social utility defense, there is an important line of reasoning which we still need to consider. Though natural law does not seem to *support* IPRs, is it possible that it might actually *mandate against* such rights?

As there is limited space here for a detailed excursion into natural law theory, we shall confine ourselves to its most prominent thinker: Thomas Aquinas (1225–1274). According to Aquinas, laws are the dictates of practical reason. Natural law is the rational, eternal order given to the universe by divine providence. Human beings, as rational creatures, are subject to natural law "in the most excellent way, in so far as . . . [they] partake . . . of a share of providence" through "an imprint on us of the Divine light" (Aquinas, 1947b [1274]). This explains why natural law and natural rights are universal, according to Aquinas, independent of local, earthly traditions that may conflict with it. For him and his followers, natural law is "our intelligent participation in God's eternal law" (May, 2004, 138–184, 132). It also explains why human beings can know or recognize what is required of them by the natural law. Given that they participate in eternal law as rational beings, they are able to identify ethical demands on themselves.

The main ethical demand on human beings, according to Aquinas, is that "good is to be done and pursued, and evil is to be avoided." In one's pursuit of the good, the most important element is the preservation of human life, or as Aquinas puts it, "inasmuch as every substance seeks the preservation of its own being, according to its nature: and by reason of this inclination, whatever is a means of preserving human life, and of warding off its obstacles, belongs to the natural law" (Aquinas, 1947a [1274]).

The protection of human life is therefore paramount to Aquinas and the right to life is part of natural law. Another part of natural law is private property. According to Aquinas, "it is lawful for man to possess property" for three main reasons (Aquinas, 1947c [1274]):

> First because every man is more careful to procure what is for himself alone than that which is common to many or to all: since each one would shirk the labor and leave to another that which concerns the community.
>
> Secondly, because human affairs are conducted in more orderly fashion if each man is charged with taking care of some particular thing himself, whereas there would be confusion if everyone had to look after any one thing indeterminately.
>
> Thirdly, because a more peaceful state is ensured to man if each one is contented with his own. Hence it is to be observed that quarrels arise more frequently where there is no division of the things possessed.

What then happens when the right to life collides with the right to property, for example, if some have more than they need and others are starving? Or if some protect their intellectual property with the result that they are depriving the poor of life-saving medication? According to Aquinas, the right to life takes precedence over the right to property. For him,

> Whatever certain people have in superabundance is due, by natural law, to the purpose of succoring the poor. . . . Since, however, there are many who are in need, while it is impossible for all to be succored by means of the same thing, each one is entrusted with the stewardship of his own things, so that out of them he may come to the aid of those who are in need. Nevertheless, if the need be so manifest and urgent, that it is evident that the present need must be remedied by whatever means be at hand (for instance when a person is in some imminent danger, and there is no other possible remedy), then it is lawful for a man to succor his own need by means of another's property, by taking it either openly or secretly: nor is this properly speaking theft or robbery. [Aquinas, 1947c (1274)]

In the natural law tradition, of which Aquinas is the most prominent proponent (Murphy, 2008), the right to property or intellectual property is therefore only valid as long as it does not interfere significantly with the right to life. Though Aquinas promotes the concept of property and hopes that the benevolence of the affluent will help the poor, he supports the acquisition of another's property without their consent in situations of imminent danger to life.

This principle has been upheld by John Locke (1632–1704), one of the most eminent Western theorists on property rights. According to Locke "charity gives every man a title to so much out of another's plenty, as will keep him from extreme want, where he has no means to subsist otherwise" (Locke, 1823 [1690], 31).

Does this mean that natural law mandates against intellectual property rights? We noted at the outset that 10 million people are dying every year due to lack of access to life-saving medicines and that this grave ill is partly due to the current IPR regime. Wouldn't this suggest that natural law forbids IPRs or at least the current regime? No. The problem is more complex than this, as IPRs also save millions of lives every year given that they provide incentives for pharmaceutical research. It might therefore be argued that IPRs are compatible with natural law so long as the number of lives saved exceeds that of lives lost. But this criterion is hard to apply. And it is also at odds with the natural law tradition, which would assign greater weight to harms suffered now by those excluded from existing medicines than to harms averted in the future through stronger innovation incentives. We therefore have to examine the social utility of IPR systems, a task we shall turn to now.

The Social Utility of Intellectual Property Rights

Given our above conclusions on natural rights, IPRs must be assessed by reference to the common good of humankind. In making this assessment, one must consider the effects of the system relative to those of its politically available alternatives. These effects depend on what the world is like: on present facts about resources and scarcity as well as on the present international economic order and distribution of wealth. Changes in the world may affect whether current IPR rules are justified—for example, the rule that gives monopoly pricing powers for twenty years to the creator of a life-saving AIDS medication.

No IPR Protection

In the context of IPRs, it is sometimes pointed out what the world would look like without rewarding pharmaceutical innovations through patents. In such a world, little innovative pharmaceutical research would exist, at least as far as private companies were concerned. Their successful research efforts would almost invariably result in economic losses as soon as competitors, unrestrained by the IPR system, copied their inventions and offered the product at low prices. Given that they would not have to recoup investment costs, their prices would be much more attractive than the prices calculated to break even by the originator. As a result, it is argued that it is better to have medicines only for the affluent now, which will become available to the less affluent after the expiration of the monopoly period, than to have none at all.

However, this comparison simplifies the problem beyond recognition. It is not sufficient to argue that the situation regarding access to life-saving medicines could be even worse. We could *all* be without access to drugs. An ethical assessment of the situation cannot focus exclusively on the worst possible scenario, but must instead consider whether the current situation can be improved upon.

The Pre-TRIPS Regime[7]

Anand Grover (2009) clearly stated that "TRIPS and FTAs have had an adverse impact on prices and availability of [generic] medicines" (28). One possible comparison to the current situation is therefore the pre-TRIPS situation, which allowed states to decide how to protect and reward their pharmaceutical industries on the basis of their own interests.

An example (Pogge and Schroeder, 2009, 202): before 2005, Indian law only allowed patents on processes, not on products. As a result, India had a thriving generic pharmaceuticals industry that supplied copies of patented medicines cheaply throughout the world's poor regions. However, in 1994 India signed up to TRIPS as negotiated in the Uruguay round of the General Agreement on Tariffs and Trade (GATT) treaty. As a result, India was required to introduce patents on products by January 2005. This change to Indian patent rules hit the world's poor in two ways, directly by undercutting the supply of affordable medicines and indirectly by removing the generic competition that reduced the cost of brand-name medicines (*New York Times*, 2005). And as Grover has pointed out, this is exactly what has happened.

It is important here to remember that the poor currently face two problems when it comes to accessing life-saving drugs. First, due to monopoly pricing powers granted to innovators for considerable lengths of time, they cannot afford medicines that are still under patent protection. One can therefore speak of an access problem (medicines are priced beyond the reach of the poor). However, patent protection is not the only problem endangering poor people's health in the context of pharmaceutical innovation. Given that the pharmaceutical industry operates almost exclusively within the profit-making sector, diseases that burden the poor are rarely investigated in the first place. These diseases are referred to as "neglected diseases," since they are often ignored by the international research community. Hence, the second hindrance could be termed an availability[8] problem (drugs are not being developed for the needs of the poor) (Selgelid and Sepers, 2006, 153).

The main argument against the pre-TRIPS regime is that it did not stimulate the development of medicines for use in less developed countries. Given the lack of patent protection in countries such as Brazil, India, or South Africa, pharmaceutical companies could not rely on market exclusivity and were therefore unlikely to take potential profits in such markets into consideration when deciding upon research programs. Yet, these and other countries have considerable and increasingly affluent sub-populations, which would be able to afford high drug prices. Such markets are estimated to include 500 million people compared to the 1 billion potential customers in rich countries.

The argument in favor of the TRIPS regime with regard to developing countries is therefore twofold: firstly, it has the potential to awaken pharmaceutical interest in diseases that were hitherto not considered profitable, in order to serve an affluent minority. Secondly, after the monopoly interval such medicines would be within the reach of the poor in relevant countries.

It is too early for success stories of this kind. Most less developed countries were required to institute TRIPS by 1 January 2005, and certain "least developed" countries still have until 1 January 2016. However, in the long run, TRIPS may bring benefits to developing countries as compared to the pre-TRIPS regime, in particular in the area of so-called type 3 diseases: diseases that occur exclusively or overwhelmingly in poor countries.

Pharmaceutical companies may well increase research into type 3 diseases, secure in the knowledge of strict patent protection and the prospect of achieving high monopoly prices from affluent patients, government agencies, and non-governmental organizations. And though access to such drugs may initially be confined to the more affluent, much larger numbers of people will be able to benefit from their existence in the long run, after the monopoly pricing interval has expired.

Thus, the current regime is likely to have advantages over its predecessor with regard to the availability problem (drugs are not being developed for the needs of the poor). However, these advantages must be weighed against problems regarding the access problem (medicines are priced beyond the reach of the poor). It is in this area that the pre-TRIPS regime has clear advantages.

Before the TRIPS Agreement was adopted, most of the less developed countries had weak intellectual property protections or none at all, which enabled them to produce or import cheap generic versions of medicines that were still under patent protection. Relative to Pre-TRIPS, the current situation therefore imposes a serious loss on the poor by pricing out of their reach new medicines that they could previously have obtained at generic prices.

It is difficult to estimate the relative effects of a set of social rules—that is, how various relevant groups of people fare differently under these rules than they would fare if other rules, or none, existed. Moreover, decisions about the design of social rules are rarely such that one option is unambiguously worse than another—that is, worse for some and better for none.

However, it is evident that the current situation is preferable for the population of affluent countries who gain access, on familiar terms, to additional medicines that would not have existed without the added market demand for patented medicines, now anticipated from less developed countries. The comparison is more complex in the case of affluent minorities in less developed countries. They are better off with regard to the availability problem; some new medicines would not have existed without the TRIPS Agreement. At the same time, they are worse off with regard to the accessibility problem. Though they are able to afford high monopoly prices, they are no longer able to benefit from the low prices of generic medicines. On balance, however, it seems plausible to argue that the additionally created medicines for local health needs make up for the financial losses.

The social utility of the poor, who cannot afford monopoly prices, is the most difficult to assess and they ought to be accorded great moral weight in any calculations, given that, according to Anand Grover, 10 million lose their lives each year due to lack of access to life-saving drugs (Grover, 2009, 6, 7, 28).

The extension of strong intellectual property rights through TRIPS into less developed countries, burdens the poor disproportionately as they lose access to generic copies of drugs that are still under patent protection. On the other hand, this extension of intellectual property rights may benefit the poor of the future, given that additional incentives are being provided to address health needs in developing countries. Initially, poor people would not be able to afford new medicines. However, they may benefit from purchases made on their behalf by aid agencies and governments, and eventually the relevant patents will have expired and prices will drop to just above the marginal cost level. This latter benefit could begin to materialize in 2025, twenty years after strong IPR protection was instituted.

The magnitude of these burdens and benefits is enormous and decisions of social utility are difficult to make. The exclusion of the poor from access to advanced medicines will exact a heavy toll of disease and death for the indefinite future. On the other hand, millions of people may survive or be healthy in the future thanks to the generic availability of medicines that would not have existed without TRIPS.

Human rights–focused philosophers may argue that it is morally impermissible to cause severe harm, including death, to poor people now for the sake of protecting millions of poor people from similarly severe harm later on. They would therefore endorse the pre-TRIPS situation, given only these two choices. Yet, one cannot be satisfied with such an outcome in view of all the harm that stimulating new drug development could avert from so many future lives. From a utilitarian perspective, one might therefore argue that TRIPS is justified if the overall gains outweigh the overall losses. However, the above two are not the only options.

Amending the Current IPR System: The Health Impact Fund

The problem of balancing strong incentives for innovators against access to life-saving medicines is not new, though it was aggravated through TRIPS. Still, various solutions have already been proposed. Due to space constraints, we cannot list or even describe them all here.[9] The most ambitious proposals are based on cooperative, open access models. An example is Michael Boylan's reform plan to transform pharmaceutical companies into nonprofit organizations with public missions, supported and overseen by affluent governments (Boylan, 2008). Most reform proposals, however, leave the market motive for pharmaceutical corporations untouched. Of those, one reform plan—the Health Impact Fund—has emerged as being superior to all others according to some analysts (Nathan, 2007; Schroeder and Singer, 2009).

The Fund has also been described as a "promising" mechanism that deserves further examination by the Expert Working Group on Research and Development Financing (2009, 16) established by the World Health Assembly in 2008. The mechanisms the EWG singled out as deserving further consideration were the Health Impact Fund, open source drug development, patent pools, priority review voucher schemes, and orphan drug legislation. Given that exemplars of the last three mechanisms are already in operation, it is most encouraging that the newer proposal of the Health Impact Fund has been included in this group. The following is a brief description of its proposed function.

The Health Impact Fund is a proposal to institute a market-based, pay-for-performance reward mechanism for innovators alongside traditional patents. Pharmaceutical innovators would be offered ten years of substantial annual rewards, based on the global health impact of a new product, on condition that they price it at the lowest feasible cost of production and distribution. In this way, they would not have to recoup R&D costs through high monopoly prices and would have a clear incentive to sell the product cheaply to achieve highest possible uptake (Hollis and Pogge, 2008).

The Health Impact Fund would be most attractive for products that are expected to have a large global health impact but relatively low profitability under monopoly pricing. For example, a drug treating a disease mainly afflicting poor people would be an excellent candidate for registration, since typically such products cannot earn high profits, though they could benefit many people. Thus, the

Health Impact Fund would provide important incentives to develop drugs for neglected diseases, thereby tackling the availability problem. At the same time, these products can be sold at low prices, because the innovator would be rewarded independently from market prices, thereby tackling the access problem.

Problems of availability and access, while critical, are not the only factors limiting the impact of medicines on the disease burden of the poor. Health systems in developing countries are often weak, with limited capacity to ensure that available drugs are on hand where they are needed, particularly in rural and remote areas, and are prescribed appropriately and used correctly by patients. In allocating rewards on the basis of health impact, the Health Impact Fund provides pharmaceutical companies with strong incentives to work with governments and other actors to address these crucial "last mile" problems.

If adequately funded by taxpayers around the world, the Health Impact Fund would lead to reduced costs for national health systems, reduced insurance premiums, and reduced prices at the pharmacy, mostly, but not exclusively, in developing countries. The scheme would run in parallel to the traditional system of patent-protected markups with the pharmaceutical innovator free to choose under which system to market each product. Firms would probably register a product with the HIF only if they expected higher profits from the Fund than from monopoly prices. For instance, a malaria drug might receive a high reward from the Health Impact Fund, whilst so-called life-style drugs (treating hair loss, acne, etc.) would fare better on the traditional patent regime.

The Health Impact Fund has a number of ancillary benefits. The low price of drugs sold under Fund arrangements would reduce incentives for counterfeiters, whose products are often of poor quality and deleterious to patients. And the more pharmaceutical companies registered their products with the Fund, the less they would incur costs associated with competitive marketing and litigation to assert patent rights, thereby freeing funds for further investment.

The Fund's greatest benefit, however, is that patients will gain access to important medicines that, without the Fund, would have been too expensive for them, or even nonexistent. In this regard, the Fund addresses both the access and the availability problem for a worldwide cost ($6 billion USD per year) that is a ridiculous 0.9 percent of the money taxpayers spent on bailing out banks during the financial crisis in England alone (£850 billion/$1,357 billion USD for two years) (National Audit Office, 2009).

Conclusion

Each year 10 million human beings die because they cannot access life-saving medicines. Some may be so poor that they cannot even afford cheap generic drugs;

others may not be able to see a doctor for prescription drugs. However, many die because the international IPR system facilitates high monopoly prices, which neither they nor their governments can afford.

As we have shown, the right to IPR protection of innovators does not trump the right to health of the poor. The former takes precedence both within international law and natural rights philosophy and on grounds of social utility. The major challenge now is to amend the international IPR system in such a way that it provides innovators with incentives strong enough to develop new medicines for neglected diseases, whilst avoiding pricing 2 billion human beings out of the market.

Only one reform plan does exactly that. The Health Impact Fund upholds strong intellectual property rights, therefore guaranteeing more medicines in the future. At the same time as preserving the advantages of the TRIPS regime, it allays its main problems for the poor. Through its two-tiered system of providing incentives for the pharmaceutical industry, the Fund meets the requirements of both social utility and natural law (focusing on the right to life) better than any existing regime.

Instituting the Health Impact Fund now would provide considerable impetus to governmental efforts to respect, protect, and fulfill the right to health. More than sixty years after the Universal Declaration of Human Rights affirmed the human right to health, the poorest third of humanity would finally have a chance to see a major reform toward its realization.

Notes

1. Lack of access to life-saving medicines also leads to serious problems of morbidity and the related human suffering. This chapter applies to both avoidable mortality and morbidity. For simplicity's sake only, we shall focus on the former.

2. See for instance, the approaches by Hart, H. L. A. (1997). *The Concept of Law, Second Edition.* Oxford: Oxford University Press; and Hohfeld, W. N. (2001). *Fundamental Legal Conceptions as Applied in Judicial Reasoning.* Surrey: Ashgate Dartmouth Publishing. A good overview is provided in Kramer, Matthew, Nigel Simmonds, and Hillel Steiner. (2000). *A Debate over Rights: Philosophical Inquiries.* Oxford: Oxford University Press.

3. By contrast to the British system of universal health care coverage without insurance, all Germans are members of a wide variety of health insurances. Those who cannot afford to pay the premiums have them covered by the state.

4. The term "judicial activism" is used in two ways. One, when referring to the professional activities of judges, the term is used pejoratively to describe the act of moving beyond the law to enforce personal or political views. For instance, a Catholic judge may rule against the use of embryonic stem cells although there is no domestic

law to support this ruling. The judge is therefore regarded as an activist. Two, when referring to the activities of attorneys and their clients (possibly NGOs), the term has been used more recently to describe legal campaigns mounted in the absence of relevant national law based on international legal instruments, such as the Universal Declaration of Human Rights. We are using the term in this second meaning.

5. Yet others asserted pressure by promising a social utility bargain independent of IPR mechanisms, namely trade liberalization (e.g., reduction of subsidies on agricultural products). However, this is not relevant here.

6. One might argue that the above example has not been explained in all its complexity given the restraints imposed on patent applicants by the Convention on Biological Diversity (CBD). However, this is irrelevant for the clash between property and intellectual property rights under discussion. In fact, one could even argue that one of the main results of the CBD is that it prioritizes physical property rights over intellectual property rights by legislating for nonhuman genetic resources to fall under the national sovereignty of states.

7. This section draws heavily on Hollis and Pogge (2008).

8. Grover uses the term differently, in all likelihood referring to the non-availability of generic drugs.

9. For a summary, see Schroeder and Singer (2009).

References

Abramovich, Victor, and Laura Pautassi. (2008). "The Right to Health at Law Courts: Some Effects of Judicial Activism on the Health System in Argentina." *Salud Colectiva 4*(3): 261–282.

African Commission on Human and Peoples' Rights. (2003). Fifteenth Annual Activity Report. Retrieved from http://www.achpr.org/english/activity_reports/activity15_en.pdf

Aquinas, Thomas. (1947a [1274]). "Of the Natural Law." *Summa Theologica.* Retrieved from http://www.sacred-texts.com/chr/aquinas/summa/sum229.htm

Aquinas, Thomas. (1947b [1274]). "Of the Various Kinds of Law. *Summa Theologica.*" Retrieved from http://www.sacred-texts.com/chr/aquinas/summa/sum229.htm

Aquinas, Thomas. (1947c [1274]). "Of Theft and Robbery." *Summa Theologica.* Retrieved from http://www.sacred-texts.com/chr/aquinas/summa/sum322.htm

Boylan, Michael. (2008). Medical Pharmaceutical and Distributive Justice. *Cambridge Quarterly of Healthcare Ethics 17*: 32–46.

Branstetter, L. G. (2004). "Do Stronger Patents Induce More Local Innovation?" *Journal of International Law 7*(2): 359–370.

Brecher, Bob. (2007). *Torture and the Ticking Bomb.* Oxford: Blackwell Publishers.

Brown, Brendan F., ed. (1960). *The Natural Law Reader*. New York: Oceana Publications.

Canadian Environmental Law Association. (No date). "Life Patents: The Oncomouse Case." Retrieved from http://www.cela.ca/collections/celacourts/life-patents-oncomouse-case. Accessed November 25, 2009.

Convention on the Elimination of All Forms of Discrimination Against Women. (1979). Retrieved from http://www.un.org/womenwatch/daw/cedaw/text/econvention.htm

Convention on the Rights of the Child (1989). Retrieved from http://www2.ohchr.org/english/law/crc.htm

Cruz Bermudez, et al. v. Ministerio de Sanidad y Asistencia Social Supreme Court of Justice of Venezuela. (1999, 15 July). Case No. 15.789, Decision No. 916. Retrieved from http://www.actionaid.org/main.aspx?PageID=780

Danzon, Patricia M., and Adrian Towse. (2003). "Differential Pricing for Pharmaceuticals: Reconciling Access, R&D and Patents." *International Journal of Health Care Finance and Economics 3*: 183–205.

Declaration of Alma-Ata. (1978). Retrieved from www.who.int/hpr/NPH/docs/declaration_almaata.pdf

Epicurus. (1925). "The Letter to Menoeceus" in *Diogenes Laertius: Lives of Eminent Philosophers Volume II, Books 6–10*, trans. R. D. Hicks. Loeb Classical Library No.185.

Expert Working Group on Research and Development Financing. (2009). "Public Health, Innovation and Intellectual Property: Report of the Expert Working Group on Research and Development Financing." Geneva: World Health Organization. Retrieved from http://apps.who.int/gb/ebwha/pdf_files/EB126/B126_6Add1-en.pdf

Finnis, John. (1980). *Natural Law and Natural Rights*. Oxford: Clarendon Press.

Grover, Anand. (2009). Promotion and Protection of All Human Rights, Civil, Political, Economic, Social and Cultural Rights, Including the Right to Development: A Report of the Special Rapporteur on the Right of Everyone to the Enjoyment of the Highest Attainable Standard of Physical and Mental Health. United Nations, A/HRC/11/12. Retrieved from http://www2.ohchr.org/english/bodies/hrcouncil/docs/11session/A.HRC.11.12_en.pdf

Hogerzeil, H., M. Samson, J. Casanovas, and L. Rahmani-Ocora. (2006). "Is Access to Essential Medicines as Part of the Fulfilment of the Right to Health Enforceable Through the Courts?" *The Lancet 368*(9532): 305–311.

Hollis, Aidan, and Thomas Pogge. (2008). "The Health Impact Fund: Making Medicines Accessible for All." *Incentives for Global Health*. Retrieved from http://www.yale.edu/macmillan/igh/#

Institute of Science in Society. (2009). Europe's Uprising Against GMOs and Patents on Life. Retrieved from http://www.i-sis.org.uk/EuropesUprisingAgainstGMOs.php

International Covenant on Economic, Social and Cultural Rights. (1966). Retrieved from http://www2.ohchr.org/english/law/cescr.htm

Irwin, Aisling. (1995). "Patent Battle over Life." *Times Higher Education*. Retrieved from http://www.timeshighereducation.co.uk/story.asp?storyCode=95686§ioncode=26

Jentzsch, Christian. (2006). *Patent for a Pig—The Big Business of Genetics: A Film*. HTTV Production for WDR (Westdeutscher Rundfunk).

Langford, Malcolm, and Aoife Nolan. (2006). *Litigating Economic, Social and Cultural Rights*. Geneva: ESC Rights Litigation Programme.

Locke, John. (1823 [1690]). *Two Treatises of Government, Book 1*. London: Thomas Tegg; W. Sharpe and Son. Retrieved from http://socserv.mcmaster.ca/econ/ugcm/3ll3/locke/government.pdf

May, William. (2004). "Contemporary Perspectives on Thomistic Natural Law" in *St. Thomas and the Natural Law Tradition*, ed. John Goyette, Mark Latkovic, and Richard Myers. Washington, DC: The Catholic University of America Press.

Millennium Development Goals. (2000). Retrieved from http://www.un.org/millenniumgoals/bkgd.shtml

Murphy, Mark. (2008). "The Natural Law Tradition in Ethics" in *Stanford Encyclopedia of Philosophy*. Retrieved from http://plato.stanford.edu/entries/natural-law-ethics/

Nathan, Carl. (2007). "Aligning Pharmaceutical Innovation with Medical Need." *Nature Medicine 13*(3): 304–308.

National Audit Office. (2009). Maintaining Financial Stability Across the UK's Banking System. Retrieved from http://www.nao.org.uk/publications/0910/uk_banking_system.aspx

The New York Times. (2005, January 18). "India's Choice." [Editorial].

Nozick, Robert. (1974). *Anarchy, State, and Utopia*. New York: Basic Books.

Nwobike, Justice C. (2005). The African Commission on Human and Peoples' Rights and the Demystification of Second and Third Generation Rights Under the African Charter: *Social and Economic Rights Action Center (SERAC) and the Center for Economic and Social Rights (CESR) v. Nigeria*. *African Journal of Legal Studies 2*:129–146.

Patent Cooperation Treaty. (1970). Retrieved from http://www.bitlaw.com/source/treaties/pct.html

Pogge, Thomas, and Doris Schroeder. (2009). "Why We Need A New Approach to Pharmaceutical Innovation: A Pragmatic Answer to a Moral Question" in *In*

Sickness and Health: The Future of Medicine, ed. Marc Noppen and Marleen Wynants: 197–213. Brussels: Vrije Universiteit Brussel Press.

Rawls, John. (1999). *A Theory of Justice*. Cambridge, MA: Harvard University Press.

Raz, Joseph. (1984). "Legal Rights." *Oxford Journal of Legal Studies 4*: 1–21.

Rifkin, Jeremy. (1998). *The Biotech Century: Harnessing the Gene and Remaking the World*. New York: Jeremy P. Tarcher/Putnam.

Schroeder, Doris, and Peter Singer. (2009). "Intellectual Property Rights Reform Plans: A Report for Innova." Retrieved from www.uclan.ac.uk/innova

Scotcher, Suzanne. (2004). *Innovation and Incentives*. Cambridge, MA: MIT Press.

Selgelid, Michael, and Eline M. Sepers. (2006). "Patents, Profits, and the Price of Pills: Implications for Access and Availability" in *The Power of Pills: Social, Ethical and Legal Issues in Drug Development, Marketing and Pricing Policies*, ed. P. Illingworth, U. Schuklenk, and J. C. Cohen: 153–163. London: Pluto Press.

Social and Economic Rights Action Center & the Center for Economic and Social Rights (SERAC) v. Nigeria. (2001). African Commission on Human and People's Rights. (October 27, 2001). Retrieved from http://www.escr-net.org/caselaw/caselaw_show.htm?doc_id=404115

Sozialgesetzbuch der Bundesrepublik Deutschland. (1975). Retrieved from http://gesetze.bmas.de/Gesetze/gesetze.htm

Tobinick, Edward L. (2009). "The Value of Drug Repositioning in the Current Pharmaceutical Market." *Drug News and Perspectives 22*(2): 119–125.

United Nations Committee on Economic, Social and Cultural Rights. (2000). E/C.12/2000/4. (General Comments) General Comment No.14. Retrieved from http://www.unhchr.ch/tbs/doc.nsf/0/40d009901358b0e2c1256915005090be?Opendocument

United States Constitution. (1787). Retrieved from http://www.usconstitution.net/const.html

Universal Declaration of Human Rights. (1948). Retrieved from http://www.un.org/en/documents/udhr/

World Health Organization Statistical Information System. (2010). Retrieved from http://www.who.int/whosis/en/index.html

World Intellectual Property Organization Patent Cooperation Treaty. (1970). Contracting Parties. Retrieved from http://www.wipo.int/treaties/en/ShowResults.jsp?lang=en&treaty_id=6

World Intellectual Property Organization. (2008). World Patent Report: A Statistical Review. Retrieved from http://www.wipo.int/ipstats/en/statistics/patents/wipo_pub_931.html#a31

World Trade Organization. (2001). Doha Declaration on the TRIPS Agreement and Public Health. Retrieved from http://www.wto.org/english/theWTO_e/minist_e/min01_e/mindecl_trips_e.pdf

Wynberg, Rachel, and Roger Chennells. (2009). "Green Diamonds of the South: An Overview of the San-Hoodia Case" in *Indigenous Peoples, Consent and Benefit Sharing*, ed. Rachel Wynberg, Doris Schroeder, and Roger Chennells. Berlin: Springer.

You, D., T. Wardlaw, P. Salama, and G. Jones. (2009). "Levels and Trends in Under-5 Mortality 1990–2008." *Lancet 375*(9709): 100–103.

PART THREE

NORMATIVE APPLICATIONS

Religion

■ Chapter 13 What Price Theocracy?
LAURA PURDY

■ Chapter 14 Global Ethics in the Academy
JAMES A. DONAHUE

PART THREE: Religion

INTRODUCTION

One of the pivotal factors in global justice is the role of religion. The two largest world religions, Christianity and Islam, are and have been for centuries key players in global politics—economics, war, and peace. The two essays in this section take quite different directions on how we are to understand religion today and its role in global justice.

Laura Purdy addresses the role of religion in governing a state: theocracy. The basic idea behind theocracy is that civil rule is done in the name of God. In such cases religious freedom trumps secular law. There are two types of theocracies that Purdy examines: first, strong theocracy (in which the state has an official or quasi official religion and the ruler—generally a dictator—interprets the will of God for the people); and second, weak theocracy, in which religious freedom is protected to such an extent that it can trump secular law.

In each instance Purdy's aim is to examine the best variety of theocracy to see whether it leads to a just society. The strategy being that if the best form of theocracy is unjustifiable, then so also will all lesser sorts.

The best type of strong theocracy would be structured around a benevolent autocrat who slashes through red tape to bring high-quality health care and education to all of her citizens. This sounds promising, but even in this sort of society there is a severe problem: the resulting shared community worldview. In any strong theocracy there is a dependency upon Divine Command Theory (DCT). DCT possesses an internal contradiction and this will result in a flawed shared community worldview. The problem with DCT is this: either whatever God says is good because God says it (the so-called *Euthyphro* problem)[1] or whenever God declares something to be good it is based upon objective criteria that rest within the action or rule. In the first case, *good* is arbitrary and in the second God is unnecessary. Neither outcome is satisfactory to sustain a proper shared community worldview. In addition, DCT requires a compliant populace that accepts the theological judgments of the leaders. This dynamic will lead to a static society because most conceptions of God are as an immutable being. Laws and policies based on such an unchanging entity must also be static. This creates a permanent status quo. However, on the other hand, democracy requires a populace trained in critical thinking that employs a mitigated skepticism in problem solving. This leads to a self-renewing community of progressive change. Thus, even the best strong theocracy possesses a fatal flaw.

The case is no better in weak theocracies. This is because of the strong emphasis upon religious freedom. Such an emphasis suggests that tenets of religion trump civil law. This can lead to the oppression of the vulnerable—such as lack of medical care for children of Jehovah's Witness and Christian Scientists and proper education for Amish children, etc. Since vulnerable populations should be protected and not harmed, and since weak theocracy leads to such exploitation, then even weak theocracy should be eschewed.

In the end, governments should be secular and should nurture and encourage an educated, critical thinking populace.

In the second essay, James A. Donahue writes about how the academy might make strides toward peaceful rapprochement. Donahue is the president of the Graduate Theological Union at the University of California, Berkeley. His essay is based upon efforts by professors at his university in just such a project that has been ongoing for several years with the goal of sowing seeds of peace in the Middle East between Muslims and Jews.

Donahue begins his essay confronting the oft-accepted role of the university as merely a theoretical think tank engaged in thought experiments that never extend beyond their boundaries. Instead, Donahue presents a vision in which the reach of the academy stretches out to society at large to integrate theory and practice. Since religion plays a major role in most of the world's societies, religious understanding can have an important role in global justice.

The first distinction to be made is between religious studies and theology. The former is value neutral concerning religious claims while the latter takes the vantage point of belief and the subsequent understanding of truth and meaning that flows from this. In both Islamic and Jewish studies, aspects of both modes of inquiry are present in a far-reaching interdisciplinary approach.

The goals of this approach are: one, the understanding of a field or body of knowledge and information that creates an encounter with the reality of the "other"; two, the encounter and development of relationships between Jews and Muslims via common problems and practical issues; and three, exploration of strategies and directives for action such as protecting the environment and economic policies.

The program at the Graduate Theological Union utilizes four models of discourse: one, engaging common text study peculiar to Islamic and Jewish traditions; two, examining popular media and the construction of Jewish and Islamic identities; three, developing ideas of business practices in the two traditions; and four, exploration of food practices across Judaism and Islam.

With respect to common textual study, Donahue has a list of key concerns and directions that have driven this effort. When looking at popular media, the task is to take apart the various *frames* that have distorted the depiction of a community via stereotypes. Business practices lead to mutual examination along the lines of international business ethics. Finally, the sharing of food together represents a bond of considerable importance. It is a cultural tie that has great potential in fostering toleration and respect.

At a recent student peace conference I attended at Georgetown University, I cited Donahue's four points at a student panel that was composed of Israelis and Muslims from the region. They were very encouraged by the thought of this sort of program becoming widespread across Israel/Palestine. It is just this sort of reaction that Donahue hopes will spread.

Note

1. In Plato's dialogue *Euthyphro,* Socrates asks the question whether some *x* is pious because the gods love it or whether the gods love *x* because it is pious.

CHAPTER THIRTEEN

What Price Theocracy?

LAURA PURDY
Wells College

Abstract

Some contemporary nation-states have theocratic governments, and secular principles are still not secure in Western countries. Yet there is little realistic assessment of the probable consequences of such government. I argue that even given the most favorable assumptions, stable, just theocracies are unlikely to survive in the contemporary world. Because of the structure of policy justification, they discourage critical thinking by citizens, have trouble with change and diversity, and foster corruption on the part of leaders. I also consider a weaker form of theocracy, one where the Free Exercise Clause of the First Amendment trumps competing laws. But that state of affairs risks harm both to third parties and to vulnerable members of religious groups. Thus, neither strong nor weak forms of theocracy are desirable forms of government.

Key Words

theocracy, democracy, autocracy, critical thinking, Divine Command Theory, Free Exercise Clause of the First Amendment

---

> *"No more can be said than that theocracy belongs to a period when men's minds were enslaved by authority."*
>
> —Heinrich von Treitschke

Many countries used to be governed by some form of theocracy, and some still are. Moreover, some contemporary religions are theocratic and hold that theocracy is the best form of government. Among them are Islam and Catholicism, both of which are powerful and boast of many adherents. In the US, too, some Christian groups overtly propound theocracy; their influence grew during George W. Bush's administration and it remains a powerful strain of politics there.[1] Hence, despite the apparent triumph of secularism in the West, scrutiny of this claim is urgent.

Oddly, there seems to be relatively little scholarly—or even popular—discussion of the pros and cons of theocracy, although closely related issues (such as the separation of church and state) garner considerable attention.[2]

The first order of business here is to define theocracy. A survey of the literature reveals some variations in the way the word is used. The basic idea is rule by God. Of course, this can mean only rule in the name of God, whether by a single sovereign, or a religiously sanctioned class of some sort.[3] A more expansive conception is suggested by Lucas Swaine: "Theocracy is, for my purposes, a form of governance under which people try to live according to a conception of the good that is strictly binding; comprehensive in range; and religious in nature" (2007, 566). I will leave this broader conception aside for now, even though it is useful for evaluating contemporary theocracies. It also seems appropriate to see as theocratic an understanding of a right to religious freedom that routinely trumps secular law. I will call the first type of political organization "strong" theocracy, and the second type "weak" theocracy.

Criticizing past and contemporary theocracies would be like shooting fish in a barrel for anyone committed to the values implied by democracy. I will therefore consider the case for a hypothetical best theocracy, showing that there are devastating objections to it. It follows that no worse theocracy could be morally tenable.

What Would the Best Theocracy Look Like?

Imagine, then, the best theocracy you can think of, one that exemplifies your favorite values, within the constraints of universalizability—the principle requiring that similar cases be treated alike unless there is a morally relevant difference between them—and basic justice.[4] For progressives, that would point to a benevolent theocratic autocrat. This autocrat establishes strongly justifiable moral principles (in the name of God) and fearlessly tackles the challenges facing humanity. She slashes through red tape and nay-saying to take on global warming and other environmental threats, eradicates corruption in government, and works consistently to protect basic human interests by such measures as ensuring access to high-quality health care and education for all.

What objections might there be to this best imaginable form of theocracy?

Structural Problems with Strong Theocracy

Change, Authority, Consistency, and Diversity: The Need for Critical Thinking

Theocratic autocracies (like other autocracies) can be swept away by opponents, no matter how appealing their policies. Therefore, it is instructive here to consider key differences between theocratic and secular autocracies with respect to change. One is that citizens in secular autocracies are more likely to have retained the intellectual tools for evaluating policies, since the official case for such rule is likely to have been the rulers' allegedly unique capacity for addressing urgent problems. In this situation, there will not necessarily have been a thoroughgoing systematic attempt to suppress citizens' capacity for critical thinking or civic engagement. If the policies adopted turn out not to work well, citizens may therefore be open to those promising other approaches and still capable of reasoning well about them.

How is theocracy different? The ground for authority is God's command, together, presumably, with the understanding that current policies are the only right ones.

This position assumes that God exists and that we could know its will. Ignoring those problems for the sake of argument, the objections to Divine Command Theory still loom large here. Either God's commands are good because its commands define the good, in which case the good is arbitrary (as it could have been the opposite). Or, God simply conveys an independently determined good, in which case God is dispensable, a mere middleperson who may add some gloss and urgency to ethical principles and actions, but brings nothing essential to their content.

Religionists tend to respond that this objection to DCT is based on a false dilemma. That is, both horns of the alleged dilemma can be true: God's commands are good both because it is good, and hence it will command only the good, and because its commanding creates goodness. But these are contradictory claims, and can't both be true. If God's commanding creates goodness, no independent grounds for judging goodness can exist. And if there are independent grounds for judging goodness, acts or states of affairs cannot be made good merely by God's fiat. This problem is exacerbated by the recognition that there are multiple competitors for recognition as God—as there in fact are, given at least three major religions making the case for their own God, not to mention potential imposters like Satan (Purdy, 1988).

More sophisticated proponents of Divine Command Theory, such as Robert Adams, seem to concede these points by giving up the claim that God is the source of value.[5] Support for God's authority is thus purchased at the cost of acknowledging the need for independent grounds for ethical claims. And, this concession will seriously weaken theocratic rulers' authority in any society where this argument is recognized by influential citizens.

For those who demand reasoned defenses of moral and political policy claims, these points should, by themselves, suffice for rejecting a theocratic defense of government power—even if they are believers of some sort. Alas, most people are not so demanding, and so governments can get away with extremely sloppy defenses, or, by appealing primarily to emotions, none at all. The consequences are frequently catastrophic.

This comparison of the possibilities for intelligent change in secular and theocratic autocracies is a special case of a more general problem about change in theocracies. As Heinrich von Treitschke points out, "it is contrary to the nature of theocracy to change and grow with the times, because it rests on the immutable rock of revelation" (1916, 26)—and the implication that the laws are the best possible. But conditions do change, of course, necessitating alterations in laws, policies, and practices. Challenges can come from uncontrollable factors such as drought, and from the evolution of assumptions and values in response to such factors.

Moreover, power must eventually be transferred to new leaders. When that happens, any policy changes not obviously deduced from broader principles (but less broad than "God's will") will be difficult to explain or justify, offending citizens' expectations and needs for continuity and consistency. This will be true no matter whether new laws are less demanding or more demanding. If less, those who struggled or suffered under the old ones will want justification for what they endured. If more, it will be difficult to show why God's demands are now so much more burdensome. Merely asserting that the previous leaders were mistaken about God's will hardly seems sufficient, and opens the door to questions about whether the current ones might be similarly mistaken.

These questions will arise no matter what the content of the laws. Suppressing such questioning is one of the motives for distancing theocratic leaders from the people (von Treitschke, 1916, 24). Yet even a benevolent leader protected by such distance is likely to grow detached from citizens' needs and concerns over time. This distancing will almost inevitably lead to policies that are less than optimal (from any perspective that has any regard for them at all); in tandem with absolute power, it also nurtures corruption.[6]

Such creeping corruption is especially likely, given the other distinctive features of theocracy—especially its need to suppress critical thinking and free inquiry (von Treitschke, 1916, 24). As von Treitschke writes, "It cannot do otherwise. Lip service at the very least must be paid to the revelation upon which the edifice of the State is founded" (24). Concomitantly, it must also resist citizen participation in decision-making: "A constitutional Pope and a constitutional Sultan are alike anomalies" (26).

Although under some circumstances societies might survive and even flourish without critical thinking, that is not the case in anything like our contemporary world. The threats facing humanity are now enormous, requiring the kind of good prudential, moral, and political decisions that require much more critical thinking, not less. Anyone with any life experience can also see that even at the individual level, misery arising from self-destructive behavior could be averted by more systematic prudential and moral critical thinking.

One might object that a theocracy needn't discourage the use of reason altogether. It might just try to shape and channel it, as most societies do in any case. And, for a variety of reasons, humans often acquiesce in these pressures. In fact, we seem to have a remarkable capacity to compartmentalize our thinking, refusing to extend critical thinking patterns we take for granted in some issues to others of equal or even more importance.

In principle, it might seem as if our best theocracy need only shield its source of authority from citizen challenges, not the policies themselves. But it hardly seems possible to detach the two, as challenges to policies will inevitably erode the authority that allegedly backs them up. And even the most defensible policies are bound to generate opposition in anything but the most homogeneous societies. Despite vigorous efforts at "ethnic cleansing," human populations are becoming ever more diverse because of increasing numbers of refugees and immigrants, and, ironically, both because of liberalism that encourages individualism, and the exuberant growth of diverse religious groups.

Openness to democratic discussion and debate is necessary to acknowledge and accommodate such diversity; otherwise government degenerates into tyranny, despite initially desirable policies. Fruitful and respectful democratic discussion and debate requires critical thinking skills, applied to a wide range of issues. But people with those skills are unlikely to be content with theocratic authority, either because its content clashes with their own convictions or because they reject theocratic authority on principled grounds altogether. Threats will also come from skeptics seeking power and control for themselves. Citizens with highly developed critical thinking skills can defend government from such deleterious challenges far more easily than those innocent of such skills.

Critical thinking skills need to be nurtured for another essential reason. The stability of even best theocracies will be challenged not only from within, but also from without. A well-run theocracy might provide a relatively high quality of life that would secure loyalty from many citizens. However, no society is immune from threats or aggression from external forces. Both internal threats (such as severe drought) and external ones tend to foster desperation, and render people vulnerable to emotional appeals. A culture of critical thinking is one of the few factors that can help to protect decent societies against the kind of mass craziness exemplified by Nazi Germany.

Cynics often note that Germany was at the time one of the most advanced countries in the world, with a highly educated population and a rich and interesting culture. Much energy has been expended trying to understand what happened, but for our purposes it suffices to note that extensive schooling doesn't necessarily imply stringent attention to critical thinking and that cultural development can be extremely uneven—very sophisticated in some ways but primitive in others, especially in dire economic circumstances. Whether having had a population more attuned to challenging authority based on its own critical scrutiny of its policies would, by itself, have been sufficient to prevent the ascent of the Nazi party is debatable, but it couldn't have hurt, and it might well have made it more difficult, perhaps even impossible.

One of the best defenses of the value of critical thinking is articulated by W. K. Clifford in *The Ethics of Belief.* His thesis is that "It is wrong always, everywhere, and for anyone, to believe anything upon insufficient evidence" (Clifford, 1901). He argues that even the apparently most trivial unfounded belief can have devastating consequences.

First, a belief will affect believers' actions, even if only to dispose them to believe similar ones, eroding others, with which it conflicts, eventually, in Clifford's colorful words, "to explode into overt action, and leave its stamp on our character for ever" (Clifford, 1901). Second, our belief "hygiene" affects the larger society. According to Clifford, allowing oneself to believe without good evidence lowers our intellectual standards, becoming, as he says, "credulous." Worse yet, if we are known to be credulous, others will cease to bother about being truthful to us, encouraging the general spread of carelessness about the truth: "The danger to society is not merely that it should believe wrong things, though that is great enough; but that it should become credulous, and lose the habit of testing things and inquiring into them; for then it must sink back into savagery" (Clifford, 1901). Clifford sees the totality of society's beliefs as a precious heritage that is influenced, being made either better or worse by each seeming tiny act of belief.

Now, it is tempting to reject Clifford on the grounds that his absolutism is itself unwarranted and indefensible—even if his language resonates eerily with contemporary brain science ("Neurons that fire together wire together" [Doige, 2007]).[7] If I allow myself to believe without evidence that the far side of the moon has or has not a certain property, it seems wildly implausible to believe that society must sink into savagery as a result.[8]

Nonetheless, it is not difficult to see how careless acceptance of more important claims could lead to such an outcome.[9] One might argue that the degraded state of public discourse—especially political discourse—in the US is both a consequence of and reinforces corrosive cynicism arising from lack of attention to our concern about the grounds for belief.

How else is it possible to explain how much traction Republican objections to current (2009) Democratic proposals for health care reform have gotten? For example, somehow, the utterly reasonable proposal to offer citizens the opportunity to consult about their end-of-life wishes has been transmogrified into death panels that will refuse care to the elderly. This claim originated and has been propagated by those—including mainstream media outlets—who apparently think that the health care system is fine the way it is, despite the widely available evidence that it costs much more and offers much less protection than those of developed countries comparable to the US in most other ways.[10] After years of living with reporters who see "he said, she said" reporting as the ultimate in objectivity, it is not surprising that people are confused by such claims and counterclaims, particularly when they perceive the issues as so vital to their well-being[11]—especially when even calm, accurate reporting takes the claim seriously in its attempt to show why it is mistaken. Leaving out of the story the political motivation from which it arose is seriously irresponsible.[12] Yet this state of affairs is now par for the course, given the fog of inaccurate and politically motivated discourse with which we are now blanketed, accompanied by little or no intelligent evaluation or analysis by the sources most Americans depend on for their news. Despite all this, it is disconcerting that so many seem unable or unwilling to make a serious attempt to sort out the truth for themselves, given that so much reliable information—including the relevant legal documents—are now easily available on the web. Clearly, this nation has failed to ensure that its citizens know how to judge claims or to care about the truth—even when their most fundamental interests are at stake.

What relevance has all this to the desirability of theocracy as a form of government? Beliefs about ethics and politics, including (most saliently) the nature of legitimate authority, are among the very most important beliefs for society that citizens hold. By its very nature, theocracy must foster fuzziness (at best) about the source and justification of moral and political beliefs. This state of affairs must undermine the culture of critical thinking, and hence even the best theocracy cannot resist the inevitable attacks on it and thus be stable, even where its policies are otherwise reasonable.

Strong Theocracy Is an Undesirable Form of Government

This conclusion is based on evaluation of structural properties of theocracy, together with well-founded assumptions about human nature, relationships, and societies.[13] It suggests that governments that can encourage critical inquiry would be superior—both more stable in the ways that matter, and more flexible in dealing with change and accommodating legitimate diverse perspectives, interests, and positions. Democracy is such a form of government. Not only can it encourage a culture of critical thinking, but it must to function well.

Do all democracies rise to this height? Alas, no. Hardly any, and only for limited periods—the struggle for good government never ends, and good government seems far more easily destroyed than constructed. Nonetheless, our focus here is on the structural properties of different types of authority, not historical examples.

If we were to focus on historical examples, it would be difficult to find a genuine democracy that could match the hell on earth created by past and contemporary theocracies. The evidence is so clear and so easily available that it hardly needs mentioning. Politically empowered religion tends to breed a kind of self-righteous and power-mad mentality that stops at nothing to impose its will. Theocrats, in the name of God, have often hunted down, tortured, and murdered those with allegedly heretical views or who they claim have failed to conform to their moral views, including, most notably, women and homosexuals. They have systematically oppressed both. Women, especially, tend to be treated as second-class citizens, at best, and at worst, treated like slaves whose lives and welfare are of no consequence whatsoever.[14] Politically empowered religionists have often also crusaded and warred against whole peoples and countries that do not share their religious views.

This behavior becomes more understandable when one pauses to consider that genuine democracy provides the religious with the space to live according to their religiously based moral convictions except where they seriously harm others. So only those who wish to impose their views on others—and who don't have good secular grounds for doing so—would yearn to be theocratic dictators.

Why the caveat about secular grounds? Because democracy, unlike theocracy, creates space for debate about morality and policy in the public square. In communities of critical thinkers, claims and positions will be taken seriously only if they can be justified in widely shared terms. At a minimum, such critical thinkers will reject moral and political positions not based on universalizability. This is a necessary, but not sufficient, principle for any reason-based moral discourse.[15] In addition, this formal standard needs to be fleshed out with substantive moral principles, including—as I suggested earlier—a basic concept of justice. In addition—and most importantly for our purposes here—there need to be principles for adjudicating competing proposals for morality-based policy, in particular proposals not based on the harm principle.

J. S. Mill's harm principle holds that legal coercion is justified only where individuals' actions threaten harm to others.[16] Although the application of the principle raises many questions about what counts as harm, what constitutes sufficient threat, and so on, it can nevertheless play an important role in protecting individual autonomy. If, for example, one party's sexual ideal precludes contraception, policies that restrict access to it for those who do not share this view cannot be put in place absent any credible showing of harm.

This approach to resolving moral difference does presuppose valuing and trusting some degree of individual autonomy. Of course, those who oppose access to contraception also oppose autonomy, as an emblem of an arrogant reliance on reason (instead of God's alleged moral authority). However, their real assessment of its value would surface soon enough were some population control group espousing enforced contraception to gain the political upper hand. In the blink of an eye, the anti-contraceptionists would be asserting the moral urgency of contraceptionless sex, retreating (in the face of their political impotence in this hypothetical case) to their right to sexual autonomy, at least implicitly supporting a like autonomy for all. In fact, Religious Right groups already appeal to their religious freedom where they judge their rights violated—even as they push for policies restricting the religious freedom of all others. It follows that a community adopting such ground rules must reject any of the claims of those who would impose policies violating them based on an alleged pipeline to God.[17]

At the beginning of this chapter, I said that theocracy can take two forms, strong and weak. So far, I have provided good grounds for rejecting strong theocracy, even one far more benign than any that has ever actually existed. What about "weak" theocracy?

Weak Theocracy

What I'm calling a weak theocracy is an apparently secular society. It has a nonreligious government that passes laws and makes policy on the usual secular grounds—adjudicating conflicting interests, facilitating transactions and economic activity, preventing harm, and advancing the general welfare. Laws and policies with moral ramifications are justified by means of moral rules, principles, values, and theories, not God's alleged authority. But it is still one where religious freedom trumps other law.

How might this happen? In the US, it could be produced by the Supreme Court upholding an absolutist interpretation of the religion clause of the First Amendment, which reads: "Congress shall make no law respecting an establishment of religion, or prohibiting the free exercise thereof." Taken at face value, this wording means that lawmakers[18] cannot limit religious freedom, even where it is in conflict with existing law. It follows that for religious individuals, secular law has no authority and they are free to follow the dictates of their religion in all matters. Their world is therefore, in many respects, a theocracy.

This might seem irrelevant for nonreligious citizens. But given some religious assumptions and practices, it is not. For this approach fails to protect vulnerable members of religious communities like children. It also fails to protect other members of society from some harmful religious activities. Such practices pose serious questions for societies that seek to honor religious freedom while regulating religious activities that threaten the welfare of others.

What might this society look like? This apparently straightforward question is trickier than it might seem, given the lack of clear guidelines for what constitutes religious activity.

Extreme Weak Theocracy

What is "religious activity"? Despite the substantial moral and legal rights and duties depending on the definition of "religion," there is great reluctance everywhere to define it. Instead, there are multiple and shifting definitions, definitions that are often used as political weapons. Some definitions are so broad that any consistent set of beliefs might constitute a religion, leaving room for claims that secular humanism, feminism, and even science be considered religions, implying that they can have no place in public schools.[19]

"Activity" can be equally vexed, given the difficulty in finding a bright line between some instances of belief and action.[20] An absolute right to freedom of religious belief (and belief generally) is essential for any decent society. On the one hand, belief cannot be coerced, only the appearance of belief. On the other, any attempt to coerce belief—as opposed to changing it on the basis of evidence and reason—is tyranny.[21]

But religious activity is another story, no matter what definition of religion should turn out to be best supported.[22] "Activity" affects others. Just to take one example—one unfortunately not imaginary—suppose adherents of a religion asserted a right to convert or kill all nonadherents?[23] The existence of one religion acting on this belief would be a nightmare, as history attests. Competing religions wedded to this principle would lead to the kind of endless religious warfare that afflicted Europe, warfare that the Founding Fathers thought could be prevented by separating church and state.

This consequentialist argument is buttressed by the requirement for universalizability. Moral and legal rights must be exercisable only to the extent that they are compatible with a like right for all. Positing a universalizable right to convert or kill others would be contradictory, in the Kantian sense.

Yet this minimal theoretical constraint on rights is not recognized by the US Christian Right.[24] Its most immoderate leaders openly assert not only their intention, but their godly right to control not only religious beliefs, but *all* aspects of American society, and, indeed, the entire world—because theirs is the one true religion.[25]

But it should be clear that even if people believe that theirs is the one true religion, it would not follow that they would be justified in using force to reshape society to suit their religious and moral convictions. Objections to Divine Command Theory are as relevant for believers as nonbelievers, especially given retreats from classical versions by philosophers such as Adams. At most, they could attempt to persuade nonbelievers of what they see as correct religious and moral views. The stance of the US Christian Right is therefore untenable, and would be a nonstarter in any state that is not already seriously undemocratic.

What about weaker claims made by those who argue, in the name of religion, that they and their communities should be left alone?

Moderate Weak Theocracy

Among those who contend that religious freedom shields them from intrusive regulation of their personal affairs are parents who shun mainstream medical treatments (Christian Scientists, Jehovah's Witnesses), or fail to provide standard, state-mandated education (the Amish), and groups (such as the Catholic hierarchy) that protect members from sexual abuse laws.

Marci Hamilton maintains that some such cases can be morally unconscionable because a key function of the law is to protect the vulnerable from serious harm. She argues that it is one thing for autonomous, informed citizens to engage in risky activities whose benefits strike them as overriding. It is another for society to allow such decisions to be made for individuals who may be, at best, partially autonomous, such as children. This judgment is based on the position that children have rights independently of their parents, and that this is necessary for their welfare.[26]

Hamilton argues that "the right balance is achieved by subjecting entities to the rule of law—unless they can prove that exempting them will cause no harm to others" (2005, 5). In her view, policies and laws that fail to reflect this view are based on a Pollyannaish lack of realism about its implications:

> What could be more important in a free society than religious liberty? When the question is left in the abstract, it is hard to think of anything more important. But when one operates from the ground and knows the facts, the answer to the question is that there are all sorts of interests that must trump religious conduct in a just and free society—such as the interest in preventing child abuse, or in deterring terrorism, or in preserving private property rights. Every citizen has at least as much right to be free from harm as the religious entity has to be free from government regulation. [8]

Much of her book is taken up with a powerful defense of this position. The surprisingly diverse cases make fascinating reading. Some involve decisions about genuinely difficult conflicts between religious freedom and accepted (and justifiable) moral and legal principles.

Others involve startlingly untenable claims of immunity from the most ordinary principles of moral decency—let alone legal responsibility. Among them, of course, are the attempts by the Catholic Church to argue that its protection of pedophile priests is a religious function. Another is the transparently self-interested claim on the part of the Contemplative Order of the Sisters of the Visitation that a novice who had developed serious (and expensive!) health problems had lost her vocation and was appropriately ejected from the order (Hamilton, 2005, 192).[27] Others involve discriminatory practices (violating hard-won labor law), where the jobs at issue had no connection with the religious activities of the employer (Hamilton, 2005, 189–195). But surely the moral case for legal immunity for religious activity must rest on the premise that it is good—or at least morally neutral.

Hamilton maintains that despite some successful defenses of such religious privilege, the trend has been generally for rulings to follow the harm principle. Nonetheless, there are enough situations where this is not true to warrant continued wariness.[28] The threats are not just from Christianity, of course: equally problematic are attempts by Muslim immigrant communities to assert their right to self-government by Sharia courts, even where Sharia law calls for barbaric punishments and discriminates against women in ways prohibited by secular law. Some such attempts have been successful, despite the harm to women, in part because of the support they have received from those who believe that respect for other cultures must trump women's equality.

Conclusion

My goal in this chapter has been to consider the claim that theocracy is the best form of government. I think I have shown that strong theocracy is indefensible, even given the most generous assumptions. It is indefensible because it has structural problems and inconsistencies that undermine its ability to deal adequately with the issues facing human societies.

Moreover, in reality, theocracy's track record is poor. It is hard to find theocracies where the rulers are benevolent and wise, and far more common to find ones where rulers are tyrants, careless of their subjects' lives and the lives of other countries. In fact, it is hard to find any theocracies that emphasize human flourishing. Instead, theocracies seem pretty universally to promote and reinforce oppressive hierarchies, rigid sex and gender roles, and harsh punishment-oriented regimes justified only by alleged commands of God. Indeed, their rules commonly violate the most basic precepts of justice, such as punishing only those guilty of wrongdoing, and in proportion to their crime. How does that justify (for example) the death penalty for raped women (Benson and Stangroom, 2009)?

Compared to the extreme practices in such theocratic states as Iran, or such theocratic-controlled areas as Afghanistan or Pakistan under the Taliban, the Christian Right platform in the US may seem moderate. And yet it calls (among other things) for dismantling the separation of church and state, the imposition of its understanding of biblical law (including criminalization of blasphemy and homosexual activity), substitution of faith-based social services for public ones, a laissez-faire economic system that, among other things, upholds private property rights against environmental legislation, repeal of all gun control laws, and withdrawal from the United Nations (Texas GOP Platform, 2005). Christian Right leaders also affirm the subordination of women and children (Scholz, 2005; Smolin, 2006). If implemented, all would erode human well-being—even survival, if recent predictions about the consequences of the most plausible global warming scenario come to pass—in exchange for adherence to principles and policies whose only justification is God's alleged commands.

Given the problems of Divine Command Theory, going along with such strictures is tantamount to abandoning reason to follow self-proclaimed religious authorities. Von Treitschke is right: this would create a society fit only for minds willing to be enslaved by authority.

Could better theocracies exist? Is this track record just a contingent state of affairs? Or do theocratic regimes appeal solely to those who yearn for the (often cruel and simplistic) rules of what they apparently think of as "the good old days"? It is plausible to think that the latter is true, and that support for theocracy is the last refuge of those unable to respond rationally to prerequisites for human survival and welfare. But that is a question for another day.

Weak theocracy fares no better. Despite its valuing of religious freedom, to the extent that it condones serious harm to vulnerable third parties, it is morally unacceptable. A last question about it is whether any religious exceptions to justified laws makes sense. Why, for example, must conscientious objection to war rest on religious grounds, when there might be far more compelling ones based on philosophical principles? But that, too, is a question for another day.

These conclusions rest, as I (and others) have suggested, on presuppositions that there are key rational and moral principles that should govern thinking about social matters. Among them are universalizability and the harm principle. Theocracies, both theoretically and in practice, fail to reflect these principles, and could be justified—even under the best possible circumstances—only by rejecting them. The price for that kind of deference to religion is too high.

Notes

1. Both elite and popular wings of the Religious Right support theocracy. See Jeff Sharlet (2009), and representatives of the more populist wing of the movement,

such as Brannon Howse (2005), and various YouTube videos (Pat Robertson, Tim LaHaye).

2. One of the few I have found is Scarlett (2004).

3. In principle, a democratic theocracy could exist, where the voice of the people is the conduit through which God speaks, but, according to the *Encyclopedia of Politics and Religion,* the ruling class has always been a small group of religious experts (Wuthnow, 2007).

4. I doubt that any society could function without at least some attention to utility, broadly defined, but will leave that constraint aside for now. Of course, it may be the case that requiring even universalizability and justice (let alone utility) would prevent prominent proponents of theocracy from even considering my arguments here. Those who doubt that I am bending over backward to be as inclusive as possible might ponder what that means for the societies advocated by them.

5. Robert Merrihew Adams (1999, Chap. 11). Thanks to my colleague Brad Frazier for comments leading me to this book, and to others relevant to my case. All the errors remain mine, of course.

6. One might attempt to rebut this point by arguing that leaders nurtured by (a true) religion would never become corrupted, but history suggests that this is implausible.

7. Thus, Clifford's principle can escape the charge that it is itself unsupported by compelling evidence because it results from strong consequentialist justification: the failure to demand good evidence for beliefs that, if acted upon, might well cause serious harm to others.

8. Although it is remarkably difficult to come up with examples that couldn't conceivably have harmful consequences under some circumstances.

9. This position presupposes that we humans are capable of critical thinking and of altering our beliefs and actions in light of it. While one might be skeptical of this, given our massive failures in these areas, I don't believe that I'm being unrealistically optimistic to think that we are capable of improvements if we finally faced this necessity in order to avoid the threats to civilization and survival humankind now faces.

10. There are also widely available compilations of how much money opponents of reform have amassed from lobbyists for the health insurance companies.

11. See Chris Mooney (2004).

12. See for example an otherwise admirable article by Alec MacGillis (2009).

13. The *Encyclopedia of Politics and Religion* lists many additional reasons why theocracies tend not to last long. Among the internal challenges are the following. First, the rulers are "experts" in religion, not the skills necessary for running a contemporary economic system; second, both the religion and the political realm are harmed by any scandal; third, the population will become bitter about inconsistent or unfair laws, and especially religious exemptions from taxation; fourth, effective government tends to be

eroded by unwillingness to negotiate caused by alleged divine authority; fifth, police brutality is common in theocracies because they are usually single-party states. Externally, other states shun states that threaten to spread a mix of religion and politics. Moreover, competing political ideals such as ideals of liberty and equality cannot be hidden from citizens; attempts to keep citizens in line tend to provoke resistance.

14. For some compelling examples, see Chapter 1 of Ophelia Benson and Jeremy Stangroom's *Does God Hate Women?* followed by lengthy analysis of the role that religion has played in these practices (2009).

15. What will count as a morally relevant difference remains to be negotiated, of course, but this principle will rule out from the outset egregious asymmetries of various sorts.

16. He did concede that such coercion might also be necessary to create some benefits. This caveat can be ignored for now, since its demands depend in part on where one draws the line between harming and failing to benefit.

17. This basic line of thinking has been developed at length by writers such as Michael Boylan (2004, Chap. 5 and 6), Kent Greenawalt (1995), and Austin Dacey (2008).

18. Although the First Amendment mentions only the federal Congress, state law now incorporates constitutional protections as well.

19. However, they do not recognize freedoms or rights equal to their own on the part of those with these perspectives and principles. And, at the same time, they work tirelessly to insert elements of their own religious views into the schools, such as school prayer, so-called Intelligent Design, and programs promoting religiously based precepts about sexuality like abstinence-only sex education.

20. All, for followers of Clifford.

21. Of course, the education of young children must include socialization into attitudes, values, and beliefs with minimal argumentation; however, as they develop intellectually and emotionally, they should be encouraged to examine them and consider the alternatives.

22. A useful and plausible definition would, I think, focus on a moral worldview predicated on the existence of a supernatural being who determines how we should act.

23. Just one example: Spaniards who asserted a right to make war on Native Americans to convert them to Christianity; then there are the Christian Crusaders. Islam has not been free of forced conversion, either. There seems to be considerable disagreement about the Qur'an's directions about forced conversion, but at least two passages seem unambiguously to promote this (9:5 and 9:29) (M. H. Shakir, trans., 2002).

24. The Vatican asserts similar rights with respect to specific issues such as reproductive rights although it does not currently claim a right to control society in general.

25. Among other things, they have floated the notion of making blasphemy and homosexuality capital crimes. In fact, they currently lobby against equal rights for

homosexuals on the basis that they, the religious, would be persecuted because of their negativism about homosexuality!

26. Because of our reliance on the nuclear family for child-rearing, and because of the emotional and economic ties that entails, it may be difficult for children to exercise such rights, of course.

27. Losing, among other things, her health insurance.

28. See, among other sources, the recent, excellent series by Diana B. Henriques on this topic in the *New York Times*, as well as unconscionable exceptions now enshrined in the law, such as states where parents who rely on faith-healing cannot be charged with abuse or neglect. In fact, a couple of versions of the health care reform bill debated in Congress in 2009 included payments for faith healing "services." See Jim Giles (2009).

References

Adams, Robert Merrihew. (1999). *Finite and Infinite Gods: A Framework for Ethics.* New York: Oxford University Press.

Benson, Ophelia, and Jeremy Stangroom. (2009). *Does God Hate Women?* London: Continuum.

Boylan, Michael. (2004). *A Just Society.* Lanham, MD, and Oxford: Rowman and Littlefield.

Clifford, W. K. (1901). *The Ethics of Belief.* London: Macmillan & Co.

Dacey, Austin. (2008). *The Secular Conscience: Why Belief Belongs in Public Life.* Prometheus Books.

Doige, Norman. (2007). *The Brain that Changes Itself: Stories of Personal Triumph from the Frontiers of Brain Science.* New York: Viking.

Greenawalt, Kent. (1995). *Private Consciences and Public Reasons.* New York: Oxford University Press.

Giles, Jim. (2009, October 22). "Faith Healing on the US Taxpayer." *New Scientist.* Retrieved from http://www.newscientist.com/blogs/shortsharpscience/2009/10/faith-healing-on-the-us-taxpay.html

Hamilton, Marci. (2005). *God vs. the Gavel: Religion and the Rule of Law.* New York: Cambridge University Press.

Howse, Brannon. (2005). *One Nation Under Man? The Worldview War Between Christians and the Secular Left.* Nashville, Tennessee: Broadman & Holman Publishers.

MacGillis, Alec. (2009, September 4). "The Unwitting Birthplace of the 'Death Panel' Myth." *The Washington Post.* Retrieved from http://www.washingtonpost.com/wp-dyn/content/article/2009/09/03/AR2009090303833.html?wprss=rss_health

Mooney, Chris. (2004, November/December). "Blinded by Science: How 'Balanced' Coverage Lets the Scientific Fringe Hijack Reality." *Columbia Journalism Review*: 26–35.

Purdy, Laura. (1988). "How Many Gods Does It Take? (To Discredit Divine Command Theory)?" *Teaching Philosophy 11*(2): 112–115.

The Qur'an Thirteenth US Edition. (2002). Trans. M. H. Shakir. Elmhurst, NY: Tahrike Tarsile Qur'an, Inc.

Scarlett, Brian. (2004). "On the Logic of Theocracy." *Sophia 3*(1): 3–22.

Scholz, Susanne. (2005). "The Christian Right's Discourse on Gender and the Bible." *Journal of Feminist Studies in Religion 21*(1): 81–100.

Sharlet, Jeff. (2009). *The Family: The Secret Fundamentalism at the Heart of American Power.* New York: Harper Perennial.

Smolin, David M. (2006). "Overcoming Religious Objections to the Convention on the Rights of the Child." *Emory International Law Review 20*: 81–110.

Swaine, Lucas. (2007). "The Battle for Liberalism: Facing the Challenge of Theocracy." *Critical Review 19*(4): 565–575.

Texas GOP Platform. TheocracyWatch.org

von Treitschke, Heinrich. (1916). *Politics,* Vol. 2, trans. Blanche Elizabeth Campbell Dugdale, Torben de Bilbe. New York: Macmillan.

Wuthnow, Robert, ed. (2007). *Encyclopedia of Politics and Religion, Second Edition.* Washington, DC: CQ Press.

CHAPTER FOURTEEN

Global Ethics in the Academy

JAMES A. DONAHUE, PHD
Graduate Theological Union, Berkeley, California

Abstract

This essay asserts that the creation of greater understanding among cultures and religions is one of the foundational goals of a global ethic and the intellectual foundations for this can and must occur within the academic disciplines that shape the substance of intellectual inquiry in institutions of higher education. Two disciplines that play a dominant role in this regard are the disciplines of Islamic Studies and Jewish Studies. Both engage not only the theoretical and intellectual aspects of Islam and Judaism, but also the practical dimensions of Muslim and Jewish life and practice.

This essay analyzes four topics from the disciplines of Islamic Studies and Jewish Studies, which have collaborated on the following topics at the Graduate Theological Union in Berkeley, California:

1. Media depictions of Muslims and Jews in popular press
2. Muslim and Jewish text study
3. Business practices in Islam and Judaism
4. Food practices in Islam and Judaism

By exploring how these disciplines engage in cross-disciplinary analysis, intellectual space is created for developing greater understandings and insights in the creation of a global ethic.

Key Words

global ethics, global justice, common ground, Islam, Judaism, interdisciplinary, pedagogy, text study, public discourse, business practices, case study, globalization, food practices, collaborations

---

This essay argues that the academy can be seen as an important resource for creating an ethics that leads to global justice. More specifically, it proposes that two academic fields, Jewish Studies and Islamic Studies, provide unique opportunities for developing a paradigm for justice work when they are in conversation with one another, exploring possibilities of commonality to create a framework for common ground, common understanding, and common purpose.

Some would contend that the role of the academy is not to create a framework for developing a global ethics or advocating for global justice but to provide the intellectual foundations that may or may not lead to the creation of a just global order. The relationship between morality and global justice may emerge as a product of intellectual inquiry, but the primary goal of academic inquiry in higher education is to create understanding from which valued actions might occur. While this "value-neutral" approach to learning is in decline these days, there are still many academics who draw a hard line between learning and developing outlooks that search for justice.[1] In this perspective, the goal of learning is *not* to point to a particular preferred value position.

I do not believe inquiry is value free, nor do I believe that the goal of inquiry is mere understanding, with advocacy relegated to another function altogether. At the same time, knowing and valuing are integrally related and I contend that the point of intellectual pursuit is to explore ideas that will lead to a world that is constructive of the human good. Global justice is just that type of social value that approximates a moral good and therefore is a desirable state to seek to create in the world.

Global justice can be comprised of many elements. The academy is that arena of intellectual pursuit where the disparate elements of human experience, ideas, and practices converge and where ideas that derive from human experience interact to provide the possibility for synthesis in the construction of possible worlds.

My argument is that religion plays an integral role in the creation of a good society and that in the context of today's intellectual climate, any global ethics or understanding of justice will require an understanding of the religious resources that are at play in the global situation. In particular, it is clear that Islam and Judaism are two of the main religious traditions that are in conflict in our global context, obligating us to find ways to dialogue in order to reduce the potential for violence and discord that global justice requires.

The claim of this argument rests on some fundamental assumptions about the nature of the academic enterprise and what intellectual inquiry entails. Some of these assumptions go against the grain of many dominant perceptions and practices in academia today. There are three fundamental assumptions that are important:

1. The nature of religious discourse in the academy
2. Theory and practice in academic discourse
3. The importance of interdisciplinarity

1. The Nature of Religious Discourse in the Academy

Though there are many ways that religion is treated in academic life, there are two formal ways that religious discourse enters the academy: through the disciplines of religious studies and theology. The distinction between these two disciplines is a matter of much interest and substantive discussion within the academy. Briefly, and perhaps simplistically stated, religious study upholds a fundamental commitment to exploring the phenomenon of religion from a variety of lenses—historical, cultural, sociological, among others—and examining its relationship and role in the development of human culture and society. It is value-neutral with regard to the claims of each religious tradition with the assumption that the scholar or teacher takes no position on issues or beliefs in any evaluative way from a faith perspective and about the relative truths or preferences of one religion over another.

Theology shares most of the fundamental assumptions of religious studies, the difference being that theology situates the inquiry and the inquirer in a context of belief that leaves critical study open to—and searches for—expressions of religious ideas and beliefs that uphold criteria for what constitutes notions of truths and meaning.

The disciplines of Jewish Studies and Islamic Studies do not fit easily under these organizational categories. These two disciplines contain elements and assumptions of both theology and religious studies. They operate under standards and criteria of objectivity and value neutrality in that Islam and Judaism are viewed as objective phenomenon, and yet there is a fundamental sense that the truths of each religion can be accessed through the lines of the believer's eye as well. It is essential for each discipline to be clear with its goals, objectives, and modes of inquiry in each investigation and analysis.

2. Theory and Practice in Academic Discourse

There has been a long-standing bifurcation between theory and practice in the academy. There are those who contend that academic inquiry is about theory and that the life of ideas is committed to modes of teaching and research in which the practical application of ideas is exactly that, a mere application. Though practical insights can be included in analysis, the point of study is to be able to theorize about ideas and issues correctly. Application is derivative from theory.

There is an increasing interest in the academy in the integration or correlation of theory and practice. This view holds that ideas and theory are informed by practice and that practice can provide important and necessary correctives and refinements of theoretical issues. This view does not hold for the dichotomization of theory and practice but rather the development of a reflexive process whereby theory and practice are in constant interaction and serve to inform and adjust one another.

Jewish Studies and Islamic Studies have a natural affinity for the correlation of theory and practice. Both disciplines are based on the practical experience of a people and the development and evolution of these people over time and history. The core of these disciplines is premised on the belief that ideas are framed and instructed by practical experience. It is important then to be open to how theory and practice do work together and to be able to explicate fundamental rules for how the two arenas of experience interact.

3. The Importance of Interdisciplinarity

There are few who would dispute the fact that the nature of academic work and analysis today requires the collaborative perspectives of multiple disciplines. Very few issues or academic disciplines operate in a way that limits the lens of analysis only to the views developed in a specific academic tradition. Issues and interpretations do not lend themselves to limited lenses of analysis. Thus, interdisciplinary work is becoming and will continue to become the way that academic analysis is done.

Having said this, it is also clear that academia is slow to organize its structures in ways that can easily accommodate the requirement of developing new lenses of interpretation and analysis.

Islamic Studies and Jewish Studies are, by their very nature, program areas that incorporate a variety of disciplines. History, linguistics, culture, social context, political and economic outlooks, philosophy, and theology, as well as many other disciplines, constitute Islamic and Jewish Studies. In that regard, they are already constitutively interdisciplinary.

The significance of this for this analysis is to suggest that a global ethic will require the incorporation of many perspectives in the search for common ground, action and understanding among competing and differing points of view. A global ethic is the achievement of multiple parties and perspectives coming together in search of constructive actions and solutions to resolve vexing issues of human ordering and choices in and across societies. For Islam and Judaism to find this common ground is the promise in the relationship between Islamic and Jewish Studies.

Goals and Outcomes

What is the point of collaborations between Jewish and Islamic Studies? The larger issue is really the point of a global ethics. Building on the premises that I have outlined above, there are certain assumptions about what academic disciplines are and what they attempt to achieve in the academic context. One goal, and perhaps the most important, is to develop an *understanding of a field or a body of knowledge and information.* The intended result of the disciplinary encounter between Islam and Judaism would be the mutual understanding within each perspective of the reality of the "other," as a discipline and as embodied in those who speak from a particular perspective. The goal of ethics in general is to reflect on the nature of the good and the right and to develop understandings of how one reasons in search of such understandings. Judaism and Islam provide shaping perspectives from which such reasoning develops.

Another goal would be the *encounter and development of relationships* between Jews and Muslims, encouraging an understanding of both similarities and differences in each tradition. While achieving common ground would not necessarily be an explicit goal of mutual study, the prospects of developing common ground in addressing common problems and practical issues and challenges would be a desirable outcome. In that we live in a time when conflicts between Jews and Muslims are profound, engagement over ideas and shared exploration of histories and traditions is a desirable means to realize the important ends that go to the heart of a global ethic.

If practices are key components for understanding Jewish and Islamic Studies, the *exploration of strategies and directives for action* are important outcomes to be achieved. This does not suggest that academic discourse across disciplines should focus on policies or actions exclusively but that a scholar is compelled to create collaborative opportunities within Jewish and Islamic studies to address problematic issues and conflicts. There are many examples of how these two traditions could find collaborations. Among these might be: collaborative actions for protecting the environment; collaboration on economic policies that address poverty and economic disparity; and ways to address political violence among peoples and nations. Again, if academic disciplines are to be both theoretical and practical in their scope, collaborations among disciplines and traditions will have both theoretical and practical outcomes.

Pedagogies in Interdisciplinary Collaborations

Teaching in an interdisciplinary context in a way that is seriously committed to the integration of theory and practice requires a certain degree of experiential pedagogy to explore relevant issues at hand. It would be important for Islamic and Jewish Studies to engage the ideas that allow each student to enter into issues in nonthreatening and inviting ways. The appropriation of ideas—and reflection on personal, social, and historical experiences—are key elements in crafting a successful pedagogy across disciplinary lines. The information presented in both Jewish and Islamic studies ought to acknowledge the potential conflicts of interpretations that might emerge and thus construct a way of viewing diverse ideas that create neutral interpretive space and encourage common ground. One way of doing this is through the exploration of issues, ideas, and objects—for example, artistic artifacts—that are both specific to *and* broad enough for Jewish and Islamic identities. This allows the student to bridge her or his context with issues or ideas peculiar to each tradition, opening forth an engagement that invites personal dialogue with both Judaism and Islam.

Another factor that is essential for collaborative pedagogy is determining how to engage differences of interpretations and practices in light of perceived historical conflicts between Islam and Judaism. Focusing on how religious interpretations differ as well as share things in common is a very helpful way of providing the necessary safe space for the successful exploration of ideas. Pedagogy is not rigid nor should it be pointed in a particular direction or one way of thinking. It should, rather, open opportunities for students to delve into the specifics of Islamic and Jewish traditions, ideas, and histories—engaging critical dialogue and encounters across traditions. Dialogue is a critical dimension of pedagogy, and the role of the teacher should be one of encouraging dialogue that allows room for both similarities and differences as well as conflicts and convergences.

Collaborative Work in Jewish and Islamic Studies at the Graduate Theological Union

I want to draw on the experience of our work at the Graduate Theological Union in Berkeley as a way of indicating fruitful ideas for developing collaborations between Islamic and Jewish studies. I will propose four models of discourse that have proven to be very important and useful for creating collaborations across disciplinary boundaries:

1. Engaging common text study peculiar to Islamic and Jewish traditions
2. Popular media and the construction of Jewish and Islamic identities

3. Developing ideas of business practices in both Jewish and Islamic traditions
4. Exploration of food practices across Judaism and Islam

An exploration of each of these will indicate how constructing understandings and encounters that are dialogical in nature has potential to bring traditions together at a common ground.

1. Engaging Common Text Study Peculiar to Islamic and Jewish Traditions

When Muslims and Jews study religious text together, it is important to have instructors who represent each tradition to ensure academic expertise and religious credibility. The choice of topics and relevant texts comprise the heart of engaging shared texts. What has proven to be constructive at the GTU is our proactive discernment of topics and issues that are most critical for mutual dialogue. In our work, there are several topics that present themselves as being particularly important for collaborative teaching. I will list these to illustrate the organizing questions that ground their search for common understanding and commitment to the common good:

- *Method of text study.* How do we determine how to interpret Jewish and Muslim texts?
- *Religious law and authority.* What is the status of authority? How do texts develop authoritative and normative status, becoming codified as laws?
- *Developing common foundational narratives.* What are the core stories that form the heart of Islam and Judaism, informing their histories, ideas, and practices?
- *Women and gender.* What is the role of women? How does one understand the influence of gender in the religious practices of each tradition?
- *Seeing "the other."* How is the notion of "the other" constructed and seen in the core historical narratives of each tradition? Who is "the other"? What status does "the other" play in each context?
- *Cultural production.* How do texts translate from the sacred to the secular? How do they develop status in the multiple arenas of a tradition?
- *Sacred place.* How do Islam and Judaism create a sense of sacred space? What challenges and opportunities does the notion of sacred space present for dialogue across traditions and disciplines?
- *Music.* How do musical practices express and propagate core understanding? How do they create communities within the tradition?

- *Social justice and the environment.* How does each tradition understand the notion of justice and its implication for issues concerning the environment?
- *Rituals and liturgy.* What is the nature of the ritual and liturgical tradition in forming community? What challenges do such practices bring across differences in practice?
- *Issues of war and peace.* How does each tradition understand peace? How does each tradition understand conflict in religious, individual, and social dimensions? How does each tradition understand violence and the use of force in contemporary contexts?
- *Economic practices across traditions.* How does each tradition understand the role of economic activity across traditions?

These items present a sampling of several criteria that could be used for choosing texts for collaborative study. Relevant texts and themes must be determined in advance by those faculty experts who are versed both in the content and the lived practice of each tradition. Our experience has demonstrated the usefulness of these core topics as successful foci for analysis.

2. Popular Media and the Construction of Identities

In the collaborative study of Judaism and Islam in the contemporary context, students and faculty need to address anti-Semitism and Islamophobia. Encouraging common understanding must take into account how stereotypes are developed and prevented. The first step in our analysis would be to name and categorize depictions that have been created of both Jews and Muslims. The central issue, however, is to determine what goes into the "framing" of these stereotypes. According to the work of George Lakoff, stereotypes arise when individuals and societies "frame" less-than-constructive representations of people that draw from prejudices, historical memory, and political agendas (Lakoff, 2002). Two examples immediately come to mind: the identification of Islam with violence and terrorism; and for Jews, the issue of victimization related to the Holocaust—its influence and implications—as a way of framing negative Jewish representation in popular media.

An analysis of how these depictions are created and how they might be addressed provides enormous opportunities to talk about each tradition and its contributions to promoting positive values for popular culture as well as the distortion that occurs in the construction of public discourses. Discussing the impacts of negative framing encourages the critical exploration of both the root of popular biases and core principles of each tradition.

What one gains in such an analysis is a critical tool for reading media representation. The study of how media produces culture—and how individuals and groups use popular stereotypes to further self-interest—has proven to be a provocative tool in our search for common ground at the GTU.

3. Developing Ideas of Business Practices in Both Jewish and Muslim Tradition

One arena in which traditions can collaborate and continue sharing experience is in the area of economic activity in business practices, specifically as it is related to religious values. No area of human experience is untouched by economic activity and the core cultural narratives that inform its application in daily life. Economics plays an important role in the evolution of religious tradition and practice and vice versa. The central issue we face is discerning how specific values and beliefs inform just business practices and economic activity. A close analysis of the correlation between economics and faith offers insight to the fundamental principles of religious claims themselves. As in other cross-disciplinary work, the critical issue for collaboration would be determining shared topics of importance for each tradition. In this regard, I offer several issues that could be helpful in providing insight to the ways Islam and Judaism address, nurture, and regulate just business practices:

- The source of authority for interpretation. How do the Koran and Torah serve as foundational texts for discerning principles for business practices?
- Issues of responsibility in business and the role of producers and consumers in the marketplace. What are the questions surrounding the limits and functions of the marketplace in terms of one extreme of unfettered activity versus various types of regulation?
- The treatment of workers in the business context. What is the range of responsibilities to which workers and business leaders are accountable both to one another and to the broader business enterprise? What are the responsibilities of businesses to stakeholders?
- Issues of fairness and transparency in business transactions. What are the roles of contracts and covenants in business organizations and agreements?
- The role of profit and its limits and possibilities. What is the role of philanthropy in the business community? What obligations do businesses have to the well-being of communities that are not necessarily addressed nor mandated by the market system?

An important method of business analysis in collaborative work between Islamic and Jewish studies is the use of case studies as a pedagogical tool. The case study method is well utilized in business school curricula within the United States and abroad. By discerning ways to deploy religious principles in actual concrete business contexts, students and teachers provide concrete and very practical solutions to the complex issues that contour the marketplace. It is in this regard that engaging issues of religious values and business practices through case studies would be extremely helpful in broadening collaborative work between Islam and Judaism.

In these days of increased interconnectedness, the globalization of business requires the exploration of business practices across transnational and transcultural boundaries. International perspectives help particular traditions bring the insights and truths of their own beliefs to the marketplace. It is critical for all religious traditions to consider developing mechanisms for global business practices. This will be a challenge for all in both the economic and religious sectors.

4. Exploration of Food Practices Across Judaism and Islam

Much has been written on the role of ritual in cultural and religious traditions.[2] The comparative study of food practices, consumption, production, and meaning-making offers a most interesting space for collaborative work between Jewish and Islamic studies. Food and the sharing of meals as ritual and sacrament is significant to both traditions. At the GTU, we have brought together experts to reflect on *kosher* and *halal* practices as specific ways to express communal and divine accountability. The celebration of holidays almost always involves food consumption—symbols of integration, hospitality, and identity construction. A close exploration of food practices opens forth opportunities to engage "the other"—dedicated space to apprehend values and practices inherent in each tradition. Such explorations constitute some of the most successful interdisciplinary and interreligious encounters between Judaism and Islam at the GTU. I argue that they offer a specific collaborative model that could be useful for interdisciplinary work.

Conclusion

My analysis has been suggestive and illustrative rather than comprehensive. My intention is to indicate how a global ethic and global justice can be cultivated in the classrooms of higher education. I have shown how two distinct religious traditions and academic disciplines at the GTU have been able to collaborate and find ways of crossing sometimes polarizing divides, developing common ground, and providing opportunities for intellectual rigor while developing understanding across disciplinary and theological differences. Fully appreciating the need to differentiate disciplines by way of content, histories, and cultures, I argue that collaborations across disciplinary lines offer enormous possibilities for the realization of a global ethic that makes concrete and practical differences in the world. It is these types of collaborations that are well worth developing in even more expanded ways than I have indicated here.

Notes

1. The "value-neutral" approach in education has its origins in the "fact/value" distinction that has been at the center of the discourse between ethics and the social sciences. For a helpful discussion of the issue, see Hilary Putnam (2002). For two classic theorists for whom the "fact/value" distinction is central, see Dorothy Emmet (1958 and 1966) and Gibson Winter (1966). Also see Boylan and Donahue (2003).

2. For some readings at this intersection of ritual, cultural/food practices, and religious identity, see Hamilton (2003), Kim (2005), Leonard, Steptich, Vasquez and Holdaway (2005), Newton (1998), Smith (2009), and Stausberg (2009).

References

Boylan, Michael, and James A. Donahue. (2003). *Ethics Across the Curriculum: A Practice-Based Approach.* Lanham, MD: Lexington.

Emmet, Dorothy. (1958). *Function, Purpose and Powers: Some Concepts in the Study of Individuals and Societies.* London: Macmillan.

Emmet, Dorothy. (1966). *Rules, Roles, and Relations.* London: Macmillan.

Hamilton, Roy W. (2003). *The Art of Rice: Spirit and Sustenance in Asia.* Los Angeles: UCLA Fowler Museum of Cultural History.

Kim, Heerak Christian, ed. (2005). *Jewish Law and Identity: Academic Essays.* Cheltenham: Hermit Kingdom Press.

Lakoff, George. (2002). *Moral Politics: How Liberals and Conservatives Think.* Chicago: University of Chicago Press.

Leonard, Karen I., Alex Steptich, Manuel A. Vasquez, and Jenifer Holdaway, ed. (2005). *Immigrant Faiths: Transforming Religious Life in America.* Walnut Creek, CA: AltaMira Press.

Newton, Derek. (1998). *Deity and Diet: The Dilemma of Sacrificial Food at Corinth.* Sheffield, UK: Sheffield Academic Press.

Putnam, Hilary. (2002). *The Collapse of the Fact/Value Dichotomy and Other Essays.* Cambridge, MA: Harvard University Press.

Smith, K. A. (2009). *Desiring the Kingdom: Worship, Worldview, and Cultural Formation.* Grand Rapids, MI: Baker Academic.

Stausberg, Michael, ed. (2009). *Contemporary Theories of Religion: A Critical Companion.* New York: Routledge.

Winter, Gibson. (1966). *Elements for a Social Ethic: Scientific and Ethical Perspectives on Social Process.* New York: Macmillan.

PART THREE

NORMATIVE APPLICATIONS

War

■ Chapter 15 The Law of Peoples
DAVID CUMMISKEY

■ Chapter 16 Cosmopolitan Revisions of Just War
GABRIEL PALMER-FERNÁNDEZ

PART THREE: War
INTRODUCTION

War in the twentieth century was very bloody. It was one of the great stumbling blocks toward global justice. Some have viewed war as an extension of diplomacy and a normal state of affairs, while others see it as an unregulated evil. In just war theory in the Western tradition, there is a distinction between offensive and defensive wars: the former being prohibited while the latter is permitted. Once one is engaged in a war, there is the further layer of analysis that governs properly carrying out a war (for example, noncombatants are generally not to be targeted). The two essays in this section will further analyze just war theory with different overlays: religious traditions (cultural worldviews) and cosmopolitanism (part/whole worldviews).

David Cummiskey starts things off by presenting two religious traditions that support a version of just war theory that belies popular conceptions. In the first case we have Islam. One popular conception in the West is that Muslims are a warlike people bent upon havoc and terrorism. In the second case is Buddhism, which is often viewed as embracing pacifism. Cummiskey contends that both of these stereotypes are wrong. The rest of the essay seeks a more nuanced understanding of each, in the process shedding light on the essential structure of the theory.

To begin, Cummiskey situates the traditional understanding of just war by referencing John Rawls's book *The Law of Peoples.* Rawls rejects war as an extension of diplomacy (advancing the self-interests of any nation). Instead, Rawls holds up the ideal of establishing democratic liberalism around the world with the conjecture that such a world order will bring an end to war.

Islamic just war theory has to be situated in reference to moral theory—here understood as Sharia. Sharia is formulated from: the Qur'an (the prophetic recitation from Allah to Muhammad), the Sunna and Hadith (stories and sayings of Muhammad), scholarly consensus on the commentaries of the Qur'an and Hadith, and a legalistic analogical reasoning from previously settled moral problems.

Obviously there is a heavy emphasis upon "consensus" and "previously settled questions" (somewhat akin to the Anglo-American doctrine of *stare decisis,* letting legal precedent stand—all things being equal). The upside of this is that cultural stability is created. The downside is that novel interpretations are difficult to come by. These novel interpretations can only come by the will of God, but that has to be interpreted (see Purdy's essay on this).

However, there are some clear restrictions. One is the use of *fire* as an offensive weapon. There is some analogical reasoning that suggests that this transfers to a prohibition on the use of nuclear weapons. This calls for an interpretation, a fatwa, by a regionally respected imam.

One controversial idea is jihad. There are two forms of jihad: Greater Jihad, the personal struggle for renewal; and Lesser Jihad, the defense of the Islamic community (including war). Just war theory obviously is interested in the lesser jihad. The Qur'an justifies fighting unbelief as a cause of war. This seems to support offensive war and terrorism. However, the Qur'an also says, "There shall be no compulsion in Religion." These interpretations are at odds. Cummiskey argues that the latter is mainstream and is a key plank in the edifice of Islamic just war theory. The prophet Muhammad, himself, is the model here. Muhammad was a political and military figure as well as a religious figure. He and his followers had been driven out of Mecca. He raised an army and conquered the city, but he did not seek revenge. Unlike the pattern of war at the time, there was no looting and killing of the vanquished.

Though there are other disputed passages and seeming contradictions that Cummiskey confronts, he concludes that the four parts of Sharia support a moderate view of warfare as only justified in conditions of self-defense (contrary to the popular stereotype).

With Buddhism, Cummiskey's task is reversed. The stereotype is that Buddhists are pacifist and will not agree to any war. As with Islam, Cummiskey begins by critically examining the religious worldview tenets. Because of Buddhism's anti-essentialism, identity is known only through relations. The key task in life is to rid oneself of illusions and to wake up to what is really around you. This involves clearing the mind of distractions. Once this is done, the essential task toward enlightenment is great compassion to all and wise insight. One of the snares in this process is *afflictive emotions*, such as anger, hatred, greed, and lust, which generate powerful desires that disrupt the proper functioning of the mind.

War is rooted in the destructive desire for territory, power, and resources. This is fueled by anger and hatred—afflictive emotions. This means at base that violence (including war) is self-perpetuating and self-defeating. But using the models of both Tibetan Buddhism and King Asoka (the ideal Buddhist king), some conflict is permissible. Armies to protect one's country are permitted in defense. Police to protect one's community are permitted. The *modus operandi* is that the doctrine of skillful means should be employed. This doctrine is similar to the *double effect* doctrine of the Western tradition. One may use means that surely will have immoral effects (under very restricted conditions) to address a greater harm. Cummiskey cites an example from the *Lotus Sutra* in which a father lies to his children who refuse to leave a burning house. He tells them that they will each have the carriage of their choice. This is a lie because he had already predetermined carriage. The children leave and are saved.

In another example a captain discovers a robber who will kill five hundred merchants and steal their goods. The captain, a holy man, knows that if the robber commits the act then he will suffer many rebirths in hell. Thus, the captain kills the robber. The captain sacrifices his own karma for that of the robber. Because of the nobleness of the act, the captain is spared punishment.

Actual cases of King Asoka and the present Dalai Lama give examples in which defensive violence is advocated as the best course.

In the end this sets up the difference between the two. The Muslims present a worldview that is meant for every day. The community worldview has some aggression built into it, but the Sharia advocates that people restrain themselves (despite various controversial passages to a defensive war posture). The Buddhists must ramp up to overcome a general pacifist worldview that is more withdrawn from daily life to return to the community and engage an attacker with the minimum force necessary to thwart the attack—including death if necessary.

Cummiskey believes that both of these traditions, Islam and Buddhism, come back to the center (somewhat Rawlsian and consonant with Obama's Nobel Prize speech), and a core might form from which all peoples of the world can create a shared community worldview for peace.

Gabriel Palmer-Fernández examines just war theory in light of the extended community worldview tenet of cosmopolitanism. Cosmopolitanism can be considered in different ways; for example, for some it means a world government, for others it is a principle of anarchism (the absence of all states), and for still others it is a way of organizing the people of the world in a new world order according to the status of their universal human rights claims. Palmer-Fernández leans to the third alternative in the context of the changing global-political structure of the world. Thus, though traditional states might remain, they are no longer the natural unit of discourse (as they used to be) but are only instrumental to communities of individuals who seek a decent life, including the basic goods and liberties necessary for this quest. The bottom line is that Palmer-Fernández's cosmopolitanism elevates the status of people and their families and their micro-communities. States become mere facilitators of the same to their citizens.

In the first part of Palmer-Fernández's essay, he carefully looks at the essential parts of traditional just war theory as it began and was developed in the Roman Catholic tradition from Augustine onward. In that account war was the province of states only. The state also possessed a real or conventional sovereignty that made it a natural unit in the environment of other sovereign states.

In the traditional theory there are two ways to judge a war as just: *ius ad bellum* (the conditions of going to war) and *ius in bello* (the conditions under which a war should be fought). In the first case, the model is that war is only justified in self-defense. A state may fight another aggressor state in order to protect its property and sovereignty. Wars of aggression are prohibited.

In the second case, soldiers may fight and kill other soldiers, but noncombatants are immune from the struggle and the killing of them constitutes murder.

The traditional account (supplemented by Michael Walzer and other contemporaries) has some fissures that suggest that it may be inadequate for the modern world, argues Palmer-Fernández. One of these fissures complicates *ius ad bellum.* This concerns wars of preemption. Country A acts belligerently and threatens country B. Country B does not want to wait until it is attacked before taking action, so country B attacks first—but because it was driven to do so by *necessity*, it may still be considered as defensive. This creates all sorts of logical conundrums that suggest these sorts of arguments and others aligned to it are no longer sufficient to judge the criteria for going to war.

Another fissure occurs in the conduct of war. For example, what is the culpability of soldiers? Are both sides on an equal footing? Shouldn't the prior immoral act by the aggressor country put its soldiers at a disadvantage? If one is fighting a burglar who has entered one's house, it might be queer to think that both parties are on a moral equal footing. (Most societies set their footing on different terms—the burglar cannot kill but the homeowner may.) This is a disputed question, as are others—such as the doctrine of supreme emergency in the justified killing of noncombatants. Again such disputations suggest that the traditional account is lacking.

The traditional account has six tenets: (1) legitimate authority; (2) just cause; (3) reasonable hope of success; (4) proportionality; (5) last resort; and (6) right intentions. Palmer-Fernández argues the most important change that cosmopolitanism has upon just war theory is rethinking (1). Since the conceptual community worldview model in cosmopolitanism has shifted according to the new world order to view citizens as primary according to their exercise of human rights, their enjoyment of freedom, and their access to the basic goods of agency (see Churchill and Gordon, Chapters 1 and 2, respectively), the legitimacy of military intervention is also changed. The legal immunity against attack by another country only applies to countries that recognize their citizens (rather than the dictators) as primary. Thus, outlaw regimes that do not afford human rights and economic opportunities to their citizens have no protection under just war theory. This is a key illustration of the difference that cosmopolitanism makes in just war theory. It is based upon the ancient right of a people to kill their tyrant: *tyrannicide.* When extended to a tyrannical regime, the rights of the people trump those of the tyrant. Thus, a state ruled by a tyrant no longer is within the global world order—it is an outlaw state that has forfeited its rights to sovereignty.

Palmer-Fernández offers examples such as these to provide a clear new direction for just war theory that should engage debate and discussion.

CHAPTER FIFTEEN

The Law of Peoples

DAVID CUMMISKEY
Bates College

Abstract

When it comes to the moral justification of war, there is a remarkable overlapping consensus: a common justification of war that is shared by contemporary secular liberalism, Islamic Sharia, and Buddhist traditions. In this age of misunderstanding, it is important to appreciate the Islamic commitment to just war theory. It is equally important to appreciate the surprising realism and pragmatism of Buddhist just war theory, which is actually much closer to Barack Obama's Nobel Peace Prize address than it is to the idealized Gandhian pacifism attributed to the Dalai Lama. For both Muslims and Buddhists, aggressive war is always wrong, but defensive war is a necessary evil in a world of violent aggressors. This shared moral response to the inevitability of human conflict reveals the deeper commonality of our humanity.

Key Words

just war, jihad, passivism, Law of Peoples, right to war, Buddhist ethics, Islamic ethics

---

When it comes to the moral justification of war, there is a remarkable overlapping consensus: a common justification of war shared by contemporary Western (secular) liberalism, and Christian, Islamic, and Buddhist religious traditions. Given the striking and widely discussed differences between these worldviews, it is worth pausing and exploring this deep and fundamental convergence on the legitimate use of ultimate violence. Of course, there are obvious deep differences between liberals, Christians, Muslims, and Buddhists; still, the moral agreement beneath important differences is, I think, more important and provides a basis for shared and fruitful connections in our evermore interconnected and interdependent world.

For the discussion here, I am assuming that liberal and Christian just war theory is reasonably familiar. We will, instead, focus on Islamic and Buddhist just war theory. In my experience, Islamic just war theory is not well known and most people seem to wrongly assume that the Buddhist tradition, with its deep commitment to Ahimsa and nonviolence, simply and categorically rejects the legitimacy of all war. In this age of misunderstanding, it is important to appreciate the Islamic commitment to just war theory. It is equally important to appreciate the surprising realism and pragmatism of Buddhist just war theory, which is actually much closer to classic Western just war theory, than it is to the idealized Gandhian pacifism attributed to the Dalai Lama. For both Islam and Buddhism, defensive war to protect one's community or nation is a necessary evil in a world of violent aggressors.

The Law of Peoples and the Right to War

The most influential proponent of contemporary Western liberalism is John Rawls, and his views on the "right to war" are found in *The Law of Peoples*. Rawls's view nicely captures contemporary Western just war theory and it thus provides our starting point for comparative reference. Rawls argues that "Liberal Democratic Peoples" should enter into a peaceful "Society of Peoples" that includes all states that respect basic human rights and limit the "right to war" to wars of self-defense—including the defense of one's allies and other peoples against aggression and gross violations of human rights (Rawls, 1999, 91). What Rawls calls "Decent Hierarchical Peoples," which are nondemocratic governments that nonetheless are committed to the good of all of the people and have a consultation system for responding to their people, are full and equal members of the Society of Peoples. "Benevolent Absolutisms" are more authoritarian nondemocratic states that still accept the basic principles of nonaggression. Although these states lack a reasonable consultation system, they are concerned with the good of their people and they respect other fundamental human rights. These benevolent authoritarian states are not accorded the same level of respect by Rawls's Society of Liberal and Decent Peoples. But despite their violations of political and participatory rights, they are nonetheless peaceful and thus should be treated in kind. These states also have a right to be treated nonaggressively and thus also a right to war in self-defense (Rawls, 1999, 92). On the other hand, "Outlaw States" are defined, one, as states that engage in aggressive expansionist foreign policies and are thus a threat to all, and two, as states that violate the fundamental human rights of their people (Rawls, 1999, 64–65, 79–81).

Rawls argues that contemporary liberal democratic states reject the right to war "in the rational pursuit of a state's rational interests" as a sufficient justification for a declaration of war (Rawls, 1999, 90). The principle of nonaggression against other states is a moral constraint that states must honor in pursuing their national interests, and the violation of this principle is viewed as a violation of enforceable international law, as essentially a crime that warrants intervention and counteraggression in defense of the peaceful states and peoples. As Rawls emphasizes, however, "the aim of just war . . . is a just and lasting peace among peoples, especially with the people's present enemy" (Rawls, 1999, 94). Even during war, we must respect, insofar as is possible, the fundamental human rights of our enemy and fight the war always with an eye to the kind of peaceful relations that we seek in a Society of Peoples (1999, 96).[1]

Is Rawls's account of a "realistic utopia," where most nation-states embrace a shared Law of Peoples and justification of war, realistic? Or, is this conception of just war distinctly Western in its orientation? In particular, is the above conception of just war also congenial to the world's approximately 1.3 billion Muslims and 400 million Buddhists?

Rawls endorses the thesis of Democratic Peace, which is the thesis that economically developed, constitutional democracies do not engage in war with each other. The idea here is that international commerce and democratic political institutions create both ideological and economic institutions that are more conducive to peace (Rawls, 1999, 47–51). In addition, nuclear weapons have radically changed the nature and calculus of war between the great powers. Randall Forsberg has argued that all these factors combine to make all-out war between the nuclear powers extremely unlikely. He explains:

> Nuclear weapons have made all-out great-power war unthinkable; mechanized warfare and the extent and fragility of modern wealth have made non-nuclear war among richest countries more costly than profitable; and the spread of democratic values has made war increasingly unacceptable as a means to any ends except the narrow goal of defending against armed attacks by others. Combined, these factors have made a major conventional war anywhere in the world (except perhaps on the Korean peninsula) highly unlikely now and for years to come. [New Democracy Forum, 1997][2]

Forsberg goes on to argue that we are thus faced with an unprecedented opportunity for a large-scale disarmament that would fundamentally change the world, and set the stage for a lasting age of world peace. The debate about the End of War was at its height before 9/11/01. The debate since the fall of New York's Twin Towers has shifted to the justification of preemptive war, and to the divide between the West and the Rest, but especially Islam, in a Clash of Civilizations. In the wake of the Afghanistan and the Iraq War, the debate about the End of War may now seem myopic and naive. Actually, however, when it comes to justification of war, Western scholars, Muslim scholars, and even the Buddhist tradition agree that only defensive war is justified. Even if we do not see the end of all war in sight, the overlapping consensus on the illegitimacy of aggressive war to advance national interest is indeed moral progress and speaks to a deep moral consensus across otherwise diverse traditions.

Islamic Just War Theory

The First Pillar of Islam is the Declaration of Faith: "There is no God but Allah and Muhammad is his messenger." In this simple declaration one embraces monotheism, rejecting the once common polytheism of the Arab peninsula, and submits oneself, dedicating one's life, to the will of God as revealed in the Qur'an, and through the example provided by God's messenger, the prophet Muhammad. The first pillar of Islam is so simple in its form but its substance actually includes all of Islamic law and ethics, called *Sharia.*

Sharia is usually translated "Islamic law" but the concept of law here is that of the moral law in the broadest possible sense. Sharia means both "law" and "the path." Similarly, the word for Islamic jurisprudence, *Fiqh,* means both "jurisprudence" and "insight." The Sharia path is a guide for one's entire life, it involves insight into the will of God for man, and it is thus much more than law in the civil and political sense of the term. Sharia is, in fact, more specific about family law (which governs marriage, divorce, and inheritance) than it is about criminal and civil law in more general terms.[3]

Sharia is based on four sources:

1. *The Qur'an*—the prophetic recitation from Allah to Muhammad
2. *The Sunna and Hadith*—stories of the life and sayings of Muhammad
3. *The Consensus of Scholars*—especially the classical commentaries on the meaning of the Qur'an & Hadith
4. *Analogical Reasoning*—from previous settled cases, interpretation, and analysis

The first and primary source of Sharia is, of course, *the Qur'an.* Since it is the directly revealed will of God, it is the primary source and trumps absolutely all other sources. Sharia, the true and straight path, simply cannot contradict the Qur'an. The Qur'an, however, is primarily focused on the articulation of the unity and majesty of God, the lessons we should have learned from the earlier prophets from Adam to Jesus, and the conflict with polytheism and idolatry. Although there are some specific guidelines in the Qur'an, especially about family law and (importantly for our purposes) just warfare, specific moral guidance, in concrete and ever new situations, can only be inferred from its broad and poetic language and its few context-specific rules.

The second source of Sharia, the *Hadith*, thus takes on extra importance. Because Muhammad was chosen by God as the messenger, he was especially favored by God, and his life thus provides a model for us to emulate. Muhammad's sayings, actions, and character thus provide a model to follow whenever the Qur'an is silent on an issue. Unlike the Qur'an, however, the accuracy and authenticity of Hadith are often sources of controversy. In early scholarship, much emphasis was placed on establishing chains of oral and eventually written transmission of the words and deeds of Muhammad. Over time, after over one hundred years of oral transmission, and after the companions of Muhammad had all long since died, the collections of Hadith took on clearer shape and authority. There are, nonetheless, distinct and equally authoritative collections of Hadith, and of course small details of stories, or of wording, can have significant impact on an overall interpretation and the crucial generalization to new situations and cases. Even when we have clear agreement on the prophet's words or actions, as we shall see below, the actual implications for us can remain unclear or controversial. As a canon of interpretation, however, the Qur'an trumps the Hadith, and the Qur'an clearly emphasizes the righteousness, mercy, equity, and justice of God. It thus follows that we should always interpret the Hadith so that it elucidates the Qur'an, and thus also so that the conclusions seem reasonable and just.

The next source of Sharia is the *consensus (Ijma)* of religious scholars that formed slowly through the shared effort of interpreting the Qur'an and Hadith. In practice, this scholarly consensus takes form, first, in the early written commentaries on the Qur'an and Hadith, and later it comes to include the four major Sunni "schools" of thought (or alternatively the Shia traditions) and other influential interpreters of the Qur'an and Hadith. (The four Sunni schools and the foundational Shia-Sunni split are not our focus here.)

Ijtihad refers to the act of novel interpretation by an individual of the Qur'an and Hadith. In the beginning, after the death of Muhammad, there was much room for independent and novel interpretation. Over time, however, a strong consensus formed on many matters of interpretation, and the consensus of the community of scholars itself takes on independent authority as a third source of Sharia. The unstated assumption of Qur'anic interpretation is that, with the help of the Qur'an and of the Prophets, the Will of God as it applies to our lives is knowable by man. Thus, if over time, after much shared reflection, scholarship, and discussion, a consensus has formed, other things equal, we have reason to trust the accumulated wisdom of the scholarly community. As a result, as consensus forms and is accepted by the Muslim community, "the gates of *Ijtihad* [novel interpretation] close," and the authority of tradition comes to trump any new interpretation. Notice that the third source of Sharia is itself based on consensus and not the Qur'an itself. It is a consensus that established consensus settles an issue and excludes new and perhaps progressive reinterpretation. As such, this is a deeply conservative principle of interpretation. This is not to deny that there is indirect support for the authority of consensus in the Qur'an and Hadith, but the support is itself based on inference and analogy, the fourth source of Sharia. Nothing in the Quran or Hadith suggests that insight and interpretation is reserved for the generations long past and closed to the wisdom of the present and living. The closing of the gates of *Ijtihad* was itself ordained by the scholars closing the gates, and it is sustained by current scholars affirming the established consensus of the past. It is thus a thoroughly conservative interpretative principle.

With each new situation, new knowledge, and new technology, we get novel problems and questions. Since the Qur'an and Hadith provide some clear cases of required actions, permissible conduct, and prohibition, we can use these examples as a basis for analogies to guide us in thinking about new situations. In addition, the consensus that has formed over time on a wide variety of moral questions provides additional settled cases that provide additional analogical insights for new and unsettled moral questions. The fourth source of Sharia is this type of *analogical reasoning* from clear cases to new cases—also called casuistry.

For example, the Qur'an states that man should not use fire as a punishment, for it is the punishment of God, and this has been interpreted by many to exclude the firing of cities in times of war. On this basis, many argue that the use of nuclear weapons is analogous to burning cities in that the bombs essentially incinerate cities, and that the use of nuclear weapons is thus also forbidden. The Qur'an, however, also says that one should arm and prepare oneself for war so as to deter aggressors. Additionally, the Qur'an states that one need not continue to restrain oneself, from otherwise forbidden means of waging war, when the enemy has not shown similar restraint. On the basis of these three different passages, many Islamic scholars conclude that the first use of nuclear weapons is forbidden, but nuclear deterrence and nuclear retaliation (in response to another's first use of nuclear weapons) in principle may be permissible.

An opinion on a moral question like the permissibility of using nuclear weapons, or other matters of theology, is called a *fatwa.* A fatwa is simply an opinion on a particular issue or question that is based on the four Sharia sources. Any Muslim who has seriously studied the Sharia may issue a fatwa, but the weight, the significance, and the influence of a particular fatwa will depend both on the quality of the reasoning, and also on the reputation and authority of the person issuing it. On new issues, there are likely, at least initially, to be competing opinions based on different sources, on different interpretations of the significance of Qur'anic passages and Hadith, or on the approaches of different traditions of interpretation. Over time, if a consensus develops as to the best opinion, then this becomes part of the Sharia itself—and a source of future analogies. In other instances, the Sharia sources may equally justify distinct and competing opinions and thus there may be a plurality of shared but distinct opinions on an issue.

When distinct subsets of the larger Islamic community come to distinct opinions on an issue, each of these opinions is entitled to respect, and thus the consensus is that the matter is underdetermined and thus each of the opinions is equally valid. Individual Muslims can then follow the opinion they believe to be most compelling. In short, the Sharia relies heavily on already established consensus on many issues, but there is also a range of acceptable positions officially represented in the distinct schools and traditions of interpretation.

An additional, secondary but still fundamental Sharia moral principle is the *principle of necessity*, which states "necessity makes permissible the prohibited." The Qur'an states, "God desires your well-being not your discomfort" (Q 2:185). In circumstances where there are serious consequences to life, health, or well-being, particular prohibitions that would block life-saving action or cause serious harm do not apply. Of course, applying the principle of necessity requires judgment and is context and situation specific. One must consider the significance and point of the prohibition as opposed to the beneficial consequences of an infringement, and decide if the prohibition is waived in that particular context. This principle inevitably plays a significant role in matters of life and death, and it is thus a central principle of Islamic practical ethics.

With this simple sketch of Islamic Sharia in hand, we can turn to the doctrine of jihad and the Islamic conception of a just war.

Jihad is sometimes called the sixth pillar of Islam, and radical "jihadists" are too often the face of Islam in the West. Although jihad is a duty, it simply is not a license to kill innocents and nonbelievers, as jihadist radicals and terrorists claim. First, "jihad" basically means struggle, and it signifies struggle in the name of Islam. There are two forms of jihad. The *Greater Jihad* is the internal struggle to follow the Sharia and to have true faith in God. The *Lesser Jihad* is the defense of the Islamic Community, which does include spreading and extending the call of Islam. Obviously, the Greater Jihad is not a source of controversy; it is the Lesser Jihad that is associated with jihadist terrorists supposedly acting in the name of Islam.

The question before us is thus over the nature of the Lesser Jihad, and this question is essentially the question of the nature of just war theory in Islam.[4] First and most importantly, *the Lesser Jihad is nothing more than defensive war; it is not supposed to be a war of conversion or a general state of war against unbelievers.* This is a point of controversy, however, and the more radical jihadists tend to divide the world into the World of Islam, the World of War, and the World of Truce. On this radical interpretation of jihad, believers are in a perpetual state of war with the unbelievers, and fighting unbelief itself can be a just cause for war.

> The broad consensus of Islamic scholars, however, clearly and unequivocally rejects this understanding of jihad as contrary to the fundamental principles of the Qur'an. First, the Qur'an explicitly states, "There shall be no compulsion in Religion" (Q 2:256). This principle is expanded and further specified in the verse of the Qur'an entitled "The Unbelievers" that states: Say: "Unbelievers, I do not worship what you worship, nor do you worship what I worship. I shall never worship what you worship, nor will you ever worship what I worship. You have your own religion and I have mine." [Q 109]

Two other important verses state, "God said 'Leave to Me those that deny this revelation'" (Q 68:44); and "Forgive them and bear with them until God makes known His will" (Q 2:109).

In all of these verses, the Qur'an expresses a "live and let live" approach to other religious beliefs. This attitude also had real political significance and was institutionalized throughout Islamic history. The first historical example occurred during Muhammad's life when he did not seek vengeance after the fall of Mecca in 630 CE (on those who had persecuted him, driven him out of Mecca and to Medina, and then attacked the new Muslim community in Medina). Additionally, in 1187 CE, when the crusaders' earlier bloody conquest of Jerusalem gave way and the city fell to Saladin, he followed Muhammad's example by taking no significant retaliation on the non-Muslim peoples of the city, and instituted a system of religious freedom. More recently, under the Ottoman Empire, the Islamic rulers instituted the "Millet" legal system that recognized three distinct systems of laws and courts for Muslims, Jews, and Christians. The Millet legal system clearly follows the Qur'an on "The Unbelievers," which states, "you have your own religion and I have mine" (Q 109). Religious tolerance, at least for Jews and Christians (People of the Book), is deeply rooted in the Qur'an, Hadith, and the traditions and history of Islam.

(As a point of clarification, because of the traditional doctrine of apostasy, according to many jurists, the doctrine of religious freedom does not extend to Muslims in that they cannot abandon Islam. Indeed, on some interpretations of Sharia, the punishment for apostasy is death. According to this tradition, for example a Muslim converting to Christianity is subject to the death penalty, and this clearly is not religious freedom. Religious toleration, so understood, provides external protections to minority non-Muslim religious communities but it also permits severe internal restrictions within religious communities.[5] The doctrine of apostasy is indeed a part of the Sharia tradition, but like the prohibition on images of Muhammad (which is not found in the Qur'an or Hadith and is instead a cultural tradition), or the subordination of women in Islam, it is not clear that it has a sound Sharia basis. The radical doctrine of apostasy is founded on (controversial) Hadith, but contradicts the explicit Qur'anic injunction that "there shall be no compulsion in religion" (Q 2:256). Recall that the Qur'an takes priority over the Hadith, and so the doctrine of apostasy is subject to criticism from Islamic progressives. Apostasy, however, is not the topic in question here.)

Given the Islamic emphasis on religious tolerance, what then accounts for the beliefs of radical jihadists? First, as a historical and sociological matter, the legacy of the Crusaders and the religious war by Christendom on Islam has a lingering impact in Islamic attitudes toward the West. Second, the Qur'an includes significant praise for war and for defending Islam by violent military means. The Qur'anic accounts of the original battles between Muhammad and the Meccans provide a rich source for the glorification of war and martyrdom for Muslims. Third, after the death of Muhammad, we have the violent battles for control of the young Muslim community and the fratricidal Sunni-Shi'a split that has lasted to the present day. Fourth, the early history of Islam is a glorious expansion which included both peaceful and militarist means. Eventually, the Islamic Empire falls to the Mongols, but Islam rises again to glory in the Ottoman Empire. Islam is a religion of peace and toleration, but its rich cultural history includes enough violent lore and legend to inspire jihadists to emulate a sometimes violent past and to strive to bring back the lost Islamic Empire.

Leaving these broad socio-historical generalities behind, let us look more directly at the Qur'an itself. Jihadists maintain that they are simply following the Qur'an, which is the clear word and will of God. Why would they claim this? The most important verse supporting the jihadists is the famous *verse of the sword*:

> And when the forbidden months are passed, slay the unbelievers wherever you find them. [Q 9:5]

And we also have these two inflammatory verses:

> Slay [the unbelievers] wherever you find them. Drive them out of the places they drove you. Idolatry is more grievous than bloodshed. [Q 2:191]
>
> Fight against them until idolatry is no more and God's religion reigns supreme. But if they desist, fight none except the evil doers. [Q 2:193]

There is much in these simple verses to incite jihadists. On the other hand, the last verse does restrict war to those who do not "desist" and in this respect suggests a more defensive stance. Similarly, the following verse makes clear that one should not "slay" those who are seeking peace:

> If they withdraw from you and fight you not, and instead give you assurances of peace, then God has opened no way for you against them. [Q 4:90]

More explicitly, the following verses do not glorify war at all:

> War is prescribed of you, though it be hateful to you. [Q 2:216]
>
> Fight in God's cause against those who wage war against you, but do not transgress [attack them first], for God loves not transgressors [aggressors]. [Q 2:190]

Here we have an explicit statement limiting war to defensive war, and this fits the more general prohibition on killing in the Qur'an:

> Do not slay the soul sanctified by God, except for just cause. [Q 6:151, 25:67]

It also fits the doctrine of religious freedom that we discussed above:

> There shall be no compulsion in religion. [Q 2:256]

Lastly, in the Qur'an, we have the doctrine of giving quarter (*aman*) to enemy troops, which is sanctuary and safe passage:

> If an idolater seeks asylum with you give him protection so that he may hear the Word of God (the call of Islam), and then convey him to safety. For the idolaters are ignorant men. [Q 9:6]

This is simply in contradiction to the idea that Islam directs the slaying of nonbelievers. It also does not cohere with the Qur'anic principle that treaties must be honored even with idolaters:

> Repose no trust in idolaters, save those with whom you have made treaties. . . . So long as they keep faith with you keep faith with them. God loves the righteous. [Q 9:7]

On the basis of all of these passages, and other Hadith, the consensus of scholars insists that just war is strictly limited to defensive wars and humanitarian wars in defense of the rights of Muslims when they are oppressed by others.

So what are we to make of the "verse of the sword" telling us "and when the forbidden months are passed, slay the unbelievers wherever you find them" (Q 9:5)? Is not the context actually quite clear? The verse is clearly about not fighting during the "forbidden months" and waiting until they are passed to return to the fight. There is no directive here that licenses the indiscriminate killing of unbelievers, and the many verses we have reviewed above demonstrate that such a reading contradicts a consistent theme of defenses and limited war that flows throughout the Qur'an and Hadith. The Islamic "right to war" is a right against aggressors and in defense of the innocent.

Because war is limited to aggressors, to those who are attacking or threatening the community, it is also limited to combatants. The targeting of innocent noncombatants is clearly prohibited and thus Muslims also recognize and endorse the principle of discrimination of combatants and innocents, and prohibits the intentional targeting of innocents. (Of course, this is a difficult distinction that is easier made in theory than in practice.) Islamic scholars also insist on the principle of efficacy (that the means used must be likely to achieve the end) and the principle of proportionality (the harm of war must be outweighed by the good end to be achieved). In addition, a violent war, a jihad, must be declared by a legitimate political authority representing the Muslim community. The Lesser Jihad is not an individual mission like the Greater Jihad, which is focused on inner faith and cultivating virtue. For all of these reasons, jihad does not justify indiscriminate terrorism aimed at innocent noncombatants.

We thus have a near perfect convergence between Islamic consensus on just war theory and the Western consensus. Of course, just as there are those who defend a militant expansionist conception of Islam and stand ready for war against all nonbelievers, so too in the West we find some who advocate war as a means to spread democracy, and indeed even those who still support war as a legitimate means to advance national patriotic interests. As a historical matter, Islam has also been spread by the sword and Christianity has had its crusades, inquisitions, and religious wars. This is not in question. But what is clear is that there is no "clash of civilizations" on the right to war and its clear limits.

Buddhist Ethics and Just War

At the core of Buddhist ethics are its dual commitments to a fundamental precept of nonviolence and to cultivating the virtue of unbounded compassion for all living creatures. In exploring the Buddhist conception of war and violence, we first need to appreciate some core doctrines of Buddhist metaphysics and philosophy of mind. The first is the *Doctrine of Inter-Dependent Origination* (also called Co-dependent Arising), which asserts that all of existence is essentially interrelated, interdependent, and interconnected. The second is the *Doctrine of No-Self,* which applies interdependent origination to the self, and thus concludes that there is no essential enduring self. These two doctrines are the core of Buddhist philosophy:

"One who sees interdependent origination sees the Dharma, and one who sees the Dharma sees the Buddha" (Strong, 2008, 109). Although the causal integration and slow transformation of the elements that make up the self create the illusion of an enduring self, the individual self is simply a momentary configuration of discreet, although causally codependent, changing elements. The self is essentially interrelated, interconnected, and interdependent on the rest of existence. There is no unitary permanent self.

In a later philosophical development, Nagarjuna (the most important Buddhist philosopher—other than the Buddha—probably from the second century CE) further develops this idea. He emphasizes that the elements (that seem to constitute the self and other things) are also mere impermanence, in the sense that they, too, lack any inherent reality. At the most basic level, there is nothing solid or substantial that makes up everything else. In this sense, the essence of everything is really empty. But this is not to deny that things exist; it is to point out the nature of their existence. This is the famous *Doctrine of Emptiness.* A simple way of thinking of this idea is that all existence is fundamentally *relational.* In understanding this concept, it helps to start with a simple obvious example. The concept of a mother presupposes the concept of a child. It also suggests a particular social relationship between the child and the mother, other than female, that is distinct from a father. In these ways the concept of mother can only be understood in its relation to other concepts. It has no meaning or referent independent from these relations—and it is thus relational. According to the doctrine of emptiness, this kind of relational dependence is true of everything. In addition, things do not have real essences that persist through time and change. There are no basic essential elements that undergo change but are themselves unchanging. Reality is just a dynamic of interrelated forces and *processes.* In more philosophical terminology, this view is a form of thoroughgoing *anti-essentialism.* Again, it helps to look at a more obvious example. What is a chair? Chairs can have four legs, three legs, or be one piece. They can be made of wood or metal or plastic. Is a barstool a chair? Is an ottoman a chair, if it is used for a chair? There seems to be no core, essential, unchanging attribute of all chairs; except perhaps that chairs are for people to sit on, but that is relational. In addition, can a chair be a piece of art that is not intended for sitting? The chair as art may still be a chair because of its relation with useful chairs. The case of mothers and chairs are easy cases. The more radical claim of emptiness is that this type of relational anti-essentialism is true of all reality without exception.

The philosophical doctrine of emptiness is complex and fascinating. It is interesting, for example, to explore the connections between the doctrine of emptiness and contemporary physics. In addition, some contemporary theories of mind and sense perception also reject the idea of a unitary mind and self. We will not here explore these connections. It is enough to note that in addition to philosophical arguments, the doctrine of No-Self is compatible with a naturalistic scientific worldview. We will focus on the implications of interdependent origination for Buddhist ethics and here it is the doctrine of no-self that is crucial.

A central thesis of Buddhist ethics is that the self is simply a particular contingent configuration of impermanent attributes and a dynamic of psychic energy. The self is constituted by physical form, sense perception, emotions and feelings, cognition, consciousness, and the forces of karmic causality that cause rebirth itself. It is the relation of these changing elements that constitutes what we call the self, and nothing more.[6]

A deep recognition of the interdependent origination (and codependent arising) of all things, and the doctrine of no-self, are at the core of the Buddhist justification for boundless compassion for all sentient life. The egocentricity that characterizes so much of human behavior is based on the illusion of the self and its alleged independence and distinctness. When these delusions are removed, the path to inner transformation is opened.

The essential core of morality for Mahayana Buddhism is *Compassion* toward all living creatures and *Equanimity* of mind that is reflected in all of one's actions, reactions, and perceptions. Wisdom and compassion are the Buddha-essence. The development of wisdom and compassion is the essence of the Path and the Middle Way, but meditation is still the means by which we develop ever greater wisdom and compassion. The ultimate goal of Buddhism is release from suffering. We all want to be happy and avoid suffering. The insight of the Mahayana tradition is that the key to happiness is developing both insight and boundless compassion. In particular, there are two insights that are essential to happiness (Dalai Lama, 1999, Chap. 6–8).

The first is that cognition, emotion, and will are all interconnected. Here we see the practical implications of the Doctrine of Inter-Dependent Origination. First, we have the dependence of emotions on cognition. The emotion of fear usually has a clear cognitive content which includes the belief that something is dangerous or harmful. To take a simple example, fear of flying in an airplane includes beliefs about airplanes, flying, and danger. Fear of flying also involves the will in that it often includes a sense of diminished autonomy and vulnerability (which is also cognitive). Some emotions may be more instinctual but most human emotions are laced with cognition. Without the underlying beliefs, it would not be the same emotion. Cognition also involves the will and emotion. If we do not take an interest in the objects of thought, we simply cannot concentrate and take in the information. Indeed, the more engaged and interesting something is, the more we can concentrate, and the more we learn and remember. Emotions essentially include cognition and cognition presupposes effective engagement. It follows that one can change one's emotions, passions, and desires by changing one's beliefs and conception of reality. This is how insight transforms character.

Second, emotion affects cognition in another important way. If we are angry or upset about something, we cannot concentrate and think clearly. Indeed, even one's capacity for perception is diminished by powerful emotions. The Dalai Lama calls the emotions that disrupt our mind in this way the "afflictive emotions." Emotions like anger, hatred, greed, and lust generate powerful desires and unsettle our minds. Indeed, they distort our judgment, undermine our will, and ruin our sleep. Furthermore, when we act on these desires, their satisfaction does not leave us satisfied at all. A person who is emotional in this way is never at peace. If one does not act on afflictive desires, the passions do not just go away; they remain and corrode from within. If, instead, the person acts on the desire and expresses hatred, for example, there is the momentary release of aggression but the person is no better off. In addition, by expressing anger, one has probably hardened an enemy who may then retaliate in turn. On the other hand, the person without anger does not suffer from its loss and is thus only a gainer.

Buddhist insight meditation aimed at anger would first help one internalize a deep awareness of the self-destructive nature of anger. It would also focus on the source of the anger and reveal its causes, its thorough interdependence, and ultimately its emptiness. Anger has a cognitive component, and is thus focused on an object, but the object has no real essence—and is itself caused by and dependent on a complex web of connections. As our idea of the essence of the object of anger dissolves, so too does the anger—because the anger was based on a distorted conception of its object. In this way, insight into interdependent origination transforms the cognition itself, and reveals that anger and hatred, and all afflictive emotions, are based on delusion and confusion.

It is not surprising that the satisfaction of these desires founded on delusion leads only to more misery and suffering—both for oneself and for others. But insight must get *into* the anger itself; the mere knowledge that anger is afflictive and self-destructive does not extinguish anger. Similarly, if I simply give someone the facts of airline safety, that does not eliminate all the fear of flying. The orientation must be shifted both cognitively and emotionally, and this is a matter of fundamentally transforming the way one thinks and feels. The moral rules (or precepts) are a first step, but without insight and understanding, rules and restraint alone leave desires to still fester within. It is thus necessary to also reflect on the causes and nature of anger and on the real nature of the object of one's animosity. It is only through greater understanding, and long practice, that established habits of thought and actions can be altered and reoriented. Buddhist insight meditation thus has a mission that was lacking in the earlier yogic practices. Indeed, insight meditation (and mindfulness of interdependent origination) is also a way of life, in that one can adopt a meditative stance almost anywhere and anytime.

War is often rooted in destructive desires for territory and power and resources. It is also caused by conflicts of interests that generate anger and hatred manifest in the dehumanization of one's enemy. But whether the conflict is interpersonal or international, it is always self-destructive and self-defeating. Violent conflicts also tear the wider fabric of relationships, harming friends and family in their wake. Wars harm combatants and noncombatants alike; the virtuous are always killed too, along with one's supposed enemies. Buddhism emphasizes the self-perpetuating and self-defeating nature of violence; aggression is rooted in afflictive emotions and delusion. Violence simply is not a path to inner peace and happiness.

For the major traditions of Buddhism, this is the core of the justification for nonviolence and universal compassion. It is noteworthy, however, that the doctrine of no-self and emptiness also inspired the Samurai ideal of Bushido. The Bushi warriors embraced the Zen ideal of "no-mind" which included clearing one's mind of distractions and responding purely and spontaneously. As Harvey explains, "The idea that life and death are empty, essenceless phenomena also helped develop a lack of hesitation, and a lack of fear of death, in battle. . . . There is only evil in killing if the person killed is not recognized as empty and dream-like" (Harvey, 2000, 266–267). If one kills without the afflictive emotions of anger or hatred, and with full awareness of the truth of emptiness, one's mind is pure and remains at peace. In this example, we see the interesting interplay between cultural conditions and Buddhist metaphysics and metaethics. Across cultures, the contours of Buddhist ethics has been influenced both by its theology and by the particular contextual circumstances. Like all else, the Buddhist ethic of war and peace seems to be subject to the principle of interdependent origination.

Tibetan Buddhism, History, and Just War

Although the commitment to passivism in Buddhism is well known, it is important to see that, in an important sense, passivism is perhaps a means and not an end in itself. We have seen that afflictive emotions like anger and hatred, although aimed at others, are self-destructive and typically misguided as well. In this sense, acting on these emotions is a mistake. Because violence is almost always rooted in afflictive emotions and delusions, it is almost always a mistake. Nonetheless, it is not the case that Buddhists reject all uses of physical coercion.

Buddhist countries have, and in earlier times even monasteries had, police and armies. Buddhist mythology includes the Four Heavenly Kings, who guard the four corners of the world, and protect the Buddha's followers from evil and also preserve the teachings of Buddhism (the Dharma). Similarly, Buddhist rulers also used their armies to protect their country and the Dharma (Kopel, 2007). We will discuss the classical Buddhist king Asoka below, but first we will briefly look at the history of a more familiar contemporary sect of Buddhism: the Tibetan Gelugpa sect led by the Dalai Lama. Even Tibetan Buddhism, which is now famous for its commitment to nonviolence, owes its original prominence to an alliance with the Mongol warlords—Genghis, Kublai, and Altan Khan.[7] Mongol armies favored and protected the particular Buddhist sectarian tradition that was ruled by the Dalai Lama, and this military support elevated the Dalai Lama to the dominant political position in Tibet; the Dalai Lama rode to power on the shoulders of Mongol warriors. Indeed, the relationship was so close that the grandson of Altan Khan was His Holiness the Fourth Dalai Lama. Indeed, even the title "Dalai Lama" was itself bestowed by the Mongol leader Altan Khan in 1578 on the Third Dalai Lama (and applied posthumously to his two earlier incarnations). *Dalai* means "ocean" in Mongolian and signified the Ocean of Wisdom manifest by the Dalai Lama. (This early relationship also spread Buddhism into Mongolia, and this is why Mongolian Buddhism is a branch of Tibetan Buddhism.)

With an unrestrained use of Mongol military might, the great Fifth Dalai Lama consolidated near total political control and religious dominance of Greater Tibet. Geoff Childs explains, "Even the Fifth Dalai Lama, considered to be an incarnation of the compassionate and fully awakened being Chenrezik, espoused the use of force to protect his political interests. When confronted with a rebellion in 1660, the Fifth Dalai Lama issued the following instructions to his Mongol allies on how to dispose of the Tibetan insurgents:

> [Of those in] the band of enemies who have despoiled the duties entrusted to them:
>
> Make the male lines like trees that have had their roots cut;
> Make the female lines like brooks that have dried up in winter;
> Make the children and grandchildren like eggs smashed against rocks;
> Make the servants and followers like heaps of grass consumed by fire;
> Make their dominion like a lamp whose oil has been exhausted;
> In short, annihilate any traces of them, even their names."[8]

More recently, the Thirteenth Dalai Lama, Thupten Gyatso (1876–1933), the year before he died, anticipated the looming confrontation with China and wrote, "[We] should make every effort to safeguard ourselves against this impending disaster. Use peaceful means where they are appropriate; but where they are not appropriate, do not hesitate to resort to more forceful means."[9] The current Fourteenth Dalai Lama fled Tibet *after* military resistance failed. The Tibetan army resisted the Chinese invasion but was soundly defeated and disbanded and sent home by the Chinese. The current Fourteenth Dalai Lama now emphasizes the futility of violent resistance and argues that nonviolence is the best means to achieve Tibetan cultural and political autonomy. In his 1962 autobiography, however, he praised the "courage and determination" of the Tibetan soldiers that defended him, and wrote, "I could not in honesty advise them to avoid violence. In order to fight they had sacrificed their homes and all of the comforts and benefits of a peaceful life. Now they could see no alternative but to go on fighting, and I had none to offer" (cited in Sperling, 2001, 325).

It is disappointing to discover that the supposed Shangri-La of Tibetan Buddhism was actually founded and sustained by military might. The romantic image of a historically peaceful Tibet, sustained by compassion and nonviolence, is a Western idealized projection. Some might even suggest that the conversion to nonviolent pacifism by the Dalai Lama in exile, and the Tibetan Diaspora, involves a complex interplay of a core Buddhist ideal and international political dynamics.

In short, Buddhist rulers have not been pacifist. Like all other states, they have used force and violence for self-defense or national defense. Nonetheless, Buddhist doctrine and teaching have emphasized that the use of force and violence is usually counterproductive, and it thus should always be the means of truly last resort. It seems that the current Buddhist stance of antiwar passivism is actually pragmatic, and not absolutist. Indeed, we will next see that all Buddhist precepts are best understood as "skilful means," and as such, they work in an indirect and pragmatic fashion to help direct one onto the path to wisdom and virtue:[10]

The Doctrine of Skilful Means

A primary text of East Asian Buddhism is the *Lotus Sutra* (Watson, 2002), and the core doctrine of the *Lotus Sutra* is the Doctrine of Skilful Means—also translated as "Expedient Means" (Pye, 2003). "The Parable of the Burning House" perhaps best captures this core doctrine of the *Lotus Sutra.* The immediate point of the parable is to explain the many sects and distinct doctrines of Buddhism, and the evolution and development of Buddhism:

> A rich man with a large house is faced with a serious problem when his house is being engulfed by fire as his children are playing happily inside, and ignoring his warning to escape from the burning house. As a skilful (or expedient) means, the rich man tells his children that there is a cart outside the house waiting for them, and in particular he tells each child that there is the type of cart outside that each child most desires—a goat-cart or deer-cart or ox-cart. In joyous anticipation each child runs out of the burning house to seize the particular desired cart. Once

> outside the burning house, there are no carts. The rich man responds to his disappointed children, however, by providing each of his children the same fabulous ox-cart, which is actually the best of all the carts, and transcends the original more limited desires of each of his children. [Watson, 2002, 34–39]

This parable was used to explain the many distinct and often incompatible Buddhist doctrines, practices, and sects that flowed into China from India. The parable tells us that the Buddha has provided different sects and doctrines to different people, but each with the goal of helping people escape the burning house, which is the treadmill of afflictive desires and delusion that lead to suffering. Once out of the fire, the more advanced doctrines and True Path, the real Vehicle of Enlightenment, can be revealed—which includes the doctrine of skilful means itself. This suggests also that the rules, precepts, and rituals of Buddhism are themselves skilful means to achieve ever greater insight and compassion, which will lead to inner peace and happiness.

The doctrine of skilful means clearly applies to many of the ethical precepts of Buddhism. For example, many of the over two hundred moral precepts for Buddhist monks serve the end of developing inner discipline and restraint, which are prerequisites to virtue, rather than being an end in themselves (Keown, 2000). The basic ethical precepts, like prohibitions on harming and lying, are also expedient means and secondary rules that help keep one on the right path, but which are not actually absolute rules. Indeed, the parable of the burning house already shows that justified deception is not a prohibited lie. The father misleads his children justifiably for their own good as the Buddha misleads his early followers to get them on the right path.

Similarly, here is an interesting example of compassionate killing from the Buddhist canon that reflects the defeasible nature of all moral rules.

> One night deities inform a Bodhisattva sea captain that one of his passengers is a robber intent on killing 500 merchants and stealing their goods. He realizes the robber will suffer many ages in hell for his deed, and that his only option is to kill the robber and take the bad karma on to himself. Accordingly "with great compassion and skilful means" he kills the robber. But by willingly accepting the karmic punishment, the bad karma is cancelled. [Harvey, 2000, 135–136]

There are several things to notice about this example of compassionate killing. First, killing is usually harming and rooted in aggression. In contrast, compassionate killing is rooted in boundless compassion both for the potential victims and for the potential victimizers. In principle, it seems that compassion can even justify preemptive violence. Second, however, the sea captain is a Bodhisattva and has foreknowledge provided by deities. Although compassion can justify killing, only enlightened beings can have the virtue and wisdom to infringe such basic norms as the prohibition on killing. Third, as a corollary, it follows that the ethical precepts are rules for the unenlightened. The moral seems to be that the less enlightened should stick to simple moral rules, but the more enlightened the being, the more judgment and compassion should guide one's actions in confronting difficult moral decisions. The right act will sometimes involve infringing rules for the greater good of all.

The resulting position is strikingly similar to recent consequentialist moral theories. For example, R. M. Hare argues that archangels, with perfect knowledge and perfect character, could follow direct consequentialist principles, but that simpler folks like us humans, "proles," need moral rules so as to generally do what's best (Hare, 1981). More precisely, we find ourselves, to varying degrees, in different contexts, and during different times of life, between the extremes of simple-minded proles and perfect archangels. So, too, for different people and contexts, moral rules can be more complex and refined; and indeed in some cases of moral dilemmas, we should directly do what seems to be best overall. Peter Railton has also defended a compelling "sophisticated consequentialist" moral theory that incorporates the virtues of character into a broader indirect consequentialist ethical system (Railton, 1984). Similarly, Robert Adams has developed a character-based moral theory, which he calls motive utilitarianism (Adams, 1976).

Asoka and the Ideal Buddhist King

In our personal lives, it is clear that we should strive to control and eliminate the psychological poison, the afflictive emotions, of anger and hatred. Insofar as is possible, of course, we should avoid harming others. However, I can use force to defend myself or others, for example, blocking a blow or restraining an attacker. Self-defense and defending others from aggression need not involve intentional harm to others. Of course, there are hard cases where I can save myself or an innocent only by harming or killing the attacker. When asked about his views on defensive actions, it is reported that the Dalai Lama responded: "If someone has a gun and is trying to kill you . . . it would be reasonable to shoot back with your own gun. Not at the head, where a fatal wound might result, but at some other body part, such as a leg" (Bernton, 2001). The guiding principle is to do as little harm as possible and to strive to maintain equanimity and compassion.[11]

When it comes to the justification of war, however, the question is directed to the rulers of nations, not individual citizens. Faced with invading armies or other aggressors, are rulers supposed to disband their armies and surrender their countries? Obama recently faced this question as he had to account for sending troops into battle as he accepted the Nobel Peace Prize.

He answered:

> As someone who stands here as a direct consequence of Dr. King's life work, I am living testimony to the moral force of nonviolence. I know there's nothing weak—nothing passive—nothing naive—in the creed and lives of Gandhi and King. But as a head of state sworn to protect and defend my nation, I cannot be guided by their examples alone. I face the world as it is, and cannot stand idle in the face of threats to the American people. . . . So part of our challenge is reconciling these two seemingly inreconcilable truths—that war is sometimes necessary, and war, at some level, is an expression of human folly. . . . The nonviolence practiced by men like Gandhi and King may not have been practical or possible in every circumstance, but the love that they preached—their fundamental faith in human progress—that must always be the North Star that guides us on our journey. For if we lose that faith—if we dismiss it as silly or naive; if we divorce it from the decisions that we make on issues of war and peace—then we lose what's best about humanity. We lose our sense of possibility. We lose our moral compass. [Obama, 2009]

It will surely be surprising to many that Obama's position harmonizes perfectly with the classical Buddhist model of the ideal ruler. (Of course, whether any particular deployment of troops is a necessary defensive action is another question.) The model Buddhist ruler is the King Asoka and his conception of just war also involves a conception of diplomacy first but defensive war when necessary to protect the community from aggressors (Strong, 1994 and 2008).

Asoka ruled the northern territories of contemporary India about one hundred years after the Buddha, 304–230 BCE. As Buddhist legend has it, Asoka converts to Buddhist after a bloody but triumphant conquest over Kalinga (modern Orissa). As a Buddhist ruler, he adopts vegetarianism, digs wells, provides medical care for humans and animals, promotes religious toleration, and in general supports public welfare. Most importantly, for our purposes, King Asoka rejects war as a means of expansion and tool of national interests and devotes his rule to spreading the teaching of the Buddha, the Dharma, and supporting the community of monks, the Sangha. Asoka writes on one of his stone pillars,

> Now [Asoka] Beloved-of-the-Gods thinks that even those who do wrong should be forgiven where forgiveness is possible. Even the forest people, who live in Beloved-of-the-Gods' domain, are entreated and reasoned with to act properly. They are told that despite his remorse [at the slaughter of innocents in his past] Beloved-of-the-Gods has the power to punish them if necessary, so that they should be ashamed of their wrong and not be killed. Truly, Beloved-of-the-Gods desires non-injury, restraint and impartiality to all beings, even where wrong has been done. Now it is

> conquest by Dharma that Beloved-of-the-Gods considers to be the best conquest. . . . This conquest has been won everywhere, and it gives great joy—the joy which only conquest by Dharma can give. [Asoka, *Fourteen Rock Edicts*, No. 13]

In other edicts, Asoka assures people on his borders that they need not fear conquest—that he only wishes to spread the Dharma (but he also insists on mutual respect between religions).

Asoka, the model Buddhist ruler, has a powerful army, and police force, but he strives to be merciful and compassionate with criminals and with other peoples within or beyond his borders. The goal is to teach and encourage virtue and wisdom, but nonetheless, aggressors, whether internal or external, cannot be passively tolerated; criminals will be punished and invaders will be repelled. It is clear that Asoka does not disband his army; he remains the dominant superpower in his region. In short, these are the political lessons we can draw from the idealized rule of Asoka: trust the people and treat them with compassion, support the Sangha, which is the community of monks that preserve and teach the Dharma, defend the innocent against all transgressors (but never with hatred or malice), and recognize and acknowledge the harm to the victims of aggression but also forgive the transgressors.

In short, we have here the familiar just war theory with which we began—with the additional Buddhist emphasis on truth and reconciliation.[12]

The Buddha as Peace-Keeper

Before we conclude this discussion of Buddhism and war, we should consider the story of the Rohini River water dispute between the Sakyas and the Koliyas.[13] The dispute is a classic dispute between two tribes sharing a river during a draught. The short version is the two sides are on the battlefield, ready to fight, when the Buddha arrives as peace-keeper. The Buddha first blocks out the sun setting darkness over the battlefield, and then reveals himself floating above them in the air, shooting six-colored rays of light out from his hair. Needless to say, the two sides are taken aback by this supernatural display and ceasefire is achieved. In the interest of lasting peace, the Lord Buddha reasons with the tribes on the harms and futility of war and also the benefits of peaceful cooperation. The Buddha knows, however, that these reasons will not lead to a lasting peace, and so he convinces the two tribes to turn over the youth that make up their armies to the Buddhist Sangha. In this way the armies are no longer available and the youth of the tribes are brought together in cooperation and Karmic transformation. Yet even this will not do! The young novice monks miss their wives and want to return to their villages, so the Buddha takes them away to the heights of the Himalayas to distract them from their passion and longing for the loving embrace and comfort of home. All attachment, even attachment to home, to country, and to one's people, leads to inevitable conflict as distinct peoples claim land, rivers, or other resources. There is surely a lesson here that could be applied to the conflict over Tibet but I will leave that aside.

There is much more to explore in this story, but what I find most striking is the clear recognition of the difficulty of avoiding tribal or factional conflict in the normal course of life. A lasting peace requires removing all of the young men, so there are no potential warriors, and completely removing them from home, love, and family. A clear message of this story is that even the Buddha cannot prevent war and maintain a lasting peace until we have all achieved enlightenment and extinguished the passions, the afflictive emotions, the greed and delusions that are the wellspring of conflict. If the Buddha cannot prevent war without conscripting all of the youth into monastic seclusion, what is a mere earthly leader to do?

For those who must rule humankind as it is (caught up in the conflicts of life, faced with so much anger, hatred, and mutual righteous recriminations, indeed faced with those set on harming, dominating, and killing others), the model offered by Rawls and Obama, Muhammad and Asoka, is indeed the most realistic utopia that one can hope for.[14]

Final Reflections

We have focused on the overlapping consensus on just war theory, but before we conclude, it is important to note that the comprehensive doctrines, the overall worldviews, of Buddhism and Islam also make a difference.

First, the distinct social-political roles of the Buddha and Mohammad make a difference. The prophet Muhammad was also the political and military leader of a people. The fledgling Muslim community was driven out of Mecca and to Medina. Muhammad was both the prophet and the political leader of Medina, and he had to defend his community in military battles with Mecca. Muhammad was triumphant in battle, conquered Mecca, but he was also merciful in peace. As a result, the Qur'an and Hadith include frank discussions of the reality of war, and the Sharia includes a detailed conception of just war. The Buddha, on the other hand, was a prince who abandoned political and social power to lead, instead, a monastic community. Despite the agreement on just war theory, as founders, the Buddha and Muhammad offer very different idealized images. Contrast the two questions: "What would Muhammad do?" and "What would the Buddha do?" The Buddha is not a political leader; indeed, in Buddhism, we must turn instead to the temporal leader of a nation, King Asoka, for an ideal of political rule. In addition, Muhammad emphasized his human, nondivine, nontranscendent nature, and in this respect, he is more like Asoka than the Buddha. If we ask, "What would Asoka do?" the answer is probably the same as the answer to the question, "What would Muhammad do?" Similarly, the Buddhist ideal of monastic withdrawal from the complexity and web of social life is not found at the core of Islam. Islam is primarily a religion of daily life. The Buddha, as leader of a monastic community, and the monastic code, does not offer much guidance for the daily life of lay Buddhists. Muhammad's followers are imbedded in families; they are fathers and sons, mothers and daughters, husbands and wives, workers and soldiers. In addition to a detailed just war theory, Islamic Sharia also presents a guide for day-to-day domestic life, marriage, romantic love, and family. These are not the core issues of monastic life. Unlike the Buddhist monastic path, the straight path of Sharia is a path for all people.

Second, Buddhism emphasizes the futility of war in a way that is not found in Islam. For Buddhists, war is sometimes justified in theory but rarely, if ever, in practice. Recall that war is always self-destructive, even when it is necessary. In contrast, for Islam war is a necessary evil that is hateful, but engaging in a just war is not sinful or wrong. Just warriors go to paradise and are favored and beloved by Allah for their commitment and sacrifice. For Buddhists, violence clouds the waters of one's mind and also sets back one's Karma.[15] With wisdom and skilful means, the harm caused may be neutralized by the good done, but it is still always unwholesome to harm a living creature, however necessary and justified. War is always a result of human folly and self-destructive attachment, even when it is necessary, and in this sense it is not part of some larger plan. I think that this difference does make a real difference in one's attitude to war, even a just and necessary war.

Third and last, the focus on nonviolence and passivism in much contemporary Buddhism is not at all foreign to Islam. Indeed, the Sufi tradition of Islam focuses on love and compassion as the purest manifestation of the divine and also focuses on transcendence and union no less than does Buddhism. In this respect, the Sufi poet and mystic Mevlana Rumi is as much of a contemporary inspiration as is the Dalai Lama. The appeal of pure boundless compassion is as universal as is the distaste for war.

Notes

1. For a clear discussion of current debates on the justification of humanitarian war, preemptive war, preventive war, and justification of the Iraq war, see O'Driscoll (2008).

2. For an extensive discussion of the contemporary reality of war and its impact, see Forsberg, et al. (1997).

3. For a comprehensive account of Islamic Sharia, and the different schools of interpretation, see Cook (2000).

4. For an excellent discussion of jihad and war, see Hashimi (2003). I am indebted throughout my discussion to Hashimi's account. On the Greater and Lesser Jihad, see Ruthven (1997).

5. See Will Kymlicka (2002), Chapter 8, "Multiculturalism," for the distinction between internal restrictions and external protections. Kymlicka also provides a clear account of the difference between a doctrine of religious toleration, like the Ottoman Millet system, and between different religious groups and freedom of conscience, which also embraces internal dissent. Any religious tradition with a conception of heresy and apostasy does accept freedom of conscience, but even the orthodox can tolerate other belief systems. Internal dissent is a challenge to the internal consensus and religious authority, and it is often treated harshly (even when freedom of *other* religions is accepted).

6. On the doctrine of no-self, see Collins (1982). In Western philosophy, these issues are explored in Hume (1896) and Parfit (1989).

7. For the history of Tibet and the Dalai Lama's rise to power, see Goldstein (1999).

8. Geoff Childs, *Tibetan Diary* (2004, 143). The quotation and translation from the Fifth Dalai Lama's letter is from Elliot Sperling (2001, 318). See Sperling for further discussion of the idealization of Tibetan Buddhism.

9. Kopel (2007) citing Smith (1997).

10. This interpretation of Buddhist ethics, and the discussion of skilful means below, are developed more fully in Cummiskey (2010).

11. On Buddhist political theory, see Harris (1994); Nandasena Ratnapala (1997); and K. N. Jayatilleke.

12. Buddhist just war theory is also focused on alternative means of conflict resolution. For a comprehensive discussion, see Harvey (2000), Chapter 6, "War and Peace."

13. The discussion that follows is based on Strong (2009). For original sources see Bollee (1970).

14. Some might argue that, in contrast to the Buddhist ideal of boundless compassion, Islam is clearly more easily distorted into an ideology that supports war and the cold-blooded killing reflected in the martyrdom of Muslim suicide bombers. In response, we should recognize the equally "cold-blooded" mindset manifest in the Buddhist Samurai ideal of Bushido, which is clearly founded on the Buddhist doctrine of emptiness and the inescapability and insignificance of death. For a brief discussion, see Harvey (2000, 264–270). In Islamic Jihadist and Buddhist Samurai warriors, we see not the essence of either view but instead the ideological malleability of all comprehensive worldviews.

15. It is noteworthy that even here we find exceptions to the rule. As Harvey (2000) explains, in Japan during the Ashikaga rule (1336–1573), "the Jodo-shin school became fortified temples, with its armed followers, both priests and laity, acting to de-

fend its single minded 'true faith' in the saving power of the Amida Buddha. They could be fanatical in battle believing that they would be reborn in Amida's Pure Land if they were killed" (266).

References

Adams, Robert. (1976). "Motive Utilitarianism." *Journal of Philosophy 73*: 467–481.

Asoka (King). (1959). "Fourteen Rock Edicts" in *Edicts*, ed. and trans. N. A. Nikam and Richard McKeon. Chicago: University of Chicago Press.

Bernton, Hal. (2001, 15 May). "Dalai Lama Urges Students to Shape World." *Seattle Times*.

Bollee, Willem. (1970). *Kunalajataka*. London: Luzac and Co.

Childs, Geoff. (2004). *Tibetan Diary*. Berkeley: University of California Press: 143.

Collins, Steven. (1982). *Selfless Persons*. Cambridge: Cambridge University Press.

Cook, Michael. (2000). *Commanding the Right and Forbidding the Wrong in Islamic Thought*. Cambridge: Cambridge University Press.

Cummiskey, David. (2010). "Competing Conceptions of the Self in Kantian and Buddhist Moral Theories" in *Cultivating Personhood: Kant and Asian Philosophy*, ed. Stephen R. Palmquist. Berlin: Walter de Gruyter.

Dalai Lama. (1999). *Ethics for a New Millennium*. New York: Riverhead Books.

Dalai Lama. (1962). *My Land and My People*. Columbus, OH: McGraw-Hill.

Forsberg, Randall Caroline, et al. (1997). New Democracy Forum: "The End of War?" *Boston Review*. Retrieved from http://www.bostonreview.net/BR22.5/toc.html

Goldstein, Melvyn C. (1999). *The Snow Lion and the Dragon: China, Tibet, and the Dalai Lama*. Berkeley: University of California Press.

Hare, R. M. (1981). *Moral Thinking*. Oxford: Oxford University Press.

Harris, Elizabeth J. (1994). *Violence and Disruption in Society: A Study of Early Buddhist Texts*. Kandy Sri Lanka: Buddhist Publication Society.

Harvey, Peter. (2000). *An Introduction to Buddhist Ethics*. Cambridge: Cambridge University Press.

Hashimi, Sohail H. (2003). "Saving and Taking Life in War: Three Modern Muslim Views" in *Islamic Ethics of Life*, ed. Jonathan E. Brockopp. Columbia: University of South Carolina Press.

Hume, David. (1896). *A Treatise on Human Nature*. Oxford: Clarendon Press.

Jayatilleke, K. N. (No date). *Dhamma, Man and Law* originally published as *The Principles of International Law in Buddhist Doctrine*. Buddhist Research Society.

Keown, Damien. (2000). *Buddhism: A Very Short Introduction*. Oxford: Oxford University Press.

Kopel, David B. (2007). "Self-Defense in Asian Religion." *Liberty University Law Review 2*: 79.

Kymlicka, Will. (2002). *Contemporary Political Philosophy: An Introduction*. Oxford: Oxford University Press.

Obama, Barack. (2009, December 12). "Nobel Prize Speech." *New York Times*. Retrieved from http://www.nytimes.com/2009/12/11/world/europe/11prexy.text.html.

O'Driscoll, Cian. (2008). *Renegotiation of the Just War Tradition and the Right to War in the Twenty-First Century*. New York: Palgrave Macmillan.

Parfit, Derek. (1989). *Reasons and Persons*. Oxford: Oxford University Press.

Pye, Michael. (2003). *Skilful Means: A Concept of Mahayana Buddhism, Second Edition*. New York: Routledge.

Qur'an (The Koran). (1999). N. J. Dawood, trans. New York: Penguin Books.

Railton, Peter. (1984). "Alienation, Consequentialism, and the Demands of Morality." *Philosophy and Public Affairs 13*(2): 134–71.

Ratnapala, Nandasena. (1997). *Buddhist Democratic Political Theory and Practice*. Ratmalana, Sri Lanka: Sarvodaya Vishva Lekha.

Rawls, John. (1999). *The Law of Peoples with Public Reason Revisited*. Cambridge, MA: Harvard University Press.

Ruthven, Malise. (1997). *Islam: A Very Short Introduction*. Oxford: Oxford University Press.

Sperling, Elliot. (2001). "Orientalism and Aspects of Violence in the Tibetan Tradition" in *Imagining Tibet: Perceptions, Projections, & Fantasies*, ed. Thierry Dodin and Heinz Rather. Boston: Wisdom Publications.

Smith, Warren W. (1997). *Tibetan Nation: A History of Tibetan Nationalism and Sino-Tibetan Relations*. Boulder, CO: Westview Press.

Strong, John S. (2009, 18 June). Account in "The Buddha as Peacekeeper: The Rohini River Water Dispute and the War Between the Sakyas and the Kosalas" presented at the Asien-Afrika Institut, University of Hamburg.

Strong, John S. (2008). *The Experience of Buddhism, Third Edition*. Florence, KY: Wadsworth.

Strong, John S. (1994). *King Asoka and Buddhism: Historical and Literary Studies*, ed. Anuradha Seneviratna. Buddhist Publication Society, Buddha Dharma Education Association Inc.

Strong, John S. (1989). *The Legend of Asoka: A Study and Translation of the Asokavadana, Second Edition*. Dehli: Motilal Banarsidass.

Watson, Burton, trans. (2002). *The Essential Lotus: Selections from the Lotus Sutra*. New York: Columbia University Press.

CHAPTER SIXTEEN

Cosmopolitan Revisions of Just War

GABRIEL PALMER-FERNÁNDEZ
Youngstown State University

Abstract

This chapter explores some revisions a cosmopolitan view brings to just war theory. The latter is, of course, the dominant moral approach to war and other forms of political violence. But it shows some important problems; for example, it is biased on behalf of one particular kind of political community, the nation-state. This bias is especially evident in two of its criteria: legitimate authority and just cause. I argue that these are seriously flawed in different ways and consequently reject the latter but expand the former to include not only the traditional nation-state but also other (non-state) groups and political communities. To support that point I introduce a moral cosmopolitanism based on the right of individuals to basic goods and other goods essential to agency, including the basic right to protect oneself from unwarranted harm.

Key Words

cosmopolitanism, nation-states, universal human rights, just war theory, legitimate authority, just cause

---

Author's note: I am very grateful to my colleagues Deborah Mower, Alan Tomhave, and Bruce Waller for their helpful comments on an earlier draft. I have not followed their good counsel in every instance. The mistakes are really mine.

For much of the first half of the twentieth century, few works were generally available on the morality of war. Almost all of them were confined to discussions among Roman Catholic scholars on the centuries-old moral tradition known as just war theory.[1] But within a decade of the nuclear bombings of Hiroshima and Nagasaki, a substantial body of scholarly work on the ethics of war began to appear, first by theologians and then by philosophers. A little later, American experience in Vietnam motivated the greatest development of the theory since the Spanish Conquest of the New World. Scores of articles appeared in English-speaking journals, and in 1977 Michael Walzer published the modern classic, *Just and Unjust War*. After the Cold War, attention went to other issues—for example, military intervention in response to humanitarian crises in Rwanda, Bosnia, Kosovo, and the 1991 Persian Gulf War. Post-9/11 discussions continue to expand the range of concern: terrorism, regime change, preemptive war, and an apparently endless global war on terror.

In response to actual events, the received tradition clearly shows new directions. Just war concepts are not timeless truths but historical elements of an ongoing discursive practice on the morality of political violence. With a chronology that begins in northern Africa with St. Augustine of Hippo during the early Middle Ages, the theory shows significant developments as it responds to challenges from technological innovations, imperial ambitions, and changing political realities, as some institutions wane in influence and power and new ones emerge—churches and nation-states, respectively. Among the most important new influences are, first, the widespread acceptance of a doctrine of universal human rights and, second, an emerging and important change in the political structure of the globe. Each of these fundamentally alters the role of the nation-state.[2] What are the implications for the ethics of war?

The traditional view is that war is the business of states and the right to war belongs to them, no matter how morally unworthy or unjust some may be—or, more properly, it belongs to the sovereign, even the brutal and criminal ones, those who oppress, maim, torture, and kill members of their own population. It never belongs to private individuals, the victims of tyrants and dictators, or to those who would rescue them. Call it the statist conception of just war: states have rights first against aggression; and then, when violated, they have the right to war. But the emergence of a cosmopolitan morality based on universal human rights and the gradual waning of the Westphalian system decenter the primacy of states and their sovereigns at the core of just war theory. Does that imply a cosmopolitan just war theory? What might that look like? Does war then become an instrument for protecting and promoting universal human rights and cosmopolitan norms rather than for rectifying cross-border aggression between states? In a cosmopolitan view, might states lose their monopoly of the right to war and might the really morally unworthy ones lose their right against aggression?

I address some of those questions in the third section below. There, I suggest that a cosmopolitan view brings at least the following two important revisions to just war theory: first, it extends the principle of legitimate authority (*who* can declare war) to persons or groups who have a just cause for war; and, second, it grants the right against aggression only to morally worthy states. I begin in the first section below with a status report on just war theory and then provide a brief description of the main features of cosmopolitanism. The reader familiar with those topics may want to go directly to the last section.

State of the Art

Just war theory consists of a set of principles that enables one to judge the morality of war. It divides into two categories (usually given in Latin): *jus ad bellum* (criteria to determine *when* it is morally permissible—or perhaps obligatory—to wage war); and *jus in bello* (criteria to determine *how* one fights a war). Following Michael Walzer, some see a moral division of labor between these categories, making it perfectly possible to fight an unjust war justly—say, a war of aggression or colonial expansion, so long as one fights in accord with the rules of war.[3] This is so, Walzer contends, because war is never the soldiers'; it belongs instead to the political leadership. Soldiers are responsible only for their conduct in war (the *in bello* portion of the theory), and so, on that account, soldiers on both sides of a war are morally equal, that is, enjoy the same war rights, including the right to kill. What has come to be known as the doctrine of the moral equality of soldiers is controversial (Primoratz, 2002; Coady, 2008; Rodin and Shue, 2008; McMahan, 2009). Consider this. Soldiers who fight on behalf of an aggressor state (unjust combatants) hardly share the moral status of soldiers who are forced to defend their victim state (just combatants). The former is like the mugger who assaults you or the burglar who breaks into your home. Without substantive justice, killing in war begins to look like crime, terror, or murder. Even lies and distortions by the political leadership to motivate popular support for a war at the very most might only excuse, never morally justify, the participation of soldiers in a given war (e.g., Iraq 2003). To be sure, soldiers never fully own the wars they fight, nor are they ever truly automatons. Still, they are moral agents and insofar as they fight they make the war their own and hence share responsibility not only for their conduct, but also for the war itself. The division contained in this doctrine has an important parallel in the law of war and perhaps is better called the legal and not the moral equality of soldiers, as the latter is surely false.[4]

Two important developments concern morally legitimate responses to perceived threats—namely, preemptive war and supreme emergency. Current discussions on preemptive war are an obvious consequence of the Iraq War of 2003 and began with the 2002 National Security Strategy of the United States of America. It says:

> [The US] will act against . . . emerging threats before they are fully formed. [We] will not hesitate to act alone, if necessary, to exercise our right of self-defense by acting preemptively against such terrorists. . . . We must be prepared to stop rogue states and their terrorist clients before they are able to threaten us or use weapons of mass destruction. . . . We must adopt the concept of imminent threat to the capabilities and objectives of today's adversaries. . . . To forestall or prevent such hostile acts by our adversaries, the United States will, if necessary, act preemptively.[5]

Had allegations by the Bush administration about Iraqi intentions to strike with weapons of mass destruction been true, there might have been a plausible just cause for the Iraq War of 2003. In response to a real and imminent threat, a nation has the right to defend itself before being attacked. Sometimes called anticipatory self-defense, a preemptive strike has an intuitive appeal. If a sworn enemy has announced the intention and taken steps to bring my death, then surely my natural right to self-defense extends to defeating his aim. Why must I wait? Even absent a wide consensus, this is a very important development in just war theory. Following Vitoria, the tradition holds that the basis of a war is a wrong done; so there must be an antecedent fault. Absent that, all is aggression. But suppose we accept the possibility of justified acts of preemption; still the concept has huge epistemic problems, not the least of which is that we really seldom know another's true intention. Is it dissimulation, bravado, or truly a readiness to attack? Daniel Webster, then secretary of state, said in 1837: there must be shown "a necessity of self-defense . . . instant, overwhelming leaving no choice of means, and no moment for deliberation" (cited in Walzer, 1977, 74). It is a high standard and even if Iraq did pose a serious threat to the United States, very many moments for deliberation were squandered in the foolish and tragic rush to war.

Another controversy, introduced by Michael Walzer, is the idea of supreme emergency: in very rare circumstances, when a nation faces imminent defeat by a horrible, evil power, it is entitled to violate the rules of war, particularly the *jus in bello* prohibition on intentionally killing the civilian population of the enemy state. Such was the case, Walzer says, early in WWII, justifying the terror bombing of German cities.[6] Currently, no state is publicly asserting a right intentionally to target and kill civilians on these grounds—not since Churchill's declaration of a supreme emergency in 1939.[7] But the fact is that states at war have always intentionally targeted the civilian population of the enemy state.[8] And supreme emergency is one plausible strategy for justifying terrorist violence against civilians, particularly when it is coupled with a doctrine of collective moral responsibility of citizens for the actions of their state.[9] If states are permitted to violate the immunity of civilians under certain conditions, then consistency requires the same license to nonstate groups, say, to political communities under serious and imminent threat of disaster.

The concern with civilian deaths is acute in asymmetric warfare, in which one side is much weaker than the other and must resort to unconventional tactics—disguising as and hiding among civilians, employing guerilla tactics and suicide attacks. Current wars in Iraq and Afghanistan are obviously of this kind, as many future wars are likely to be. Such wars challenge just war theory by blurring the distinction between combatant and civilian, or legitimate and illegitimate targets of death in war. An important concern that has not received sufficient attention is the overall international context in which these wars occur. In asymmetric war, powerful nations like the US, though they insist that other nations abide by conventions and agreements, often run roughshod over them. And in a world dominated by a single power—a "hyper-power"—with a very wide and deep arsenal of military and other war-related capabilities, the United States gets to do things other nations do not get to do at all. That dominance, says David Luban, "marks a dramatic change in the political organization of the earth . . . [in which] the moral principles appropriate to one system of political organization may turn out to be senseless or even destructive applied in another system."[10]

Cosmopolitanism

Nations are a product of European history and first appeared some two hundred years ago. Taking a bird's-eye view of history, they stand somewhere between the age of knights, kings, and queens and a new age of larger political units or regional confederations, as Kant called them, gradually developing in various parts of the globe today. In any one of them, Thomas Paine's phrase "my country is the world" is quite intelligible as a description not only of a certain moral sentiment or loyalty to universal humanity but also of an emerging political reality, just as it was perfectly intelligible to eighteenth century intellectuals on both sides of the Atlantic.[11] But the nation is now under threat. Some argue that it is too narrow and constrained a concept, that it is poorly suited to the growing integration of the globe, and is unable to address many of the pressing problems we face.[12] They see a world without borders, without walls. Against this backdrop, a global movement of universal human rights has emerged, expressing the fundamental conviction that how human beings are treated is of concern to everyone, everywhere, and challenging the traditional concept of national sovereignty. In the post-WWII international order, the idea of human rights has become part of humanity's common vocabulary—formal expressions of them are found, for example, in the Nuremberg Charter, the UN Universal Declaration on Human Rights, the Convention on the Prevention and Punishment of the Crime of Genocide, and in its most recent progeny, the report of the International Commission on Intervention and State Sovereignty.[13]

This international movement provides a model for thinking about a universal, global morality that is cosmopolitan in scope and in which, as Kant put it, "a violation of right on one party of the earth is felt in all" (1996, 330). It views human beings, rather than states, as the fundamental unit of moral concern, enjoying equal moral worth, and possessing rights to certain basic goods and freedoms crucially important for human life.[14] Despite differences (say, of culture, religion, gender, or class) all humans share certain basic needs—for nourishment, shelter, safety; for respect, literacy, society, among others. These are minimally essential for a decent human life and constitute, as Michael Boylan puts it, a "hierarchy of claims" upon others to respect, protect and, when necessary, provide.[15] These rights are typically explained by reference to some property of human beings. Though the relevant property can differ (for Boylan it is the desire to be good; for Gewirth it is purposive action; for Okin it is needs and capacities; for Jones it is vital interests), it is nonetheless universal, along with the claims it makes. The nature of these claims is controversial and the body of scholarly literature on the subject is vast and very impressive. Whether they are natural or fictions, they are for us today quite palpable and useful features of what we know of the moral world.

Many cosmopolitan views emphasize the *individual* rights of persons to basic goods and freedoms. But an individualism of rights can contain a mistaken anthropology and render cosmopolitanism subject to powerful and important objections. "Living in society," Taylor rightly observes, "is a necessary condition of the development of rationality . . . of becoming a moral agent . . . a fully responsible, autonomous being. . . . Outside society . . . our distinctively human capacities could not develop."[16] A fuller, more adequate cosmopolitanism considers also the common life of persons sustained through political organizations and social practices among those basic goods crucially important for the development of the human personality. The primary political organization in the modern period having responsibility to protect and promote the rights of persons and their common, social life has been the nation-state. But the state has largely failed in that very important task. At present there are nearly two hundred states in the world.[17] Only some of them are able to provide basic nutritional, educational, social, and political goods—that is, protecting people from internal and external threats, delivering education and basic individual and public health services, and providing institutions that respond to the needs of the population. Of 177 states ranked by the Failed State Index of the Fund for Peace, 38 are under "Alert" and another 93 under "Warning," for a total of 131 or nearly 75 percent of all states considered as experiencing significant troubles.[18] The list of critical, fragile, weak, or failed states includes nations from all continents except North America and Australia—from Pakistan to Peru, Haiti to Indonesia, Senegal to Afghanistan and Iraq. While there are some successes—the very affluent and privileged few in Western Europe and North America—for the most part the state has failed as the responsible agent to meet human rights to basic goods and freedoms.

It is generally assumed that because people are organized around the globe into separate, independent states, the duty to respond to those rights belongs to them. It sounds like a reasonable proposal, but it is fundamentally flawed. Prior to states, other kinds of political associations met these needs—or were assigned responsibility for them—and it may no longer be the case that states can best meet those needs in a changing globe. Because (most) states have failed in their responsibility to meet the rights of their population, new responsible agents must be identified. This is the view Robert Goodin calls the "assigned responsibility model." Start with the assumption that we all have certain basic human rights of the sort we have been dealing with as well as certain general duties toward each other, not only of a negative but also of a positive kind. Duties will be appointed either in a "quasi-naturalistic" fashion—say, the family—or in a more socially constructed way—the institutions of a particular state (Goodin, 2002, 153). Neither family nor state creates new duties. They are instead localizations of those general duties we all have toward each other, specified in particular, special institutions. Sometimes those institutions fail. And when they do, the duties otherwise belonging to them will have to be reallocated, to other states, regional confederations, or the world community.

So conceived, cosmopolitanism is a normative approach that takes seriously the universality of morality without limiting its scope to borders or walls and gives moral primacy to persons rather than states. Such an unbounded morality will present important challenges to just war theory.

Cosmopolitan Revisions of Just War Theory

In this final section, I consider some fundamental revisions cosmopolitanism brings to contemporary just war theory at the level of *jus ad bellum*. As a global, political theory cosmopolitanism must develop principles that apply when groups, nations, or other larger political communities violate the rights of others. Specifically, it must provide principles for the defense of the rights of persons to basic goods and freedoms, as well as the just rectification of wrongs committed against them by external or internal political actors. The standard, that is, statist, account of a morally justified war requires the following: (1) legitimate authority; (2) just cause; (3) reasonable hope of success; (4) proportionality; (5) last resort; and (6) right intentions.

On this standard account, a war is unjust if it is aggressive—Germany invades Poland, for example. Aggression is the only crime states can commit, says Walzer. Everything else is a misdemeanor (1977, 51). Consequently, Poland has a just cause against Germany; so too any allies Poland might have: defense from unwarranted aggression. Though necessary, having a just cause is not sufficient for a just war, as other conditions also must be met—the war must be publicly declared by the sovereign, have a reasonable chance for success, consider and balance the evils produced by war to its political objectives, exhaust available nonviolent means for resolving the conflict, and seek to return to conditions prior to aggression.

A cosmopolitan account of just war does not challenge all the standard principles. Principles (3) to (5) remain unchanged; (6), however, seems unnecessary, with or without cosmopolitanism. Why the political leadership of a nation waging a defensive war must have a subjectively right intention is unclear. Is it not enough to have an objectively just cause and to seek only rectification of a wrong? Grotius rightly omits this Augustinian requirement for two very good reasons: first, war is a condition between states and states are not the kind of thing that can have intentions; and second, when a war is otherwise just, whatever intention the political leadership holds cannot invalidate it.[19] Numerous writers question Principle (5). It is very hard to tell exactly when the last resort is reached. There is often something else one can try, some additional nonviolent means of resolving a dispute; a totally necessary war is exceptional. But a perilous point might be reached as one looks for one last chance to avoid war. And if a nation has already been unjustly attacked, last resort is hardly a relevant, necessary condition. The proportionality principle (4) is one of the most neglected in the scholarly literature, perhaps because it is one of the most challenging to define. It wants us to weigh the expected benefits of going to war—for example, defeating an evil aggressor—against the expected costs in blood and treasure.[20] But whose costs and benefits are to be considered, weighed, and balanced—those of the belligerents or of the entire world?

In part, the balance and weighing are to be made in relation to the political objectives of the war—whether the evils produced by war are proportional to its justified objectives. When those objectives are unclear—for example, as is the case in the current war in Afghanistan—proportionality determinations are difficult, if not impossible to draw. But even when the political objectives are clear, calculations become extremely complex, as one must consider not only evils and costs we can quantify, like body counts, but also qualitative ones, like life under foreign rule.

Matters are different with the remaining two principles, (1) and (2). Here a cosmopolitan view brings important revisions. I begin with (1), the principle of legitimate authority. It is among the oldest in the theory, appearing prior to St. Augustine and at least as early as Cicero. We understand it today as requiring the declaration of war by the legitimate sovereign of a state, say, the Congress of the United States (as required by our Constitution), and in other nations whoever is the proper ruler as determined by their own political organization, usually the president or prime minister. Elizabeth Anscombe captures the core of the statist conception of the principle when she says: "The right to attack with a view to killing is something that belongs only to rulers and those they command to do it. . . . It does belong to rulers precisely because of that threat of violent coercion exercised by those in authority which is essential to the existence of human societies" (Anscombe, 1981, 53). But the principle is more flexible than normally thought, showing at least three possible conceptions: statist, nonstatist, and poststatist.

Statist Conception. The political situation in the high middle ages, when Thomas Aquinas came on the scene, was quite fluid. Not only did the Roman Church exercise considerable political power, with the pope as its legitimate ruler enjoying war-making authority (which it used against Muslims in Spain, pagans in Prussia, and political opponents in Italy), but also national kings in Sicily, France, and Cyprus; city-states, some of which Aquinas himself visited, of Milan, Pisa, and Lucca, each with its own sovereign; aristocrats who challenged kings for their thrones; and wealthy trading conglomerates that advanced their interests with large private armies. It was a daring move on Aquinas's part to limit legitimate war-making authority to prince or church, but especially to prince. He writes:

> Since the responsibility for the commonwealth has been entrusted to rulers it is their responsibility to defend the city, kingdom or province subject to them. And just as it is legitimate for them to use the material sword to punish criminals in order to defend it against internal disturbances . . . so they have also the right to use the sword to defend the commonwealth against external enemies. [Aquinas, 1947, II-I, q. 40]

A centralized authority over a territory is obviously important to Aquinas, and in that sense he provides material for the modern nation-state. But it is the idea of a political community or Aristotelian *polis* that is crucial. The political unit of importance to Aquinas he called a "perfect community": perfect as it was sufficient to meet all of an individual's earthly needs, which could well be a city, kingdom, or province. Today we might think of a nation, regional confederation, or world state. Later just war theorists followed Aquinas in using the idea of a perfect community and granting war-making authority to their legitimate ruler. Suárez, for example, would say: "External hostilities that are opposed to peace are properly called war, when undertaken between sovereigns or between states. . . . By natural right the sovereign, without temporal superior, holds legitimate power to declare war, or the republic which reserves a similar jurisdiction for itself."[21] Here sovereignty and legitimate authority to declare war rest in one and the same person.

Nonstatist Conception. It is natural to think of the principle of legitimate authority as necessarily tied to the concept of the nation-state. Most of us have known little else. But it is mistaken. The discussion above shows that the principle has been tied to political organizations other than the state—to cities and provinces, kingdoms and church. It is all the more clear that legitimate authority and the state are not in any deep way essential for the other when we consider the pervasive global force of post-WWII anticolonial struggles, as well as indigenous national and separatist movements all seeking political self-determination. In Africa and the Middle East, in India and elsewhere, people were encouraged by promises of independence and self-rule made by Allies during WWII, particularly as expressed in the Atlantic Charter: UK and US promises to "respect the right of all peoples to choose the form of government under which they will live" (Churchill and Roosevelt, 1941, 352). More often than not, the exercise of this right meant an armed struggle against a colonial power. It was usually declared by persons lacking official state sovereignty, yet who represented the rights and interests of a political community and thereby enjoyed *de facto* legitimate authority to declare war for the cause of national liberation and establish a state of their own. Here the state and legitimate authority are independent concepts.

Poststatist Conception. It is of course impossible to say whether the state will persist, perish, or take new forms. Consequently, we cannot say what kind of wars we'll fight in the future, who will wage them, with what kinds of weapons, and for what reasons. There are some studies, however, that provide thought-provoking suggestions—for example, Martin Van Creveld's *The Transformation of War* and Mary Kaldor's *New and Old Wars.*[22] For the past two hundred years, nations have been the primary war-making organization. But their monopoly over violence is now faltering and gradually other groups of an entirely different nature have emerged. "Should present trends continue," Van Creveld writes, "then the kind of war that is based on the division between government, army, and people seems to be on its way out. . . . Over the long run, the place of the state will be taken by warmaking organizations of a different type" (1991, 192). Similarly, Kaldor maintains that in the context of globalization, as the state becomes an anachronism, new types of wars will emerge. These new wars—or Network Wars, as she aptly calls them in *Global Civil Society*—will take place in the disintegration or ruins of states. They will be fought by hybrids of state and non-state armies (including private security groups—Blackwater in Iraq), without uniforms or pitched battles, directing violence almost entirely against civilian populations. The rules codified for states during their ascendency and dominance in Geneva and Hague Conventions will (likely) give way as other practices and rules develop in the transition to a poststatist world, or we might have different (and not necessarily compatible) coterminous practices. Here the state and legitimate authority coincide in some but not in all cases—perhaps not even in most.

In the new cosmopolitan context, (partially or totally) freed from its statist moorings, the principle of legitimate authority to declare war will likely take different forms. We can identify at least two. The first one is hardly novel; indeed, its origin lies in antiquity and it is perhaps the oldest theory of justifiable use of lethal force in the West. It is the doctrine of tyrannicide, introduced into medieval Catholicism by John of Salisbury, and addresses violence not between states, but between a community and an unjust ruler. Because tyrants do not obey the law and in their disobedience are, John wrote, the "likeness of wickedness . . . it has always been an honorable thing to slay them" (John of Salisbury, 1963, 370). In his early writings Aquinas agreed (though later he demurred). Other medieval and early modern writers went along with the doctrine, adding an important qualification—in all cases, however evil a tyrant is, representatives of the community must be consulted. Jean Gerson, chancellor of the University of Paris in the early fifteenth century, put it: "Wise philosophers, expert jurists, legists, theologians, men of good life, of natural prudence, and of great experience should be consulted and confidence should be placed on them" (cited in Jászi and Lewis, 1957, 31). The last Catholic theologian to write on the topic was Juan de Mariana in 1599, who recounts with total approval the story of the young monk, Jacques Clement, who assassinated Henry III, king of France, as he laid siege to the city of Paris.

One might balk at this doctrine, declaring it extremist, bombastic, anarchic. There's something to that. Yet it has survived the centuries and nearly all forms of political communities—from small city-states to the largest empires. Modern European philosophers have certainly endorsed it, particularly the seventeenth century British resistance theory of Locke, Sidney, and Milton, for example, each establishing the right of the people to subdue, rebel, and finally execute tyrants. The second form and perhaps a more appropriate formulation of the principle from a cosmopolitan perspective is this: a person, group, nation, or supranational entity has legitimate authority to declare war when it has a just cause for war, for example, defending itself from unwarranted aggression. Here a justified cause is sufficient for the kind of authority traditionally required by the principle. It sounds radical but is not that far removed from current practice. The statist conception attaches the right to war to states. A cosmopolitan view can endorse that conception. It does so not on grounds that only states as such have this right, but rather on grounds of human rights—that is, on the view that all human beings have rights to certain goods and freedoms, including the right to defend those goods and freedoms from unwarranted aggression.

Suppose once again the US invades the small island socialist republic of Cuba, as it did forty years ago and as some Cuban-Americans hoped the Bush administration would. Impoverished by decades of an economic and trade embargo and having lost economic aid from the former Soviet Union, the government of Cuba is unable to defend itself and its population from American aggression. Under such circumstances, the right of self-defense reverts back to individuals who now, as private persons and without direction of their government, have just cause and are therefore the legitimate authority to declare and fight a defensive war. Vitoria is clear on this point. He writes: "Any one, even a private person, can accept and wage a defensive war . . . without authority from any one else, for the defense not only of his person, but also of his property and goods" (li). The only relevant difference Vitoria notes between a private person and a state is that the former may wage war only "to defend himself and what belongs to him," but not to punish, recapture property, or correct a wrong, as does the state.[23] Suarez concurs.[24] And Grotius expands on his predecessors by first distinguishing between two kinds of war—private and public—allowing the first on the basis of natural right even against one's own state when no legal recourse is available, as "by natural right, war may be denied to no one" (Grotius, 1962, parts I, III, IV).

Cosmopolitanism brings a second revision. It concerns which states have the right against aggression and, when violated, have the right to war. The statist conception holds that no matter how oppressive, brutal, or tyrannical a state is toward its members, it enjoys those rights, just as every other (morally worthy) state does. In that regard all states are morally equal. But the doctrine of the moral equality of states is surely false, or false from a cosmopolitan view. Among the first to press this point is David Luban in an illuminating article, "Just War and Human Rights." For Luban, states have no intrinsic but rather instrumental value. They serve important functions—for example, protection and promotion of the rights and interests of their members. When a state fails to do so or becomes tyrannical, it cannot assert those rights. It lacks legitimacy. A "tyrannical state," Luban says, "cannot derive sovereign rights against aggression from the rights of its oppressed citizens, when it itself is denying them those same rights."[25] Why would anyone think that the group or party with the most power or its monopoly in a territory represents the interests and rights of its people, is their legitimate sovereign, and therefore has the right against aggression and, when violated, has the right to war? On the cosmopolitan view, only states that protect and promote the rights and interests of their members are morally worthy and enjoy the right against aggression and, when violated, the right to war. Cambodia's Khmer Rouge and Germany's Third Reich did not enjoy those rights, nor does any other morally unworthy state.

Darrel Moellendorf provides an illustration of this approach in a discussion on the war to defend Kuwait against Iraq in 1991. Given the moral equality of states assumed in the statist conception of just war theory, Kuwait had a just cause to defend itself; so too did any other state with which Kuwait had a defensive alliance or which honored a request by Kuwait to assist in self-defense, as did the US-led coalition. Moellendorf disagrees. On a cosmopolitan perspective, a state can have a just cause against aggression "if and only if the intervention is directed towards advancing justice in the basic structure of the state or the international effects of its domestic policy" (2002, 159). Restoring the Kuwaiti regime would do neither. Most of its population (consisting of guest workers) would never receive, or their children born in Kuwait enjoy, rights to citizenship or property. These are certainly marks of a morally unworthy state, one that lacks the right against aggression as well as the right to war. Given these facts, Moellendorf says, "the restoration of the Kuwaiti government would do nothing to advance the cause of justice for most of its residents" (161). In no way does this judgment imply some justice in Iraq's aggression. There was none. Nor was there any justice in the intervention of the US-led coalition, but for another reason—namely, it sought to retain an international order favorable to our economic interest while allowing economic injustice in Kuwait to go unchecked.

Conclusion

Cosmopolitanism not only revises some of the fundamental principles of just war theory, it redefines the meaning of a just war. The implications are perhaps troubling, but the implications of denying cosmopolitanism are much more troubling. To reject cosmopolitanism would deny the equality of persons, regardless of their membership in particular groups or nations, the importance of fundamental human rights to basic goods and liberties, and the individual's right to defend them. It would, in effect, deny the contemporary foundations of morality.

Notes

1. A pre–WWII bibliography would contain few titles. Some of the most significant are the following: Alfred Vanderpol (1911); John Eppstein (1935); G. E. M. Anscombe (1939). A very useful and comprehensive bibliographical essay on works published prior to 1969 can be found in Ralph B. Potter (1969). An up-to-date nearly exhaustive (annotated) bibliography on just war and very many related topics is available on M. Rigstad's website www.justwartheory.com.

2. I use *nation*, *state*, and *nation-state* interchangeably. My expression "morally (un)worthy state" refers to a regime in power, its bureaucratic apparatus, perhaps also its ideology but never to a nation—that is, a people.

3. Michael Walzer (1977) says: "The two sorts of judgment are logically independent. It is perfectly possible for a just war to be fought unjustly and for an unjust war to be fought in strict accordance with the rules" (21).

4. The division is a modern one. Vitoria (1917) says, "For although I may doubt whether the war is just, yet the next point is that I may lawfully serve in the field at my prince's command." "*On the Laws of War*," trans. John Pawley Bate, in *The Classics of International Law*, ed. James Brown Scott (Washington, DC: Carnegie Institution: 177, Proposition V). Grotius (1962) says: "It does not fall within the province of the general to conduct negotiations with regard to the causes or the consequences of war. . . . Even though the general has been placed in command with absolute power, that must be understood to apply only to the conduct of the war" (848). In calling the moral equality "false," I follow Jeff McMahan (2007, 98).

5. Retrieved from http://www.whitehouse.gov/nsc/nssall.html, pages 2, 7, 12, 14. Accessed on September 30, 2002.

6. Walzer, *Unjust Wars*, Chapter 16. Others have endorsed the idea. See John Rawls (1998). Rawls says, "there are occasions when civilians can be attacked directly . . . [for example] when Britain was alone and desperately facing Germany's superior might . . . and the enormous moral and political evil it represented for civilized society" (476).

7. However, statements by John Reid, former British defense secretary, and Donald Rumsfeld, former US secretary of defense, on the war on terror come perilously close. David Frumm and Richard Perle raise the specter of supreme emergency when they write: "There is no middle way for Americans: it is victory or holocaust" (cited in Coker, 2008, 3).

8. Some 231 million people were killed in wars and conflict of the twentieth century. For a comprehensive examination of the scientific literature, see Milton Leitenberg (2006). The risk of death in war for civilians increased from 15 percent in WWI to 90 percent in Vietnam. See Gabriel Palmer-Fernández (1998).

9. See Burleigh Taylor Wilkins (1992); Tony Coady and Michael O'Keefe (2002); Gabriel Palmer-Fernández (2005); Seumas Miller (2009).

10. David Luban. (2004). See the very interesting discussion on disparity of power in the last section of Luban's article.

11. Of special value on Paine's cosmopolitanism is Staughton Lynd (1968). The same sentiment is captured by Tertullian's expression "Nothing is more foreign to us [Christians] than the state (*res publica*), for there is only one state that we recognize and that consists of the entire world" (1953, 204). Of course, Marcus Aurelius, Diogenes, and other figures of the ancient world said much the same.

12. Whether the nation-state is waning, shifting, or weakening does not have to be determined here, although I believe the former provides a more plausible account of many observable phenomena. A world history written in the early twenty-first century, E. J. Hobsbawn (1990) writes, "will inevitably have to be written as the history of a world which can no longer be contained within the limits of 'nations' and 'nation-states' as these used to be defined, either politically, or economically, or culturally, or

even linguistically. It will largely be supranational and infranational, but even infranationality, whether or not it dresses itself up in the costume of some mini-nationalism, will reflect the decline of the old nation-state as an operational entity" (191). For a similar conclusion from a different set of assumptions, see Kenichi Ohmae (1995).

13. *The Responsibility to Protect* (Ottawa, ON: International Development Research Centre, 2001).

14. The expression "a universal, global morality that is cosmopolitan is scope" is redundant but necessary, as a troubling feature may be noted in some contemporary liberal moral and political philosophy—it limits the scope of our obligations to our compatriots. Though morality is universal for liberals, it is neither global nor cosmopolitan for them and instead is bounded by national borders. See the chapters by Christopher Lowry and Udo Schüklenk, John-Stewart Gordon, and Gabriel Palmer-Fernández (2009) in *Morality and Justice: Reading Boylan's* A Just Society.

15. Michael Boylan (2004). See also Edward H. Spence (2007); C. Jones (1999); D. Moellendorf (2002); and Henry Shue (1996). Of course, the work of Martha Nussbaum, Amartya Sen, Alan Gewirth, Susan Okin, and others is quite compatible with this view.

16. Charles Taylor (1985). See also Yael Tamir (1993), especially Chapter 1, "The Idea of the Person."

17. There is no agreement on the exact number.

18. Retrieved from http://www.fundforpeace.org/web/index.php. Accessed on 2 September 2009.

19. In the words of Grotius: "With these words [on intentions] you may rightly associate the passage of Augustine: 'The eager desire to injure, the cruelty of vengeance, the unappeased and unappeasable mind, the savagery of rebellion, the lust of ruling, and whatever else there is akin, these are the things which are justly censured in warfare. However, when a justifiable cause is not wanting, while these things do indeed convict of wrong the party that makes war, yet they do not render the war itself, properly speaking, unlawful. Hence no restitution is due as a result of a war undertaken under such conditions'" (*Law of War and Peace*, 566). However, intention does play a very important role in a Christian ethics. Aquinas (1947), for example, says: "It can happen that even if the authority declaring a war is legitimate, and even if there is a just cause, nevertheless war is rendered unlawful (*illicitum*) on account of perverse intention" (Vol. II, II-II Q 40, Art. 1). Without a right intention, there could be no Christian participation in war. In spite of the importance of intention Aquinas does not say that a perverse intention renders a war unjust. A recent defense of this principle is given by Anthony Coates (2006).

20. Again, Grotius is a good guide. He says, "The king who undertakes a war for trivial reasons, or to exact unnecessary penalties, is responsible to his subjects for making good the losses which arise therefrom. For he perpetuates a crime, if not

against the foe, yet against his own people, by involving them in so serious an evil on such grounds" (*Law of War and Peace*, 575).

21. Francisco Suárez (1956, 47, 59). My translation.

22. Martin Van Creveld (1991); Mary Kaldor (2007).

23. Francisco De Vitoria (1934, Appendix B, li–lii, or "Second Principal Question, Propositions I and II").

24. Francisco Suárez, *Guerra*. He says: "We should not concede license to any member of the state to seek vengeance, but only within the limits imposed by just defense. . . . Positive law cannot prohibit [the right of self-] defense which has been given by natural law" (1956, 62, 67; my translation).

25. Luban (1985, 204). See also Charles Beitz (1979) and Brian Orend's discussion (2006) on what he calls "minimally just states." Limitations of space preclude a fuller discussion on this important matter.

References

Anscombe, G. E. M. (1981 [1939]). "The Justice of the Present War Examined" in *Collected Philosophical Essays, Volume III: Ethics, Religion, and Politics*. Minneapolis: University of Minnesota Press.

Aquinas, Thomas. (1947). *Summa Theologiae*. New York: Benziger Brothers.

Beitz, Charles. (1979). *Political Theory and International Relations*. Princeton, NJ: Princeton University Press.

Boylan, Michael. (2004). *A Just Society*. Lanham, MD and Oxford: Rowman and Littlefield.

Churchill, Winston, and Franklin Roosevelt. (1941, August 14). *The Atlantic Charter*.

Coady, C. A. J., and Michael O'Keefe. (2002). *Terrorism and Justice*. Melbourne: Melbourne University Press.

Coady, C. A. J. (2008). *Morality and Political Violence*. Cambridge: Cambridge University Press.

Coates, Anthony. (2006). "Culture, the Enemy and the Moral Restraint of War" in *The Ethics of War: Shared Problems in Different Traditions*, ed. Richard Sorabji and David Rodin. Burlington, VT: Ashgate.

Coker, Christopher. (2008). *Ethics and War in the 21st Century*. New York: Routledge.

De Vitoria, Francisco. (1934). "De Juri Belli," trans. John Pawley Bate, in *The Spanish Origin of International Law*, ed. James Brown Scott. Oxford: Clarendon Press.

Eppstein, John. (1935). *The Catholic Tradition of the Law of Nations*. London: Burns, Oates, and Washbourne, Ltd.

Fund for Peace. (2009). "Failed States Index, 2009." Retrieved from http://www.fundforpeace.org/web/index.php

Goodin, Robert E. (2002). "What Is So Special About Our Fellow Countrymen?" in *Patriotism*, ed. Igor Primoratz. New York: Humana Press.

Gordon, John-Stewart. (2009). "On Justice" in *Morality and Justice: Reading Boylan's A Just Society*, ed. John-Stewart Gordon. Lanham, MD: Lexington Books.

Grotius, Hugo. (1962). *The Law of War and Peace*. New York: Bobbs-Merrill Co.

Hobsbawn, E. J. (1990). *Nations and Nationalism since 1780: Programme, Myth, Reality*. Cambridge: Cambridge University Press.

Jászi, Oscar, and John D. Lewis. (1957). *Against the Tyrant*. Glencoe, IL: Free Press.

Jones, C. (1999). *Global Justice: Defending Cosmopolitanism*. Oxford: Oxford University Press.

Kant, Immanuel. (1996). "Perpetual Peace" in *Practical Philosophy*, ed. Mary J. Gregor. Cambridge: Cambridge University Press.

Kaldor, Mary. (2007). *New and Old Wars: Organized Violence in a Global Era, Second Edition*. Stanford, CA: Stanford University Press.

Leitenberg, Milton. (2006). *Deaths in War and Conflicts in the 20th Century*, Cornell University Peace Studies Program, Occasional Paper #29.

Lowry, Christopher, and Udo Schülenk. (2009). "Justice and Global Health" in *Morality and Justice: Reading Boylan's A Just Society*, ed. John-Stewart Gordon. Lanham, MD: Lexington Books.

Luban, David. (1985). "Just War and Human Rights," in *International Ethics*, ed. C. Beitz, et al. Princeton: Princeton University Press.

Luban, David. (2004). "Preventive War." *Philosophy & Public Affairs 32*(3).

Lynd, Staughton. (1968 [2009]). *Intellectual Origins of American Radicalism, New Edition*. Cambridge: Cambridge University Press.

McMahan, Jeff. (2007). "The Sources and Status of Just War Principles." *Journal of Military Ethics 6*(2).

McMahan, Jeff. (2009). *Killing in War*. Oxford: Oxford University Press.

Miller, Seumas. (2009). *Terrorism and Counter-terrorism*. Malden, MA: Blackwell.

Moellendorf, D. (2002). *Cosmopolitan Justice*. Boulder, CO: Westview.

"The National Security Strategy of the United States of America." (2002). Retrieved from http://www.globalsecurity.org/military/library/policy/national/nss020920.pdf

Ohmae, Kenichi. (1995). *The End of the Nation State: The Rise of Regional Economies*. New York: Free Press.

Orend, Brian. (2006). *The Morality of War*. Ontario, CA: Broadview Press.

Palmer-Fernández, Gabriel. (1998). "Civilian Populations in War, Targeting of" in *Encyclopedia of Applied Ethics*, ed. Ruth Chadwick: 505–525. San Diego: Academic Press.

Palmer-Fernández, Gabriel. (2005). "Terrorism, Innocence, and Justice." *Philosophy and Public Policy Quarterly 25*(3): 22–27.

Palmer-Fernández, Gabriel. (2009). "Public Policy: Moving toward Moral Cosmopolitanism" in *Morality and Justice: Reading Boylan's A Just Society*, ed. John-Stewart Gordon. Lanham, MD: Lexington Books.

Potter, Ralph B. (1969). *War and Moral Discourse*. Richmond, VA: John Knox Press.

Primoratz, Igor. (2002). "Michael Walzer's Just War Theory: Some Issues of Responsibility." *Ethical Theory and Moral Practice 5*: 221–243.

Rawls, John. (1998). "Fifty Years after Hiroshima" in *Hiroshima's Shadow*, ed. Kai Bird and Lawrence Lifschultz. Stony Creek, CT: The Pamphleteer's Press.

The Responsibility to Protect. (2001). Ottawa, ON: International Development Research Centre.

Rigstad, M. Retrieved from www.justwartheory.com

Rodin, David, and Henry Shue. (2008). *Just and Unjust Warriors*. Oxford: Oxford University Press.

Salisbury, John of. (1963). *Policratus*, trans. John Dickenson. New York: Russell & Russell.

Scott, James Brown, ed. (1917). "On the Laws of War," trans. John Pawley Bate, in *The Classics of International Law*. Washington, DC: Carnegie Institution.

Shue, Henry. (1996). *Basic Rights: Subsistence, Affluence, and U.S. Foreign Policy*. Princeton, NJ: Princeton University Press.

Spence, Edward H. (2007). "Positive Rights and the Cosmopolitan Community: A Rights-Centered Foundation for Global Ethics." *Journal of Global Ethics 3*(2): 181–202.

Suárez, Francisco. (1956). *Guerra, Intervencion, Paz Internacional*, trans. Luciano Pereña Vicente. Madrid: Espasa-Calpe.

Tamir, Yael. (1993). *Liberal Nationalism*. Princeton, NJ: Princeton University Press.

Taylor, Charles. (1985). "Atomism" in *Philosophy and the Human Sciences: Philosophical Papers 2*. Cambridge: Cambridge University Press.

Tertullian. (1953). *Apology, De Spectaculis*, trans, T.R. Glover. Cambridge: Harvard University Press.

Van Creveld, Martin. (1991). *The Transformation of War*. New York: Free Press.

Vanderpol, Alfred. (1911). *Droit de guerre d'après les Théologiens et les Canonistes du Moyen Age*. Paris: A. Tratin.

Walzer, Michael. (1977). *Just and Unjust Wars: A Moral Argument with Historical Illustrations*. New York: Basic Books.

Wilkins, Burleigh Taylor. (1992). *Terrorism and Collective Responsibility*. New York: Routledge.

PART THREE

NORMATIVE APPLICATIONS

Gender, Identity, and Family

■ Chapter 17 Women on the Move
ROSEMARIE TONG

■ Chapter 18 Gender and Sex Development
SIMONA GIORDANO

■ Chapter 19 Duties to Children
MICHAEL BOYLAN

PART THREE: Gender, Identity, and Family

INTRODUCTION

As we learned earlier in Wanda Teays's essay, the *other* is often overlooked and exploited. Three classes of people generally fit into this class of invisibility: women (particularly those who live in poverty); those whose gender identity is not identical to the mainstream; and children (who often are neither seen nor heard). These three classes and their stories constitute this last section of the book.

In Rosemarie Tong's essay, we begin with a fact about the changing world: people are living longer—particularly in the G-20 nations. In years past people often worked until they died. But now in many countries there are social insurance plans that allow for retirement from work. However, often the health and mobility of these people fails before they actually die, creating a need for eldercare beyond what may have been the case in the past. Who should provide this care? Who will pay for it? These questions create the backdrop for Tong's essay.

Tong cites Zimmerman, Litt, and Bose (ZLB) as setting out four dimensions of this problem: one, the deficits in care to the caregiver's own family when the caregiver must leave home for hours each day or even months and years in the case of immigrant caregivers going abroad for work; two, making caregiving a commodity that is sold like any other commodity in the marketplace; three, the creation of a gendered division of labor that exploits women; four, a tendency to exacerbate race-based, class-based, and gender-based inequities that already exist. Tong's essay emphasizes the first point (with some discussion in passing about the others).

Tong situates her discussion with a case study about providing care to her own father. Because there are no public solutions for this increasingly frequent problem in the United States (save for less-than-optimal Medicaid coverage for the indigent), a private solution is required. After a few missteps, Tong hired an African-American nurse aide named Sharon and allowed Sharon to bring her family to live in Tong's father's house (thus addressing much of ZLB's first point). The foundational principle behind this solution was the application of *caring maternal thinking*. This should be put on par with the normative principles set out in Part One of this book.

However, any private solution to a public problem is flawed in four ways, argues Tong. Too often around the world caregiving is not valued and so it is relegated to the *other*—often female, foreign, and poor. The wages paid are among the lowest since *care* is not valued in power-driven competitive societies: it smacks too much of feminine maternal thinking.

Some countries, such as Germany, Japan, Denmark, and Norway, offer public solutions to this public problem. Tong argues that this is the best approach to take. This is because if a need is important to society, then society should address it, paying decent wages in the process. If this policy were brought about, then societies would be integrating *care* into national social policy. Following Virginia Held, Tong believes that there can be no justice without care. Moving forward on this single policy front will also address societal issues concerning the role of women, immigrants, and the underclass—all of which are necessary for every country to transform itself into a just world order. The use of feminist thinking, therefore, in this one case study is an emblem of how the global community should approach common problems to improve the lot of all the parties involved.

In the second essay, Simona Giordano introduces another group that is treated as the *other,* those with gender dysphoria or gender variance. Around the world there are laws and customs that discriminate and persecute those who are not heterosexual. Lesbian, gay, bisexual, and transsexual people (LGBTs) are oppressed in a number of ways: homosexual acts are illegal in more than seventy countries and in Iran, Kuwait, and Saudi Arabia *it is a capital crime!* Unjust treatment of LGBTs is thus an important issue that global justice must address.

Part of the problem is conceptualizing gender variance. This is because, Giordano argues, it implies value-laden terms such as *normal* and *abnormal. Sex*, as a term, indicates a phenotype with a particular chromosomal makeup. *Gender* is defined as the fulfillment of certain social roles. In this way, gender is a socially constructed term. As with all socially constructed terms, it is subject to social criticism and modification.

Another way of thinking about gender is via clinical psychology and endocrinology. Under this approach gender identity would be the congruence between the phenotype and the person's behavior and his or her feelings about him- or herself. But psychology and endocrinology tend to overemphasize an etiology that is either nurture or nature. There is some evidence for both sides (compare the two case histories), but just like the general debate on nurture versus nature, Giordano believes that some combination of the two is probably correct.

Given Giordano's *biosocial* approach, the question of gender identity individualizes itself as a part of the epistemological question of personal identity. Just as each person's personal identity is understood differently (individually) so also is one's way of being female or male. Thus, gender variance is really better understood as a complex nonlinear continuum through an ongoing process of negotiation that continues throughout life. This model belies the common mutually exclusive static judgment that all females understand their femaleness in the same way and will do so forever (and the same holds true for males). Such an understanding would clearly lift gender variance out of the pathology model because everyone negotiates with essentially the same variables throughout her or his life.

The ethical dimensions of the issue come about when one considers that, because gender variance is not pathological, it should not be treated as such by either medicine or society. If one widens the purview of what medicine *is* to include the relief of suffering and creating a better quality of life (as Giordano suggests), then doctors should assist when they can. This would not be endocrinal treatment (to make them un-gay, for example) but might exhibit itself in helping lesbians procreate via IVF (in vitro fertilization) if they so choose.

When considering international policies, Giordano offers six suggestions: (1) internationally share data from clinical experience and research professionals on how a more liberal context for gender variance can be achieved—the wider the network, the more powerful will be the message to restrictive areas; (2) since gender identity is a complex nonlinear continuum, employ a multidisciplinary approach toward relieving suffering; (3) revise medical opinions in many areas of the world that classify gender variance as a pathology by setting out the epistemological case (outlined above); (4) stay away from embracing any single model as the standard; (5) recognize the individuality involved in gender identity as a subcategory of personal identity in an ongoing process; and (6) eliminate endocrine treatment of gender variance.

Giordano argues that these six international policy suggestions will help protect individuals from unjustly being labeled with a psychiatric diagnosis. Gender has no univocal meaning and thus epistemological contextualism is in order. This will lead to the use of converging models that link gender identity to general personal identity, which is dynamic and part of one's existential state. All these goals are couched in the broader mission of medicine beyond merely curing disease and attending to injuries, toward a mission of addressing human suffering around the world.

In the last essay in this section, I examine another invisible population: children. Every six seconds a child dies from health-related causes. One third of all children on earth are underfed and children are very susceptible to violence through child labor, land mines, war, sex trafficking, and other sorts of exploitation. The first part of the essay defends both positive and negative duties to children. The former exist as the result of a justified rights claim and the latter are due to rectifying bad consequents from an agent, institution, or country (compare to Lillehammer, Illies, and Miller).

In the second part of the essay, the community context of children is examined. The first sort of duty we have toward children flows from their being potential agents in the world. As such they fall under the protection of the shared community worldview imperative and the extended community worldview imperative.

The second sort of duty that we have toward children comes from the actual community in which the child is raised. Several different sorts of communities are outlined and various community-relative standards derive from this examination.

However, one thing clear beyond community standards is that positive duties to children can be understood via the convention of univocal contracts (a third source of duty). A univocal contract is one in which one party sets the terms of the contract. These, in turn, come in two flavors: *unrestricted,* in which a "take it or leave it" approach is taken, and *restricted,* in which one party sets down all the rules and the other has no option but to accept. The moral duty incurred by the contract maker of the restricted univocal contract is rather high. It is the contention of this essay that parenthood is rather like the restricted univocal contract.

A fourth source of positive duty to children is that of love. This creates a conceptual conundrum. Duties are the sort of thing that can be commanded: "*X* must do *y*." In order for *x* to be ordered to do *y*, doing *y* must be under *x*'s control. But love seems to be out of one's direct control; therefore, it seems that it cannot be a duty. The essay contends that there is an understanding of love that can be commanded and so would constitute another justification for positive duties to children.

The last section of the paper constitutes a number of policy suggestions on how the international community might fulfill its positive duties to the children of the world.

CHAPTER SEVENTEEN

Women on the Move

ROSEMARIE TONG
The University of North Carolina at Charlotte

Abstract

The rapid aging of the world's population warrants a response from developed and developing countries as to who should care for elderly people and for how much compensation, if any. A growing trend that requires scrutiny is that of relatively poor immigrant women who leave behind their families and countries to provide elderly people in wealthier countries with care services. As a result of meeting the eldercare needs of rich people, relatively poor immigrant women may create a "deficit of care" among the dependents they leave behind. In this chapter, I argue that ordinarily care deficits should not be viewed as mainly the fault of individual women, but primarily as the fault of uncaring marketplaces, governments, or individual men who do not do their fair share of carework.

Key Words

carework, deficit of care, immigrant women, long-term eldercare

---

The world's population is aging in a dramatic manner. In 2006, more than 500 million people were at or above age sixty-five. By the year 2030, that number will swell to 1 billion (Department of State, 2007). More specifically, in the year 2030, 20 percent of the US population will be age sixty-five or older (Daniels, 2006). Ten years later, the number of US people in their eighties will be larger than the number of US people under the age of five (Daniels, 2006). In Japan, where life expectancy is already 77.6 for males and 84.3 for females (McCallum, 2001), there are predictions that the Japanese government will no longer be able to fund long-term eldercare by the year 2050 (Tsuno and Homma, 2009, 9). The situation is not much different in many developing countries. For example, on the continent of Asia, which holds about 60 percent of the world population, those who will be sixty-five and older by 2050 will increase by 314 percent to a total of 857 million. Eastern Asia's aged sixty-five and over population will increase by 243 percent; Southeast Asia's will increase by 430 percent; and South Asia's will increase by 393 percent (Goh, 2005, 90–91).

Although increased life expectancy is in many ways a cause for global celebration (Daniels, 2006), the benefits of large numbers of people living longer lives are accompanied with significant costs, some of them financial, but others social and personal. From where will the funds come to meet the heavy long-term care needs of increasingly aging populations? More pointedly, who will and who *should* provide the actual day-to-day care that elderly people require? Whose responsibility are they, and may that responsibility be shifted from the shoulders of family members (if they exist) to the shoulders of strangers or the state? May relatively rich people rely on relatively poor people to do their carework for them? May men expect women to do their carework for them, as in China where the wives of first-born sons do their filial labors for them? Finally, may the burden of eldercare in developed countries be transferred from the laps of "their" women (Hooyman and Gonyea, 1995, 326) to the laps of immigrant women from developing countries?

From a feminist point of view, the questions I have just posed are particularly pressing. Specifically, Mary K. Zimmerman, Jacqueline S. Litt, and Christine E. Bose (2006, 10) observe that we are undergoing a "global crisis in care." As they see it, this world trauma has four dimensions: one, the deficits in care that families experience when some or all of the women in them leave home for hours each day, or even years or months at a time to do paid carework either in their own country or in other countries; two, the "commodification" of carework as just another product to be sold in the marketplace; three, the power of large, multipronged organizations as well as ubiquitous "structural adjustment policies" to create systems of carework that add to already unfair "gendered divisions of labor"; and four, a tendency to reinforce race-based and class-based as well as gender-based inequities, thereby increasing the divide between rich and poor countries (10–11). In this chapter, I focus primarily on the first of these dimensions. I argue that care deficits should not be viewed as mainly the fault of individual women, but primarily as the fault of uncaring marketplaces, governments, or individual men who do not do their fair share of carework.

A Personal Anecdote

Although anecdotes are not always a good method to use in a scholarly essay, one of the motivating factors behind this chapter is the set of challenges that I faced for nearly five years as I tended to my progressively ill father's healthcare needs in his own home. At first, my father's care was manageable for me even though I had a full-time job and my own household to maintain. He could get around on a walker, drive to the store to get groceries, get in and out of bed, make simple meals, and so forth. But as my father weakened and fell prey to the disease consequences of diabetes—congestive heart failure, arthritis, irritable bowel syndrome, and more—he gradually lost his ability to take care of himself. Before I knew it, my father was bound to a wheelchair, unable to perform basic "activities of daily living," the long-term care industry's term for the things people need to be able to do on their own to function in society (Kane and Kane, 1987, 4). Like it or not, people who cannot toilet, bathe, dress, and feed themselves are in trouble. Unless others help them, they will deteriorate and most likely die.

Because my father was very obese (around 265 pounds), I could not turn him over in bed or diaper him. Desperate for help, I called upon my two adult sons (at that time, single, employed men in their late twenties) for assistance. They did as much as they could, but it soon became apparent to me that they were sacrificing their life plans (for example, further schooling in one instance and marriage in the other) to help me out with their grandfather. I then asked my husband for help, but he told me, very honestly, that he simply could not "get involved." My father's condition was more than his psyche could stand. He thought my father should be in a skilled nursing home, especially because keeping him up in his own home was jeopardizing my job. Why should I, let alone he, risk losing our jobs because of too many absentee days spent caring for my father? Didn't I understand that if either of us lost our jobs, let alone both of us, we could wake up one day without the funds for our own long-term care?

I understood my husband's position all too well. Like him, I was concerned about being able to finance our eldercare as well as my father's eldercare. But I had promised my father that he would die in his own home no matter what. Moreover, even if I reneged on my promise, I simply could not afford to put my father in a skilled nursing home, not at the cost of about $70,000 a year (Andrews, 2009). Admittedly, because my father had next to nothing left in his life savings, he would have swiftly qualified for Medicaid, the US welfare program for impoverished people. But because most good skilled nursing homes shun Medicaid patients (Mann and Westmoreland, 2004, 417), I worried that I would have to place my dad in a less-than-good, perhaps even bad skilled nursing home. Soon that thought started to drive me crazy.

So after identifying what personal costs I could cut from my budget (new clothes, beauty salon visits, doctor's and dentist's appointments, pleasure trips, generous gift-giving, expensive foods, and so forth), I decided to contact a home healthcare agency for help. Although their price for eldercare was high, it was not as high as a skilled nursing home's would be. I thought I could afford eight to twelve hours of it daily for my father. That care, combined with just a bit of help from my boys, could provide my father with decent homecare, even though he would be without any help in his home for some of the night.

I wish I could say this arrangement worked. But it did not. In the first place, I felt badly that most of what I paid my father's caregivers went to their agency or for government taxes. Second, some of the careworkers the agency sent my way were not all that reliable, mostly because they were trying to take care of their own families or working another job on the side. Third, some of the careworkers were not really suited for carework. They were simply doing it because they could not get any other paid work. Fourth, some of the careworkers were very fearful that if they did not follow the agency's rules and regulations to the T, they would either get fired or be sued by me if anything bad happened to my father. I wound up having heated arguments with some of these caregivers. For example, one of my father's first home helpers, whom I eventually discharged, would not let him use his walker to get to and from the bathroom toilet. She insisted that is was safer for him to defecate and urinate in a bedpan or a diaper. My father and I objected, insisting, first, that the bathroom was less than thirty feet from his bed and, second, that she could slowly walk with him to and from the bathroom. But she did not like our solution to my father's problem. I suspected that her convenience rather than concerns about my father's safety were her real reason for not wanting him to go down the hall to the bathroom.

Before too long, I realized the home-health agency arrangement was not working for me or my father. Not only did I find it difficult to work with some of my father's professional caregivers, I also found the agency's bills increasingly too steep for my overall budget. It occurred to me that I could lessen the total cost of care for my father if I directly advertised for a careworker and paid that person a bit over the minimum wage for however many hours of help I could afford. Within a short time, an immigrant Filipino woman with a visa and an immigrant Mexican woman with no legal documents came to my door. They offered to work for less than the minimum wage if necessary. They also stressed that they had no family obligations in this country, a plus from my way of thinking at the time. I could also tell that their cheerful personalities would brighten my father's day. Yet I felt uncomfortable about hiring either of them, particularly the immigrant Mexican woman without documents. I worried how long they would stay in the United States. I also worried about finding myself in some sort of Zoë Baird situation. In 1992, then president-elect Clinton nominated Baird to the post of attorney general. Soon after, news came to light that she and her husband had for years employed a Peruvian couple to live in their home, one serving as their nanny and the other serving as their driver. Because the couple was not in the country legally, Baird's nomination was challenged. Clinton's opponents asked whether Baird would be able to uphold US immigration policy, a policy that prohibits people from doing what she and her husband did. Soon after the crisis erupted, Clinton accepted Baird's withdrawal of her nomination, having no choice under the circumstances (Krauss, 1993, 122).

As I mulled over my options, Sharon, an African-American nurse aide who helped care for my father when he went to a skilled nursing home for rehabilitation subsequent to surgery, contacted me. She said she had established her own home healthcare business, and was willing to take care of my father for a price I could afford. Because Sharon lived nearby my father, she could even structure her work schedule (she had other clients at the time) so that she could check in on my father throughout the day and at least once during the night.

My father liked Sharon very much. He told me she massaged him, cooked his favorite meals, watched television with him, played cards with him, diapered him in a way that did not shame him, and so forth. I felt relieved. Yet I felt badly that I could not pay Sharon more than she charged, though she pointed out that I paid her better than her other clients. So I let her bring her youngest child and her new grandchild, an infant, to my father's home. She met their needs as well as my father's in an amazingly cheerful, calm, upbeat way. I was literally in awe of Sharon's capacity to provide care attentively. Her actions were instances of what feminist philosopher Sara Ruddick calls maternal thinking, the kind of thinking those who do the work of good mothers display. Maternal thinkers are emotionally as well as intellectually engaged in preserving their children's very lives, helping them grow, and teaching them how to be socially acceptable people who can properly respond to others' needs and interests (Ruddick, 1995). So good was Sharon's care of my father, however, that at times I was threatened by it. I felt I had let my father down because of my unwillingness to quit my job to focus totally on his needs in the way that Sharon did.

Before long, I let Sharon move herself and her family into my father's house (which, by the way, I owned). I also gave her an old automobile. In turn, Sharon stopped charging me for my father's care. All of her and her family's basic needs (shelter, food, transportation) were now covered. However, I still felt badly about the situation, even though Sharon told me that life in my father's home was far better for her and her family than life in the apartment they had left behind. Periodically, I would give Sharon a cash gift or buy presents for her family members. By the time my father died, Sharon had become spouselike in stature. I found it difficult to ask her to move out of my father's house so that I could sell it to offset the expenses I had incurred providing eldercare for him. Eventually, I got the courage to tell Sharon that she and her family had six months to relocate. I was thrilled when, one day, she told me she had found employment for good money. I gave Sharon all of my father's furniture, plus moving expenses. Every once in a while, I think about Sharon and her family, wondering if they are indeed faring well. I also wonder about what happened to the immigrant Filipino woman and the immigrant Mexican woman who came to my door. Did they ever find work? Were they still in the country? How much better, or worse, was their situation because I chose to employ Sharon instead of them?

Guilt Trips

As is my tendency, my personal experience prompted me to do considerable research about both native-born and immigrant eldercare workers in the United States. I soon found empirical data that confirmed my suspicion: namely, that the way I solved my father's eldercare needs was not that unusual. The demand for *affordable*, community-based or home-based healthcare and personal care workers is very high, and it is being supplied primarily by women who are willing to do eldercare work for relatively low wages. Although some of these women are native-born women of color, an increasing number of them in the United States, for example, are immigrants (Polverini and Lamura, 2004; Browne and Braun, 2008, 17). Interestingly, Ron Hoppe, a founder of Worldwide Health Staff Associates, points out that Americans are not much interested in working for his company, which cannot pay its workers any more than fast-food businesses do. The only people, continues Hoppe, who do seem to want to work for him are immigrants, many of whom come from caring cultures and all of whom are accustomed to working long hours for less money than Americans are.

Thinking about Hoppe's observation, the fact that the women who came to my door were an African-American, a Filipina, and a Mexican did not seem accidental. Carework is, as Dawn Lyon claims, increasingly "racialized." It is work for which women of color supposedly have particular gifts. Observes Lyon:

> In a recent study of women migrants from Bulgaria and Hungary in Italy and the Netherlands, interviews with native women expose some of the characterizations of migrant women working in the field of care as "naturally" gifted for such a role . . . in contrast to their Italian counterparts. Several interviewees made much of their employees' willingness to labor without complaint and celebrated their apparent subservience as personal (or national) characteristics—rather than, for instance, an indication of their relative powerlessness. The migrant women were applauded for their acceptance of low wages by the native women, who at the same time admonished their Italian counterparts who would demand double for similar work. Furthermore, distinctions were made between different migrant groupings, based on stereotypes that appear to be widespread. For instance, women from some Latin American countries, according to the interviewees, have "sweet" temperaments making them good carers (but not as good cleaners). [Lyon 2002, 222–223]

The operating assumption of many people is that careworkers should work "for free" and that they should keep smiling no matter how adverse their work environment may be. Asking to be paid for carework is somehow a sign of ethical deficiency, as is drawing limits about how much care one will provide a client.

Relying on immigrant women to do low-paid carework seems to be the order of the day, all things considered. No matter how poor a country is, if there is a country poorer than it, then that country may be a source for female caregivers willing to work for very low wages. And, of course, countries high up on the economic ladder see no reason not to rely on poor countries to supply them with careworkers. For example, in the United Kingdom, 35 percent of the nurses who work in the eldercare environment are immigrants and most of them work for low wages. In London, more than 60 percent of the people who do eldercare work are immigrants (Cangiano, Shutes, Spencer, and Leeson, 2009, 182). These workers are nearly exclusively women, and they come from Zimbabwe, Poland, Nigeria, the Philippines, and India. Their employers like their "work ethic" and their "warmth, respect, empathy, trust and patience in the care relationship" (Lan, 2002, 184). They also like the fact that they are willing to work for wages that native-born eldercare workers find outrageously low.

As in the United Kingdom, in Taiwan there is an exceptionally high demand for immigrant careworkers. Since the early 1980s, significant numbers of immigrant women without legal papers have worked in Taiwanese households (Lan, 2002, 188) thereby enabling Taiwanese women in the paid workforce to keep their jobs. Comments Pei-Chan Lan: "The filial duty of serving aging parents is transferred first from the son to the daughter-in-law (a gender transfer); later, it is outsourced to migrant careworkers (a market transfer)" (Lan, 2002, 188). As a result of citizens' pressure, the Taiwanese government has decided to legalize large numbers of immigrant careworkers. Specifically, in 1992, Taiwan started to grant work permits to "domestic caretakers" who agreed to care for severely ill or disabled people, children under the age of twelve, or elders over the age of seventy (Lan, 2002, 171). Moreover, it began to describe the importation of careworkers from the Philippines and Indonesia in particular "as a solution to the growing demand for paid care work among both nuclear households and the aging population" (Lan, 2002, 172).

Interestingly, Taiwanese female employers sometimes bond with their Filipina employees. They ally with them against husbands who are viewed as tyrannical or exclusively demanding: men who either refuse to do carework or do not appreciate its value. But, at other times, no such bond is created and the Filipina employee is treated poorly by her Taiwanese employer(s) or client(s). She may be abused verbally or discriminated against on account of her race. Not having any way to defend herself against mistreatment, the Filipina employee, like other migrant eldercare workers, may do what she is told to do and leave it at that.

The fact that she has legal documents does not mean she can quit and secure another job that pays well enough to support herself and her family back home.

If it is easy to take advantage of immigrant elder careworkers with proper legal documents, it is far easier to intimidate, harass, or bully immigrant elder careworkers without legal documents. Fearing deportation or slipping into jobs as sex workers, undocumented eldercare workers are a particularly vulnerable group of careworkers. Earlier in this chapter, I mentioned that during the period I cared for my father, I did not want to follow Zoë Baird's lead. Baird could have easily afforded to hire a nanny with legal papers to care for her children. Her decision to instead hire an undocumented worker opened her up to harsh criticism. The media portrayed her as nearly as heartless as the rich New York businesswoman who said that her ideal careworker would be a person who could not "leave the country, who basically [did] not know anyone in New York, who basically [did] not have a life" (Change, 2006, 43–45). The words of this wealthy woman are, of course, disconcerting. They seem to reduce the "ideal careworker" to a mere means: that is, a thing or instrument to serve one's own interests with no concern for the interests of the person one is using. Clearly, all too many relatively advantaged women are oblivious to the fact that their advantages are made possible by other women's disadvantages.

Women Are in This Situation Together

Reflecting on everything I have written above, I comfort myself with the thought that I did not use Sharon as a mere means to my goal of being able to provide my father with cost-effective, good care—that is, care inexpensive enough to allow me to stay in the paid workforce *and* meet his care needs well. To be sure, I did not pay Sharon nearly enough for her valuable eldercare work. Still, I paid her more than the going rate, and I gave her fringe benefits like food and lodging, though not healthcare insurance and a pension plan. Moreover, I made it easy for her to care for her own child and grandchild even as she cared for my father. Her children did not suffer from a deficit of care because she was caring for my father. Still, I felt guilty, and understandably so. My residual guilt had two sources: one, my espousal of care ethics, and two, my belief that private solutions to public problems just make those public problems worse.

As an exponent of care ethics, I agree with Virginia Held that care is more fundamental than justice insofar as social functioning is concerned. According to Held, there can be care without justice, but not justice without care in the sense that "without care no child would survive" and, therefore, no society, capable of developing just policies, would be possible (Held, 2006, 17). Moreover, like Carol Gilligan and Nel Noddings, two of the feminist thinkers most associated with an ethics of care, Held thinks that women are far more linked to caring ways of thinking and acting than are men. She emphasizes, however, that men need to develop their caregiving skills. It is simply not fair to burden women, many of whom work a full day outside the home, with a disproportionate share of society's unwaged caregiving tasks. Finally, and most relevant to this article, Held presents an exceptionally demanding view of care according to which a person cannot be truly caring unless he or she has the feelings and emotions appropriate to care. If a daughter, for example, cares for her aging father simply because it is her duty to do and not because she loves her father and is attuned to his feelings, then her actions are morally incomplete.

Why, then, was I not willing to give up my job in the paid workforce in order to care for my father full-time for one to five years? Was it for the *feminist* reason that when a woman in the paid workforce leaves it, she substantially erodes the economic progress women have made the last quarter century? Or was it for the *filial* reason that my parents—two Czech immigrants—had sacrificed ever so much for me to get the kind of well-paying job I had? Or was it for the *human-hearted* reason that Sharon begged me to keep my job so that she could keep hers? Or was it for the *capitalist* reason that somewhere along the line, I had forgotten my 1970s desire to content myself with living a sustainable life? Did my husband and I really need the kind of upper-middle class we have, complete with large house, two high-end cars, costly vacation trips to far-away places, and so forth?

To be honest, I do not know which of the reasons above accounted most for my unwillingness to quit my job in the paid workforce. But I do know that I would not have had to ask some of the questions I just raised had the United States joined other developed countries and offered its citizens universal healthcare insurance, including universal long-term eldercare insurance. Regrettably, the United States does not view long-term eldercare as "a public resource and responsibility" (Tronto, 2005, 135). For this reason, it "privatizes" long-term eldercare—that is, it transforms it into a market commodity that people can purchase. But this way of meeting people's needs for long-term eldercare does not work well for poor people. On the contrary, "privatizing" long-term eldercare best serves rich people who, like I, have the income to hire someone like Sharon.

Sadly, by taking care of my father "privately," I may have served four unworthy goals, according to feminist thinker Joan Tronto. First, because I had enough money to hire Sharon and stay fully employed in my well-paid job, I increased social inequality. Specifically, I was able to work more productively, thereby gaining merit pay that widened the economic gap between me and Sharon. Second, by handling my eldercare problem the way I did, I increased the chances that workers would be exploited. In other words, by employing Sharon in the way I did, I made it more difficult for Sharon to forge connections with similarly situated workers to lobby for things of importance to them. Third, whether I like to admit it or not, I encouraged myself to think that I was doing Sharon a "favor" by hiring her. I made myself willfully "ignorant" about the fact that my choice to hire Sharon made me part of the problem of social inequality rather than part of the solution to social inequality. Fourth, and perhaps most importantly, by hiring Sharon to care for my father, I made it harder for all of us to engage in meaningful dialogue about the difference between "necessary care" and "personal service." Did Sharon really *need* to provide my father with all the care I purchased for him, or could he have done without some of it? Did I really need all the help Sharon gave me, or was I just trying to make my life easy? (Tronto, 2005, 136–137).

If the United States had a *public* system of long-term eldercare—a system like the ones that exist in other developed countries—I might not have found myself in the quandary I did. I would not have had to hire Sharon with private money; instead, I could have used public money to hire her or the Filipina woman who came to my door. Moreover, if the United States had a public system of long term eldercare, then it could provide women like Sharon and the Filipina woman not only with decent wages and benefit packages but also with ways to protect themselves from exploitation and discrimination.

Consider that although Germany and Japan are distinct countries culturally speaking, they provide remarkably similar publicly mandated long-term eldercare programs (Harrington, Geraedts, and Heller, 2002; Ihara, 2000), programs that countries like the United States could adopt without too much trouble. Germany inaugurated its mandatory long-term eldercare program in 1994. The program is financed by contributions from employers, employees, and pensioners. It offers benefits either in the form of home-based services provided by publicly authorized caregivers (domestic or immigrant) or cash subsidies that beneficiaries may use to pay either familial caregivers (Harrington, Geraedts, and Heller, 2002) or privately contracted caregivers. Interestingly, far more immigrant careworkers than domestic careworkers appear on elderly Germans' doorsteps. Apparently, most Germans view caring for the elderly as particularly onerous work—work better suited for Eastern European migrant women than German women. In a bid to interest at least some German women in caring for the elderly, one entrepreneurial German eldercare agency decided it could solve two social problems with one initiative: namely, hiring prostitutes eager to do any sort of decent work that permits them to get off the street and out from under the thumbs of pimps. Warding off critics of this recruitment initiative, Rita Kuehn, head of the agency, pointed out that prostitutes are well-equipped to serve as excellent eldercare workers. They have, she stated, "good people skills, aren't easily disgusted, and have zero fear of physical contacts" (Duke, 2006, 685). In short, German prostitutes are willing to do the kind of taxing eldercare that many other German women (and, of course, German men) are not willing to do. It is not easy to care for disintegrating bodies that smell of death in many cases.

Like Germany, Japan has a publicly mandated long-term eldercare program. The program came into existence partly in response to the publication of *Yellow Fall*, a novel that hit Japanese bookstores in 1995 (Sae, 1995). The novel tells the story of a middle-aged man who cannot get his wife to help him care for her frail and demented in-laws. The point of the novel is that Japanese women can no longer be expected to care for elderly relatives, most especially mothers-in-law. Unlike traditional Japanese women, "modernized" or "Westernized" Japanese women do not think they have an obligation to sacrifice personal pursuits to wait on their elders hand and foot.

Although the Japanese long-term eldercare program is remarkably similar to the German program, it does not permit elderly Japanese to use public funds to pay familial caregivers (World Health Report, 2002). Responding to Japanese women's fears that were such familial payments permitted, Japanese women would be pressured by elderly in-laws to come to work for them, the Japanese government decided it would be best not to permit money to pass between the hands of family members. The issue here is not whether the only reason holding a woman back from caring for her elderly family members is monetary, but whether she wants to care for them or any other elderly persons at all. Not all people want to do paid carework. They would rather do other paid work. For example, a Japanese woman might prefer working as an administrative assistant for less money than working as a caregiver for her mother-in-law for more money (Ihara, 2000).

Perhaps the most enthusiastic supporters of long-term eldercare are Norway and Denmark. Their policies are even more elder-friendly than those of Germany and Japan. Unlike many other citizens of developed countries, Norwegians and Danes are willing to pay the high taxes that make such a benefit possible. However, they do not abuse the benefit of long-term eldercare, viewing it as some sort of "entitlement" they should use even if they do not really need it. On the contrary, they try to use the least amount of this benefit as possible so that their descendants will be able to enjoy it in the future. For this reason, most Norwegians and Danes work well into their seventies; they maintain a healthy lifestyle; and they live as independently as possible. Most remarkably, Norwegians and Danes are, as a population, "feminist." In other words, they truly value carework as *worthy of pay* (Williams, 2000). For example, the Danish state "is based on the explicit principle of social inclusion for older people and women of working age, who are relieved of any *duty* [sic] to provide unpaid care work" (Blackman, 2001, 84). Still, Danes do not view their country's "social inclusion principle" as excusing them from providing any type of "free" family caregiving whatsoever. Most Danes feel obligated to enhance the care their elderly family members receive from paid careworkers in ways that only family members can (Stuart and Weinrich, 2001).

Long-term eldercare as it is implemented in Norway and Denmark is, I realize, an ideal that is attainable only in countries that are both affluent and populated by relatively frugal people—that is, by people willing to settle for less than the best when it comes to health care. Moreover, the kind of long-term eldercare Norway and Denmark offers its citizens can work only if people are willing to let the state come into their homes, and there are all sorts of problems with the state coming into one's home. As soon as someone opens their door to state-subsidized services, they subject themselves to a level of scrutiny and supervision that may lead to misunderstandings. For example, familial caregivers may find themselves asked some uncomfortable questions about loved ones' cuts, bruises, burns, weight loss, and the like. Accusations may be made on the basis of little solid evidence and families may rue the day they asked for public assistance (Tornstam, 1988).

Another source of tension and stress between familial caregivers and publicly paid home care providers is disagreement about what is best for the person needing care. For example, publicly paid home care providers may think it is in the best interest of a diabetic client to adhere to a very low carbohydrate diet, a diet that families as well as the client may find overly restrictive. When told they should stop giving favorite foods to their loved one, families may protest that their father is eighty-eight years old and that one of his few remaining pleasures is eating a hot fudge sundae. A small gain in health status is simply not worth denying dad his favorite treat, not when he does not have many more years to live, the last of which may be spent in a semiconscious state. Unimpressed by such reasoning, publicly paid home care providers may chide families. They may say something like, "You don't want your father to get worse, do you?"

Making Long-Term Eldercare a Priority

If the United States were to follow Norway's and Denmark's example and provide its aging population with publicly mandated long-term care, who would step forward to deliver that care? Paid family members? Paid domestic professionals? Paid immigrant professionals? Except in countries like Norway and Denmark that acknowledge carework as valuable public work worthy of decent compensation, there is at present a growing tendency to use immigrants as elder careworkers. Sadly, even when carework is recognized as *public* work, it is not necessarily also recognized "as highly skilled and valuable work" (Willett, 2001, 94)—as work just as important to society's well-being as the kind of work lawyers, physicians, engineers, information technologists, etc. do. If it were so recognized, more men as well as women would want to do it and more people like me would want to do it. The fact that fewer and fewer family members *want* to care for their aging relatives is not a good sign. On the contrary, it is a sign that an increasing number of people may, truth be told, think that service work is "low-class" work—work best done by a "class of poor, black, Third-World, mainly female workers who provide commodities, fast food, and other services for the wealthy" (Weir, 2005, 320–321). Although there is nothing inherently wrong for a woman like me to hire a woman like Sharon or a woman like the Filipina immigrant, there is something fundamentally wrong about not valuing carework enough. Women like me must demand that our governments use public funds to pay decent wages to those who do carework, and women like me need to do our fair share of carework or, in lieu of carework, work that makes an equal contribution to the formation and maintenance of "meaningful human relationships" (Willett, 2001, 96). Somehow or another we have to create the kind of world in which carework is *good* work—the kind of work for which one might reasonably leave one's home country to migrate to another country. Regrettably, we do not live in such a world yet, and so women like me must continue to wonder whether we do more harm than good by hiring women like Sharon or like the Filipina immigrant who came to my doorstep.

References

Andrews, Michelle. (2009). "4 Ways to Cover the Cost of Long-term Care." *U.S. News and World Report.* Retrieved from http://health.usnews.com/articles/health/best-nursing-homes/2009/03/11/4-ways-to-cover-the-cost-of-long-term-care.html?msg=socialweb_

Blackman, Tim. (2001). "Conclusion: Issues and Solutions" in *Social Care and Social Exclusion*, ed. Tim Blackman, Sally Brodhurst, and Janet Convery: 20–84. New York: Palgrave Publishers.

Browne, Colette V., and Braun, Kathryn L. (2008). "Globalization, Women's Migration, and the Long-Term-Care Workforce." *The Gerontologist 48*(1): 16–24.

Cangiano, Alessio, Isabel Shutes, Sarah Spencer, and George Leeson. (2009). "Migrant Care Workers in Ageing Societies: Research Findings in the United Kingdom" Report, COMPAS: ESRC Centre on Migration, Policy, and Society: University of Oxford 182.

Change, Grace. (2006). "Disposable Domestics: Immigrant Women Workers in the Global Economy" in *Global Dimensions of Gender and Carework*, ed. Mary K. Zimmerman, Jacqueline S. Litt, and Christine E. Bose: 43–45. Stanford, CA: Stanford Social Sciences.

Curry, Natasha. (1998). "Elder Care Across the Globe. CareGuide@Home." Retrieved from http://69.20.9.230/modules.php?op=modload&name=CG_Resources&file=article&sid=965

Daniels, Norman. (2006). "Equity and Population Health: Toward a Broader Bioethics Agenda." *Hastings Center Report 36*(4): 22–35.

Department of State and the Department of Health and Human Services, National Institute on Aging, National Institutes of Health. (2007). *Why Population Aging Matters: A Global Perspective.*

Duke, Katy. (2006). "Project Retrains Prostitutes as Care Workers for Elderly People." *British Medical Journal 332*: 7543.

Gilligan, Carol. (1982). *In a Different Voice.* Boston: Harvard University Press.

Goh, Victor H. H. (2005). "Aging in Asia: A Cultural, Socio-Economical and Historical Perspective." *The Aging Male 8*(2): 90–91.

Gostin, Lawrence O. (2008). "The International Migration and Recruitment of Nurses." *JAMA 299*(15): 1827–1828.

Harrington, Charlene A., Max Geraedts, and Geoffrey V. Heller. (2002). "Germany's Long Term Care Insurance Model: Lessons for the United States." *Journal of Public Health Policy 23*(1): 44–65.

Held, Virginia. (2006). *The Ethics of Care: Personal, Political and Global.* New York: Oxford University Press.

Hooyman, Nancy, and Judith Gonyea. (1995). *Feminist Perspectives on Family Care: Policies for Gender Justice.* Thousand Oaks, CA: Sage Publications.

Ihara, Kazuhito. (2000). "Japan's Policies on Long-term Care for the Aged: The Gold Plan and the Long-term Care Insurance Program." New York: International Longevity Center. Retrieved from http://unpan1.un.org/intradoc/groups/public/documents/APCITY/UNPAN023659.pdf

Kane, Robert A. and Rosalie L. Kane. (1987). *Long-term Care: Principles, Programs, and Policies.* New York: Springer Publishing Co.

Kingma, Mireille. (2007). "Nurses on the Move: A Global Overview." *Health Research and Educational Trust 42*(3): 1291–1292.

Kittay, Eva F., and Ellen K. Feder. (2002). *The Subject of Care: Feminist Perspectives on Dependency.* Lanham, MD: Rowman & Littlefield.

Krauss, Clifford. (1993, 17 January). "The New Presidency: Justice Department; Nominee Pays Fee for Hiring of Illegal Aliens." *New York Times*: 122.

Lan, Pei-Chia. (2002). "Among Women: Migrant Domestics and Their Taiwanese Employers across Generations" in *Global Woman: Nannies, Maids, and Sex Workers in the New Economy*, ed. Barbara Ehrenreich and Arlie Russell Hochschild. New York: Holt Paperback.

Lyon, Dawn. (2002). "The Organization of Care Work in Italy: Gender and Migrant Labor in the New Economy." *Indiana Journal of Global Legal Studies 207*(18): 212–213.

Mann, Cindy, and Tim Westmoreland. (2004). "Attending to Medicaid." *Journal of Law, Medicine, and Ethics 32*(3): 417.

McCallum, John. (2001). "Health in the 'Grey' Millennium: Romanticism versus Complexity?" in *Aging: Culture, Health, and Social Change*, ed. David N. Weisstub, David C. Thomasma, Serge Gauthier, and George F. Tomossy: 29–42. Boston: Kluwer Academic Publishers.

Mills, Edward J., et al. (2008). "Should Active Recruitment of Health Workers from Sub-Saharan Africa be Viewed as a Crime?" *The Lancet 371*: 687–688.

Noddings, Nel. (1984 [2003]). *Caring: A Feminine Approach to Ethics and Moral Education, Second Edition.* Berkeley: University of California Press.

Polverini, Francesca, and Giovanni Lamura. (2004, April). "Labour Supply in Care Services," National Report on Italy, by the European Foundation for the Improvement of Living and Working Conditions (Ancona, Italy: INRCA).

Romoren, Tor Inge. (2003). "The Carer Careers of Son and Daughter Primary Carers of Their Very Old Parents in Norway." *Ageing & Society 23*: 471–85.

Ruddick, Sara. (1995). *Maternal Thinking: Toward a Politics of Peace.* Boston: Beacon Press.

Sae, Shuichi. (1995). *Koraku* [*Yellow Fall*]. Tokyo: Shincho-Sha.

Schmid, Hillel. (2005). "The Israeli Long-term Care Insurance Law: Selected Issues in Providing Home Care Services to the Frail Elderly." *Health and Social Care in the Community 13*(3): 191–200.

Stuart, Mary, and Michael Weinrich. (2001). "Home-and Community-Based Long-Term Care: Lessons from Denmark." *The Gerontologist 41*(4): 474–80.

Tornstam, Lars. (1988). "Abuse of the Elderly in Denmark and Sweden: Results from a Population Study." *Journal of Elder Abuse and Neglect* 1(1): 35–44.

Tronto, Joan. (2005). "Care as the Work of Citizens" in *Women and Citizenship,* ed. Marilyn Friedman. New York: Oxford University Press.

Tsuno, Norifumi, and Akira Homma. (2009). "Ageing in Asia—The Japan Experience." *Ageing International* 34(1): 1–14.

Weir, Allison. (2005). "The Global Universal Caregiver: Imaging Women's Liberation in the New Millennium." *Constellations 12*(3): 308–330.

Willett, Cynthia. (2001). *The Soul of Justice: Social Bonds and Racial Hubris.* Ithaca, NY: Cornell University Press.

Williams, Joan. (2000). *Unbending Gender: Why Family and Work Conflict and What to Do about It.* New York: Oxford University Press.

World Health Report. (2002). "The Payer Systems." *Hospitals & Health Networks 77*(7): 54.

Zimmerman, Mary K., Jacqueline S. Litt, and Christine E. Bose. (2006). *Global Dimensions of Gender and Carework.* Stanford, CA: Stanford Social Sciences.

Zivotofsky, Ari Z. and Naomi Zivotofsky. (2009). "Are Healthcare Workers Chained to Their Country of Origin?" *AJOB 9*(3): 16–18.

CHAPTER EIGHTEEN

Gender and Sex Development

SIMONA GIORDANO
University of Manchester

Abstract

People with gender identity disorder (GID) are victims of various forms of injustice: discrimination, abuse, violence. Moreover, GID is classified as a psychiatric condition. The classification is inherently stigmatizing. Yet, should GID disappear from diagnostic manuals, access to publicly funded medical treatment could be restricted. In order to understand how gender variance should be understood and treated, we should understand what 'gender' is, and what a 'normal' versus an 'abnormal' gender development and identification are. This essay puts some order in the vast literature on sex and gender development and identification. It discusses the notion of gender, and explores the vexed question of whether gender is a primarily biological or psychological acquisition. The ethical implications in terms of access to treatment are also discussed.

Key Words

gender, sex development, gender identity disorder

Author's note: I wish to thank the sociologist Monica Santoro for her comments on this paper, and John Harris for telling me that all this actually makes sense.

> *"Man is double. There are two beings in him: an individual being which has its foundation in the organism . . . and a social being. . . . This duality of our nature has as its consequence in the practical order . . . and in the order of thought. . . . In so far as he belongs to society, the individual transcends himself, both when he thinks and when he acts."*
> —Emile Durkheim (1912, 13)

People with gender dysphoria, or gender variance, are often the victims of great injustice. Many are subjected to abuse and violence (GLSEN, 2005), and many (sometimes even children) are murdered only for reasons related to their gender identity (Warwick, Chase, and Aggleton, 2004; Di Ceglie, 2000).

Laws and social policies across the world are often oppressive against non-heterosexual people. Lesbian, gay, bisexual, and transsexual people (LGBTs) generally earn less and suffer discrimination in a number of other ways. Homosexuality had been outlawed by about half the US until the early 1990s, and homosexual acts are still illegal in more than seventy countries. In some countries, they are punishable with execution (Iran, Kuwait, Saudi Arabia) (Kitzinger, 2001, 273). In countries where sex and gender variance is not outlawed, social policies appear to be strongly heterosexual, and this reinforces the idea that gender variance is a 'deviance' (Kitzinger, 2001, 280).

People with gender variance also suffer another great injustice. They are labelled as suffering from a psychiatric disorder, as gender variance is classified both in the ICD-10 (WHO, 1992) and in the DSM-IV-TR (APA, 2000). Thus, they are condemned to a stigma that follows them through life. But the diagnosis of psychiatric illness also sentences them to another paradox. In some cases, because gender variance is classified as a mental illness, it is difficult for people to obtain endocrinological treatment. It is in fact sometimes argued that endocrinological treatment should not be given for a condition that is not endocrinological in nature. However, should gender identity disorder (GID) be removed from the ICD-10 and the DSM-IV-TR, sufferers risk seeing reduced their chance to obtain publicly funded treatment or health insurance coverage for the medical treatments they need (Dreger, 2009).

What is gender variance? Is it appropriately regarded as a disorder, or as a mental disorder? And what are the consequences, in terms of access to medical treatment, should the answer to either question be 'no'?

In order to understand what a disorder of gender is, it seems crucial that we know what we mean when we talk about 'gender'. So, firstly, I examine the notion of gender. Because disorders of gender are taken to refer to 'abnormal' development of gender or abnormal gender identification, if we want to understand what a disorder of gender is (or what we mean by 'disorder of gender'), we need to understand what a 'normal' gender development is thought to be. We therefore look at the main theories of gender development.

In attempting to clarify the conceptual issues identified above, this chapter brings clarity and order to the vast literature on gender and gender identity disorders.

The conclusion of this analysis is that there is no sound epistemological reason to consider gender variance as a disorder. It is an existential condition, a series of facts and occurrences, and a way of being. Gender variance is no more and no less of a disorder than 'female' or 'male' gender.

There might be pragmatic reasons to maintain the classification of gender variance in the DSM and ICD, but there are no principled or epistemological reasons to do so.

The Notion of Gender

The notion of gender, according to Archer, was 'first used by Greek Sophists in the fifth century BC to describe the threefold classification of the names of things as masculine, feminine, and intermediate' (Archer and Lloyd, 2002, 17; Boylan, 1984). Originally, thus, gender is a grammatical notion. Now, as Archer points out, 'gender' is used as a more 'politically correct' (Archer and Lloyd, 2002, 17) way to refer to 'sex'. But whereas the grammatical meaning of 'gender' is not equivocal or ambiguous, the vast literature on gender and gender identity disorders shows that the notion of gender has different meanings in different research contexts.

Gender in Sociology, Psychology and Feminist Studies

In sociology, developmental psychology, and feminist and gender studies, the term 'gender' is generally associated with the roles that an individual covers in a given context (family or society). These roles, behaviours, and attitudes reflect the expectation that a society in a given historical and geographical context has of men and women.

Gender studies differentiate between 'sex' and 'gender'. Sex is the sum of biological traits that produce a phenotype. Sex refers to the genetic and chromosomal makeup of an individual, to the anatomy and the physiology of the individual. Gender, instead, is a set of social and cultural norms. Gender is the 'social interpretation' (Gross, 2009, 631) of the biological facts. Gender, in this meaning, is a social construct that applies to biological sex.

In a given society, individuals must continually testify their gender belonging through language, behaviour, and social roles. The concepts of 'man' and 'woman' are dynamic concepts, to be understood in the specific historical, geographical, and cultural context. It is society that determines what it is to be man or woman (Rubin, 1975).

The common denominator of these studies is that many features of gender are the result of implicit and/or explicit social and cultural norms. Gender is not biologically given: it is a social and political construct, and reflects normative ideas of how society should be organized.

Gender studies oppose the idea that the classification of genders is purely biologically determined, and denounce the social consequences that this has had, in particular, for women. 'Naturalistic', 'biological', or 'essentialist' claims (such as that women are 'empathic and nurturant' by nature and therefore they are 'by nature' best suited for childrearing) have a precise political significance: these claims are, or can be, forces of social and political oppression.

Background: Critique of Social Institutions

Some of the works by Marx and Engels constitute the background for the critique of gender roles. Whereas Marx and Engels are mostly known for their contribution to the communist ideology, and Marx in particular for his reflection on Hegel's political thought, both Marx and Engels have, perhaps more broadly, contested the fabric of society with its various institutions, including the family.

In *The Origin of the Family, Private Property and the State*, Engels argued that the relationships that we know within a society (including the relationships between women and men, and their respective roles) are neither given by nature nor the produce of a teleological predefined or divine plan. Social institutions, such as the family, evolve historically and are influenced, in different ways, by economical forces (Engels, 1884). Engels was in turn profoundly influenced by the studies of Morgan, who applied the evolutionary criteria of Darwinism to the study of the family across time (Morgan, 1877). The nuclear monogamic family, in which intimate cross-generational relations (incest) are taboo, is the product of evolution, argued Morgan.

According to Engels, the differentiation of roles and powers between man and woman are contradictions, in the same way as capital and labour, city and countryside, working class and owners, among others. He writes:

> The modern family contains in germ not only slavery (servitus), but also serfdom, since from the beginning it is related to agricultural services. It contains in miniature all the contradictions which later extend throughout society and its state. [Engels, 1884, Chap. 2]

If social institutions (including the relationship between woman and man) are not given by nature or god, but are the result of a complex process of *becoming*, entirely based on material conditions (interrelationship of economic forces and social relations), it follows that these social institutions are not fixed, and that they have no intrinsic normative value. They are amendable to review and criticism, as amendable to review and criticism as are the other forms of polarization that result from modern economy.

Gender in Clinical Psychology and Endocrinology

In clinical psychology, psychiatry, and endocrinology the notion of gender has acquired an apparently more specific meaning.

In these contexts, gender and gender identity refer to the congruence between phenotype and the person's behaviour and feelings about oneself. Gender identity, thus, is the sense of 'belonging to one sex' (Zucker, 2001, 102).

Disorders of gender identification refer to complex conditions in which individuals experience discomfort with their own biological sex.[1] In this sense, gender dysphoria has been referred to as 'sense of estrangement' from one's body (not from one's society) (Di Ceglie, 1998).

Due to the fluidity of the notion of gender within various contexts, and due to the variety of models of gender development,[2] it is difficult to reconcile different ways of understanding gender, gender identity, and gender identity disorders.

I shall not discuss in detail various theories of gender development. I discuss the vexed question of whether gender is a primarily biological phenomenon, or a social construct. This can in turn give a key for understanding gender identity disorder.

It is not necessarily true that GID is a biological disorder *if gender is primarily biologically given*. Vice versa, it is not necessarily true that GID is *not* a biological disorder *if gender is primarily a social construct*. We could configure the possibility of, for example, a social construct (or a biological datum) that is rejected by an individual due to biological forces (or to social forces). However, a 'dis-order' presumes the existence of 'order', and the knowledge of the 'orderly' mechanisms is preliminary to the understanding of the 'disorder' under analysis.

I will argue that, as the binomial classification of 'man', 'woman' (consequently trans *as the man trapped in a woman's body and vice versa)*, also the binomial classification of *biological versus social explanations* is a misrepresentation of a more complex set of occurrences.

How Does Gender Develop?

If we want to understand what is an 'abnormal' or 'disordered' gender identification, it seems necessary to understand what is a 'normal' or 'healthy' gender identification.

Sex typing is the process by which children learn their gender identity. 'A permanent gender identity is usually acquired by age five' (Gross, 2009, 631). How does gender develop? Is gender identity based on biology or is it the result of upbringing? Several theories try to explain how gender identity develops.[3] We focus here on the three main models, the Social, the Biological, and the Biosocial model.

The Social Model

The main assumption of social models of gender development is that both gender role and identity are social constructs. For this reason, social models of gender are also called 'constructionist' models. Against 'essentialist models', these argue that gender roles are not *a datum*, an inner state relating to one's biology. In many understated and implicit ways, gender roles and identities are created by the parental and social responses to the *sex* appearance of a baby.

Children learn the behaviour that their society expects of people of their sex. Parents model gender behaviour, encourage children to behave appropriately, and reinforce them when they do (Lorber, 1994). Adults, often without realising it, behave in a different way with the same baby depending on whether they think the baby is male or female. From the time that parents learn whether the new baby is a boy or girl, many aspects of the way it is treated will be influenced by its sex (Will, Self, and Datan, 1976).

Case History 1: Baby X (readapted from Archer and Lloyd, 2002, 60–71)

In this study new parents were invited to play with a six-month-old baby, dressed as a boy or a girl. Gender-stereotyped toys were present in the room. The parents were invariably seen as behaving toward the child in a gender-stereotyped way, according to what they believed the sex of the child to be. Later studies confirmed these findings.[4]

Bandura observed that gender development is heavily based on external sanctions—for example, parents in many cultures provide play experiences that are sex-typed. According to Bandura (and his *social learning theory*), children learn to behave differently if they are boys and girls, because they are treated differently. Children monitor their behaviour against the expected standards and feel pride in performing gender role–consistent behaviour, even if there is no explicit external sanction or praise (Bandura, 1965).

Psychology studies have shown that gender roles are internalized by very young children, and that the environmental (implicit or explicit) sanctions shape the children's response.

Bussey and Bandura studied three- to four-year-old nursery children. They asked the children to evaluate gender-typed behaviour of peers (from videotape) playing with 'masculine' or 'feminine' toys. Even younger children showed disapproval of gender-inconsistent behaviour (for example, boys playing with dolls) (Bussey and Bandura, 1992). Lloyd and Duveen studied 120 children aged eighteen months to three years, and arrived at similar conclusions (Lloyd and Duveen, 1990).

The Social Model and Clinical Practice

These studies have guided for a few decades the treatment of children born with ambiguous genitalia, at least in the US.

John Money (1921–2006), a psychologist and sexologist specialised in sexual identity and gender development, for example, treated a number of intersex children, based on the idea that, if gender is reassigned within a critical period (normally two-and-a-half to three years), there is no psychological harm to the child (children whose gender is assigned later are less likely to adjust without complications). Insofar as parents also believe in the gender of rearing, a child raised in a certain gender will typically conform to that gender. Gender is mainly a matter of nurture, and not nature. Regardless of the chromosomal heritage, gender will develop without ambiguity in the gender of rearing. Clinical literature reports cases of people who are chromosomal males, with external phenotype as females, who are raised according to genital appearance and who identify unequivocally with the gender of rearing (Gross, 2009, 624).

Zucker writes:

> In a study of 105 hermaphrodites, Money et al. (1957) found that only 5 of 105 patients had a 'gender role and orientation [that] was ambiguous and deviant from the sex of assignment and rearing'. . . . Thus, Money et al. concluded that 'the sex of assignment and rearing is consistently and conspicuously a more reliable prognosticator of a hermaphrodite's gender role and orientation than is the chromosomal sex, the gonadal sex, the hormonal sex, the accessory internal reproductive morphology, or the ambiguous morphology of the external genitalia.' [Zucker, 2001, 105]

However, some unsuccessful clinical cases have not only challenged the practice of early surgical treatment for intersex, but also the validity of the social model (especially as a basis for clinical practice).

The case of John/Joan became sadly famous (Colapinto, 2000).

Case History 2:
John/Joan

During a circumcision operation carried out at eight months on two twins, the penis of one of the boys was severed. Money, the surgeon, advised on reconstructing a vagina and raising the child as a girl. The boy was never happy being 'a girl'. He later took the name of David Reimer and had reassignment surgery to male. David accused Money of having condemned him to a childhood of humiliation and misery. David wrote: 'The organ that appears to be critical to psychosexual development and adaptation is not the genitalia but the brain' (Ben-Asher, 2004). David committed suicide in 2004.

Analyses of this and other similar cases indicate that gender identity cannot in all cases be moulded by upbringing.

Biological Explanations for Gender

The biological model suggests that gender is mainly determined by biological forces. John Bowlby (Bowlby, 1969), for example, argued that some differences in the attitudes and behaviours of males and females are genetically transmitted instincts. At least some of the roles linked to gender are, according to Bowlby, instinctual—biologically and not socially determined.

On this line, Simon Baron-Cohen writes: 'The female brain is predominantly "hard-wired" for empathy. The male brain is predominantly "hard-wired" for understanding and building systems' (2003, 1).

Gender role is innate and biologically determined, according to the biological model. The preference for different toys and activities between girls and boys is an indication of this. The differences are also physical: male babies are generally bigger; boys often sleep less, cry more, and are generally more active, whereas girls start talking earlier than boys and so on. Many studies have explored the psychological attributes belonging to each sex (Fenson et al., 2007; Maccoby and Jacklin, 1974; Ruble and Martin, 1998; Schaffer, 2004). Studies on the sex differences in children indicate that boys and girls have traits that are specific to their biological sex, and these cannot always be modified by rearing.

Other studies have focused on the influence of prenatal hormones in gender development. Animal studies suggest that prenatal hormonal influences can affect both gender identity and gender role. Prenatal exposure to androgens 'plays a role in the pattern of masculinisation that has been observed across a variety of behavioural domains' (Zucker, 2001, 105).

Experimental evidence from animal studies suggests that altering the balance of various hormones changes the gender-role behaviour. The behavioural systems that appear affected include nurturance ('maternalism') affiliation (nonsexual peer relations), aggression, and activity levels, all of which show normative sex differences and which, at least in lower animals, have been shown to be affected by experimental manipulations in exposure to prenatal sex hormones, including androgens.

The social model not only does not account for these findings, it also fails to consider differences in individuals, according to Zucker. In a detailed review of animal studies and studies of gender identification of people with various forms of sex disorders, Zucker found that women with Congenital Androgen Hyperplasya (CAH), for example, have less satisfaction with their gender than control groups, regardless of upbringing. But Zucker also notes that studies on rats show that 'the average number of neurons in the corpus callosum of rats shows a significant sex difference. However, this typical sex difference is exquisitely sensitive to, and modified by, the rearing environment' (Zucker, 2002, 104; see also, Chung et al., 2002; Kruijver et al., 2000; Van Kesteren, Gooren, and Megens, 1996; Zhou et al., 1995). Zucker concludes that the development of gender encompasses both biological forces and social norms. Others, as we now see, get to the same conclusion.

Biosocial Models

> Of course, no one really thinks that such [social and biological] influences operate in isolation. Development is a complex process that must ultimately involve the interplay of both. But, for the purposes of identifying specific influences that really make a difference, researchers have tended to forget this wider picture. For example, the social learning tradition involves concentrating on the process of imitation and ignoring the impact of prenatal androgens because these are regarded as unimportant in explaining what is imitated and under what circumstances. Biological approaches concentrating on the influence of prenatal androgens would tend to ignore details of the social environment, since these are regarded as unimportant compared with the hormonal influence. What is implicit in both research strategies is a belief that the variable under investigation is the main controlling influence on the behavioural outcome being investigated. [Archer and Lloyd, 2002, 75–76]

We have also seen above that the 'split' between models is somehow sharp and that the implications for clinical practice can also be significant. Thus, it is very important to remind ourselves that both models contribute to our understanding of gender, and cannot be taken in isolation. None of these models should be applied with absolute deference to clinical practice.

Gender development is a complex process that is the result, variable and dynamic (open to changes over time), of an interplay involving both biological and social factors.

Gender identity is a part of a broader notion of identity, which is formed in a unique way based on biology, on social interactions, and on the original manner in which each individual makes sense of what it is to be him- or herself within the context in which he or she lives. The notion of 'identity', like the notion of 'gender', has been widely debated both in psychology and in philosophy. In psychology, the notion of identity is generally used in concomitance with 'self-concept.' Several studies have provided various accounts of when and how people, as well as animals, acquire a sense of 'who they are.' Murphy writes: 'the self is the individual as known to the individual' (Murphy, 1947). Researchers have studied the cognitive structures that allow self-reflection and organization of information about oneself (Gross, 2009, Chap. 33). Studies on animals and children have attempted to disentangle the way in which, and the phases of life at which, individuals form a concept of their own identity (who they are, how they are differentiated from others, and what responses they can elicit in others and in the surrounding environment). Identity, in broad terms, is thought to comprise self-image, social roles, personality traits, self-esteem, autobiographical memory, age, and gender.

Gender is thus only one aspect of 'who one is', and wedges in the concept of self with various other facts and interpretations. Acquisition and awareness of gender develop thanks to a combination, which is bound to be unique in each individual, of biological and social forces.

Gender includes activities and interests, relationships, verbal and nonverbal communication styles, and even values (Deaux and Stewart, 2001, 85). Gender, thus, cannot be regarded as a stable concept. Both the concept of gender and how people identify and express themselves, change over time and according to social and cultural values and norms (Deaux and Stewart, 2001).

Males and females thus are not, and cannot be, a homogeneous group. As each individual is unique and different to any other, his or her way of being 'a male' or 'a female' will necessarily be unique and different. There are thus, inevitably, different masculinities and femininities. Not only will 'being a male' or 'a female' mean different things to different individuals. It will also mean different things to the same individual at different points in time.[5]

Biosocial Models and GID

If gender identity is a unique process, which each individual develops according to a complex interplay of subjective features and preferences, biology, and social forces, it follows that gender variance is not a purely intrapsychic phenomenon, a condition that belongs to the individual, but is a relational condition, neither simply caused by biology, nor purely socially constructed. Gender variances are *ways of being*, and thus position themselves along a continuum of legitimate[6] expressions of *who one is*.

It follows that variations in gender identifications are as 'normal' or as 'deviant' as it is to be unequivocally 'woman' or 'man'. All processes of gender identification are equally complicated. They all require a complex and long process of negotiation between preferences, inclinations, biological makeup, social expectations, personal experiences, and acquisition of social roles. If variation is pathology, then unequivocal gender identification is also pathology. If unequivocal gender identification is not pathology, then equivocal gender identification ought not to be.

Not coincidentally, a large part of the suffering in people with GID and in those born with various forms of intersex (and also in those who care for these sufferers) is related to the often understated assumptions about how each of us is expected to be—namely, a man or a woman with adoption of roles that are congruent with the biological sex. At the most, one might be 'in the wrong body', with the assumption that s/he will be happy in the other. The very notion of 'transgender' or 'transsexual' contains thus the germs of a profound misunderstanding, as it is based on implicit normative assumptions of unequivocal definition. These notions fail to capture the complexities of how each of us is, as unique individuals, and of how each individual, his or her unique biological makeup, adapts to one's body and one's various roles within different areas of social and relational life.

Ethical Implications

If the arguments of this chapter are persuasive, it follows that there is no sound reason to regard anything that has to do with gender and gender identification as pathological. As anticipated in the introduction, this could have the effect of limiting access to medical treatment. Why should doctors treat with hormonal and surgical treatment conditions that are not endocrinological or medical in nature?

This raises a more general question of what medicine is for. Should medicine only intervene to treat disabilities, or illnesses? (For the purposes of this essay I use 'disability', 'illness', and 'disorder' as synonymous.) Or should doctors also intervene to treat 'existential conditions' of suffering? One additional and related problem is what the state should pay for. These more general issues cannot be explored fully in this chapter. However it is important to at least address some concerns relating to the implications of what has been said so far, in terms of access to medical treatment.

I have argued elsewhere (Giordano, 2008b) that medicine is an enterprise aimed at releasing people's suffering and ameliorating people's quality of life.[7] *Prima facie* it is unethical to let someone suffer, when we have the means to alleviate their suffering. Each person should have an equal opportunity to obtain healthcare assistance, regardless of age, gender, and other arbitrary features, and only according to need and prognosis (Harris and Giordano, 1999). The main role of medicine, thus, is not 'curing illnesses' (Giordano, 2005), creating the greatest number of welfare units, or enhancing the overall welfare of society, but helping individuals to live the best life that is attainable to them.

The view that medicine should 'cure diseases' creates more problems than it resolves. What is 'a cure' and what is 'a disease' are highly contentious issues (Giordano, 2005; Boorse, 1987, 372; Imrie, 2004; Oliver, 1996; Dewsbury et al., 2004; Harris, 2000). If it is unclear what should count as a 'disease', and medicine should only treat diseases, then obviously it is not clear what conditions medicine should treat.

Moreover, if endocrinological treatment should not be offered for GID if GID is not an endocrinological disorder, then by consistency many other conditions should not be treated for similar reasons. It is in fact normal clinical practice to offer medical treatment for conditions of suffering that are not caused by physical or biological imbalances. Treatment in many cases is offered regardless of the quandaries surrounding definitions of disability. The treatment of children with retarded growth, or with excessive growth, is an example of how endocrinology intervenes to treat conditions that involve no somatic dysfunction, and whose distress is associated more with 'expectations' relating to what is 'normal', than with pain or physical inability or illness.

The treatment of fertility and infertility is another example of this. Infertility is arguably not a disorder. For some people it is an advantaged state. For others being infertile is indifferent. Lesbians and single women who apply for assisted reproduction often have no underlying pathology, and yet need and can obtain medical assistance to procreate. Medical treatment, in these cases, is provided without an analysis of the reasons why people suffer. Some people suffer from being childless because of social expectations, because of understated acquisition of social roles. It cannot be up to the endocrinologists to perform an analysis of the more profound psychological or social reasons why some people want children, or suffer being childless. Medicine cannot scrutinize whether the desire for maternity is a biological instinct, or rather a social construct, and provide fertility treatment accordingly. There is no reason to apply different standards to treatment relating to gender identity (unless a morally relevant difference could be found, which justifies differences in treatment).

Even more clearly, sometimes people obtain 'mutilations' and physical damage at request. Without going into the more extreme examples relating to requests for amputation of healthy limbs, or male and female circumcision (which raises different ethical issues in that they are often requested for minors), vasectomy and other surgical interventions performed to become infertile, are clear examples of medical interventions not given to repair physiological damage. On the contrary, what to some would be 'damage' is inflicted in order to improve the person's overall welfare.

There might be ethical and pragmatic issues of resources allocation, which could explain why the state might not publicly fund some treatments. Some might, for example, raise questions as to whether these types of medical interventions (medical interventions that aim at alleviating suffering or enhancing quality of life, in absence of known physical damages to repair) should be paid by the state at all (Brassington, 2007, 77; 2009), or should be paid by the state *on an equal footing* with treatments for other and possibly more threatening medical conditions. However, these concerns are not principled reasons to deny medical treatment for conditions that are not 'medical' in a strict sense.

Of course, healthcare professionals have a right (which is both moral and legal) not to treat. However, this right is not absolute, and has to be balanced against the right of the applicant not to suffer. UK abortion law, for example, establishes that a doctor can legally refuse to perform an abortion based on conscientious objection notwithstanding a 'duty to participate in treatment which is necessary to save the life or to prevent grave permanent injury to the physical or mental health of a pregnant woman' (Abortion Act, 1967, Section 4(2)). Thus, healthcare professionals are to some extent responsible (ethically and legally) for their omissions (Giordano, 2007; 2008a). They are not only responsible for their actions. Responsibility for omissions is not unique to healthcare professionals, but applies to us all. When healthcare professionals deny medical treatment, knowing that as a consequence, a person will suffer serious psychological, physical, or social harm, or even death, they are to some extent responsible for that harm. This is so regardless of the nature and origins of the applicant's condition. Moreover, the healthcare professionals' moral right not to treat is proportionate to the applicant's capacity to access alternative services. When alternative services are not available, healthcare professionals have a more stringent responsibility to accept requests for treatment (Giordano, 2008c).

There is evidence that hormonal and, in some cases, surgical treatments alleviate the suffering of people with gender variance (Delemarre-van de Waal and Cohen-Kettenis, 2006). People with gender issues might suffer enormously, and some would rather die than be left without medical and psychological treatment. The consequences of delayed or no treatment are wide-ranging and hideous in many ways (Giordano, 2008b). Treatment should be offered if it is in the patients' best interests, if it is likely to ameliorate their lives, to promote their psychological and social adjustment, and to save their lives, according to the best available empirical evidence. This should be so, regardless of whether the condition is primarily biological or intrapsychic or social.

I am now going to assess the implications that this all has on international clinical practice.

Implications for International Practice

One of the pioneers in the field of treatment of gender identity problems was Harry Benjamin, an American sexologist. The Harry Benjamin International Gender Dysphoria Association (now called World Professional Association for Transgender Health: WPATH) published, in 2001, the sixth version of *The Standards of Care for Gender Identity Disorders,* originally named after Harry Benjamin. Other national guidelines have been issued, normally in coherence with the Harry Benjamin Standards of Care (a review of various guidelines can be found in Giordano, 2007).

The Endocrine Society, which involves clinicians coming from different countries (Hembree et al., 2009), has provided renewed guidelines, based on the clinical experience gained by healthcare professionals in various countries in the last decade.

These new international guidelines mainly discuss the clinical issues associated with gender identity disorders. Yet, it is important to address some of the ethical implications that the arguments of this essay could and should have, in terms of international clinical policy and practice.

First, although some countries issue 'national' guidelines,[8] it is important that networks of professionals share international criteria. This has two advantages: one is that healthcare professionals operating in less liberal contexts can benefit from the clinical experience and research of professionals operating in countries where greater clinical freedom is allowed. The other advantage is that sharing scientific results internationally also allows assessment of social variables that might be involved in the onset of gender identity problems.

Second, it should be recognised (as all the major international guidelines do—see WPATH, 2001, 8) that gender identity issues are complex phenomena. Suffering is associated with several variables. Some are intrapsychic, some are relational, and some are social in nature (see Giordano, 2007). It is therefore important that a multidisciplinary approach is taken, to tackle the various aspects of people's suffering.

Third, international bodies of medical opinion should begin to recognise that there is no epistemological and no known clinical reason to regard gender variance as pathological. This can release the stigma associated with having atypical gender identity development and should not in principle impact upon access to treatment. It should be simply acknowledged that the formation of gender identity is a complex and partly unexplained process, and that for some people it might be more complicated than for others.

Fourth, each model of explanation of gender and gender identity development has strengths and weaknesses. Clinical practice should not be informed by any of them in isolation. Absolute deference should not be paid to any of the models of explanation of gender identity and GID, because none of them, taken in isolation, has provided a conclusive argument for gender development and for gender dysphoria.

Fifth, professional guidelines should recognise individual differences in gender development, and, as a consequence, individual differences *in response to treatment.* Guidelines should be flexible enough to allow adaptation to the needs of each individual patient in each national or local context in which the dis-ease is manifested. They should recognise the breadth of various gender expressions and the differences in national, social, and family contexts in which the condition appears, and allow professionals to offer interventions that are best suited to each individual case.

Sixth, the argument that, because there is no known biological cause for gender identity disorders, endocrinological treatment should not be offered is mistaken conceptually and morally dubious. The healthcare profession has a moral responsibility to release people's suffering, insofar as it has the instruments to do so.

Conclusions

People with atypical gender identity development suffer a number of forms of injustice. One of these is being nailed to a psychiatric diagnosis, which seems necessary in order to be eligible for treatment.

There is vast disagreement around what gender identity disorders are, around their causes, and around the way it is best to treat them. This chapter has attempted to bring clarity to the vast literature on gender and gender identity disorders.

We have seen that the notion of gender does not have univocal meaning, and is used differently in different research contexts. We have also looked at theories of gender identity development. If we want to understand what 'abnormal' gender identity development is, it seems necessary to understand what 'normal' gender identity development is and what it encompasses.

Different models of explanations of gender identity development all seem to capture some of the complexities involved with the acquisition of gender identity. I have argued that identity of gender is a part of a broader sense of personal identity, and, as such, biological, intrapsychic, and relational elements all cooperate in its formation. In this sense, atypical and typical gender identity developments have the same origins, namely a complex interplay of various factors, which all contribute to the articulation of 'who one is'.

The sense of belonging to one gender is not fixed. It is dynamic, and it changes in different people and across one's lifetime: what it means to be a woman is different for different people, and different for the same person at different points in time. In this sense, there is no epistemological reason to regard some forms of gender identity development as pathological. Gender identity, whether typical or atypical, is part of who one is, is an existential state or condition, and not a pathology. This in principle should not negatively affect people's eligibility for treatment.

A broader discourse on what medicine is for could not be undertaken in this essay. This chapter thus lays the basis for further reflection on the medical legitimate sphere of intervention. I have suggested, here and elsewhere, that the role of medicine is not to cure diseases, but to alleviate peoples' suffering, and that insofar as healthcare professionals have the instruments to alleviate suffering and prevent people from dying prematurely, they have a moral obligation to do so, regardless of the nature and origin of people's afflictions.

Notes

1. It could be argued that the differentiation of these two characterizations of gender identity is not as stark as this. It is in fact possible that 'a body' symbolises 'a set of roles and rules'. It is thus possible that incongruence with one's phenotype is somehow expressive of a more general sense of incongruence with all that 'having that body' entails. The same reasoning can apply to cases of ambivalent gender identification, where people feel they have both masculine and feminine sides to their selves.

2. An account of various theories of gender identity development can be found in Gross (2009, Chapter 36).

3. There is the Freudian model, for example, that we do not analyse for reasons of space and consistency.

4. A comprehensive account of socialization is found in John Archer and Barbara Lloyd (2002, 60–71). Archer and Lloyd also offer an interesting critical account of Kohlberg's theory of gender identity development and gender constancy (66–69).

5. One implication of this is that, at least to some extent, sexual and gender "deviance" (homosexuality as well as transsexuality) is generated by normative models of sexual and gender 'normalcy'. In this sense, the 'anomaly' is created by cultural and social norms and expectations.

6. They are 'legitimate' in two senses: because their existence can be explained and justified with reason, and ethically legitimate because they concern the individual only.

7. One additional aim is prolonging life.

8. For example, in the UK, in 1998 the Royal College of Psychiatrists issued the *Guidance for the management of gender identity disorders in children and adolescents.* Available at http://www.rcpsych.ac.uk/files/pdfversion/cr63.pdf

References

Abortion Act. (1967). Available at http://www.statutelaw.gov.uk

American Psychiatric Association (APA). (2000). *Diagnostic and Statistical Manual of Mental Disorders, DSM-IV-TR (Text Revision), Fourth Edition.* Washington: APA.

Archer, John, and Barbara Lloyd. (2002). *Sex and Gender.* Cambridge: Cambridge University Press.

Bandura, Albert. (1965). "Influence of Model's Reinforcement Contingencies on the Acquisition of Imitative Responses." *Journal of Personality and Social Psychology 1*: 589–595.

Baron-Cohen, Simon. (2003). *The Essential Difference: Men, Women and the Extreme Male Brain.* London: Penguin/Basic Books.

Ben-Asher, Noa. (2004). "Paradoxes of Health and Equality: When a Boy Becomes a Girl." *Yale Journal of Law & Feminism 16*: 275–312.

Boorse, Christopher. (1987). "Concepts of Health" in *What Is Disease?* ed. D. Van De Veer and R. F. Almeder: 359–393. Totowa, NJ: Humana Press.

Bowlby, John. (1969). *Attachment and Loss. Volume 1. Attachment.* Harmondsworth: Penguin.

Boylan, Michael. (1984). "The Gelenic and Hippocratic Challenges to Aristotle's Conception Theories." *Journal of the History of Biology 17*: 83–112.

Brassington, Iain. (2007). *Public Health and Globalisation. Why an NHS is Morally Indefensible.* Exeter: Societas Imprint Academic.

Brassington, Iain. (2009). Journal of Medical Ethics Blog. Retrieved from http://blogs.bmj.com/medical-ethics/2009/01/29

Bussey, Kay, and Albert Bandura. (1992). "Self-Regulatory Mechanisms Governing Gender Development." *Child Development 63*: 1236–1250.

Bussey, Kay and Albert Bandura. (1999). "Social Cognitive Theory of Gender Development and Differentiation." *Psychological Review 106*: 676–713.

Chung, Wilson C. J., Geert J. De Vries, and Dick F. Swaab. (2002). "Sexual Differentiation of the Bed Nucleus of the Stria Terminalis in Humans May Extend into Adulthood." *Journal of Neuroscience 22*(3): 1027–1033.

Colapinto, John. (2000). *As Nature Made Him: The Boy Who Was Raised as a Girl.* New York: Harper Collins.

de Beaufort, I., I. Bolt, M. Hilhorst, and H. Wijsbek. (1998–2001). "Beauty and the Doctor: Moral Issues in Health Care with Regard to Appearance: Report to the European Commission Directorate General XII." Rotterdam: Erasmus University. Retrieved from http://ec.europa.eu/research/biosociety/pdf/bmh4_ct98_3164.pdf

Deaux, Kay, and Abigail J. Stewart. (2001). "Framing Gender Identities" in *Handbook of the Psychology of Women and Gender*, ed. Rhoda K. Unger. Wiley: New Jersey.

Delemarre-van de Waal, A. H., and T. P. Cohen-Kettenis. (2006). "Clinical Management of Gender Identity Disorder in Adolescents: A Protocol on Psychological and Paediatric Endocrinology Aspects." *European Journal of Endocrinology 155*(1): 131–137. Retrieved from http://www.eje-online.org/cgi/content/full/155/suppl_1/S131#F2

Dewsbury, Guy, et al. (2004). "The Anti-Social Model of Disability." *Disability & Society 19*(2): 147.

Di Ceglie, Domenico. (1998). *A Stranger in My Own Body*. London: Karnak Books.

Di Ceglie, Domenico. (2000). "Gender Identity Disorder in Young People." *Advances in Psychiatric Treatment 6*: 458–466.

Dreger, Alice. (2009). "How and Why to Take 'Gender Identity Disorder' Out of the DSM." Bioethics forum. Retrieved from http://www.thehastingscenter.org/Bioethicsforum/Post.aspx?id=3602

Durkheim, Emile. (1912 [2001]). *The Elementary Forms of the Religious Life*. Oxford: Oxford University Press.

Edley, Nigel, and Margaret Wetherell. *Men in Perspective: Practice, Power and Identity*. Hemel Hempstead: Harvester Wheatsheaf.

Engels, Frederick. (1884 [2001]). *The Origin of the Family, Private Property and the State*, trans. Ernest Untermann. Honolulu: University Press of the Pacific.

Fenson, L., V. A. Marchman, D. J. Thal, P. S. Dale, J. S. Reznick, and E. Bates. (2007). *MacArthur-Bates Communicative Development Inventories: User's Guide and Technical Manual, Second Edition.* Baltimore: Paul H. Brookes Publishing Co.

Giordano, Simona. (2005). "A Heaven Without Giants or Dwarfs," invited for publication in *Edited Collection,* ed. S. Holm [details not yet available].

Giordano, Simona. (2007). "Gender Atypical Organisation in Children and Adolescents: Ethico-Legal Issues and a Proposal for New Guidelines." *International Journal of Children's Rights 15*(3–4): 365–390.

Giordano, Simona. (2008a). "Gender Atypical Organisation in Children and Adolescents" in *International Public Health Policy and Ethics*, ed. Michael Boylan: 249–272. Springer: Dordrecht.

Giordano, Simona. (2008b). "Lives in Chiaroscuro. Should we Suspend Puberty of Children with Gender Identity Disorder?" *Journal of Medical Ethics 34*: 580–584.

Giordano, Simona. (2008c, 28 September). "Suspension of Puberty in Adolescents with Gender Identity Disorders" invited presentation at the International Conference on Gender Identity Disorder in Children and Adolescents, Imperial College, London.

GLSEN. (2005). "National School Climate Survey Sheds New Light on Experiences of Lesbian, Gay, Bisexual and Transgender (LGBT) students." Retrieved from http://glsen.org/cgi-bin/iowa/all/library/record/1927.html

Gross, Richard. (2009). *Psychology*. London: Hodder Education.

Haiken E. (1997). *Venus Envy. A History of Cosmetic Surgery*. Baltimore: Johns Hopkins University Press.

Harris, John. (2000). "Is There a Coherent Social Conception of Disability?" *Journal of Medical Ethics 26*: 95–100.

Harris, John, and Simona Giordano. (1999, June). "Pari opportunita` nella distribuzione delle risorse sanitarie." *Keiron*: 26–28.

Hembree, Wylie C., et al. (2009). "Endocrine Treatment of Transsexual Persons: An Endocrine Society Clinical Practice Guideline." *Journal of Clinical Endocrinology & Metabolism*. Retrieved from http://jcem.endojournals.org/cgi/content/abstract/jc.2009-0345v1

Imrie, Rob. (2004). "Demystifying Disability: A Review of the *International Classification of Functioning, Disability and Health*," *Sociology of Health & Illness 26*(3): 287–305.

Kitzinger, Celia. (2001). "Sexualities" in *Handbook of the Psychology of Women and Gender*, ed. Rhoda K. Unger. Hoboken, NJ: Wiley.

Kruijver, F. P., J. N. Zhou, C. W. Pool, M. A. Hofman, L. J. Gooren, and D. F. Swaab. (2000). "Male-to-Female Transsexuals Have Female Neuron Numbers in a Limbic Nucleus." *Journal of Clinical Endocrinology & Metabolism 85*(5): 2034–2041.

Lloyd, Barbara, and Gerald Duveen. (1990). "A Semiotic Analysis of the Development of Social Representations of Gender" in *Social Representations and the Development of Knowledge*, ed. Gerald Duveen and Barbara Lloyd: 27–46. Cambridge: Cambridge University Press.

Lorber, Judith. (1994). *Paradoxes of Gender*. London: Yale University Press.

Maccoby, E. E., and C. N. Jacklin. (1974). *The Psychology of Sex Difference*. Stanford: Stanford University Press.

Morgan, Lewis Henry. (1877 [2000]). *Ancient Society*. London: New Brunswick.

Murphy, G. (1947). *Personality: A Bio-Social Approach to Origins and Structure*. New York: Harper and Row.

Oliver, Michael. (1996). *Understanding Disability: From Theory to Practice*. Basingstoke: Palgrave Press.

Royal College of Psychiatrists. (1998). *Gender Identity Disorders in Children and Adolescents. Guidance for Management*. London: Royal College of Psychiatrists.

Rubin, Gayle. (1975). *The Traffic in Women*. New York: Monthly Review Press.

Ruble, D. N., and C. L. Martin. (1998). "Gender Development" in *Handbook of Child Psychology Volume 3*, ed. W. Damon and N. Eisenberg. New York: Wiley.

Schaffer, H. R. (2004). *Introducing Child Psychology*. Oxford: Blackwell.

Van Kesteren, P. J., L. J. Gooren, and J. A. Megens. (1996). "An Epidemiological and Demographic Study of Transsexuals in the Netherlands." *Archives of Sexual Behavior 25*(6): 589–600.

Warwick, I., E. Chase, and P. Aggleton. (2004). "Homophobia, Sexual Orientation and Schools: A Review and Implications for Action." University of London, 2004, Research Report No 594. Retrieved from www.dfes.gov.uk/research/data/uploadfiles/RR594.pdf

Will, J. A., P. Self, and N. Datan. (1976). "Maternal Behavior and Perceived Sex of Infant." *American Journal of Orthopsychiatry 46*: 135–139.

World Health Organization (WHO). (1992). *ICD-10, International Statistical Classification of Diseases*. Geneva: WHO.

World Professional Association for Transgender Health (WPATH). (2001). *The Standards of Care for Gender Identity Disorders*. Originally named *The Harry Benjamin International Gender Dysphoria Association's Standards of Care for Gender Identity Disorders*.

Zhou, J. N., M. A. Hofman, L. J. Gooren, and D. F. Swaab. (1995). "A Sex Difference in the Human Brain and Its Relation to Transsexuality." *Nature 378* (6552): 68–70.

Zucker, K. J. (2001). "Biological Influences on Psychosexual Differentiation" in *Handbook of Psychology of Women and Gender*, ed. R. Unger: 101–115. Hoboken, NJ: Wiley.

Zucker, K. J. (2002). "Intersexuality and Gender Identity Differentiation." *Journal of Pediatric and Adolescent Gynecology 15*(3): 3–13.

CHAPTER NINETEEN

Duties to Children

MICHAEL BOYLAN
Marymount University

Abstract

This essay argues for the recognition of children's rights to the basic goods of human agency and the ensuing duties that fall upon every citizen of the world to provide all children these goods. These duties are not restricted to national boundaries because the justifying arguments rest upon the basis of rights claims, univocal contracts, philosophical love, and the extended community worldview imperative. Collectively these reasons support a strong commitment to providing all children these goods.

Key Words

children, rights, duties, international, cosmopolitanism

Children are the most vulnerable general population of people on the planet. They are very prone to poverty, illness, and death via disease and violence. Every six seconds a child dies from health-related causes (prominent on the list are malaria and HIV/AIDS). One third of all children on earth are underfed (among the youngest this expresses itself through: underweight, stunting, and wasting [Child Fund, 2009]).[1] Though many children are enrolled worldwide in some sort of primary education program, attendance is often much lower and secondary school attendance is sometimes around 25 percent or less.[2] Children are also very susceptible to violence through child labor, land mines, war, sex trafficking, and other sorts of exploitation (no good data are available, but anecdotal data are frightening).

What we owe to children, and how we can philosophically justify our position, will be the subject of this essay.

First, we need to define "children." "Children" will be taken to apply to all from birth until some age of socially accepted independence from the family. This age of independence will vary from society to society. In some societies the age may be thirteen, while in others it may be younger or older (DeLoache and Gottlieb, 2000). Often several dates are given. For example, in the United States, some religions have a date of being recognized as an adult around twelve to thirteen, driving privileges are often extended at sixteen, voting and military service at eighteen, drinking alcohol at twenty-one, and the ability to rent a car at twenty-five. Clearly there are biological points that are less relative, such as cognitive development that sets minimal levels of rationality at between ten and twelve years old (Shaffer and Kipp, 2009, Part 3). For the purposes of this essay, we will accept the United Nations Convention on the rights of the child as setting the age as below the age of eighteen (Part 1, Article 1).

Positive and Negative Rights and Duties

"Duties" will be seen as being of two sorts: positive and negative. Positive duties will be those moral or legal obligations that are a correlative response to a legitimate claim right. In this case we have a duty to *do something* in response to a legitimate claim right. Negative duties will be understood as refraining from harm or compensating for an existing harm (committed by the agent). In medicine the Hippocratic Oath enjoins physicians to do no harm. This is an example of a negative duty of the first sort. Environmental cleanup laws that require companies that cause contamination of the environment to pay the costs of cleanup are examples of the second sort. In these cases we have a duty either to refrain from certain sorts of action that will directly or indirectly harm another agent or to compensate him for our prior harmful activity.

With these definitions in hand, let us proceed to the general foundation of positive and negative human rights and duties. We begin with rights because rights and duties are correlative and because rights are logically prior to duties (we have positive duties *because* of the procedure of legitimating a positive rights claim). After we do this, then we will examine what variations might apply to children.

It is this author's contention that the most important category of human rights is that covering what is generally termed "basic rights." Basic rights are a category within *human rights* that cover the strongest rights claims (Shue, 1996). A list of the basic rights might include: food, water, sanitation, clothing, protection from unwarranted bodily harm, basic health care, education, liberty rights, and the autonomy (and opportunity) to do with one's life as one likes. This is a large list. Which of these rights are most basic? Which stand out before the others? In order to answer this question we must examine first the definition of a claim right and then how it is justified.

What Is a Claim Right?

Claims rights are legitimate claims that an agent may make against some other agent or community. Since rights claims are always against some responding party, it is important to distinguish two different conceptions about who might have the correlative duties that correspond to the legitimate basic rights claims. On the one hand are those supporting a nationalist perspective (such as John Rawls). In this case the claim is against fellow citizens of a nation. On the other hand are those supporting a cosmopolitan perspective (such as Thomas Pogge). In this case the claim is against all those on earth in a position to satisfy the claim (the ought implies can standard).

How Are Claim Rights Justified?

There are three principal justifications for human rights: legal, interest-based, and agency-based. Let us address these in order. First, there are legal-based justifications for human rights. This approach depends upon either contractarianism (via some international body such as the United Nations) or intuitionism. Under these paradigms we have documents that are agreed upon by certain representative individuals because of mutual interest or because they are intuited to be valid claims. Two key examples of a contractarian basis are the Universal Declaration of Human Rights (agreed to by representatives to the member nations); and the United States Bill of Rights (agreed to by representatives of the first United States Congress). To answer our generating question, the list of human rights would be pared to basic rights by general agreement (Singer, 1993).

However, a downside to this approach is that these legal regulations require a measure of specificity. This means a level of interpretation. When one enters the international sphere, the force of the legalistic approach can be compromised because the various nation-states that sign some particular agreement (contractarianism) often represent a particular constituency at a particular moment in history. The time span of the human signers is short. When a new head of state comes into power, he or she does not necessarily feel bound personally by the acts of a predecessor. Because there is no World Government with executive or judicial power of enforcement, the signatories to international treaties are really subject to an honor system. In practice this often means that weak countries must comply while rich and powerful countries comply at their pleasure. When there is no one with the power to enforce contracts (including binding penalties), then the only reason any nation would comply would be self-interest on a changeable basis. This reality leaves the legal option with a significant gap.

The second approach to human rights seeks a moral justification via the interest-based approach. Jonathan Mann suggests, "The implicit question of the modern human rights movement is: 'what are the societal (and particularly governmental) roles and responsibilities to help promote individual and collective well-being?'" (1996, 166). If human rights are fundamentally concerned with well-being, then following Raz, "'X has a right' if and only if X can have rights, and, other things being equal, an aspect of X's well-being (his interest) is a sufficient reason for holding some other person(s) to be under a duty" (1986, 166). The key point here is how we are to assess *x*'s well-being. Turning to our generating question, the list provided would be pared in accordance with the conditions of well-being. Much like Sen's capabilities approach, the focus is upon some end state. Whatever it takes to achieve well-being (in some minimal way) within a society constitutes a ground for a legitimate rights claim.

Advocates for this approach say that over and against the legalistic approach, the interest-based grounding of human rights in well-being gives a more theoretical foundation so that hard cases will be solved by theoretical principles and not by hair-splitting legal decisions. Detractors will say that well-being is too far down the food chain to be effective. They would assert that well-being is the responsibility of the agent.

This leads us to the third justification for human rights, agency-based arguments. Those who take aforementioned objection to the well-being position (including this author) will say that policy is best served by outlining specific goods[3] (the most fundamental for action are biologically based: food, water, clothing, sanitation, protection from unwarranted bodily harm, including basic health care).[4] Once one knows what these goods are, then the generating question is answered about what constitutes basic rights—it is the claim to these fundamental goods of human action. The force of the agency basis of human rights rests upon the conditions necessary for humans to commit purposive action. On the agency account, desiring to commit purposive action amounts to something close to human nature. Under the agency account, the correlative duty of others is to give a person what she needs to be a minimally effective actor in the world. The rest is up to her.

There are certainly some overlaps between the interest-based and agency accounts. They each approach the problem with a different foundational aim. The interest-based account looks at an end product of well-being and tries to figure out what is needed to get there. The agency account looks at an end product of committing purposive action and tries to figure out what is necessary to allow voluntary, purposive action to take place. Each theory describes a primitive level that would stand as a justificatory basis of basic rights from the standpoint of that theory: legal, interest-based, or agency-based.

Positive and Negative Duties

There are two sorts of duties: positive and negative. Claim rights entail positive duties. In this case, one is enjoined to perform an action on behalf of another because that other person has a legitimate rights claim against him/her. Let's look at a concrete example. If we understand the structure of a claims right as "*x* has a right to *y* against *z* in virtue of *m*" (where *x* is a person, *y* is a good of agency, *z* is a person or community, and *m* is a legitimating moral institution), then this rights claim can be rewritten as a duty: "*z* has a duty to *x* to provide *y* in virtue of *m*."[5] If *y* is "the right to vote in the United States by all citizens who have registered," then we can imagine the situation in 1964 in which Maya Jones (an African American citizen of the United States) was turned away at the polls due to a poll tax or a literacy test that was excessive and not given to European-descent individuals in her state. Maya was denied the right to vote. This means her legitimate rights claim was denied. This incurs a duty against all the peoples of the United States to enable her to vote. The 1965 Voting Rights Act was a public response to this duty. This is an example of a positive right that Maya had and which was later recognized because of the correlative duty.

An example of a negative duty would look like this. In the first instance, "*x* has a duty to refrain from harming *z* by action *a* in virtue of *m* (a legitimating moral institution)." In the second instance, "*x* has a duty to provide *y* (a compensatory good proportional to what was lost through the commission of *a*) to *z* in virtue of *m* (the principle of retributive justice)."[6] Under these scenarios, any agent (*x*) must account for the harm he or she does to others. This sounds straightforward enough, but what constitutes a harm?

In United States law a *harm* is contrasted with a *nuisance*. The former has legal (moral) status while the latter does not. For example, if someone on a bus were to pick his nose, that might constitute a nuisance, but it would not be a legitimate harm. On the other hand, if someone on the bus were to spill his coffee onto the person's white skirt who is seated next to him on the bus, then this might constitute a harm and demand some sort of recompense (such as the cost of cleaning the skirt).

Negative duties fit into retributive justice because they describe a *giving back*. However, since there is a boundary of tolerance (the so-called nuisance), then there can be many gray areas. For example, what if a multinational company acts within the laws of the land in which it is incorporated, and the company builds a chemical factory and there is a chemical spill that doesn't kill anyone, but affects the drinking water of the children of the region. In this hypothetical case let us suppose that over time the children suffer mental retardation of varying degrees. Since children don't speak up for their own grievances, they cannot move into the realm of the legalistic model that might dictate retribution. Thus, they languish in their injury (many times, unknowing).

It is also the case that what constitutes a "harm" is disputable. In the administration of George W. Bush, a regime of "enhanced" interrogation techniques were employed on prisoners (some of whom were under eighteen years old [Mayer,

2009]). The Bush administration's standard of *harm* varied from the Army's manual of conduct and the Geneva Conventions (Mayer, 2009). *Harm*, under Bush, became loss of bodily function or death (Yoo, 2003). This constituted a rather extreme line (Weisberg, 2009; Brecher, 2008).

Regarding children, the same extreme standards are often applied: if they can continue to function, everything is thought to be fine (by society). However, this is not always the case. Since children from the beginning of time have had the hardest path to follow, and because developmentally they are very positive people, it is sometimes very hard to ascertain when they are suffering. One example of this is the sexual abuse scandals of the Roman Catholic Church—abuse by a small percentage of priests against children in various parishes (Robinson, 2008; Bartunek, 2005). The children who were abused generally did not report the abuse at the time. They waited and suffered—sometimes as long as twenty or thirty years. This is because children are not programmed to be their own advocates or to question adult authority figures. They will endure abuse by a parent or an authority figure because that is all they know how to do. It is a simple strategy of survival: endurance.

Because of this endurance strategy of survival, negative duties are not as effective as positive duties at protecting the vulnerable. This is because positive duties set out conditions of goods attainment before something goes awry. The Table of Embeddedness sets out a blueprint. On the other hand, negative duties look at life in a rearview mirror and try to rectify wrongs already committed. But in the case of children (poor advocates for their own cause), it is already too late. There is no effective remedy for the loss of nutrition, medicine, clothes, shelter, or protection from abuse. The unfortunate victims live with the consequences all their lives.

It is the conclusion of this author that because of this dynamic with children the leading emphasis should be on positive rights and duties and only secondarily upon negative rights (refraining from harm—hard to assess except retroactively) and retributive justice (negative rights and duties). We need to protect children *before* they are harmed.

Models That Support Duties to Children

Agents and Potential Agents

Because agency is set out as a defining characteristic in human rights claims (positive rights and duties), and because agency seems to suggest adult homo sapiens who fall within the so-called normal range,[7] then the default subject stand-in is adult homo sapiens. Seen on an Aristotelian continuum of potentiality => adult actuality => perfect adult actuality, children fall in the realm of potentiality. They are potential agents (Gewirth, 1978, 141; see also, Beyleveld, 1991; Spence, 2006). As such their potential purposiveness is not yet fully presented. We expect them to develop into actual purposive agents (all else being equal). In the interim, the potential purposive agent needs protection to develop according to nature. The very fact that we respect our ability to commit purposive action above all else creates a deep respect for this primary aspect of our personhood (understood as a species-level predication). This disposition grounds our respect for potential agents in an analogous way to our necessary duties to respect and protect the legitimate claims of actualized adult purposive agents. This duty of protection is proportional to the degree of agent actualization. Thus, for example, the duty to protect an infant is higher than the duty to protect a seventeen-year-old. This is because the seventeen-year-old is at the cusp of being an actualized adult (who can protect himself, ceteris paribus), while the infant has most of the process before her and is thus more vulnerable.

The first ground of duties to children can be summarized in this way: Children are potential agents and because of this all others owe them respect and protection in direct proportion to their actualized demonstrated ability to commit rationally based purposive action. This is a general duty against all agents according to the shared-community worldview imperative and the extended community worldview imperative.[8]

Communities and Children

All children are born in a geographical context. This means that the shared community worldview often comes into play in the raising of children. This can be for the good or for the bad. It sometimes takes a bit of detective work to find out how the community worldview situates children. This is because children are often formally invisible. For example, "children" and "family" are not found in the United States Constitution. They did not rise to the level of official recognition. The ways that communities openly view children has an effect upon the way children are treated.[9]

Let us examine a few different ways that communities view children. Our first example comes from a community in the puritan Massachusetts Bay Colony (seventeenth century). If we were to consult them, they would say that infants are born into sin and require very strict direction in order to steer them clear of the Devil. This would create a framework in which exact rules and close supervision were the norm—because on their own the community could expect the worst possible outcome. Under this view improperly raised children can poison and destroy the community as they become adults (DeLoache and Gottlieb, 2000, 29–54). This is similar to the Fulani in West Africa who see raising children like cattle farming. The cattle are constantly at risk from wild predators, and the children are at risk from diabolical forces. Children are raised along the same standards as cattle farming to protect the village from destruction (DeLoache and Gottlieb, 2000, 171–198).

The Beng in West Africa exhibit another community worldview. Parents go through ceremonies to lure children (residing in a netherworld) into the uteruses of the wives. Because of this relationship, the community believes that their children *choose* their parents. Parents who have strong, healthy children are the lucky ones because powerful nether children *chose them*. Because of this balance of power, children are well respected and thought to know all the world's languages initially so that there is almost constant communication with them (as opposed to the Ifaluk peoples from the Pacific atoll who think babies can understand nothing so they largely ignore them (DeLoache and Gottlieb, 2000, 199–220)). In time, say the Beng, development saps these special gifts. This creates a framework in which rules are gradually phased in—because in the process of development children descend to the lower level of adults (DeLoache and Gottlieb, 2000, 55–90). This creates a community worldview that views "childlike" as akin to godly—something toward which to aspire.

In Bali babies are thought to be reincarnated ancestors and gods. Infants are treated with the respect and deference owed to a deity. Upbringing consists in trying to hold onto this holiness as long as possible through family and community balancing of opposing forces (such as hot and cold) so that a middle, holy ground might be maintained. This puts forward the notion that proper childcare can save an entire village and keep them pure. Children are at the forefront of creating happy and healthy lives (DeLoache and Gottlieb, 2000, 1–28).

In most of these communities, children are seen to be the future. Through different models, children are pivotal to this process. Whether it is through keeping the Devil out of them, retaining the holiness within them, or teaching them special skills (such as "dreaming" for the Australian Walpiri, necessary for the culture to exist (DeLoache and Gottlieb, 2000, 148–170)), children are viewed as important (via different models). However, it does make a difference whether you view children as inherently sinful, neutral like cattle, or godlike. The sorts of positive goods of agency afforded to the children are often (descriptively) a function of the existing community worldview.

Univocal Contracts

A key ground of duties to children comes from the nature of univocal contracts. A univocal contract is one in which one party sets the terms of the contract. In a free (unrestricted) univocal contract the other party can take or leave the terms of the contract. So, for example, an insurance company has a contract for their car insurance policy. You may examine the policy, but there is no negotiation on the wording of the coverage—only on the amount purchased (or not).

In restricted univocal contracts one party sets down all the terms and the recipient must accept the terms without recourse. For example, this is the sort of contract that is given to citizens of states that do not allow emigration. The individual must accept the terms of living within the society without any recourse. It is also the sort of contract that conscripts its young people into the army: they must train and enlist in the army or face very serious consequences.

The moral duty that arises from univocal contracts is that the one offering such a contract should extend greater care than the recipient. In free univocal contracts within the United States, this moral principle is observed in our legal system (Casenotes, 2007, Chap. 5). There has been very little study of restricted univocal contracts since in most cases they are set within repressive public contexts that do not have a robust rule of law (and in that sense are only nominally contracts). However, if we were to use the same principle of ensuing duties that applies to free univocal contracts, viz., that the one-sided nature of the contract conveys more responsibilities to the contract originator than to the individual confronted by the contract, then, by extension, the duties upon the contract originator under restricted univocal contracts would be even higher. If this logic is correct, then we have another model by which to understand duties to children: restricted univocal contracts. No child is consulted by the parents about being brought into the world. We find ourselves born into a family, a community, and a nation—none of which we had any power over. This condition of being *thrown into the middle of things* by the power of our parents constitutes a restricted univocal contract. It is univocal because the parents created the context of our existence and set all the rules. It is restricted because (in the case of young children) they cannot just walk away from the contract. (Infants cannot walk or crawl. Toddlers have a very limited sense of their environmental options. Young children and preteens generally cannot successfully fend for themselves without assistance. In the case of teenagers below the age of eighteen, the "restricted" nature of the contract becomes less pronounced.)

If children find themselves on the receiving end of a restricted univocal contract, then under the above paradigm, the parents have strong consequent duties to protect and defend their children according to what the shared community worldview says is the best environmental conditions for the child (see the communities section). Such a duty flows from the nature of restricted univocal contracts. The community worldview standards must be tempered by the Table of Embeddedness that is universally valid (see the third endnote). Thus, if some society thinks that female genital mutilation is part of the shared community worldview, but there is no intersubjectively agreed-upon enhancement in action potential for the child (viewed on international empirical medical standards), then this particular societal duty will be morally prohibited.

However, in the case of the level-one basic goods of agency—food, water, sanitation, clothing, shelter, protection from unwarranted bodily harm (including health care)—there is an incumbent duty on the parents' part to provide these to their children (along with the other basic goods as they are able to provide these). This is not an act of charity, but a firm ought that stems from their decision to have these children.[10]

No child was ever consulted about being born to this or that family or situation. As such he or she does not deserve the advantage or disadvantage of such an outcome. The contract originators, the biological parents, have a contractual duty (based upon the nature of univocal restricted contracts) to provide to their children as many of the goods of agency (measured against the Table of Embeddedness) as possible (at least through level-one secondary goods). This is a third sort of duty to children that flows from parents. This description of duty is often called the right to an open future (Feinberg, 1992). In this context we have a conflict between the rights of parents and children about what is in their best interests. A pivotal US legal case in this regard was *Wisconsin v. Yoder* (406 U.S. 205 [1972]). In this case the dispute concerned Amish parents who would not allow their children to attend school past the eighth grade in violation of Wisconsin state law, which required all children to attend school until sixteen.

Kenneth Henley challenges the contention that such rules were necessary for the Amish way of life to continue in the modern age, saying, "If this claim is true, then such traditional ways of life have no right to survive" (1979, 262). Feinburg (1992) concurs, saying that in the modern world "an educable youth whose parents legally withdraw him from school has suffered an invasion of his rights of trust" (86). Other writers such as Giroux (1999) and Malvern (2000) come to similar conclusions using the ideas of "promise" and "innocence." But *mere* provision of the structural goods necessary for as many options as possible is not the best of all possible worlds. As we will see in the next section, *love* and doing well for the child are also necessary (Prusak, 2008). All of these various terms can be worked into the concept of restricted univocal contracts. It is this author's opinion that this moral-legal approach is superior to the anticipatory rights approach that is the actual ground of Feinburg's argument. Though they may predict many similar outcomes, the advantage of my approach is that it is always seen within the context of the Table of Embeddedness and a parent's ability to perform (the ought implies can caveat).[11] When parents cannot provide those goods that a child can legitimately claim (basic goods and level-one secondary goods), then other institutions must step in: the local community, the state, and the international community—in that order. The inability of a parent to execute the duties incumbent from restrictive univocal contracts because of legitimate lack of resources creates an unfulfilled positive duty. When such a situation occurs, these other contextual bodies have a duty to step in because at the end of the day, the children of the world have legitimate rights claims to at least the basic goods of agency. This right is proximately *against* the parents and then successively against the local community, the state, and the international community in that order.

Love and Children

There is something queer about declaring a duty to love. This is because love is often considered to be under the genus of the emotions. Emotions are often taken to be out of one's direct control—"like over-hasty servants who run out before they have heard all their instructions, and then carry them out wrongly" (Aristotle, 1894, 1149a 25) and "love out of inclination cannot be commanded" (Kant, 1785, 399). One cannot be commanded to perform a deed that is out of one's direct control. If love is an emotion, and emotions are out of our direct control, then QED: one cannot be commanded to love.

In commanding what is out of one's direct control, I am reminded of the fictional command given by Miss Havisham to Pip that he should *play*! (and fall in love with Estella) in Charles Dickens's *Great Expectations*. Pip was in a rather constrained environment with Estella. He ends up engaged in the card game "beggar thy neighbor" (Pip came from the working class).

Certainly there are different sorts of love. Some aspects of these various meanings of love may be more or less in our power. If being friendly and cordial to others is a sort of love, then surely that is roughly in our control to create such a habit. On the other hand, sexual attraction (sometimes referred to as love) is biologically based. We cannot force ourselves to be sexually attracted to someone who biologically repels us.

The sort of love that is *a propos* here is one that has connections to morality that we *can* control. This process begins with a *disposition* to connect emotionally to others: sympathy.[12] One can voluntarily create habits that dispose her to regard others in such a way that (for the most part) she tries to view all people she comes into contact with as individuals possessing personal stories that are grounded in human dignity. Because of this disposition to regard others in the context of dignity, an *openness* occurs in the emotional connection. This openness implies evenhandedness. Each party is on par. It is this author's conjecture that sympathy that is open will lead to a response of *care* (Tong, 2009, 163–199; see also Noddings, 1984). Care is an action-guiding response. When another person is in need (with whom one has open-sympathy), then care will require an action response in the other's best interest. This solves the issue of moral motivation. Care ensures that those with whom one has a relationship of open sympathy will receive an action response that the care giver understands through her sympathetic, open relationship to be in the other's best interest (meaning what the other would want if he were to consider *his* own best interest).[13] It has been my contention that the triad of sympathy, openness, and care constitutes philosophical love (Boylan, 2004, 34–43). Since this definition of philosophical love begins in a disposition that one consciously and voluntarily nurtures, one can be commanded to engage in the process (since anything within one's direct power to perform can be commanded).

Thus, philosophical love of people we come into contact with directly (via the shared community worldview imperative) or indirectly (via the extended community worldview imperative) can be commanded without incurring the aforesaid difficulties.

All persons on earth must consider with love the lot of all other people on earth. However, when we consider children, the dynamics change a bit. *Children* (depending upon where they are on the purposive agent continuum) are not fully agents. We often adopt an *unequal* sympathy when we confront them directly or by extension. This is generally a mistake (Benporath, 2003; Ariès, 1962). This is because children possess (in actuality) many characteristics that deserve respect (despite their status as protected individuals). Thus, children possess a dual rights claim: one, from their status as protected potential agents; and two, from their actual personal ground of dignity that is born from their individual narratives (autonomy). Only children possess this dual rights claim;[14] thus this claim requires *more* and not *less* moral consideration in providing them with at least the basic goods of agency based on love with the ultimate purpose of enabling as many possible futures as the society and history can offer (an open future).

In closing this section, it should be noted that I have avoided situating love in a traditional parental context that rests upon biological determinism. The reason for this is that this sort of love is fickle because its biological origin is out of one's control and because of this it is often overridden by other egoistic concerns on the part of parents (due to the parents' own personal pleasures, on the one hand, and on the other hand to the parents' anger that often translates into domestic violence against the weakest member on the food chain: the children). To remedy this, I have appealed to a command to philosophical love that all parties—parents, society, and the world—owe to children everywhere.

The International Context

The basis of rights claims, univocal contracts, philosophical love, and the extended community worldview imperative all support a strong commitment to children's rights that may or may not be recognized by existing community worldviews. Since the aforesaid reasons argue for recognizing basic goods of agency for all children, it seems productive to make a list of the most pressing action items that the world must address:

- Providing all the children of the world the level-one basic goods of agency (including specifically all of the following):
  - Providing all children at least 500 calories a day (the very minimum level to stay alive) with the aspirational goal of 1,000 calories a day (the very minimum to avoid stunting, wasting, or being underweight—level-one basic goods)
  - Providing clean water and sanitation (level-one basic goods)
  - Educating families on the nutritional needs of young children, including the value of breastfeeding and the importance of introducing suitable complementary foods at the right age (level-one basic goods)
- Protecting children from infection by immunizing them against common childhood diseases and by providing safe water and sanitation (level-one basic goods)
- Protecting the children of the world from being born with HIV/AIDS though public health measures such as distributing condoms and medicating HIV-positive mothers so they will not transmit the disease to their children (level-one basic goods)
- Providing malaria nets for all families at no cost to them (level-one basic goods)
- Supporting research toward medical vaccines for malaria and HIV/AIDS (along with other various water-washed and waterborne diseases)
- Paying special attention to the nutritional needs of girls and women, since chronically undernourished women tend to bear low-birthweight babies, perpetuating the vicious cycle of undernutrition (level-one basic goods)
- Removing land mines from war areas (level-one basic goods)
- Creating safe havens in war-torn areas for families (level-one basic goods)
- Protecting children from being sold as slaves in the sex-trafficking industry (level-one basic goods)
- Providing all the children of the world level-two basic goods (including specifically all of the following):
  - Taking measures to increase attendance at primary and secondary schools for males and females alike (level-two basic goods)
  - Enforcing child labor laws (level-two basic goods)

- Seeking the establishment of general public policies that recognize the dignity of children and take steps to protect their interests in law through: (for example) child-friendly accommodations required in new building construction, family-nurturing work rules for parents (childcare and parental leave policies), monetary support for children in poverty (level-two basic goods), targeted programs for special needs children, etc.

This is a very modest list. Of course other level-two basic goods and level-one secondary goods *ought* to be available to all (Boylan, 2004, Chap. 7). But if we are concerned with aspirational, concrete goals that can be realistically set before us for action within a short time horizon, the aforesaid bullet points offer a steep but realizable goal.

Conclusion

This essay has argued for the recognition of the rights of children and the ensuing duties upon us all to the children of the world. This is not restricted to national boundaries because the arguments based upon the basis of rights claims, univocal contracts, philosophical love, and the extended community worldview imperative all support a strong commitment to children's rights at least including level-one basic rights (as judged on the Table of Embeddedness). It is up to the rest of us to respond through the four channels of international action: one, governmental action; two, United Nations action; three, nongovernmental organizational action; and four, committed personal action. The time to act is now. We must hurry for the time is growing late.

Notes

1. These three categories describe three states caused by malnutrition: *Underweight*: proportion of under-fives falling below minus 2 standard deviations (moderate and severe) and minus 3 standard deviations (severe) from the *median weight-for-age* of the reference population; *Stunting*: proportion of under-fives falling below minus 2 standard deviations (moderate and severe) and minus 3 standard deviations (severe) from the *median height-for-age* of the reference population; *Wasting*: Proportion of under-fives falling below minus 2 standard deviations (moderate and severe) and minus 3 standard deviations (severe) from the *median weight-for-height* of the reference population (definitions from the Child Fund, accessed 01 December 2009: www.childfund.org/).

2. Education

Countries and Territories	Primary School Net Enrollment Rate, 2000–2007 (percent)		Primary School Net Attendance Rate, 2000–2007 (percent)	
	Male	Female	Male	Female
Sub-Saharan Africa	75	70	64	61
Eastern and Southern Africa	83	81	66	66
West and Central Africa	67	58	63	56
Middle East and North Africa	86	81	88	85
South Asia	88	83	81	77
East Asia and Pacific	98	97	92[e]	92[e]
Latin America and Caribbean	94	95	90	91
Central and Eastern Europe, CIS	92	90	93	91
Industrialized countries	95	96	–	–
Developing countries	89	86	80[e]	77[e]
Least developed countries	79	74	65	63
World	90	87	80[e]	77[e]

Countries and Territories	Secondary School Net Enrollment Rate, 2000–2007 (percent)		Secondary School Net Attendance Rate, 2000–2007 (percent)	
	Male	Female	Male	Female
Sub-Saharan Africa	28	24	26	22
Eastern and Southern Africa	30	27	20	18
West and Central Africa	26	20	31	26
Middle East and North Africa	67	62	54	52
South Asia	–	–	51	43
East Asia and Pacific	60[e]	62[e]	60[e]	63[e]
Latin America and Caribbean	69	74	–	–
Central and Eastern Europe, CIS	79	75	79	76
Industrialized countries	91	92	–	–
Developing countries	51[e]	49[e]	48[e]	43[e]
Least developed countries	30	26	26	24
World	58[e]	57[e]	48[e]	44[e]

[e] Excludes China.

SOURCE: *The State of the World's Children 2009*, UNICEF.

3. See the Table of Embeddedness in Chapter 8 for my view of this hierarchy of goods necessary for purposive action.

4. My argument for this is as follows:

1. All people, by nature, desire to be good—Fundamental Assumption
2. In order to become good, one must be able to act—Fact
3. All people, by nature, desire to act—1, 2
4. People value what is natural to them—Assertion
5. What people value they wish to protect—Assertion
6. All people wish to protect their ability to act—3–5
7. Fundamental interpersonal "oughts" are expressed via our highest value systems: morality, aesthetics, and religion—Assertion
8. All people must agree, upon pain of logical contradiction, that what is natural and desirable to them individually is natural and desirable to everyone collectively and individually—Assertion
9. Everyone must seek personal protection for her own ability to act via morality, aesthetics, and religion—6, 7
10. Everyone, upon pain of logical contradiction, must admit that all other humans will seek personal protection of their ability to act via morality, aesthetics, and religion—8, 9
11. All people must agree, upon pain of logical contradiction, that since the attribution of the basic goods of agency are predicated generally, it is inconsistent to assert idiosyncratic preference—Fact
12. Goods that are claimed through generic predication apply equally to each agent and everyone has a stake in their protection—10, 11
13. Rights and duties are correlative—Assertion

---

14. Everyone has at least a moral right to the basic goods of agency and others in the society have a duty to provide those goods to all—12, 13

5. This analysis of claim rights comes from Wesley N. Holfeld, *Fundamental Legal Conceptions* (New Haven, CT: Yale University Press, 1919).

6. Boylan (2004: 181–187).

7. Aristotle, the first systematic biologist in the Western tradition, used the expression *epi to polu* ("for the most part") to describe the realm of what needs to be proven. Today this can be viewed from the eyes of statistics as proving the null set between 0.5 to .05 percent (the standards used in pharmaceutical trials). We need not see the extremes as a telling counterexample, as some counterexample in physics (which aspires to 100 percent) might be. For physics, one counterexample falsifies the model. For discussions of social philosophy the super majority of 75 percent is more reasonable.

8. These imperatives are: the shared community imperative—"Each agent must contribute to a common body of knowledge that supports the creation of a shared

community worldview (that is itself complete, coherent, and good) through which social institutions and their resulting policies might flourish within the constraints of the essential core commonly held values (ethics, aesthetics, and religion)," and the extended community worldview imperative—"Each agent must educate himself as much as he is able about the peoples of the world—their access to the basic goods of agency, their essential commonly held cultural values, and their governmental and institutional structures—in order that he might individually and collectively accept the duties that ensue from those peoples' legitimate rights claims, and to act accordingly within what is aspirationally possible." A more detailed account of these imperatives can be found in Boylan (2011, Chap. 2).

9. I would like to thank Linda Cote-Reilly, a developmental psychologist, for steering me toward DeLoache and Gottlieb and discussing the significance of this in light of contemporary developmental psychology.

10. This argument does not apply to those women who did not choose to have children but find themselves pregnant, such as those who were raped or subject to domestic incest or in any other way did not intend to become pregnant.

11. As I have said in the past, the ought implies can caveat should not be used as an excuse to get out of fulfilling real duties owed to others (Boylan, 2004, 162 et passim).

12 .This *disposition* is not too dissimilar to Joseph Raz's version of love as an *attitude* (1994, 11) except that in this context the disposition is toward the first step in a sequential process—toward sympathy. The ability to control this disposition would be similar to the three steps toward habits outlined by Matthew Liao (2006b, 5–7; 2006a, 426–430); however, unlike Liao, I focus exclusively on the first step in the process—sympathy—and contend that the other steps will follow.

13. This can sound a bit like paternalism/maternalism, but it need not be viscous. Viscous paternalism/maternalism stems from the caregiver's own personal worldview and not that of the receiving party. In this sort of care, the prior relationship of open sympathy puts everyone on an even level.

14. The disabled also possess a dual claim, but the grounding of it is somewhat different. In some ways disabled children possess a triple claim, but an analysis of this is beyond the scope of this essay.

References

Ariès, P. (1962). *Centuries of Childhood: A Social History of Family Life.* New York: Knopf.

Aristotle. (1894 [1985] from Bywater's text). *Nicomachean Ethics*, trans. Terence Irwin. Indianapolis, IN: Hackett.

Bartunek, Jean M. (2005). *Church Ethics and Its Organizational Context: Learning from the Sex Abuse Scandal in the Catholic Church (Boston College Church in the 21st Century Series).* Lanham, MD: Rowman and Littlefield.

Benporath, Sigal R. (2003). "Autonomy and Vulnerability: On Just Relations Between Adults and Children." *Journal of Philosophy of Education 37*(1): 127–145.

Beyleveld, Deryck. (1991). *The Dialectical Necessity of Morality.* Chicago: University of Chicago Press.

Boylan, Michael. (2004). *A Just Society.* Lanham, MD and Oxford: Rowman and Littlefield.

Boylan, Michael. (2011). *Morality and Global Justice: Justifications and Applications.* Boulder, CO: Westview.

Brecher, Robert. (2008). *Torture and the Ticking Time Bomb.* Oxford: Blackwell.

Casenotes. (2007). *Casenote Legal Briefs Contracts: Keyed to Knapp, Crystal, and Prince, Sixth Edition.* New York: Aspen Publishers.

Child Fund. ChildFund.org. Data constantly updated. Figures for this paper are from 01 December 2009. Retrieved from www.childfund.org

Churchill, Robert Paul. (2006). *Human Rights and Global Diversity.* Upper Saddle River, NJ: Prentice Hall.

DeLoache, Judy, and Alma Gottlieb. (2000). *A World of Babies: Imagined Childcare Guides for Seven Societies.* Cambridge: Cambridge University Press.

Dickens, Charles. (1862 [1998]). *Great Expectations*, ed. Margaret Cardwell. London: Oxford University Press.

Feinberg, Joel. (1992). "The Child's Right to an Open Future" in *Freedom and Fulfillment: Philosophical Essays*: 76–97. Princeton, NJ: Princeton University Press.

Gewirth, Alan. (1978). *Reason and Morality.* Chicago: University of Chicago Press.

Giroux, H. (1999). "Public Intellectuals and the Challenge of Children's Culture: Youth and the Politics of Innocence." *The Review of Education, Pedagogy & Cultural Studies 21*(3): 193–225.

Griffin, James. (2008). *On Human Rights.* Oxford: Oxford University Press.

Henley, Kenneth. (1979). "The Authority to Educate" in *Having Children: Philosophical and Legal Reflections on Parenthood,* ed. Onora O'Neill and William Rudick: 254–264. New York: Oxford University Press.

Kant, Immanuel. (1785 [1964]). *Groundwork of the Metaphysics of Morals*, trans. H. J. Paton. New York: Harper and Row.

Liao, S. Matthew. (2006a). "The Right of Children to Be Loved." *Journal of Political Philosophy 14*(4): 420–440.

Liao, S. Matthew. (2006b). "The Idea of a Duty to Love." *Journal of Value Inquiry 40*: 1–22.

Malvern, S. (2000). "The Ends of Innocence: Modern Art and Modern Children." *Art History 23*(4): 627–632.

Mann, Jonathan. (1996). "Health and Human Rights." *British Medical Journal 312*: 924–925.

Mann, Jonathan. (1997). "Medicine and Public Health: Ethics and Human Rights." *Hastings Center Report 27*(3): 6–13.

Mayer, Jane. (2009). *The Dark Side: The Inside Story of How the War on Terror Turned into a War on American Ideals.* New York: Anchor.

Noddings, Nel. (1984). *Caring: A Feminine Approach to Ethics and Moral Education.* Berkeley: University of California Press.

Pogge, Thomas W. (2008). *World Poverty and Human Rights, Second Edition.* Oxford: Polity Press.

Prusak, Bernard. (2008). "Not Good Enough Parenting: What's Wrong with the Child's Right to an Open Future." *Social Theory and Practice 34*(2): 271–291.

Rawls, John. (1971). *A Theory of Justice.* Cambridge, MA: Harvard University Press.

Rawls, John. (1999). *The Law of Peoples.* Cambridge, MA: Harvard University Press.

Raz, Joseph. (1986). *The Morality of Freedom.* Oxford: Clarendon Press.

Raz, Joseph. (1994). *Ethics in the Public Domain: Essays in the Morality of Law and Politics.* Oxford: Oxford University Press.

Robinson, Bishop Geoffrey. (2008). *Confronting Power and Sex in the Catholic Church.* Collegeville, MN: Liturgical Press.

Scanlon, T. M. (1998). *What We Owe Each Other.* Cambridge, MA: Harvard University Press.

Sen, Amartya. (2000). *Development as Freedom.* New York: Anchor.

Shaffer, David R., and Katherine Kipp. (2009). *Developmental Psychology: Childhood and Adolescence.* Belmont, CA: Wadsworth.

Shue, Henry. (1996). *Basic Rights, Second Edition.* Princeton, NJ: Princeton University Press.

Singer, Beth. (1993). *Operative Rights.* Albany, NY: SUNY Press.

Spence, Edward. (2006). *Ethics Within Reason.* Lanham, MD: Lexington Press.

Tong, Rosemarie. (2009). *Feminist Thought, Third Edition.* Boulder, CO: Westview.

Weisberg, Jacob. (2009, May 2). "All the President's Accomplices: How the Country Acquiesced to Bush's Torture Policy." Slate.com. Retrieved from http://www.slate.com/id/2217359/

Yoo, John. (2003, March 14). "Memorandum for William J. Haynes II, General Counsel of the Department of Defense: Re: Military Interrogation of Alien Unlawful Combatants Held Outside the United States." Washington, DC: U.S. Department of Justice [Office of the Deputy Assistant Attorney General].

ABOUT THE CONTRIBUTORS

Michael Boylan received his PhD from the University of Chicago. He is professor of philosophy at Marymount University. Boylan is the author of ninety-five articles on philosophy, the history of science, and literature and twenty-four books, including *A Just Society* (2004), *The Extinction of Desire* (2007), *Basic Ethics,* Second Edition (2008), *The Good, The True, and The Beautiful* (2008), *Philosophy: An Innovative Introduction* (with Charles Johnson, 2009), and *Morality and Global Justice* (2011). He was a fellow at the Center for American Progress 2007–2009 and has lectured in nine countries around the world.

Robert Paul Churchill is professor of philosophy at The George Washington University and served for many years as chair of the department, and director of the Peace Studies Program. He earned his doctorate at Johns Hopkins University with a dissertation on civil disobedience. He has published on a wide range of issues centering on human rights, global ethics, just war theory, genocide, crimes against humanity, weapons of mass destruction, and nonviolence and toleration, as well as logic and political philosophy more generally. His published works include *Becoming Logical, Democracy, Social Values and Public Policy* (ed.), *The Ethics of Liberal Democracy* (ed.), and *Human Rights and Global Diversity.* He is presently working on two books: *Universal Human Rights: A Defense* and *Consuming Desires: An Analysis of Greed.*

David Cummiskey, PhD, is a professor of philosophy at Bates College. He teaches moral philosophy, medical ethics, philosophy of law, and political philosophy at Bates College. Cummiskey is also a medical ethics consultant at Mid Coast Hospital, Brunswick, Maine, and at Central Maine Medical Center, Lewiston, Maine. His primary research interests are contemporary Kantian ethics, consequentialism, and international and crosscultural approaches to issues in medical ethics. He is the author of *Kantian Consequentialism* (Oxford University Press, 1996).

James A. Donahue is president and professor of ethics of the Graduate Theological Union. Before coming to the GTU, he served as professor of theology and ethics, dean of students, and vice president of Student Affairs at Georgetown University. Donahue is the coauthor of *Ethics Across the Curriculum: A Practice-Based Approach*, and coeditor of *Religion, Ethics and the Common Good.* His research is focused on the construction of religious identity in a global world. Donahue holds a BA from the College of the Holy Cross, an MDiv from Princeton Theological Seminary, and a PhD from the Graduate Theological Union.

Simona Giordano is a reader in bioethics at the Centre for Social Ethics and Policy, and Institute for Science Ethics and Innovation, in the School of Law of the University of Manchester. Simona was awarded the degree of Dottoressa in Filosofia with a dissertation on Henry Sidgwick and Aristotle at the University of Rome in 1996 and a PhD in Psychiatric Ethics in Manchester in 2001. She is the author of *Understanding Eating Disorders* (2005) and *Exercise and Eating Disorders* (2010). She has worked on gender identity studies since 2005, and obtained the award for the best ethics research on gender identity in the year 2007 by the Gender Identity Research and Education Society (GIRES), UK.

John-Stewart Gordon holds an MA and BA in philosophy and history from Konstanz University (2001) and a PhD in philosophy from Göttingen University (2005). He is currently professor and chair for anthropology and ethics at the University of Cologne and is conducting a research project on "human rights in bioethics" which is funded by the Heinrich Hertz-Stiftung. Furthermore, he is a member of the board of *Bioethics* as well as area-editor of the Internet Encyclopedia of Philosophy (IEP). John published several books as single author and editor and is currently coeditor of *Bioethics and Culture* (2011). In addition, he has published peer-reviewed articles in journals, encyclopedias, and volumes such as *Bioethics, Journal for Business, Economics,* and *Ethics and IEP.* John taught philosophy at Tübingen University, Ruhr-University Bochum, Duisburg-Essen University, and Queen's University, Kingston Canada.

Christian F. Illies, PhD, is the chair in philosophy at the Otto-Friedrich University, Bamberg, Germany. Illies studied in Heidelberg, Konstanz, École Normale Supérieure, Fontenay/St. Cloud, and at Oxford (as a Rhodes Scholar). His research focuses on ethics and metaethics, philosophy of biology, philosophical anthropology, and philosophy of culture and technology. He is the author of *Darwin* (1999, coauthored with V. Hösle), *The Grounds of Ethical Judgement* (2003), and *Philosophische Anthropologie im biologischen Zeitalter* (2006).

Julie E. Kirsch received her PhD in philosophy at the University of Toronto. She teaches philosophy at D'Youville College. She has published journal and encyclopedia articles on moral epistemology and moral psychology—particularly on the problem of self-deception.

Hallvard Lillehammer teaches moral and political philosophy at Cambridge University, where he is Sidgwick Lecturer and University Senior Lecturer in the Faculty of Philosophy. He is the author of *Companions in Guilt: Arguments for Ethical Objectivity* (Palgrave Macmillan, 2007).

Seumas Miller is professor of philosophy at Charles Sturt University and the Australian National University (joint position), as well as being a research fellow at Delft University of Technology. He is also foundation director of the Centre of Applied Philosophy and Public Ethics (an Australian Research Council Special Research Centre). He is the author of over a hundred academic articles and twelve books including: *Social Action* (2001), *Ethical Issues in Policing* (with John Blackler, 2005), *Corruption and Anti-Corruption* (with Peter Roberts and Ed Spence, 2005), *Terrorism and Counter-Terrorism* (2009) and *The Moral Foundations of Social Institutions* (2010).

Nien-hê Hsieh is an associate professor in the Legal Studies and Business Ethics Department at the Wharton School, University of Pennsylvania with a secondary appointment in the Department of Philosophy. He also serves as codirector of the Wharton Ethics Program. He writes about ethical issues in economic activity and ways to structure economic institutions to meet the demands of justice. Current research topics include the moral dimensions of work, incommensurable values, and the responsibilities of managers and corporations in relation to the support of just political institutions. Hsieh holds a BA in economics from Swarthmore College, an MPhil in politics from Oxford University, and a PhD in economics from Harvard University. He was a Postdoctoral Fellow at Harvard Business School, and has held visiting fellowships at Harvard University, Oxford University, and the Research School for Social Sciences at the Australian National University.

Gabriel Palmer-Fernández is director of the Dr. James Dale Ethics Center and professor in the Department of Philosophy and Religious Studies at Youngstown State University. His publications include several books, the most recent of which is the *Encyclopedia of Religion and War*, and numerous scholarly articles in the ethics of political violence, medical ethics, and the history of Christian ethics.

Thomas Pogge received his PhD in philosophy from Harvard and writes and teaches widely on Kant and in moral and political philosophy. He is Leitner Professor of Philosophy and International Affairs at Yale, professorial fellow at the Australian National University Centre for Applied Philosophy and Public Ethics (CAPPE), research director at the Oslo University Centre for the Study of Mind in Nature (CSMN) and adjunct professor of political philosophy at the University of Central Lancashire. His recent publications include *Politics as Usual* and *World Poverty and Human Rights*, Second Edition (2010 and 2008). With support from the Australian Research Council, the BUPA Foundation and the European Commission, Pogge's current work is focused on a team effort toward developing a complement to the pharmaceutical patent regime that would improve access to advanced medicines for the poor worldwide (see www.healthimpactfund.org).

Laura M. Purdy received a PhD from Stanford University; she is professor of philosophy and Ruth and Albert Koch Professor of Humanities at Wells College, where she has been based since 1979. She was a postdoctoral associate in the Program on Science Technology, and Society at Cornell University (1975–1977), Irwin Chair at Hamilton College in 1988–89, and a bioethicist and professor of philosophy at the University Health Network and University of Toronto Joint Centre for Bioethics from 1997 to 2000. Her areas of specialization are applied ethics, primarily bioethics, reproductive ethics, family issues, and feminism. She is author of *In Their Best Interest? The Case Against Equal Rights for Children*, and *Reproducing Persons: Issues in Feminist Bioethics;* and coeditor of *Feminist Perspectives in Medical Ethics* (with Helen B. Holmes), *Violence Against Women: Philosophical Perspectives* (with Stanley French and Wanda Teays), *Embodying Bioethics: Recent Feminist Advances* (with Anne Donchin), and *Bioethics, Justice, and Health Care* (with Wanda Teays), as well as many articles.

Doris Schroeder is professor of moral philosophy and director of the Centre for Professional Ethics at the University of Central Lancashire, UK, and professorial fellow in the Centre for Applied Philosophy and Public Ethics at the University of Melbourne, Australia. Her background is in philosophy, politics, and economics. Prior to joining academia, she worked as a business planner for Warner Music. Her main areas of interest are international justice, human rights, dignity, and benefit sharing.

Michael J. Selgelid earned a BS in biomedical engineering from Duke University and a PhD in philosophy from the University of California, San Diego. He is a senior research fellow in the Centre for Applied Philosophy and Public Ethics (CAPPE) at the Australian National University (in Canberra), where he is also director of a World Health Organization (WHO) Collaborating Centre for Bioethics and deputy director of the National Centre for Biosecurity. He held previous appointments at the University of Sydney (Australia) and the University of the Witwatersrand (Johannesburg, South Africa). His research focuses on ethical issues associated with infectious disease and genetics. He coauthored *Ethical and Philosophical Consideration of the Dual-Use Dilemma in the Biological Sciences* (Springer, 2008) and coedited *Ethics and Infectious Disease* (2006). He has over a hundred publications in total.

Peter Singer is Ira W. DeCamp Professor of Bioethics in the University Center for Human Values at Princeton University and Laureate Professor at the University of Melbourne. His books include *Animal Liberation, Practical Ethics, Rethinking Life and Death, One World,* and most recently, *The Life You Can Save.*

Klaus Steigleder is professor of philosophy at Ruhr University Bochum in Germany. He works principally on theoretical and applied ethics with a special emphasis upon Kant and Gewirth (in theoretical ethics) and economic ethics, ethics of risk, and bioethics (in applied ethics). His most recent books are *Geschichte, Theorie, und Ethik der Medizin* (2006, coeditor with Stefan Schulz, Heiner Fangerau, and Norbert W. Paul), *Die Aktualität der Philosophie Kants* (2005, coeditor with Kirsten Schmidt and Burkhard Mojsisch), *Bioethik* (2003, coeditor with Marcus Düwell), *Kants Moralphilosophie* (2002), and *Grundlegung der normativen Ethik: Der Ansatz von Alan Gewirth* (1999).

Wanda Teays, PhD, from Concordia University, Montreal, is a professor of philosophy and department chair at Mount St. Mary's College in Los Angeles. Her books include: *Second Thoughts: Critical Thinking for a Diverse Society,* Second Edition (2009). She coedited (with Laura Purdy) *Bioethics, Justice, and Health Care* (2001) and (with Stanley G. French and Laura Purdy) *Violence Against Women: Philosophical Perspectives* (1998). To accompany her bioethics anthology, she selected film clips on bioethics in the news for a CNN-produced video. Her most recent articles are "Torture and Public Health," published in Michael Boylan, ed., *International Public Health Ethics and Policy* (2008) and "Extinguishing Desire: Not Such a Simple Plan After All," in John-Stewart Gordon, ed., *Morality and Politics: Reading Boylan's* A Just Society (2009). She also wrote "From Fear to Eternity: Violence and Public Health" in Michael Boylan, ed., *Public Health Policy and Ethics* (2004); "The Ethics of Performance Enhancing Drugs" in Teays and Purdy, ed., *Bioethics, Justice & Health Care* (2001); and other articles in the area of bioethics, justice, and the law. She is currently working with John-Stewart Gordon and Alison Renteln on an anthology in the area of bioethics and culture.

Dr. Rosemarie Tong is Distinguished Professor for Health Care Ethics in the department of philosophy and director of the Center for Professional and Applied Ethics at the University of North Carolina at Charlotte. She received her PhD in philosophy from Temple University in 1978 and her MA in philosophy from Catholic University in 1971. Dr. Tong joined the UNC Charlotte faculty in 1999. Previously, she taught for a decade at Davidson College, NC, and before that a decade at Williams College, MA. Dr. Tong has over 150 publications, including books, book chapters, journal articles, and reviews. Her most recent book is *New Perspectives in Health Care Ethics: An Interdisciplinary and Crosscultural Approach*. Other books include *Feminist Thought: A More Comprehensive Introduction*; *Globalizing Feminist Bioethics: Crosscultural Perspectives*; *Linking Visions: Feminist Bioethics, Human Rights, and the Developing World*; *Feminist Philosophy: Essential Readings in Theory, Reinterpretation, and Application*; *Feminine and Feminist Ethics*; *Feminist Approaches to Bioethics*; and *Ethics in Public Policy*. Much demanded as a speaker on feminist concerns and healthcare ethics issues, Dr. Tong has given close to three hundred presentations, regionally, nationally, and internationally. Within the past four years she has addressed audiences in Beijing, Taipei, Helsinki, London, Mexico City, and Sydney.

INDEX

Abassi, Feroz, 73
Abu Ghraib prison scandal, 72
Academy, 146–147
  global ethics in, 281–291
  goals and outcomes in, 285–286
  interdisciplinarity and, 284–285
  nature of religious discourse in, 283
  theory and practice in, 283–284
Action
  belief and, 4–5, 52–53
  collective, 129, 130
  freedom and, 34
  motivation and, 4
  social institutions and, 129
  well-being and, 34
Adams, Robert, 265, 317
Afghanistan, 71, 302, 329, 332
Africa, 17, 28, 187–191, 192, 196, 213, 217–218, 222
African Commission for Human and People's Rights, 233
Aguilar, Maria del Socorro Pedro de, 69
AIDS, 187–191, 192, 196, 215, 217–218, 219–220, 221–222, 385, 397
Allah. *See* Islam
Amnesty International, 30
Anscombe, Elisabeth, 86, 105–106, 117–118, 333
Anthropology, 87, 106, 119–120, 330
Antigone (Sophocles), 31
Apartheid, 29, 217
Aquinas, St. Thomas, 209, 242–244, 333, 335
Arab American News, 70
Arar, Maher, 72, 73
Archer, John, 367
Arendt, Hannah, 22
Aristotle, 4, 30–31, 32–33, 87, 113, 390
Asoka, King, 296, 314, 317–319, 320–321
Augustine, St., 297, 326, 332–333
Australia, 142
Australian National University, 208

Baird, Zoë, 356
Bandura, Albert, 370, 371
Baron-Cohen, Simon, 372
Basic Rights (Shue), 11–12
Beauchamp, Tom, 42
Begg, Moazzam, 73
Beitz, Charles, 28
Belief
  action and, 4–5, 52–53
  bias and, 5
  consequentialism and, 52, 62
  direct and indirect control of, 5, 54
  education and, 5
  ethics of, 5, 52–57
  extended-community worldview imperative and, 5, 61
  formation of, 5
  freedom of, 69–70
  hierarchy of, 5
  ignorance and, 5, 57–63
  involuntary nature of, 53
  management of, 5, 55
  moral significance of, 52–57

Belief *(continued)*
  nature of, 5, 54
  personal worldview imperative and, 5, 57–60
  shared-community worldview imperative and, 5
Beneficence, 187
  ethics of, 86, 93–95, 97–98
  morality of, 93
Benjamin, Harry, 378
Bill of Rights, U.S., 29, 387
Bin Laden, Osama, 67
Bose, Christine E., 345, 350
Botswana, 188
Bowlby, John, 372
Boy Scouts of America, 6, 76
Boylan, Michael, 4, 35–36, 248, 330
  belief and, 61
  deontological ethics and, 108, 115
  extended-community worldview imperative and, 22
  ignorance and, 60
  personal worldview imperative and, 57
Bradbury, Steven, 72
Branstetter, Lee, 238
Brazil, 159
Britain, 209
Brookings Institution, 130, 157
Buchanan, Allen, 10, 13, 14
Buddhism
  Asoka, King and, 296, 297, 314, 317–319, 320–321
  Dalai Lama and, 299, 300, 312, 314, 317
  Doctrine of Emptiness and, 310–311
  Doctrine of Skillful Means and, 315–317
  just war theory and, 295, 296–297, 299, 300, 309–321
  pacifism and, 295, 296, 299, 315
  Tibetan, 296, 313–315
  Zen, 313
Burkina Faso, 188
Bush, George W., 72–73, 222, 264, 328, 389–390
Business ethics, 134, 169
Bussey, Kay, 371
Bybee, Jay, 72

CAH. *See* Congenital Androgen Hyperplasya
California, University of, Berkeley, 260, 281, 286–290
California Supreme Court, 76–77
Caney, Simon, 10, 14–15, 17
Capitalism, 132
Caregiving, 345–346, 349–361
Categorical Imperative, 17
Catholic Church, Catholicism, 264, 273, 274, 295, 326, 333, 335, 390
Cellar, Edward, 70
Center for American Progress, 130, 157
Central Intelligence Agency (CIA), 71, 72, 74, 222–223
Chakrabarty, Ananda, 241
Children, 345
  communities and, 348, 391–392
  definition of, 386
  duties to, 348, 385–398
  extended-community worldview imperative and, 396–397
  global poverty and, 136–137
  international context and, 396–398
  love and, 395–396
  shared-community worldview imperative and, 393–394
  univocal contracts and, 392–395
Childress, James, 42
China, 3, 9, 10, 350
Choice
  ethics of, 93–94, 95, 97
  freedom of, 113
Christian Right, 272, 275
Christian Scientists, 260, 273
Christianity, 32, 104, 259, 309
  See also Religion
Churchill, Robert Paul, 3, 4

Churchill, Winston, 328
CIA. *See* Central Intelligence Agency
Cicero, 32, 333
Claim rights, 4, 29–30, 386–389
Clash of Civilizations, 302
Clement, Jacques, 335
Clifford, William Kingdom, 4–5, 268
  ethics of belief and, 52–57
Climate change, 105, 149
Coast Guard, U.S., 68
Cohan, Deborah, 70
Cold War, 326
Collective responsibility
  collective action and, 129
  global poverty and, 135–150
  moral, 130
  needs-based rights approach to, 130
  See also Responsibility
Committee for Refugees and Immigrants, U.S., 68
Communities, 146
  children and, 348, 391–392
  deontological ethics and, 106–107, 121
  duties and, 4
  needs-based rights and, 143
Community of nations, 3
Conditional cash transfers, 131, 157, 159, 161–164
Congenital Androgen Hyperplasya (CAH), 373
Consequentialism, 317
  belief and, 52, 62
  equality and, 89, 92–97
  global ethics and, 89–100
  global poverty and, 99
  good, promotion of and, 85–86, 90, 108
  human rights justification and, 13
  implications of, 89
  indifference and, 89, 90, 93, 97–100
  morality and justice and, 85
  motivation and, 90–91
  permissions and constraints and, 86, 95–97
  practical reason and, 89, 90
  shallow pond example and, 85, 86, 90, 91, 92, 100
  utilitarianism and, 85, 115–116
Constitution, U.S., 69, 70, 391–392
  Bill of Rights, U.S., 29, 387
  First Amendment, 263, 271
  progress of science and, 237
  same-sex marriage and, 76
Contractarianism, 231
Convention on the Elimination of All Forms of Discrimination against Women, 234fig
Convention on the Prevention and Punishment of the Crime of Genocide, 330
Convention on the Rights of the Child, 234fig
Copernican Revolution, 21
Corporate responsibility, 133, 185, 186, 189
Cosmopolitanism, 295, 297, 298, 325–337
Council for Scientific and Industrial Research (CSIR), 242
Cruz Bermudez et al. v. the Ministerio de Sanidad, 233
CSIR. *See* Council for Scientific and Industrial Research
Cummiskey, David, 295–297

Dalai Lama, 297, 299, 300, 312, 314–315, 317
Daniels, Norman, 207, 212, 213
Davies, Christie, 22
DCT. *See* Divine Command Theory
Declaration of Alma-Ata, 234, 234fig
Denmark, 359–360
Democracy, 9, 264, 267, 269–270, 309
Deontological ethics (DE)
  anthropology and, 87, 106, 119–120
  appeal of, 104–105, 115–122
  communities and, 106–107, 121
  definition of, 104

Deontological ethics (DE) *(continued)*
duties and, 103–122
efficiency and permanence and, 111–113
environment and, 103, 104, 112–113, 119
extended-community worldview imperative and, 115
freedom and, 107–110, 113–115
God and, 86
good and, 87, 103, 107, 108
justification and, 106, 107, 115–118
law and, 117–118
moral stance and, 103, 110–111
morality and justice and, 85, 86–87
objections to, 86–87, 103, 105–107, 118–122
reason and, 107
Descartes, Rene, 104
Desert theory, 153, 154–157, 207, 214–215
Detainees, 5, 6, 65, 66–67, 71–74
Dickens, Charles, 395
Disease
collective moral responsibility and, 142
economic interests and, 221–222
global health and, 207, 208, 212, 215, 219–220, 222–223
MNEs, moral responsibility of and, 187–191
refugee camps and, 5
Divine Command Theory (DCT), 259, 265, 273, 275
Doha Declaration, 238
Donahue, James A., 260–261
Donaldson, Thomas, 19, 133–134, 188, 196
Doxastic voluntarism, 54
Durkheim, Emile, 366
Duties
to aid, 147–150
to children, 348, 385–398
communities and, 4
corporate social, 133
deontological ethics and, 103–122
extended-community worldview imperative and, 87
human rights and, 3
libertarianism and, 208
to love, 395–396
of MNEs, 133–134
morality and, 51–52, 106
motivation and, 130
negative, 130, 197, 208, 386–390
not to harm, 147–150
positive, 130, 386–390
rights and, 3, 4, 30, 104, 386–390
toward future generations, 103, 121–122
typology of, 188–189, 194
Dworkin, Ronald, 15, 28–29

Economic mobility, 131, 153, 153–154, 157–161, 159, 163
Education, 157
belief and, 5
bias and, 5
global ethics in the academy and, 281–291
Islamic and Jewish Studies and, 281–291
morality and, 60
See also Academy
Egalitarianism, 207, 211, 212–213, 225
Egoism, ethical, 4
Eldercare, 349–361
The Elements of Politics (Sidgwick), 89
Emotivism, 105
The End of Violence (film), 66
Enemy women, 65
Engels, Friedrich, 368
English common law, 69
Enlightenment, 4, 104, 117, 316
Environment, 103, 104, 112–113, 119, 149, 386
Epistemic obligations, 3, 4–5
EPO. *See* European Patent Office

Equal opportunity, 207, 211, 212–213, 213, 225, 376
Equality
  consequentialism and, 89, 92–97
  responsibility and, 139, 141
Ethics
  of belief, 5, 52–57
  of beneficence, 86, 93–95, 97–98
  beneficence in, 86
  business, 134, 169
  care, 356–358
  of choice, 93–94, 95, 97
  global finance and, 169–182
  macro-, 131–133
  meta-, 66
  micro-, 170
  of nature, 94, 95, 97
  of reciprocity, 43–44
  of risks, 180–181
  of special ties, 94–95
  of war, 326
The Ethics of Belief (Clifford), 52, 268
Ethnic cleansing, 267
EU. *See* European Union
European Court of Human Rights, 9
European Patent Office (EPO), 241
European Union (EU), 9
Everson v. Board, 70
Extended-community worldview imperative
  belief and, 5, 57–59, 61
  children and, 348, 396–397
  deontological ethics and, 115
  duties and, 87
  human rights and, 3–4, 23
  motivation and, 3–4

"Famine, Affluence, and Morality" (Singer), 5, 60
FBI. *See* Federal Bureau of Investigation
FDI. *See* Foreign direct investment
Federal Bureau of Investigation (FBI), 70
Feinburg, Joel, 394
Feminism, 60, 346, 350, 357, 359
Financial crisis of 2007–2009, 173–174, 179, 181
Financial ethics
  basic normative orientations of, 173–178
  fundamental tasks of, 178–182
  guiding principle of, 170–173
  risks, evaluation of and, 180–181
Financial markets
  dynamics of, 174–175
  efficiency of, 169, 170–173, 173–174
  globalization and, 178–179
  human rights and, 173
  laissez-faire approach to, 132
  liberalization of, 178–180
  macroethics and, 131–133, 169–182
  moral hazard and, 179
  moral importance of, 170–173
  permanence of, 132
  permanently sustainable, 132
  purpose of, 147, 171
  regulation of, 132, 172, 175, 176–177
  sustainability of, 132, 170–173
First Amendment, 263, 271
Forsberg, Randall, 301
Free Exercise Clause, 263
Free Trade Agreements (FTAs), 230
Freedom, 15
  action and, 34
  of belief, 69–70
  of choice, 113
  deontological ethics and, 107–110, 113–115
  good, promotion of and, 103, 109–110
  intellectual property rights and, 241
  moral, 103, 109–110, 113–115
  moral stance and, 103
  morality and, 104
  religious, 69–70, 260, 264, 271
  right to, 145
French Declaration of the Rights of Man and the Citizen (1789), 29
FTAs. *See* Free Trade Agreements

GATT treaty. *See* General Agreement on Tariffs and Trade treaty
Gays and lesbians, 5, 65, 67
  LGBTs, 346, 366
  military and, 6
  same-sex marriage and, 74–77
  societal and legal recognition of, 6
Gender, 157
  notion of, 367–369
  social institutions and, 368–369
  studies of, 367–368
Gender development, 365
  biological model for, 372–373
  biosocial approach to, 373–375
  clinical practice and, 371–372, 373–374
  ethical implications of, 375–378
  normal vs. abnormal, 367, 369–370
  social model for, 370–371, 371–372
Gender identity, 345, 365, 366, 369, 374
  biosocial approach to, 346–347
  policy and, 347
  as social construct, 370
Gender identity disorder (GID), 369, 374–375
  biological cause for, 379
  as psychiatric condition, 365
  treatment for, 366, 376–379
Gender variance, 346, 365, 366, 375
  as disorder, 367
  implications for international practice and, 378–379
  as pathological, 378–379
  as psychiatric condition, 366
  treatment for, 366, 376–378
General Agreement on Tariffs and Trade (GATT) treaty, 245
Generic Consistency, 34–35
Geneva Conventions, 6, 71, 72, 74, 334, 390
Genocide, 9
George, Ronald M., 76–77
Germany, 208–209, 231, 232, 267–268, 346, 359–360
Gerson, Jean, 335
Gewirth, Alan, 4, 28, 34–35, 41, 120, 330
GI Education Bill, 131, 160, 163
GID. *See* Gender identity disorder
Gilligan, Carol, 356
Giordano, Simona, 346, 347
Global ethics, 66
  academy and, 281–291
  consequentialism and, 89–100
  See also Ethics
Global Financial Crisis, 149
Global health
  access to life-saving medicines and, 208–210, 229–250
  desert theory and, 207, 214–215
  disease and, 207, 208, 212, 215, 222–223
  economic interests and, 212, 221–222
  egalitarianism and, 207, 211, 212–213, 225
  equal opportunity and, 207, 211, 212–213, 376
  funding for, 207–208, 211–226
  global justice and, 207
  global security and, 208, 212, 222–223
  good and, 211, 223
  Health Impact Fund and, 248–249
  intellectual property rights and, 209, 229
  justice and, 207, 211–226
  libertarianism and, 208, 211, 217–219
  motivation and, 207–208, 211–212
  policy and, 207
  prudential (self-interested) arguments and, 208
  rights and, 207, 213, 229, 231–235
  utilitarianism and, 207, 211, 215–217
  well-being and, 211, 215, 223
The Global Infectious Disease Threat and Its Implications for the United States, 223
Global justice
  academy and, 281–291

epistemic obligations and, 3
global business and, 185–198
global health and, 207
human rights and, 3
morality and, 282
Other and, 3
religion and, 259, 260, 263–275
theocracy and, 263–275
war and, 295
See also Justice
Global poverty
collective responsibility and, 135–150
conditional cash transfer and, 131
consequentialism and, 99
economic mobility and, 131, 163
human capital investment and, 130–131
indifference and, 99
international institutions and, 135
responsibility and, 130, 219
rich, moral obligations of and, 135–138
social institutions and, 192
wealth building and, 131, 153
women and, 345
See also Poverty
Global security, 208, 212, 222–223
Globalization, 8, 173, 178–179, 181–182, 290
God, 105, 209
authority of, 265, 271
deontological ethics and, 86
human rights and, 32–33
natural law and, 31
theocracy and, 259, 264, 265
will of, 4, 32, 266, 296, 302
Good
collective, 146, 147
consequentialism and, 85–86, 90, 108
deontological ethics and, 87, 103, 107, 108
freedom and, 109–110
global health and, 211, 223
public, 146
universal notion of, 110
Goodin, Robert, 331
Gordon, John-Stewart, 3, 4
Gould, Carol, 3, 18
Graduate Theological Union (Berkeley), 260, 281, 286–290
Great Expectations (Dickens), 395
Greenberg, Karen J., 72
Griffin, James, 3, 9–10, 11, 12, 15–19, 28, 39, 196
Grotius, 332, 336
Groundwork for the Metaphysics of Morals (Kant), 4, 36–37
Grover, Anand, 230, 235, 237, 245, 247
Gyatso, Thupten, 314

Hadith, 295, 302, 303
The Hague, 9
Haitians, 12, 68
Hamdi, Yaser, 71
Hamilton, Marci, 273–274
Harding, Sandra, 78
Hare, R. M., 317
Harm
duties not to, 147–150
needs and, 144
Hart, Herbert, 28
Harvard University, 240
Health care. *See* Global justice
Health Impact Fund, 210, 248–249, 250
Hegel, George Wilhelm Friedrich, 86, 87, 104, 106, 111, 114, 119
Heil, John, 54
Held, Virginia, 346, 356, 357
Henley, Kenneth, 394
Henry III, King of France, 335
Higher education. *See* Academy
HIV/AIDS, 187–191, 192, 196, 215, 217–218, 219–220, 221–222, 233, 385, 397
Hobbes, Thomas, 33, 34
Holy Scriptures, 32
Homeland Security Department, U.S., 67
Hoppe, Ron, 353
Hsieh, Nien-hê, 133–134, 194

Human capital investment, 130–131, 163–164
Human rights
claimability and, 3, 11–12
coherency and, 3, 11
determinacy and, 3, 11
duties and, 3
epistemic obligations and, 4–5
extended-community worldview imperative and, 3–4
feasibility and, 3, 12
financial markets and, 173
foreign policy and, 213
global justice and, 3
globalization of, 8–10
health care, funding for and, 211
inflation of, 9–10
internalization of norms of, 3, 8, 9, 23
international institutions and, 30
international law and, 9
just war theory and, 298
justification of, 3, 4, 7–23, 27–45
law and, 29
MNEs and, 186–187
motivation and, 7
nature of, 27, 28–30
needs-based, 143–145
"other" and, 5–6
as rational rights, 28
scope of, 3, 4, 12, 17
separability and, 3, 12, 13
social institutions and, 193
theories of, 3, 10–13
universality and, 3, 4, 7, 8, 10, 16–18, 28
war and, 301, 326, 329–330
"Human Rights and Capabilities" (Sen), 39–40
Human Rights First, 68
Human rights justification
agency-based approach to, 3, 4, 16, 18–19
Buddhism and, 296–297
capability approach to, 39–40
categories of, 4
claimability and, 3
coherency and, 3
determinacy and, 3
divine rights approach to, 4, 27, 32–33
feasibility and, 3
first-person arguments and, 17–18, 19–20
fundamental interests approach to, 27, 33–34
human rights, globalization of and, 8–10
human rights, scope of and, 3, 17
human rights theories and, 10–13
interest-based approach to, 3, 4, 14–16
is-ought problem and, 36, 43
motivation and, 8, 20–23
natural rights approach to, 4, 27, 30–32
"other" and, 7, 8, 65–78
personal autonomy approach to, 27, 34–36
pluralistic approach to, 3, 13–14
rational rights approach to, 27, 36–44
traditional, 4
tyrannicide and, 335
universality and, 16–18, 18–20
Human Rights Watch, 30, 62
Hume, David, 21

Ignorance
belief and, 5, 57–63
morality and, 57–63
veil of, 4, 27, 37, 45, 133
Illies, Christian, 86, 87
Imagination. *See* Moral imagination
Immigration and Nationality Act (INA), 70
Immigration and Naturalization Service (INS), 69
INA. *See* Immigration and Nationality Act
India, 29
Indifference, 89, 90, 93, 97–100
Individualism, 267

Infectious disease. *See* Disease
INS. *See* Immigration and Naturalization Service
Intellectual property rights, 192
- access to life-saving medicines and, 229, 230, 241, 245–248
- antitrust laws and, 236–237
- Health Impact Fund and, 248–249
- as human rights, 239
- monopoly pricing powers and, 236, 239, 244, 247
- natural rights and, 239–244
- purpose of, 230, 235–239
- reform of, 248–249
- right to health and, 230, 235
- social rules and, 239–240, 246
- social utility of, 244–248
- types of, 236fig

Intellectual property rights (IPRs), 209
International Bill of Human Rights, 7
International Commission on Intervention and State Sovereignty, 330
International Court of Justice, 30
International Covenant on Civil and Political Rights (1966), 29
International Covenant on Economic, Social and Cultural Rights, 232, 234, 234fig, 239
International Covenant on Economic, Social and Cultural Rights (1966), 9, 29
International institutions
- global poverty and, 130, 135
- human rights and, 30
- responsibility of, 130

International law, 9
International Monetary Fund, 163
Internet, 5, 62
IPRs. *See* Intellectual property rights
Iraq War, 302
Iraq War (2003), 327–328, 329
Islam, 70, 264
- business practices in, 260, 281, 287, 289
- *fatwa* and, 304–305
- food practices in, 260, 281, 287, 290
- global politics and, 259
- Hadith and, 302, 303
- identity and, 260
- Itijihad and, 303–304
- jihad and, 296, 305–306, 309
- just war theory and, 295–296, 299, 302–309
- media depictions of, 281, 286, 288–289
- religious toleration and, 306–307
- Sharia and, 274, 295, 297, 302–305
- text study of, 281, 287–288
- Verse of the Sword and, 307–308
- women and, 274, 307

Islamic Studies, 281–291
Israel/Palestine, 260

Japan, 346, 359–360
Jehovah's Witnesses, 75, 260, 273
Jewish Studies, 281–291
Jihad, 296, 305–306, 309
John of Salisbury, 335
Jonas, Hans, 121–122
Jones, C., 330
Journey of Hope (film), 68
Judaism, Jews, 32, 69, 260
- business practices of, 260, 281, 287, 289
- food practices of, 260, 281, 287, 290
- identity and, 260
- media depictions of, 281, 286, 288–289
- text study of, 281, 287–288

A Just Society (Boylan), 4, 35–36
Just and Unjust War (Walzer), 326
"Just War and Human Rights" (Luban), 336
Just war theory
- Buddhism and, 295, 299, 300, 309–321
- Catholicism and, 326, 333

Just war theory *(continued)*
cosmopolitanism and, 295, 297, 298, 325–337
human rights and, 298
Islam and, 295–296, 299, 302–309
Obama's Nobel Prize speech and, 297, 299, 317–318
preemptive war and, 327–328
religious traditions and, 295
status of, 327–329
supreme emergency and, 327–329
terrorism and, 328
traditional, 297–298
tyrannicide and, 298
Justice
compensatory, 12
consequentialism and, 85
corporate responsibility and, 133, 185, 186
deontology and, 85, 86–87
distributive, 12, 13
efficiency and permanence and, 173
equal opportunity and, 212, 213
global, 173
global health, 211–226
health care and, 207
legal, 30
MNEs and, 194–197
nations and, 133
natural, 30
policy and, 173
restorative, 217–219
retributive, 12, 389
separability and, 3
social, 173
social institutions and, 133, 197, 213, 217
See also Global justice
Justification. *See* Human rights justification

Kaldor, Mary, 334
Kant, Immanuel, 61, 104, 272
Categorical Imperative of, 17
cosmopolitanism and, 329
deontological ethics and, 87, 104, 106, 107–108, 113
deontology and, 86
human rights justification and, 4, 14, 17, 21, 27, 36–37, 38, 41, 42, 45
morality and, 111
rationality and, 27, 42
Kirsch, Julie, 4–5
Koh, Howard, 10
Koran. *See* Qur'an
Kuehn, Rita, 358
Kymlicka, Will, 15

Lagouranis, Tony, 72, 73
Lakoff, George, 288
Lan, Pei-Chan, 353
Lane, Melissa, 189
Law
deontological ethics and, 117–118
English common, 69
harm and nuisance and, 389–390
human rights and, 29
international, 9
natural, 27, 30–32
reason and, 242
secular, 259
The Law of Peoples (Rawls), 295, 300–302
Lesbian, gay, bisexual, and transsexual people (LGBTs), 346, 366
Levander, Carl W., 70
Leviathan (Hobbes), 33
LGBTs. *See* Lesbian, gay, bisexual, and transsexual people
Liberalism, 107, 267, 300
Libertarianism, 208, 211, 217–219, 225
Lillehammer, Hallvard, 85–86, 208
Lindh, John Walker, 71
Litt, Jacqueline S., 345, 350
Locke, John, 31, 105, 107, 209, 240, 244, 335
Luban, David, 329, 336
Lyon, Dawn, 353

MacIntyre, Alasdair, 106, 120
Macroethics. *See* Financial ethics
Malvern, S., 394
Mann, Jonathan, 387–388
Marriage, same-sex, 74–77
Marx, Karl, 368
Masri, Khaled el-, 72
Mbecki, Thabo, 217
McNamara, Robert, 65, 76–77
Media, 260, 281, 286, 288–289
Mele, Alfred, 56
The Methods of Ethics (Sidgwick), 91–92
Mill, John Stuart, 106, 270
Millennium Development Goals, 234fig
Miller, Richard, 192–193
Miller, Seumas, 129, 134, 208
Minersville School District v. Gobitis, 75
Mishkin, Frederic S., 182
MNEs. *See* Multinational Enterprises
Moellendorf, Darrel, 213, 336
Mohammed, Khalid Sheikh, 73
Money, John, 371
Moore, G. E., 85
Moral hazard, 179
Moral imagination, 3, 7
Moral motivation. *See* Motivation
Moral relativism, 10, 57, 105, 118
Moral stance, 103, 110–111
Morality
  belief and, 57
  consequentialism and, 85
  deontology and, 85, 86–87
  duties and, 51–52, 106
  epistemic obligations, 3
  freedom and, 104
  global justice and, 282
  human rights, 3
  ignorance and, 57–63
  justification and, 104
  "other" and, 3
  rationality and, 4, 42
  reciprocity and, 30, 43–44
  rights and duties and, 30
  of war, 327
Morocco, 72
Motivation
  accountability and, 4
  action and, 4
  consequentialism and, 90–91
  duties and, 130
  emotions and, 21
  epistemic obligations and, 4–5
  extended-community worldview imperative and, 3–4
  health care, funding for and, 207–208, 211–212
  human rights and, 3, 4, 7, 8, 20–23, 27
  love and children and, 396
  moral, 207–208
  moral imagination and, 3, 7
  personal worldview imperative and, 3
  reason and, 21
Muhammad, 295, 296, 302, 303, 306, 307
Multinational Enterprises (MNEs)
  as artificial persons, 194–195
  duties of, 133–134
  global economy and, 185, 186
  global justice and, 185
  harm, avoiding and preventing and, 191–194
  human rights and, 186–187
  justice and, 194–197
  moral agency of, 190–191, 194–196
  as natural persons, 195, 197
  policy and, 186
  principal of rescue and, 190
  provision of assistance and, 187–191
  purpose of, 190–191
  regulation of, 186
  responsibility and, 133, 185–198
  shareholders and employees, roles of in, 197–198
Murphy, G., 374
Muslims. *See* Islam

Nagel, Thomas, 107
NATO. *See* North Atlantic Treaty Organization

Natural law
divine providence and, 242
God and, 31
human rights and, 27, 30–32
intellectual property rights and, 240–244
objections to, 105
Natural rights
human rights and, 4
intellectual property rights and, 239–244
Nature, 4
ethics of, 94, 95, 97
Navy SEALs, 72
Nazi Germany, 267–268
Neal, Mark, 22
Needs, 144–145
New and Old Wars (Kaldor), 334
NGOs. *See* Nongovernmental organizations
Nicgorski, Sister Darlene, 70
Nickel, James, 12, 13, 14, 16, 28
Nicomachean Ethics (Aristotle), 4, 30
Nietzsche, Friedrich, 111
Niger Delta Development Commission, 233
Nigeria, 233–234
Nigerian National Petroleum Company, 233
Nihilism, 110
Noddings, Nel, 356
Nongovernmental organizations (NGOs), 10, 30, 398
North Atlantic Treaty Organization (NATO), 9
Norway, 346, 359–360
Nozick, Robert, 106, 118
Nuclear weapons, 301, 304, 326
Nuremberg Charter, 330
Nussbaum, Martha, 13, 15, 43

Obama, Barack, 74, 297, 299, 317
On Human Rights (Griffin), 39
On the Basis of Morality (Schopenhauer), 27
OncoMouse, 240–241
O'Neill, Onora, 119, 134, 189, 195
Orend, Brian, 28
The Origin of the Family, Private Property and the State (Engels), 368
Other
caregiving and, 345–346
detainees, 5, 6, 65, 66–67, 71–74
enemy women, 65
gays and lesbians, 5, 6, 65, 67, 74–77
gender variance and, 346
global justice and, 3
human rights and, 5–6, 8, 65–78
LGBTs, 346
morality and, 3
refugees, 5–6, 65, 66, 67–71
treatment of, 65–66
women, 345, 349–361

Pacifism, 295, 296, 299, 315
Packard, Randall, 217
Padilla, Jose, 71, 73
Paine, Thomas, 329
Palmer-Fernández, Gabriel, 297, 298
Patent Cooperation Treaty, 237, 238
Persian Gulf War (1991), 326, 336–337
Personal worldview imperative, 3, 5, 57 60
Pharmaceutical companies, 188–191, 192, 196, 209, 248
Pogge, Thomas, 86, 147–148, 192, 207, 208, 210, 213, 219, 225, 387
Policy
gender identity and, 347
global health and, 207
justice and, 173
MNEs and, 186
wealth building and, 153
Poverty. *See* Global poverty
Procrustes, 106, 119
Pufendorf, Samuel, 105
Purdy, Laura, 259

Qahtani, Mahammed al-, 73
Qur'an, 289, 295, 296, 302, 304, 306, 307–308, 320

Railton, Peter, 317
Rationality, 6, 42, 76–77
 duties and, 4
 human rights justification and, 36–37, 37–38, 45
 morality and, 4, 42
Rawls, John, 28, 107, 115, 197, 239, 387
 deontological ethics and, 104, 106
 egalitarianism and, 225
 equal opportunity and, 207, 212–213
 just war theory and, 295
 justice and, 133–134
 right to war and, 300–302
 veil of ignorance and, 4, 27, 37, 45, 133
Raz, Joseph, 15, 231
Reagan, Ronald, 70
Reason
 consequentialism and, 89, 90
 deontological ethics and, 107
 law and, 242
 motivation and, 21
 theocracy and, 267
Reciprocity, 30, 43–44
Red Cross, 74
Refugees, 5, 65, 66, 67–71, 267
 asylum seekers and, 5, 67
 definition of, 5, 6
 economic betterment and, 6, 67
 sanctuary and, 6, 69, 70–71
 terrorism and, 6, 70
Regulation
 of financial markets, 132, 172, 175, 176–177
 MNEs and, 186
Relativism, 10, 60, 105, 118
Religion
 decline of, 104
 democracy and, 270
 economics and, 289
 freedom of, 69–70, 259, 260, 264, 271
 global justice and, 259, 260, 263–275
 society and, 282
 theocracy and, 263–275
 tolerance and, 306–307
Religious Right, 271
Reno, Donald, 69
Responsibility, 129
 collective, 135–150
 corporate, 133
 doxastic, 5, 51–52
 duties and, 130
 global poverty and, 130, 135–150, 219
 Imperative of, 122
 individual vs. collective, 129–130
 of MNEs, 133, 185–198
 modes of, 129, 138–139
 moral, 129–130, 138–141
 natural, 129, 138
 "other things being equal" clause and, 139
 of pharmaceutical companies, 188–191, 192, 196
 social institutions and, 141–143
Rifkin, Jeremy, 241
Rights
 basic, 386
 claim, 4, 29–30, 386–389
 democracy and, 9
 divine, 27, 32–33
 duties and, 3, 4, 30, 104, 386–390
 health care and, 207, 213, 229, 231–235
 inflation of, 14
 intellectual property, 192, 209
 legal, 4, 29, 231–235
 liberty, 4, 29–30
 to life, 145, 209, 241, 243–244, 250
 manifesto, 14
 moral, 4, 29, 231
 natural, 4, 27, 30–32, 209
 needs-based, 143–145, 149
 negative, 149
 positive, 148, 149

Rights *(continued)*
rational, 27, 36–44
as trumps, 29
to vote, 389
war and, 300–302, 326, 336
Rodrik, Dani, 182
Rorty, Richard, 28, 105
Ruddick, Sara, 353
Rumi, Melvana, 321
Russia, 9
Ryder, Richard, 41–42

Sachs, Jeffrey, 216–217
Saladin, 306
Same-sex marriage, 74–77
Sanctuary, 6, 69
Sandel, Michael, 107
Sanger, Lawrence, 62
Santorum, Rich. *See* Immigration and Nationality Act
Scepticism, 111
Scheffler, Samuel, 216
Schopenhauer, Arthur, 27, 37, 106
Schroeder, Doris, 208, 210
Segupta, Arjun, 10
Selgelid, Michael J., 207–208
Sen, Amartya, 13, 15, 39–40
Seneca, 32
September 11, 301
SERAC. *See* Social and Economic Rights Action Centre
SERAC v. Nigeria, 233
Setiya, Kieran, 54
Shallow pond, 85, 86, 90, 91, 92, 100, 129, 136, 208
Shared-community worldview imperative, 5, 348, 393–394
Sharia, 274, 295, 297, 302–305
Shue, Henry, 11–12, 28, 133–134, 188, 194
Sidgwick, Henry, 85–86, 89, 91–92, 97, 110
Sin Nombre (film), 68
Singer, Peter, 5, 41–42, 60–61, 96, 98, 147, 148, 210, 216
global poverty and, 135–136
shallow pond and, 85, 90–91, 92, 100, 129, 136, 208
Snell, Karen, 69
Social and Economic Rights Action Centre (SERAC), 233
Social institutions, 135
action and, 129
collective responsibility and, 141–143
gender and, 368–369
global poverty and, 192
human rights and, 193
justice and, 133, 197, 213, 217
moral foundations of, 129, 145–147
needs-based rights and, 143–145
responsibility and, 129
Social rules, 239–240, 246
Somalis, 5
Sophists, 367
Sophocles, 31
South Africa, 5, 29, 68, 217–218
Speciesism, 41–42
Status. *See* Other
Steigleder, Klaus, 131–132
Strohmeyer, Sister Marian, 69
Suárez, Francisco, 333, 336
Subramanian, Arvind, 182
Sub-Saharan Africa, 187–191, 192, 196, 213, 222
Sunna, 295, 302
Swaine, Lucas, 264

Table of Embeddedness, 35–36, 157, 158–159fig, 390, 398
Taguba Report, 72
Taking Rights Seriously (Dworkin), 28–29
Taylor, Charles, 107, 330
Teays, Wanda, 5–6, 345
Technology, 51, 238, 326
Ten Commandments, 4, 32

Terrorism, 66–67
just war theory and, 328
refugees and, 6, 70
war on, 72, 326
Theocracy
critical thinking and, 265–269
definition of, 264
diversity and, 267
Divine Command Theory, 273
Divine Command Theory and, 265, 275
global justice and, 263–275
God and, 259, 264, 265
reason and, 267
religious freedom and, 259, 260, 264, 271
strong, 259–260, 263, 265–271, 275
structural problems with, 265–271
weak, 259, 260, 263, 271–274, 275
A Theory of Justice (Rawls), 212–213
Theodosian Code of 392, 69
Tong, Rosemarie, 345–346
Torah, 107, 289
Torture, 145, 240
Trade-Related Aspects of Intellectual Property Rights Agreement (TRIPS), 209–210, 230, 235, 237, 240, 245, 246, 247, 250
The Transformation of War (Van Creveld), 334
TRIPs. *See* Trade-Related Aspects of Intellectual Property Rights Agreement
Tronto, Joan, 357
Tuberculosis (TB), 142, 208, 215, 218, 219–220
Turner, Adair, 178
Two Treatises of Government (Locke), 31
Tyrannicide, 298, 335

UN. *See* United Nations
UN Committee on Economic, Social and Cultural Rights, 234fig
UN Convention (1951), 67
UN General Assembly, 10, 232
Underground Railroad, 68
Unger, Peter, 95
UNICEF, 62, 114
United Nations (UN), 5, 6, 7, 9, 30, 73, 114, 163, 209, 398
United States, 153
economic mobility in, 157
eldercare in, 358, 360–361
human capital investment and, 130–131
human rights and, 10
United States of America v. Maria Del Socorro Pardo De Aguilar, 68
Universal Declaration of Human Rights (1948), 9, 29, 188, 209, 213, 232, 234fig, 250, 330, 387
Universality, 3, 4, 7, 8, 10, 16–18, 18–20, 28, 86
Universities. *See* Academy
Utilitarianism, Utilitarians, 42, 61, 105
consequentialism and, 85, 115–116
global health and, 211, 215–217, 225
health care and, 207
risks, evaluation of and, 180

Van Creveld, Martin, 334
Veil of ignorance, 4, 27, 37, 45, 133
Venezuela, 233
Vietnam War, 160, 326
Voluntarism, 54
Von Treitschke, Heinrich, 263, 266, 275
Voting rights, 389

Walzer, Michael, 28, 42, 297, 326, 327, 328, 332
War
defensive, 308–309
democracy and, 309
end of, 301
ethics of, 326
global justice and, 295

War *(continued)*
human rights and, 301, 326, 329–330
just war theory and, 295
morality of, 327
preemptive, 301–302, 326, 327–328
right to, 300–302, 326, 336
on terror, 72, 326
See also Just war theory
Wealth building, 131
conditional cash transfers and, 153–166
desert theory and, 153
economic mobility and, 157–161
essential mission to, 132
personal wealth funds, 161–164
puzzle-maker model and, 154–156, 162–163
wealth, definition of and, 160
Webster, Daniel, 328
Well-being, 34, 211, 215, 223
White Plague, Black Labour (Packard), 217
Whitt, Clayton, 73–74
WHO. *See* World Health Organization
Wiggins, David, 130, 143
Wikipedia, 62
WIPO. *See* World Intellectual Property Rights Organization
Wisconsin v. Yoder, 394
Wittgenstein, Ludwig, 19, 33
Women, 270, 287
caregiving and, 349–361
enemy, 65
immigrant, 349–361
Islam and, 274, 307
in poverty, 345
World Bank, 30, 135, 220
World Health Organization (WHO), 220, 230, 232
World Intellectual Property Rights Organization (WIPO), 238
World Trade Organization (WTO), 238
World War II, 22, 69, 131, 160, 163, 328
World Wildlife Foundation, 112–113
Worldview. *See* Personal worldview imperative; Shared-community worldview imperative; Extended worldview imperative
WTO. *See* World Trade Organization

Yemen, 5
Yoo, John, 72

Zimbabweans, 68
Zimmerman, Mary K., 5, 345, 350
Zizek, Slavoj, 73
Zubaydah, Abu, 73